CRIMEAN QUAGMIRE

GREGORY CARLETON

Crimean Quagmire

Tolstoy, Russell and the Birth of Modern Warfare

HURST & COMPANY, LONDON

First published in the United Kingdom in 2024 by
C. Hurst & Co. (Publishers) Ltd.,
New Wing, Somerset House, Strand, London, WC2R 1LA
© Gregory Carleton, 2024
All rights reserved.

A Cataloguing-in-Publication data record for this book
is available from the British Library.

ISBN: 9781911723639

www.hurstpublishers.com

Printed in Great Britain by Bell & Bain Ltd, Glasgow

For Gina and Alessandro

CONTENTS

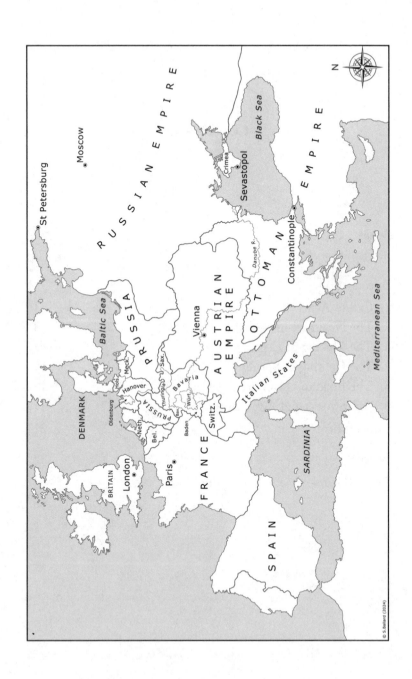

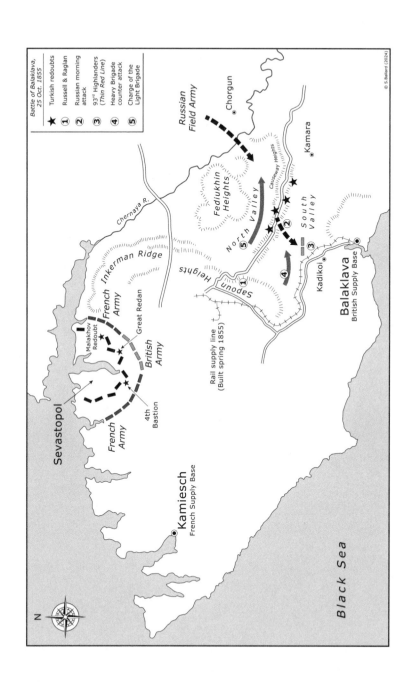

Battle of Balaklava,
25 Oct. 1855

★   Turkish redoubts

①   Russell & Raglan

②   Russian morning
     attack

③   93rd Highlanders
     (*Thin Red Line*)

④   Heavy Brigade
     counter attack

⑤   Charge of the
     Light Brigade

© S. Ballard (2024)

N

Russian Field Army

Chorgun

Kamara

Fediukhin Heights

Causeway Heights

North valley

South valley

⑤

②

③

④

Kadikoi

Sapoun Heights

①

Balaklava
British Supply Base

Chernaya R.

Inkerman Ridge

French Army

Malakhov Redoubt

Great Redan

British Army

4th Bastion

French Army

Rail supply line
(Built spring 1855)

Sevastopol

Kamiesch
French Supply Base

Black Sea

ACKNOWLEDGMENTS

In the course of researching and writing this book—a longue durée if there ever was one—I have incurred many debts that the following words cannot begin to cover. On Russian history, particularly its military aspects, I am most grateful for the insight and input of Jonathan Brunstedt, Adrienne Harris, Dan Mulholland, Stephen Norris and the two anonymous reviewers for Hurst Publishers. I would also like to thank the organizations and institutions that hosted various conferences and talks which allowed me to air my ideas, both big and small. These include the Association for Slavic, East European and Eurasian Studies as well as Baylor University, Columbia University, Harvard University, Radboud University Nijmegen, Tufts University, University College London and the University of Nottingham. To all, I express my sincere gratitude. Any mistakes or errors, however, originate with me and are mine alone.

I would also like to express my sincerest gratitude to Lisa Adams of the Garamond Agency for her continuing support of my efforts. Working with her has been a blessing and has made bringing *Crimean Quagmire* to print—which at times seemed to me an improbable thing—a most smooth (and sane) process. Her exemplary professionalism and patience is something to which I can only aspire, and I would like to underscore that

ACKNOWLEDGMENTS

without her this book would likely not have appeared. To the publishers and editors at Hurst, especially Daisy Leitch and Mei Jayne Yew, I would also like to extend my deepest thanks for their confidence in my work and contributions in giving it its present shape. They and their ever-courteous staff have been a joy work with. My gratitude extends as well to Tufts University for providing time off necessary to conduct much of the book's research and to the staff at Tisch Library for being most helpful in assisting me in the same.

As with my previous books, the classroom has been the major driver behind *Crimean Quagmire* and I am most grateful to all my students at Tufts who have taken "war courses" with me in various iterations for providing a crucial platform to present, test and modify the book's theses. They might not have known it at the time (and still likely do not) that, without their engaging discussions and feedback, this whole project might never have seen the light. Teaching is why I entered this profession and it remains the backbone behind my research—not the other way around. In this regard I must also champion the unfailing support of my colleagues in the Department of International Literary and Cultural Studies, especially Charles Inouye and Vida Johnson, and how working there—my only professional home after graduate school—has truly been a pleasure.

Finally—and here words truly fail me as they did once for Tolstoy and Russell on the battlefields of Crimea—I cannot express how grateful I am to my wife, Gina, and our son, Alessandro. Never could I have imagined two people bringing such joy and happiness into my life, and I humbly offer this book as recompense for whatever 'quagmires' I might have caused during its writing. I dedicate it unreservedly and unequivocally to both of them.

INTRODUCTION

In the middle of the nineteenth century, the two greatest empires in the world, Britain and Russia, went to war with each other. Given the tides of history, this might seem an inevitable turn of events. After all, as rivals for global supremacy, how long could the two hold off before coming to blows? Much as the ancient world bore witness to the existential showdown between Rome and Carthage, the esteemed Russian poet Fyodor Tiutchev observed at the time that history seemed to be shaping up along the same lines and, so he hoped, with the same result. Two thousand years ago the master on land, Rome, defeated the ruler of the seas, Carthage. Surely today, with Russia possessing the largest army in the world and Britain the largest navy, destiny would repeat itself.[1]

Of course the Crimean War never came close to anything like that even if, as Tiutchev and others believed, the same superlatives were in play again. The fighting between Russia and Britain began in 1854 and ended in 1856 with the two countries occupying the same positions and with the map of Europe virtually unchanged. Why the war never took on an existential tenor can be traced, arguably, to the simple fact that there was no clearcut, overriding reason for the two to be fighting each other in the first place. If Herodotus stated at the very beginning of his

1

opus that its principle objective was "to show why" the Greeks and Persians went to war in an even earlier great power rivalry, the father of history would have been hard pressed to do the same, nearly two and a half millennia later, when it came to the British and the Russians.

Moreover, by the mid-nineteenth century peaceful co-existence between the two seemed a likely possibility since the last time the two empires took up arms in Europe, it had been as allies against Napoleon. Indeed, in the years running up to the Crimean War, both had more pressing international concerns. Britain was still in the grip of a French invasion scare led by their old arch-enemy's nephew, Louis Napoleon Bonaparte, following a coup in 1851 that had turned him from a democratically elected president into a dictatorial monarch. So too what Russia feared most—nationalist revolutions and democratic uprisings—had come true three years before when Hungarians, Germans, Poles and others rose up in revolt in 1848. In short, if at century's midpoint the dogs of war in both empires were straining at the leash, then their quarry would seem to lie elsewhere. Even after the war its origins remained a puzzle and that situation has continued to the present day, with consensus among scholars occurring only on one point. It was mercifully short, like a waystation between the greater conflagrations of the Napoleonic Wars and the First World War—except for one troubling fact: Crimea changed forever the face of modern warfare.

It did so by introducing to the world a plethora of technological "firsts." At the top of this list was the rifle, which made its destructive power on the battlefield truly known. Along with it came long-range artillery, the railroad and the telegraph, photography, chloroform and triage surgery. Ironclads, steam-powered ships and the explosive shell also appeared, making sails and wooden hulls obsolete overnight. The war also witnessed the first use of landmines or "man-traps," as one British officer called them, presciently described by another as "scarcely fair" in the annals of war since they continued to kill even after the enemy had quit the field; his dream—something the Germans would actually do on Russian soil in 1941—was to drive prisoners out in front so as to clear the ground. Even poison gas gained attention as a novel way to flush the enemy out of the trenches. A chemist with the improbable name of Lyon Playfair felt that cyanide, shot from a cannon, would be a most humane method to accomplish this since it "would kill men without suffering." The British War Office, unlike in the next century, thankfully disagreed. Yet taken together, whether experimental or not, this collection of new weaponry and its supporting systems represented the greatest revolution in warfare since the introduction of gunpowder.[2]

This infusion of technology has rightfully made the Crimea the first "modern" war, coming a decade before the American Civil War and serving as a harbinger of the industrial slaughter of the First World War. This conflict, however, bore witness to another revolution, one that has received far less attention, though it is arguably of equal significance. It has to do with the ways in which we try to understand war and our attempts to represent and convey its horrors. For the first time the public at home learned from the soldiers themselves of war's true destructive impact—that is, how their bodies were torn apart by new weapons or drowned in the mud of trenches; how minds were lost in harrowing bombardments that drove some to suicide; or how others wasted away from gangrenous rot in foul-smelling hospitals.

The consequence of this knowledge, once it reached home, should not be underestimated, especially when seen alongside official attempts from the government, the military and their abettors to sweep such horrors under the carpet, to obfuscate and distract and, ultimately, to lie to their own people. But once the genie was out of the bottle, as it were, there was no turning back. The Crimean War was the first in which public opinion helped push Britain to the negotiating table, whereas in Russia it drove the state, headed by the tsar, to such depths of despair that it too eventually sought the same. Crimea, in short, catapulted the world into a new, unprecedented type of war, as much one of words as weapons.

Two men, eyewitness participants from opposite sides of the trenches, paved the way for this revolution in words and set the stage for how we try to make sense of war—even when today the media at hand extend far beyond pen and paper. One was an Irish correspondent destined to become the father of modern journalism; the other, a Russian noble, whose work would make him one of the world's greatest writers. Together, over 150 years ago, William Howard Russell and Lev Tolstoy introduced to the world images of war it had rarely—if ever—seen before, images that clashed with a centuries-old tradition derived from Homeric models that had made the battlefield an exalted place, knowing only glory, courage and worthy sacrifice. In newspaper dispatches home and in short stories published while the war was ongoing, Russell and Tolstoy offered instead graphic scenes of appalling slaughter centering on the siege of Sevastopol, the port city on the Crimean Peninsula that for eleven months was witness to most of the war's fighting. Neither had gone to Crimea with that intention and neither, to be sure, could wholly shed the influence of that Homeric tradition, but because of their impact at that time and the careers they both subsequently had—becoming two of the most celebrated names in the world of letters for that century—never again would war enjoy its exalted status as a purely noble affair.

What gave their revolution in words such a decisive push, especially in the case of Russell, was another seismic change occurring in society at this time: the rise in literacy rates, particularly among recruits in the British army. If they could now read in unprecedented numbers, they could also write, and this power transformed them overnight from an abstract collective into individuals who gave voice to what they faced on the battle-field, in the camps and in the hospitals. Letters, diaries and memoirs from rank-and-file soldiers give us an acute, unfiltered sense of how they fought and died; how they suffered, hungered and labored; how their nerves and endurance were driven to the edge; and how too often their fears and anxieties brought them to despondency. For the first time, these "voices from below" recorded for posterity what war meant on an everyday basis out-side the purview of generals, commanders and politicians.

The pictures these soldiers drew confirmed the accuracy of Russell's reporting—and by extension what Tolstoy was also writing—despite official protestations and attempts to control the "story" of the war. The train, steamship and telegraph accel-erated this transmission of information from the frontlines back home to a matter of days and, by war's end, to one of mere hours—again, at least for Britain. This landmark moment in history meant that the public, over 1,500 miles away, learned essentially in real time how the war was progressing—or not; something no government had to contend with before.

All of these factors—technological breakthroughs, the lethal-ity of new weapons, increased literacy rates, the courage of people like Russell and Tolstoy—bring us to a final "first" for the Crimean War that returns us to the question of why it was fought. The sheer number and scope of participants—the British, the French, the Ottoman Turks and, eventually, the Sardinians allied against the Russians—made it a global affair, indeed, the greatest international crisis of the Victorian era, yet it neither matched the dynastic struggles for various European thrones from the eighteenth century, nor did it repeat the epic battle with Napoleon from the beginning of the nineteenth. Instead, several lines of clashing ideological and geo-strategic interests erupted almost without warning at mid-century, and delineating them is perhaps the best place to begin.

As we might expect, the initial spark came from religious differences. Of the five participants, Russia was the sole Orthodox Christian nation (though as an empire stretching from Europe across Asia it was, of course, also multi-confessional) and this exclusivity was something both sides drew upon. Russia saw itself as the protector of other Orthodox Slavs, such as the Serbs and the Bulgarians who, for the most part, were under the thumb of Muslim Turks or Catholic Austrians. At the same time, this difference made Russia a pariah in the eyes of the West, especially Protestant Britain and Catholic France, who preferred to paint it as a fount of heresy, obscurantism and superstition. Russia's official religion was a backwards one, so ran this reasoning, which made all the more sense since it was also a backwards country held up by the chains of serfdom and an autocratic system.

In the first half of the nineteenth century, this isolation and Russia's own imperial ambitions helped turn the country, in the West's estimation, into a mortal threat. After the fall of Napoleon in 1815, it didn't take Britain long to substitute Russia in his place as the tyrant du jour. From Whitehall to the popular press and streets of London came the image of the Russian bear threatening to claw its way through Europe—but with none of the French emperor's enlightened mindset. Instead, the only gift Russia could offer its victims was Eastern despotism and enslavement. By mid-century its imperial drive seemed to confirm this as it marched through the Caucasus and Central Asia en route to ruling nearly a sixth of the world. Certainly the oppressed peoples of Eastern Europe, such as the Poles, could attest to Russia's implacable predatory nature. It did not take much for Britain— while still fearing French invasion—to see that expansion as a direct threat to its own empire, in particular its terrestrial links to

India. Ironically it was Karl Marx, certainly no friend of capitalist Britain, who gave voice to the fears of many in the West. One could never trust Russia, he warned at the time, since "its methods, its tactics, its maneuvers may change, but the polar star of its policy—world domination—is a fixed star."[3]

Russia did little to assuage such fears. With pride it stood solidly and stubbornly as the "gendarme of Europe," its army always ready to pounce on any expression of freedom or liberty no matter where such sentiments might be found—even outside its borders. The latest to discover this had been the Hungarian nationalists in their struggle for independence from their Austrian overlords. When revolution flared across Europe in 1848, including in Budapest, Russia had sent an army across its border to quash them since it could not countenance any threats to Europe's political order.[4]

Russia's preternaturally militaristic reputation had been further bolstered by its longstanding struggle with Turkey. Conflict between the two, from petty raids to full-scale invasions, extended back hundreds of years and was fueled by the usual mix of differing faiths and clashing interests that stretched across a shared border from southeast Europe, across the Black Sea and through the Caucasus. If one were to keep count, outright war had flared up between them three times in the eighteenth century and twice already in the nineteenth. In fact, if an immediate cause for the Crimean War were to be identified, then it was, first and foremost, their rivalry and mutual suspicion that triggered it.

That spark came unexpectedly in 1850 when the Turkish sultan, whose territory included the Holy Land, gave France the keys to the Church of the Holy Sepulchre, built on the site of Jesus's crucifixion and the most sacred place of pilgrimage in Christendom. Since Orthodox monks had held them before, transferring control to another faith was a personal insult to the

Emperor of Russia, Nicholas I, in his role as protector of the Orthodox. Not only was Russia's national prestige at stake, France was in his eyes a fraudulent newcomer to the imperial circle since its emperor was self-anointed, just like the original Napoleon, his usurper uncle from forty years before. (Initially elected president of France's Second Republic in 1848, less than four years later Louis Bonaparte seized power and brazenly awarded himself the title of Napoleon III.)

The Turks' shift in allegiances was not due to any religious epiphany that might favor Catholicism over Orthodoxy but rather to France's aggressive diplomacy as its pushy new emperor tried to muscle his way onto the world stage. Russia, not surprisingly, responded in like fashion but, unable (and unwilling) to retaliate directly against France, decided to browbeat the Turks by moving troops in the summer 1853 into the territories of present-day Romania, then under Ottoman control. Negotiations taken half-heartedly by both sides failed to reach a compromise. Proud, arrogant, self-righteous, Nicholas refused to back down, as did the Turks. The impasse continued until October of that year when the latter, assured of support by Britain and France, declared war against Russia. Desultory fighting on the Danube and in the Caucasus yielded marginal results. Marginal, that is, until the next month when the Russians decimated the Turkish fleet at Sinope, a port on the southern shore of the Black Sea. Of the new technologies that would make their debut in the war, here the explosive shell made its first appearance when it pulverized the wooden hulls of the Turkish ships.

The Turkish defeat shocked the British, who feared that the Russians might proceed unimpeded to the ultimate prize, Constantinople, the capital of the Ottoman Empire and gateway between the Black Sea and the Mediterranean. Their long-simmering Russophobia caught fire and, along with France, in March 1854, Britain declared war on Russia. That move, in turn, came as a shock to Nicholas since Christians allying with Muslims against another Christian nation was something of a rare occurrence in European history. Moreover, Austria and Prussia, the two other major powers bordering Russia, did not come to Nicholas's aid; instead, they remained neutral while keeping their armies at the ready.

As noted, the war never reached the epic proportions one might have expected. While there were engagements in the Baltic and even the Pacific, for the most part the primary fighting between Russia and the West was confined to Crimea in the Black Sea and its port of Sevastopol, home to the Russian fleet. The allies laid siege to the city, and it is there that the war's most significant events took place and where its legends and legacy were born. During the showdown at Sevastopol, several bloody battles occurred which dominated the public's attention back home in both Britain and Russia, and they now serve as chronological signposts to chart the course of the siege. The list begins with the Alma River in September 1854 when the allies, having just landed in Crimea, first faced the Russian army and revealed the devastating power of their new rifles. Their victory cleared the way to the city, and the next month witnessed the start of the siege proper with the so-called Great Bombardment of its defenses by over 1,000 of the allies' cannon. A few weeks later came a Russian counter-attack at the Battle of Balaklava in which the Charge of the Light Brigade and the Thin Red Line gained mythic status. In November, the stalemated slaughter of the Battle of Inkerman dispelled any thoughts of quick victory while helping give birth to another legend, Florence Nightingale, the hero of modern nursing.

After a catastrophic hurricane, both sides settled in for the winter, which nearly destroyed the ill-prepared British army, and while the spring of 1855 brought some relief, it was marked by another fruitless bombardment by the allies. In June they launched a frontal assault on the entrenched Russians, which ended in a failure that foreshadowed the Somme in 1916. Only in September, a year after they had landed, could the British and French muster the overwhelming forces to push the exhausted Russians out of the southern half of the city and bring the siege to a close. That gave rise to still another legend, this time for the Russians: the epic of Sevastopol, the city which stood up to the West for 359 days without surrendering.

As compelling as these legends were, they could not compensate for the inability on either side to answer a simple question: what was it all for? Why did nearly a million people die in a war begun for such murky reasons and that ended with so little to show for it? It is what we continue to ask and why Crimea earned the scorn of a diplomat at the time—from the winning side no less—as "the only perfectly useless modern war that has been waged."[5]

Yet it is in these words, spoken by Robert Morier, who would later become the British ambassador to Russia when the two empires were on course to become allies once again, that the real story of the Crimean War and its significance for today lie. A war of choice initiated by nations infatuated with their own exceptionalism, a stalemate resulting in ghastly losses, the shifting and often contradictory rationales employed to justify its conduct, governments caught in lies and deception, an outcome leaving both sides embittered and embattled with unprecedented domestic blowback—what is all of this but the recipe for the quagmires that have plagued great powers ever since, from the trenches of the First World War, to the jungles of Vietnam, to America's invasion of Iraq in 2003 and Russia's of Ukraine twenty years later? That the Crimean War was the first of its kind for the modern age—the only distinction being its brevity—is perhaps its most consequential and compelling legacy.

This final "first" that Crimea enjoys is inseparable, once again, from the revolution in words the war engendered and the central role Russell and Tolstoy played in it. Through their work they kept returning readers to the fact that the war made no sense; it lacked, put simply, a convincing story. It was not a war for national survival, as might be said of the Napoleonic Wars; nor did it stem from dynastic conflicts like those from a century before. The Crimean War stood out for its time as an anomaly, but one that demonstrated to the world a valuable lesson: victories, like that over Napoleon (or, we could say later, Hitler) are generally easy to write; they tend to script themselves. Few debates arise over decisions made or paths taken since the laurels waiting at the war's end tend to make the preceding events justifiable or, at least, understandable. So too, one could say, with defeat. Here debates over why failure occurred may always continue, but the surety of that outcome offers cohesion and coherence to any narrative one might propose.

Yet quagmires—like the one into which the Crimean War quickly descended—upend both scripts. Since they are almost always wars of choice, the motivating story of "why" becomes paramount. However, if that story changes or loses its footing during the course of the conflict then most likely something has gone seriously awry. Moreover, quagmires lack the decisive closure of absolute victory or defeat—either of which gives a final, definitive chapter from which one can grow and learn. That is why the impact of quagmires often lingers far beyond the end of any fighting. Their aftereffects, as we see time and again in history, can break nations, bring down governments or lead to revolutions, both social and political.

Russell's reporting and Tolstoy's stories drove the idea of the quagmire into the public mainstream like never before. What made their writing particularly powerful—radical even—was its honest treatment of death, the veritable sine qua non of all conflicts. Both directly challenged and upset the received norms of how men die in battle and revealed them to be hollow clichés.

Instead of resorting to Homeric glosses and rhetorical paeans to god and country, Russell and Tolstoy sought in words and imagery to foreground death in the most raw, unadorned state possible, no matter if it ran afoul of censors or went against public taste. In short, thanks to them, after Crimea death in war became different—both how we record it and how we represent it.

What motivated them was not only their penchant for upending artistic and journalistic conventions—that is, their sheer skill and imaginative creativity as writers—but also the profound injustices they saw behind the war's unprecedented losses. For Crimea was the last major European war in which most of the fatalities occurred off the battlefield. Disease, exposure and hunger were the greatest killers, as in previous conflicts. However, by mid-century, with the concomitant revolutions in science, medicine and transport, that should not have been the case. The causes, cures and preventions of such deaths were, for the most part, known—which is something Russell, in particular, never let his readers forget. Untold thousands lost their lives because of such simple wants as a blanket or overcoat or because of the neglect of rudimentary hygiene. Thousands died, in other words, because of avoidable breakdowns in planning and logistics; in the failure to apply advanced science and medicine; in the stubbornness of doctors to part with traditional ways; and because of apathy, incompetence and indifference at the command level.

Russell, working for the *Times* as an embedded journalist (as we would call him now), led the way in exposing how much of this tragedy was due to human agency, and when the government tried to cover up and deny this, it was his words that brought it down—literally, as the prime minister resigned while the siege of Sevastopol was still ongoing. Not for nothing did the *Times*, the preeminent newspaper of the empire, conclude when the war was over, "Never was so great an effort made for so worthless an object. It is with no small reluctance that we admit a gigantic effort and an infinite sacrifice to have been made in vain."[6] After Russell, one might even say, British politics and journalism would never be the same.

Tolstoy's impact was different—Russia of course had none of the freedoms of speech Russell enjoyed—but no less important. As a junior artillery officer, he experienced and witnessed the horrors of trench warfare, and his short stories, which also appeared during the siege, confounded censors but won over readers due to their unconventionality and set him on his path to greatness, later crowned by *War and Peace* and *Anna Karenina*. By war's end he, like Russell, could not say what all the bloodshed was for, and his disgust with the conduct and lies of his government led him to resign his commission and devote himself to writing—the effect of which, especially on chroniclers of war, cannot be overestimated.

That Russell and Tolstoy together had such an influence on how the world now sees war—and quagmires in particular—constitutes the primary focus of what follows. In this sense, one could see it as a precursor to Paul Fussell's landmark *The Great War and Modern Memory* which demonstrated that after 1914 the world—particularly how we imagine it through language and literature—was forever altered. The seeds for that change, however, were already being sown sixty years before in Crimea when the nature of war itself crossed a threshold and so too the writing it generated.

The fighting in Crimea differed from its predecessor, the Napoleonic Wars, and yet its battlefield tactics were still beholden to that earlier era with predictable—and tragic—results. Russell and Tolstoy played an essential role in crafting the two greatest myths to emerge from the war (the Charge of the Light Brigade and Sevastopol, the City That Never Surrendered), but their outlooks took a sharp turn by the spring of 1855, raising fundamental questions about the siege, particularly through the lens of its tremendous losses. Both writers, independently of each other, not only carved out new territory to understand the human face behind the death of soldiers but also ensured how unprecedented yet consequential that break-through was. Their writing was particularly impactful on the home front in light of the increasing sense of the war's point-lessness on both sides, a defining feature of quagmires. Russell and Tolstoy thus laid the groundwork for veterans of the First World War and later conflicts to try to understand and cope with their own experiences.

As they set out for Crimea, Russell and Tolstoy could not have known what awaited them. Both were young, but because of their experiences there they would become in their lifetimes international icons and undisputed masters in their fields. Most importantly for our purposes, they would also become the drivers of a revolution in war writing as they tried to understand and convey what happened in the trenches of Sevastopol. Perhaps that is the only thing of lasting value we can now take from "so worthless an object."

1

CALL TO ARMS

While William Howard Russell and Lev Tolstoy both hailed from Europe, the worlds they lived in could not have been more different. By mid-century Britain and Russia were peerless rivals in the game of empire building but shared little beyond that. Britain was the world's preeminent democracy, its leading economic, industrial and financial power, whereas Russia stood as its opposite, an autocracy openly and unabashedly hoping to stem any liberalizing currents. One was a bastion of free speech and free labor; the other was mired in despotism and servitude. If Britain sought to lead the world in technological and scientific innovation, Russia's mission was to freeze progress and cut off the wings of enlightenment. Indeed, while Thomas Macaulay, the eminent historian of the time, could champion his countrymen "as the greatest and most highly civilized people that ever the world saw," a minister for Tsar Nicholas I let it be known that he "could die in peace" if he could "keep Russia in check for the next fifty years."[1]

Details only bring out the differences more. If one of the most salient signs of progress in the nineteenth century was the railroad, then Britain reigned supreme. Less than fifty years after its introduction, it had transformed the island, including Scotland and Wales, into a close-knit land, traversable in mere hours. A majority of its population now lived in or around cities and the literacy rate for both men and women was well on its way to percentages close to the nineties, a mark reached by century's end. In Russia, by contrast, not only did peasants make up most of the population, but nearly eighty per cent were serfs, that is, the property of landowners or the state. This was slavery not by race (which the British Empire had abolished in 1833) but through a caste system in which Russians could be bought, sold, beaten and abused by their own. Literacy could be a dangerous weapon, which is why the state viewed any attempts to educate them with suspicion and fear—something Tolstoy would learn firsthand when he tried to set up schools for peasants' children just before the war.

As for railroads, by mid-century Russia could show only a paltry, single connection between the capital St. Petersburg and the tsar's summer palace, twenty-five kilometers in all; if Britain's rail system sought to unite all its people into a single polity, Russia's only carried the royal family to escape the city. After all, as the tsar's minister of finance let it be known, an expanded railway network would allow discontents and troublemakers to gather and spread subversion that much more easily. Thus, by 1853, the year the war began, the vast country's railway network had expanded to less than 600 miles, whereas Britain's stood at a mighty 8,000.[2]

The Russian government's fear of movement could be felt most readily at the border where ingress and egress were severely restricted. Britain, conversely, opened its doors to virtually all, including revolutionaries bent on its own destruction. Karl Marx needed neither a mask nor a false identity to sit openly in the libraries of London while he wrote *The Communist Manifesto*, calling for the overthrow of the capitalist system, in 1848. Such was not the case in Russia, where a veil of secrecy and suspicion loomed over all—including the tsar himself. When Nicholas had traveled to Britain four years earlier on a diplomatic mission to ease continental tensions, it was incognito as "Count Orloff" in order to throw off would-be assassins lurking in London—first and foremost Polish exiles fighting for their nation's liberation. Such was the Russian court's fear of assassination that histories of ancient Rome were censored to remove references to such acts lest anyone get the wrong idea. Students would learn instead that emperors back then merely "perished"—a paranoia that was replicated in math textbooks as well since, some officials believed, equations with ellipses and other strange symbols might harbor a secret code for subversives. Not for nothing had Nicholas's Russia earned its title as the "gendarme of Europe."

How much the two empires differed from each other was put on full public display at the Great Exhibition, which opened in 1851 and was later heralded as the first World's Fair. Held in London, the building that housed the event was itself a veritable monument to progress. Made solely of iron and glass, the Crystal Palace extended nearly 2,000 feet and rose to a height of over 40 yards—so tall, in fact, that the sturdy oaks of Hyde Park, where it was constructed, were not moved but simply enclosed within its towering ceiling. Inside was the most dazzling array of technological innovations and marvels of industry the world had ever seen, all of which had one aim: to improve life by making it more efficient from farm yard to factory, safer and longer-lasting, and, at the same time, full of leisure. From massive steam engines, textile machines, cameras and prototypes of powered tractors to microscopes and surgical instruments—all attested to humans' ongoing conquest of nature, shrinking the planet ever more while uncovering its deepest secrets. Britain, France and the United States led the way with most of these showstoppers whereas other places from around the world, often their colonies, delighted visitors with colorful displays of native cultures and the like. In all, nearly 100,000 objects were to be seen in the Crystal Palace.

Amid this parade of empires, Russia's exhibit stood alone. It offered none of the forward-thinking inventions favored by the West but rather the exotica, for example, of the Cossacks and colonized peoples of Asia or of its raw agricultural products, particularly grain, which constituted its principal export and fed so many in Europe. And while its addition to the exhibition certainly was popular—the event drew over 6,000,000 visitors in the six months it ran in Hyde Park—to any observer it was clear that Russia's contribution to the pyramid of progress was to sustain its base rather than lead from its top.

Nothing from the Victorian age could rival the Crystal Palace and the Great Exhibition as symbols of a new world dawning, and this was especially true for the hosts, who relished the impression that only Britain could put on such an event. Indeed, this period was arguably the first to be conscious of itself not only as one of transition but also as transformational. Breaking with the confines of the past—with its limits on locomotion, communication, knowledge, science, medicine—was the calling card of the day, with the host country at the forefront. Taking stock at this time, one enthusiastic British man could readily proclaim that "within the last half century there have been performed upon our island, unquestionably, the most prodigious feats of human industry and skill witnessed in any age of time or in any nation of the earth." Its inventions and innovations were remaking the world so that nature no longer presented any foreseeable barriers or limitations; instead of being slaves to its whims and caprices, humankind had finally liberated itself from nature's chains and stood over it as its conqueror. Indeed, martial imagery was not off-mark, as Macaulay's fellow historian,

Thomas Carlyle wrote: "We remove mountains, and make seas our smooth highway; nothing can resist us. We war with rude nature; and, by our restless engines, come off always victorious, and loaded with spoils."[3]

The ever-victorious march of progress was the quintessence of the Victorian mindset. With Britain at its fore, events could go in only one direction, following a single path from the darkness of the past to the light of the present, and dreams come true in the future. Known as the Whiggish interpretation of history, with Macaulay and Carlyle as its chief practitioners, this school of thought had only one place for the likes of Russia: to be left behind in history's dustbin as the symbol of all that was retrograde. Of course, for Nicholas this was precisely where he wanted Russia to be; in fact, the gendarme metaphor did not necessarily circulate in his court as a negative. If autocracy stood as the clearest indication of God's desire for political order and stability, then what other role could he and, by extension, the state assume? Indeed, as the celebrated historian Mikhail Pogodin would argue, *pace* the Whigs of London, was it not time for Russia to break free from the "yoke" of the West's so-called civilizing mission and find its true place as the leader of the Slavs, "brothers in blood and faith?" For Russia, in other words, the proper way for history to go might be in the opposite direction.[4]

* * *

Yet for all their differences, one thing linked the two empires and it played a crucial role in how they approached war in Crimea: they shared the laurels for defeating Napoleon Bonaparte forty years before. This achievement, as understood then, was more than just another victory in their respective histories. It not only confirmed a heightened sense of exceptionalism for both, it was also an epoch-defining triumph—on par, for example, with Rome conquering Carthage or the Franks stopping the Muslims at Tours at the beginning of the Middle Ages. If the first had secured Rome's dominance of the Mediterranean and thereby allowed the fruits of the classical world to flourish, the second, so ran the thought, had made certain that Europe would remain Christian and enjoy its gifts as well. For the nineteenth century, the Anglo-Russian defeat of Napoleon had saved Europe from an existential threat to its civilization once again. After all, the Corsican upstart was a tyrant seeking to destroy the established political order and reshape the continent with him at its center. This ambition made Napoleon, at least in the eyes of the Russian Church, nothing less than the anti-Christ himself, as he was officially designated. If those were the stakes, what could be more prestigious than the bragging rights for his ultimate defeat?

Russia made its claim first. In 1812 when Napoleon invaded at the head of the largest army the world had ever seen, the Russians faced him alone with no one coming to their aid. They shed their own blood by the thousands at the Battle of Borodino, the bloodiest single day of all the Napoleonic Wars, and sacrificed their villages and fields while luring the enemy deep into their country's wintry grip. They even gave up Moscow, the capital of the motherland, to the foreign invaders and let it burn as the ultimate sacrifice. This they did willingly and, with God shining on them, they broke the back of the French army and thus became the only country invaded by Napoleon to successfully defend itself without outside help. For devout Russians, this was nothing short of a miracle because until that time Napoleon's forces had seemed invincible, roaming freely across the continent. Yet their triumph did not end there. The next year Russia led a coalition, including Austria and Prussia, that ended in the occupation of Paris in 1814 and Napoleon's abdication and exile to Elba. Russia, in short, had delivered the mortal blow to the anti-Christ on its own soil.

The British, on the other hand, looked to Waterloo a year later in 1815 as the truly decisive victory. There, in a small field in Belgium, the Duke of Wellington crushed the would-be tyrant after he had escaped from his island exile and destroyed any remaining military ambitions he might have harbored. That victory, instead of the Russian campaign, was what had put the final nail in Napoleon's coffin.

With the prestige of each nation at stake, the contest over laurels was no small matter. The Russians could make the counter-claim—as Tolstoy himself would a decade after Crimea in *War and Peace*—that Waterloo was anti-climactic, that is, merely the final chapter in the story of a tyrant whose defeat was preordained by the disaster of 1812. Indeed, for many of his compatriots, that year—fortuitously when romantic nationalism was sweeping Europe—marked the moment their nation was reborn into a new life. For crushing Napoleon gave Russians *the* central place in one of history's greatest stories, and the effect on the country's mood was nothing less than transcendent. Thus when the veteran and celebrated poet Denis Davydov thought of that year, it awakened in him a special feeling he could proclaim to the world: "Now my head rises with pride knowing that I am Russian." Indeed, amid the ashes of Moscow, set aflame as the ultimate sign of Russians' willingness to sacrifice themselves in such a titanic struggle, was born "the spirit of our great people." The event was almost Christ-like in its beneficence, for the cross Russians bore that year became, as another observed, "the salvation of Russia and of Europe."[5]

Yet Britain was not to be outdone in the superlatives it could take from Waterloo and, in fact, from the whole of the Napoleonic Wars. After all, was not the entire conflict with Bonaparte, from 1805 to 1815, bookended by British triumph? In that first year at Trafalgar its fleet had smashed the combined French and Spanish one—a victory which ensured its command of the seas, as Waterloo did its command of the land ten years later. That was a dual triumph to which no other nation could lay claim. Thus by 1850 it was clear to many in Britain that victory over Napoleon was the culminating point not just of British history, crowning its meteoric rise as the dominant power on the globe, but of world history as well. In the aftermath of that war, no other people had spread their influence so profoundly over its six continents. It almost went without saying, therefore, that when Sir Edward Creasy's bestselling *Fifteen Decisive Battles of the World* first appeared in 1851, only Britain could lay claim to being the driver behind nearly half of them, with the final one, of course, being Waterloo.

The mantle of exceptionalism—divinely given and proven in battle—thus shone over both nations when they declared war on each other in 1854. Not surprisingly, each army looked with nostalgia on that golden time, no matter how much new technologies should have demanded more of their attention. Crimea, in other words, was no exception to the tendency that victors enter their next war beholden to their previous one. In fact, veterans of the Napoleonic Wars could still be found in the ranks of both armies—a full forty years later. This was most notable in the British officer corps where the man chosen to lead the expeditionary force against Russia was Lt. General Fitzroy Somerset, Lord Raglan, who first served with Wellington as his secretary during the Peninsular Wars and then again as his aide at Waterloo where he lost his arm to a French cannonball (which is why in Crimea he had the bad habit of referring to the Russians, now his enemy, as "the French").

More symptomatic of calcified policies in the British army was the continued practice of officers purchasing their own commissions. With the exception of the substantially smaller artillery and engineering branches, in the infantry and cavalry only a young gentleman of means could afford to buy entry, even at the level of ensign, the lowest commissioned rank. Moving from there up to lieutenant, captain and so forth was predicated on openings appearing because of death and retirement or because those in the higher ranks would, essentially, put their positions up for sale—often at the price of several years' salary. Yet by the 1850s, this system, which derived from the seventeenth century in order to ensure that officers owned property (and were thus less likely to rebel against the state), flew in the face of the emerging Victorian ethos of meritocracy and, more than anything, guaranteed that class divisions and the attendant snobbery carried over from civilian society to the military. To be sure, officers from other armies at this time were also drawn from the aristocracy—witness Tolstoy's own rise in the ranks—however, in Crimea the system's glaring deficiencies and built-in recipes for incompetence would become impossible to ignore.

For Russia the embrace of the past was seen most readily in the rank-and-file soldiers, the building blocks of both the army and navy that were still made up of serfs, the illiterate peasants conscripted on an annual basis from villages according to a quota system. Initially serving for life, the term was later amended to twenty-five years. Nevertheless, even this was tantamount to a death sentence, which is why a village would hold a funeral for a new recruit. Once inducted, he became the property of the state and was often marched away in chains to prevent desertion.

As chattel, the conscripted serf was typically treated by officers as an animal or even worse. Beatings and other kinds of corporal punishment were part of the daily norm, while thievery and exploitation were also extremely commonplace—something Tolstoy learned to his shock and disgust. Using government funds, officers short-changed their own soldiers in provisions, uniforms and other supplies while pocketing the difference; even the cartridges they were given for their obsolete muskets were sometimes known to contain sand because the gunpowder had been sold off. It is little wonder that their hostility towards officers was so great—and often greater than that for the enemy—that in combat it was not unheard of for officers to be killed by their own. Outside consensus only confirmed this. Before the war, an American observer declared that "a Russian private is the most wretched creature upon earth," whereas a Polish captain who had deserted to the British reported that "the Russian soldier is perhaps the most unhappy being in the world." Few would disagree.[6]

Yet despite the deprivation and abuse they faced, Russian peasants also enjoyed the reputation of ranking among the most formidable of soldiers. Stories of their unbreakability, their willingness to die standing in their ranks, dated from the eighteenth century when during the Seven Years' War their most famous adversary, Frederick the Great, declared that "it is not enough to kill the Russian soldier; he must be knocked down as well." Apocryphal or not, the conclusion of a British observer when that war ended certainly wasn't: "Experience has proved that the Russian infantry is far superior to any in Europe."[7]

The wars with revolutionary France and Napoleon only furthered that reputation. If the British were known for their "pluck," a word coming into currency around this time and denoting the national trait of perseverance in the face of adversity, then for the Russians it was the idea of *stoikost*, their tenacious ability to withstand anything—hunger, cold, enemy bullets—until death. That fatalistic trait would be seen time and again at Sevastopol, and the reasons behind it have led to mixed speculation on its sources. The harsh conditions of a serf's life and the military's ferocious discipline certainly played a role. However, there was something else, much closer and simpler to the peasants' understanding of the world, that also contributed to their fortitude: an intense and unfailing belief in themselves as foot soldiers in the Army of God defending Holy Rus, the mystical designation of the motherland hearkening back to the Middle Ages.

This faith could readily be seen at the siege, for instance, with Russian gun crews placing icons next to their cannon or with priests in cassocks marching and sometimes fighting alongside their soldiers. It manifested itself as well in the superstitions virtually all peasants held, particularly with regard to the devil, who seemed to figure as often as Christ or Mother Mary in their collective imagination. In fact, very often the greatest danger in their eyes was not any redcoated infantryman but cholera and typhus since those diseases were believed to the devil's favorite weapons. Not surprisingly for an army of bachelors, the evil one could also appear in the bodies of young women or take the shape of animals like wolves, pigs, snakes and even flies. Moreover, the Russian soldier had to contend not just with a single demonic force but with devils in the plural, including those who lived in families and married witches. As a sign of their infernal ubiquity, Vladimir Dal, the famed lexicographer of this era, recorded that peasants had over forty words to signify "unclean spirits." That is why for every Russian soldier the cross around his neck was often more valuable than the musket in his hands.[8]

That little had changed in the Russian army since the days of Napoleon was equally due to the fact that the person in command, Tsar Nicholas, preferred it that way. From his childhood at the beginning of the century—he was fifty-seven when the Crimean War began—the army and everything attached to it was his obsession. To the dismay of his tutors and nurses, he could often be found building forts from pillows and cushions, but, unlike most boys his age, he never grew out of it; fortifications continued to fascinate him through adulthood. He enjoyed the soldier's life so much that his preferred attire was a military uniform and his favorite place to sleep was a military cot that servants transported from palace to palace. Nothing excited him more than to be on the parade ground where his soldiers would train endlessly so as to perform elaborate maneuvers in tight precision—something that made for great spectacle but which was nearly useless on the battlefield. To him that was of no concern—much to the consternation of his advisors as war approached. Instead, in the tsar's eye it was as if his soldiers should be judged solely on how well their smart ranks and glittering uniforms compared to the toy ones of his youth.

When his real soldiers were counted together, along with militias and auxiliaries, Nicholas's army was the largest in the world. Numbering over 1,000,000 men, it dwarfed those of both France and Britain, even with the latter's colonial troops included. Yet from that massive figure, only a little over a 100,000 would be available to fight in Crimea. Not only did the rest have to defend the longest border in the world, thousands had to be kept on alert internally to quell uprisings, whether of serfs or oppressed minorities.

This reduced number put the Russian army on par, more or less, with the allied one that would invest Sevastopol. While the latter force fluctuated over the year-long siege, the initial British contingent sent there numbered just over 25,000. (The French would always provide substantially more throughout the war.) This number was quite large for the island empire, representing approximately a fifth of all those available from across the globe. Organized into six divisions (five infantry and one cavalry), it was less than the total number in Wellington's army at Waterloo, but it still represented a sizeable expeditionary force, approximating the population of a mid-level city sent with mid-century logistics nearly 2,000 miles away.

The men Britain sent to Crimea were also not too distant from their Napoleonic forebears. No one would question their bravery, yet they still served under the "scum of the earth" label Wellington had bestowed on them before Waterloo. Nor was their lot one to be envied, especially as flogging continued as a principal means of punishment. Besides one surprising change, a new generation of rifles which would have a tremendous impact on the battlefields of Crimea, when it came to the other particulars of a soldier's life—uniform, drill, tactics, supply—little had changed from the days of Waterloo.

In short, with rare exceptions the armies that Russia and Britain deployed to Crimea were similar to the ones used against Napoleon. Indeed, many assumed that the fighting there would be just like before too. However, when they first faced off on the battlefield, both were quickly disabused of that notion. This was a new kind of war in which the experiences at Borodino or Waterloo quickly became irrelevant.

The Writer and the Correspondent

Just like the countries they came from, the lives of Tolstoy and Russell before Crimea could not have been more different. The first grew up near the top of his society. He was a count from a well-connected family with an illustrious surname that, at least through legend, could be traced back to the fourteenth century whereas his mother's name, Volkonskaya, was even more famous and went back further via a different legend to the time of Riurik, the ninth-century Scandinavian who ruled over the eastern Slavs in the lands of modern-day Russia, Ukraine and Belarus. With such a lineage came wealth—his father had estates on which labored over 1,500 serfs—and Lev Tolstoy, born in 1828, enjoyed all the privileges that came with it: a formidable education in languages and the arts through private tutors; a personal serf given to him as a companion (and who accompanied him to Crimea); and, upon entering adulthood, his own land, though he frittered away a good share of it in gambling debts. In a society structured just for the likes of him, one full of cards, women and wine, his life was well set—except for one thing. It promised nothing special and he hated himself for indulging in its frivolous banalities.

We have intimate knowledge of how Tolstoy felt at this time because he kept a diary since age eighteen—begun, he freely admits in its opening lines, while lying in a clinic recovering from venereal disease. The self-portrait he paints conforms, on the one hand, to that of a dandy and aspiring rake and rarely rises above such expectations. On the other, however, he was also acutely introspective and quite willing to step on tradition. Moreover, he believed that destiny had carved out for him a special place, one that his present life had not yet fulfilled. The ego that emerges from this last sentiment is characteristic of a Byronic pose from that period. Yet even with that caveat, his impression of himself can be excessive: "there is something in me," he wrote a year before the Crimean War began at the age of twenty-four, "that has me believe that I was born not to be like everyone else."[9]

At first, Tolstoy sought to find that "something" by dedicating himself to improving conditions for his serfs on his estate at Yasnaia Polyana, about 125 miles south of Moscow. He had inherited it from his father who died when Tolstoy was nine, but short of abolishing the institution itself, his insistence on knowing what was right—not the only time this would happen—only met with suspicion from the peasants he intended to help, and they resisted him at nearly every step. Tolstoy next tried enrolling in the University of Kazan, but neither of his chosen subjects, foreign languages and law, answered his calling and he left without earning a degree. A return to his estate, where he would end up spending most of his life, saw him try to help peasants once more, this time through educating their children, but his efforts failed for lack of finances, primarily because his gambling continued to eat them away.

Frustrated and restless, in the summer of 1851—precisely when the attractions of the Crystal Palace were dominating London—Tolstoy threw it all to the wind and went south to the Caucasus with his eldest brother, an artillery officer. At that time no other place in the Russian Empire combined the attractions of an exotic land with the excitement of war, and Tolstoy, in the capacity of a civilian observer, fell fully in love with it. It was the place where the idols of his teenage years, like Alexander Pushkin and Mikhail Lermontov, were exiled and where the most Byronic of Russia's novels, the latter's *A Hero of Our Time*, was set.

Tolstoy himself was by now also experimenting in literature and though he tried to live the romantic cliché—throwing himself into the passions, mountains, and wild fighting of the Caucasus—as a writer he saw that life for the predictable artifice that it was, just like his introspective self from before at Yasnaia Polyana. Already he was driven in these early works to get it "right," that is, to be as authentic in his fiction as possible, and so he rebelled against the excesses of the prevailing cult of Romanticism with its hackneyed characters and plots.

It was a rebellion that soon paid off, for the next year, 1852, was a momentous one for Tolstoy. Not only did he shed his observer role and join the army as a junior officer in the artillery, it also saw the publication of his first novel, *Childhood*, in which he used an introspective lens to peel back the conventions of upper-class life through the eyes of an impressionistic boy. Based loosely on his own childhood, it culminates in the death of the mother—Tolstoy's own had died when he was two—and show-cased his powers of observation bolstered by mature reflection. *Childhood* was an unqualified success and it appeared in one of the premier journals of the time, *The Contemporary*, founded by Pushkin nearly twenty years before. Showing a boldness that would later help carry him through the unpredictable world of Russian censorship, Tolstoy had sent the manuscript unsolicited to its editor, the progressive Nikolai Nekrasov, who immediately recognized the talent in the twenty-four year old. So began a most productive relationship between the two that would be of immense benefit to the young writer in his Crimean years. Tolstoy's name quickly circulated among the greats of his time, most notably Ivan Turgenev, despite the fact that he was absent from the literary circles of St. Petersburg and for now published only under the initials "L. N."

That year, 1852, was also an eye-opener for Russian literature, yet for different reasons. It showed new writers like Tolstoy what it really meant to live in a society bound by censorship and under the watchful eye of the secret police. Scandal was triggered by Nikolai Gogol or, more precisely, his death in March by suicidally starving himself. How one should mark his passing would seem straightforward; after all, the famed writer's personal views were highly conservative and soundly Orthodox. He was an extreme Slavophile who defended serfdom and believed that the tsar was placed on earth by god to lead Holy Russia. However, in his literary endeavors, particularly his masterpiece of a decade before, *Dead Souls*, many saw something else, a satiric indictment of Russian society, and in that gap lay a political minefield for the unwary.

One writer who had already fallen into that trap while Gogol was still alive was Fyodor Dostoevsky, the author so far of two novels, *Poor Folk* and *The Double*. When he read out loud in a private circle of pseudo-socialists the letter of another progressive who had attacked Gogol's arch-conservatism, Dostoevsky himself was denounced, arrested and sentenced to a firing squad in 1849. Only on the field of execution did he learn his life was to be spared. Hard labor in a Siberian prison camp was his new fate where, when 1852 began, he still lingered.

Upon Gogol's death the trap continued to ensnare writers, including Turgenev himself, who had had the temerity to call him "great" in a eulogy. For this he was sent to jail and then exiled—but spared Siberia—and kept under house arrest outside the capital. Other dominoes began to tumble under the thumb of the state, including the very censor who allowed Gogol to be called "a great Christian satirist," for he was harshly disciplined by his superiors. As another censor confided in his diary, what to an outsider might seem a comedy of excess was in Russia deadly serious, and the turmoil raised by Gogol's death froze the literary world. "Every day, every hour you feel that the axe will fall," the censor wrote, "because of some secret denunciation or slander."

This glimpse into the inner workings of the censorship bureau belongs to Aleksandr Nikitenko, a unique figure for his time given the contradictions between his social origins and career path. Born a serf, he gained literacy by training as a clerk and subsequently earned his freedom through the intervention of influential writers like Vasily Zhukovsky. He then became a professor of history and closet liberal who decried the absence of free speech in Russia—all the while working for the state he privately criticized. His secret diary is thus an invaluable exposé of the astonishing, illuminating and absurd lengths the government would go to in order to suppress anything that might be seen as threatening. After all, as he and most of Russia's reading public realized, Gogol himself was no subversive and the crackdown on the reaction to his death ultimately backfired. Bringing the heavy arm of the police down on Turgenev, one of the most popular writers at that time, only spotlighted its own excesses. In fact, so many people came to see and support the writer while under arrest that the police ended up banning all visitors. Moreover, at a deeper level, this episode—one of many under Nicholas's reign—exemplified the difficult position in which Nikitenko and others, including soon Tolstoy as well, would find themselves: full of patriotism and love for Russia but hating the state and the intolerance of its regime. After all, who would want to live in a country where the government, Nikitenko observed, "has treated us like stupid cattle"?[10]

As an insider, Nikitenko soon found out what was behind the storm over Gogol's death. It was due to the caprice of one man, Nikitenko's superior, Mikhail Musin-Pushkin, chair of the censorship committee in St. Petersburg who, despite the second half of his surname, was no relation to the nation's most famous poet. Notorious for bullying people as "jerks," "blowhards," and "empty heads"—epithets others would use equally on him—Musin-Pushkin, somewhat inexplicably, held a diehard animus against Gogol. So much so that a simple sign of respect for the deceased, a customary move in any culture, not to speak of one of its greatest writers, could bring out his wrath and terrorize the literary world, seemingly unchecked by anyone else.

For now, all this scandal passed Tolstoy by. Far away in the south, his time that year was spent reading and hunting—primarily snipe and pheasant—and wrestling with his three admitted weaknesses: gambling, vanity and sex. The only hint of problems to come is in a diary entry for August 1852 where he proposed to "expose the evil of the Russian government" through literature. Little did he know that in two short years, that ambition would put him squarely in the sights of Musin-Pushkin and that he himself would face the same wrath when one of his stories from Crimea landed on the desk of the head censor.

* * *

Russell, born eight years before Tolstoy in 1820, had no such claim on either wealth or social status. Irish, but of mixed Protestant-Catholic background, his family was always hovering on the brink of financial hardship. For that reason he grew up with his grandparents in Dublin, gaining an education good enough to enter Trinity College to study law. Like Tolstoy, he never got his degree but a cousin, working for the *Times*, set him up with a side job reporting on Irish politics. The combination proved quite fortuitous. Not only was the *Times* the British Empire's foremost newspaper, the subject of his reporting, being something of a blood sport, never lacked for a story. Success soon brought Russell to London where he worked freelance as the Irish liaison and parliamentary reporter under the tutelage of its new editor, John Delane (who had just taken that post at the remarkable age of twenty-three).

The next decade, spent primarily in the capital, saw Russell get married and have children, make friends with such luminaries as Charles Dickens and William Makepeace Thackeray, and move full time into journalism, though sometimes working for a rival London paper, *The Morning Chronicle*. It was under the auspices of the latter that he returned to Ireland in 1846 for his grimmest assignment to date: the Famine. As he recalled later in life, even with the experience of several wars behind him, nothing could compare with what he saw in his homeland, particularly the dying children with "arms and legs dwindled" but with bellies "enormously swollen."[11] That their deaths were generally avoidable—or would have been with planning and foresight—made it all the worse and unwittingly helped prepare him for when he would see such death on a massive scale once again in Crimea.

Upon his return to London, Russell settled down professionally, moving back to the *Times* but now as a salaried employee. His next prominent assignment took him in 1850 to Denmark for his first war where two duchies with German-speaking majorities on its southern border, Schleswig and Holstein, sought independence from Danish control. Neither the war nor his reporting on it was anything special. Russell succeeded in witnessing only one battle, a victory for the Danish government, and his coverage displayed little of the narrative flair and eye for detail for which he soon would become famous. That foretaste would come instead in 1852, a defining year for him just as much as for Tolstoy, when he received the golden ticket of journalistic assignments: reporting on the funeral of the Duke of Wellington for the *Times* or, in the words of the Queen, "the greatest man this country ever produced."[12]

No one in Britain's history had ever been sent off in a such a fashion. The procession, fronted by 10,000 soldiers and led by the Queen's Consort, Prince Albert, took four hours to go through the streets of London where it was seen by upwards of 1,500,000 people who crowded its balconies, rooftops and viewing stands, all covered in black bunting and mourning crape. Russell's coverage was equally massive, a 14,000-word piece taking up the entire front page of the *Times*. That space allowed him to indulge in the most purple of prose as befitting, in his words, "England's greatest son" whom "Providence" had sent to save the world from the "days of darkness" when Napoleon threatened.[13]

Russell's reporting also showcased an acute eye for detail, of which there was an abundance to report on, starting with the Duke's funeral carriage, 25 feet long and cast from the bronze of cannon captured at Waterloo, which required twelve horses to pull. Yet it also allowed him to record the mishaps that occurred during the affair such as when the carriage got stuck in the mud and required over sixty men to push it out. All in all, it showed how much he had matured as a reporter and how much faith the newspaper had in him, for the assignment was no rush job. It had obviously been bantered back and forth behind the scenes, since Wellington had died in September—coincidentally the month when Tolstoy's *Childhood* appeared—and, after several weeks lying in state, was laid to rest only in November. It served as confirmation, in short, of someone who had begun to make his name in the field of journalism—much like his Russian counterpart had in literature.

* * *

If the year 1852 was transformative for both men, it was also the last in which peace among the great powers reigned in Europe, though neither Tolstoy nor Russell—nor anyone else—knew it at the time. There is no mention of disputed church keys or clashing strategic interests in either's diary or correspondence. Instead, Russell continued to move up in the ranks of London's literati while Tolstoy continued to serve in the Caucasus, gathering material and writing as the fighting there continued with the native peoples. Yet when war was declared, both made the quick decision to go to Crimea since both likely recognized that this was to become the international event of their age. Moreover, it allowed both the best opportunity to realize a shared dream: a chance to truly make their name outside the traditional paths endorsed by society.

How Russell got there is better told by himself, for it reads like the beginning of an adventure tale when he recalled it some forty years later:

> As I was sitting at my desk in the *Times* office one evening in February 1854, I was informed that the editor, Mr. Delane, wished to see me, and on entering his sanctum I was taken aback by the announcement that he had arranged a very agreeable excursion for me to go to Malta with the Guards. The Government had resolved to show Russia that England was in earnest in supporting the Sultan against aggression, and that she would, if necessary, send an expedition to the East. It was decided, he said, that I was the best man to represent the paper on the occasion.

Russell was told that he would be back by Easter since the Russians, once they saw the British display of military muscle, would no doubt back down. Either way, his task was clear and straightforward: accompany the troops wherever they might go. Yet for all its simplicity, never before had a journalist been given such an assignment combined with the freedom to write as he pleased. Not surprisingly, it would be over two years before he would see home again.[14]

As for Tolstoy, his route to Crimea was more circuitous and hewed closely to his continuing belief in destiny's special call. When the Ottoman Empire declared war on Russia in 1853, he was reassigned from the Caucasus to the front lines on the Danube which Russia, as a deliberate provocation, had crossed with its troops. There he witnessed the siege of Silistria, a Turkish fortress on the river, and wrote exuberantly to his aunt (who was something of a surrogate mother) in French about the shelling and the strange pleasure he took in seeing people kill each other. (*"Il est vrai que c'est un drôle de plaisir que de voir de gens s'entretuer."*) A desire to see more bloodshed on a grander scale and, as he explained later to his brother, a commensurate burst of patriotism led him to request action in Crimea where the allies had already landed and begun to lay siege to Sevastopol. Family connections helped push his request through a labyrinth of bureaucracy and in November 1854, when the siege had begun in earnest, he arrived in the city. Tolstoy would remain there and in its environs for nearly a year, resigning from the service only when it fell in the early fall of 1855. St. Petersburg— and international fame nearly second to none—would be his next destination.[15]

2

THE NEW FACE OF WAR

The Crimean War was the last in which the great powers of Europe saw themselves through the lens of romanticized pomp and pageantry. It was the last in which the men marched into battle in parade uniforms adorned with all their regimental finery; and it was the last in which they fought in tiered ranks accompanied by drums and bugles like their fathers at Waterloo and Borodino.

The war was also the swansong of the chivalry that had marked centuries of combat on the continent's battlefields; the final time officers extended courtesies to each other across the trenches. During the siege, correspondence between them on both sides was ongoing, the language typically being French. Protocol for nobility who were captured was also preserved. At their first meeting at the Battle of Alma, for instance, the Russians gallantly offered to send for the personal effects of a French colonel they had taken prisoner. For appearance's sake he refused, but his captors insured that, due to his rank, servants would continue to attend him.[1]

The Crimean War was also the last when both sides engaged in joint, on-the-spot commemorations for the fallen, a practice reminiscent of Homeric funereal rites. In the summer of 1855, ten months into the siege, a ceasefire was observed to honor the deaths of Lord Raglan, the British commander who succumbed in the field to dysentery, and his counterpart, Admiral Pavel Nakhimov, beloved commander of Sevastopol's defenses who was felled by a sniper just weeks later. The guns fell silent while separate funeral parades conveyed their bodies to their final resting place—Raglan's to a ship bound for Britain; Nakhimov's to a spot next to his predecessor, Admiral Vladimir Kornilov, himself killed during the Great Bombardment in October 1854. The procession for Raglan, a British surgeon noted in his diary, was nearly a whole-day affair involving thousands of soldiers representing the four allies, all of whom were allowed to pay their respects in peace: "French cavalry took the lead, then French artillery, English cavalry, English artillery, Turkish cavalry, Sardinian cavalry, [with] the body on a gun-carriage drawn by 8 horses." The honorary pall-bearers marching behind were the four commanders of each army while "the whole road was lined by English and French regiments of the Line with bands at intervals playing funeral dirges."[2]

Even soldiers of lesser rank could earn such respect if their behavior spoke to the same code of honor. At the Battle of Inkerman, for instance, Henry Clifford earned the Victoria Cross for leading his men in a charge during which he lopped off a Russian man's arm with his sword. The next day, passing a line of prisoners, he was startled when the same man ran up to him, swathed in bandages but laughing. "Bono Johnny!" he shouted while extending to Clifford his only good arm, now to shake hands. And when it came to the dead, something of the same fealty to past ritual could extend to them as well. When deep in the winter hundreds of French troops fell assaulting a redoubt, the commander of the Russian garrison, General Dmitry Osten-Sacken, a veteran of the Napoleonic Wars, wrote to their commander—in French and using their calendar, the Gregorian and not the Julian—"I consider it my duty to inform you that your dead brave soldiers, remaining in our hands after the affair of the 23rd of February, were buried with full honors commensurate with their exemplary courage." While many of the fallen from other "affairs" would, instead, be laid in mass graves with no such recognition, gestures like this one showed a desire to adorn this war with the vesture of previous ones.[3]

Finally, it was a war the last generation of romantics, men such as Thomas De Quincey, famous for his earlier work, *Confessions of an English Opium Eater*, could wed to the Victorian ethos of progress and prosperity. War could only be a "positive good," he wrote just before Britain declared it in 1854, especially when waged for "human rights" and "human dignity." His language sounds strikingly modern just as does his belief that recent advances in technology would render war a "magnificent and enlightened science." No longer would the battlefield yield "horrid tale[s] of butchery"; instead, combat would become "indefinitely humanized and refined" with an almost salutary effect by ridding the world of despotism and bondage—which was a less than subtle jab at Britain's newest enemy, Russia. In addition, De Quincey predicted that these efficiencies would make war an event that could be dispensed with relatively quickly, following the Victorian passion for speed and motion.[4]

De Quincey's exuberance over the direction of modern warfare was right on only one count: the Crimean War was much shorter than the decades-long struggle against revolutionary France and Napoleon. Other than that, however, as the fighting ground down to a siege so too did the potential for powerful stories that had animated earlier conflicts. Was there anything to match the dramatic sweep of Wellington's Peninsular Campaign that ran from Portugal, through Spain and across the Pyrenees to strike France in its soft underbelly? Or the epic tale of Napoleon's 1812 invasion that took his army to Moscow only to have it disintegrate as the Russians lashed back?

A Siege Like No Other

Sevastopol, where tens of thousands of troops were bottled up in just a few square miles, offered none of those dramatic storylines. To underscore that point, in one dispatch home Russell lamented how four months into the siege they felt "deprived of the peculiar attractions of most wars in Europe"—a clear reference to popular accounts of the struggle with Napoleon's forces like Sir William Napier's *History of the War in the Peninsula* (1828–1840). Himself a decorated veteran of that successful campaign, the narrative flair of Napier's six-volume account made it a bestseller in the interwar years and served as a shining example of what a British expeditionary force fighting overseas could achieve. Full of lightning strikes and decisive victories orchestrated by the Iron Duke himself, that campaign was everything Crimea was not. Comparing those glory days with the current siege of Sevastopol, Russell let readers know of the disappointment surging through the ranks: "There is none of the romance of the Peninsular campaigns about it. We are all shut up in one dirty little angle of land...[with] nothing but the drudgery of the trenches and of fatigue parties."[5]

It is not that sieges were unknown in Britain or Russia. Rather, the major ones that stood out from earlier wars were either of a decidedly different quality or distant enough in time so as to pass into legendary status and thus make the present one at Sevastopol seem deficient—at least in its narrative potential. For the Russians, the most famous siege in recent memory had occurred in a war with Turkey at the fortress of Izmail, on a tributary of the Danube. Taken by storm in 1790 by Alexander Suvorov who, like Wellington, was the country's greatest general of that era, it had gained iconic status in Russia's military lore. It had even been commemorated in an ode written by the preeminent court poet, Gavriil Derzhavin, which, when set to music, had become the nation's unofficial anthem until replaced by "God Save the Tsar" later in the nineteenth century.

Not to be outdone, the British could just as well cite the 1812 siege of Badajoz, a fortress-city in Spain whose name, while unfamiliar today, rang out for readers then as a glorious affair— so much so that forty years later Russell could still reference it without needing to provide context. Badajoz was another of Wellington's showcase victories culminating, as had Russia's siege of Izmail, with a frontal assault on the city's walls led by officers who had volunteered for the near-suicidal, nighttime mission. Though costing several thousand casualties, they took the city, a feat that became a defining moment in the Peninsular campaign—especially for one of its heroes, a young officer who was among the first to breach the walls. The person so honored was then known as Major Fitzroy Somerset; forty years later he was none other than Lord Raglan, commander of the Crimean expeditionary force.

Instead of such exciting engagements, the only things Sevastopol could offer, Russell observed less than two months into the siege, were dead horses and mud. Indeed, the closest comparison he could draw was not with Izmail or Badajoz but with "what sort of view Noah might have had" looking down from the Ark on Mount Ararat onto the land as the flood waters receded:

> The whole plateau on which stands 'the Camp before Sebastopol' [his usual lead-in tag]...is a vast black dreary wilderness of mud, dotted with little lochs of foul water, and seamed by dirty brownish and tawny-coloured streams running down to and along the ravines. On its surface everywhere are strewed the carcasses of horses and miserable animals torn by dogs and smothered in mud. Vultures sweep over the mounds in flocks; carrion crows and 'birds of prey

obscene' hover over their prey, menace the hideous dogs who are feasting below, or sit in gloomy dyspepsia, with drooped head and dropping wing, on the remnants of their banquet.

Whatever the biblical allusions, Russell was not exaggerating. Such desolation was due to that peculiar turn the weather takes in Russia during the fall and spring, known as *rasputitsa*, the in-between period between winter's freeze and the dry ground of summer. Just as it would halt Hitler's panzers a century later, it immobilized the British army in Crimea as well.[6]

To be sure, *rasputitsa* affected both sides. The Russians had no special powers to overcome it; they just knew to expect it. Eduard Totleben, the engineer in charge of Sevastopol's defenses, noted in his memoirs that during that time the ground literally "dissolves," leaving a morass that for the unsuspecting British greatly hampered—and often stopped completely—the delivery of food and ammunition to the frontlines. One aide-de-camp to Raglan, who due to his position enjoyed substantially better quarters than the enlisted man, even turned "mud" from a noun ("you sit in mud, you live in mud, you eat mud") into a verb, as in to "mud your dinner." Such conditions, one could say, also made dinner of the soldiers' boots. When it rained—almost a daily occurrence during that period—"the thick heavy clay," Russell observed, "sucked the soles off" them, swallowing everything up. That last point was not meant in jest for it could include horses, mules and men—Crimea being one of the few places where one could drown on high ground in the mud and rain.[7]

As the siege dragged on, so did the effects of the weather. Tolstoy, in fact, began to think that only it—and not the Russian army—might drive the allies home, and he privately invoked Nicholas the Wonderworker, the patron saint of Russia, to save the city. His wish almost came true on 14 November when a colossal hurricane struck, nearly wiping out the British camp, which consisted mainly of tents. The wind, unlike any seen

THE NEW FACE OF WAR

before, snapped their poles and tore the canvas to shreds. It also blew out windows and even blew the roofs off the few buildings where the British soldiers tried to escape its wrath. It staved in barns and knocked over horses and wagons, with the latter tumbling through camp like wooden rollers. Anything and everything went up, filling the air "with blankets, hats, great coats, little coats, and even tables and chairs" and hurling them into the sea while the men, dazed and senseless, Russell reported back to readers of the *Times*, "had to cling to the earth with all their might to avoid the same fate."[8]

Equal violence came to the fleet at Balaklava, the small, fjord-like port used by the British to offload supplies for their army. Ships foundered or were dashed against the rocks as hundreds drowned and their cargoes were lost forever. None was more devastating than the destruction of *Prince*, which went to the bottom of the Black Sea along with thousands upon thousands of bullets and shells and, worst of all given the cold weather soon to follow, over 50,000 heavy coats, 50,000 pairs of woolen underwear and socks, and over 30,000 blankets and rugs. As November came to a close, Frances Duberly, the 25-year-old wife of a cavalry captain, famously described their plight in her memoirs, copying Russell's oft-used rhetorical tactic of back-home analogies to make sense of Crimea for his readers:

> If anybody should ever wish to erect a 'Model Balaklava' in England I will tell him the ingredients necessary. Take a village of ruined houses and hovels in the extremest state of all imaginable dirt; allow the rain to pour into and outside of them, until the whole place is a swamp of filth ankle-deep; catch about, on an average, 1,000 Turks with the plague, and cram them into houses indiscriminately; kill about 100 a day, and bury them so as to be scarcely covered with earth, leaving them to rot at leisure—taking care to keep up the supply. Onto one part of the beach drive all the exhausted *bât* ponies, dying bullocks, and worn-out camels, and leave them to die

of starvation. They will generally do so in about three days, when they will soon begin to rot, and smell accordingly. Collect together from the water of the harbour all the offal of the animals slaughtered for the use of the occupants of above 100 ships, to say nothing of the inhabitants of the town,—which, together with an occasional floating human body, whole or in parts, and the driftwood of the wrecks, pretty well covers the water—and stew them all together in a narrow harbour, and you will have a tolerable imitation of the real essence of Balaklava.[9]

Yet just as the army began to recover, as its "careworn, threadbare, ragged men" struggled to put their lives back together, as one officer wrote, winter struck with a bone-crippling freeze that was one of the coldest on record. With many, if not most, troops still in their summer uniforms, its deadly ravages recalled Napoleon's retreat from Moscow forty years before. And while Raglan, it should be noted, did request winter clothing, little was forthcoming—a want felt more acutely by the destruction of *Prince* and other stores during the hurricane. This proved fatal to many who, bereft of overcoats, could be found in the morning frozen solid in several feet of snow. Even frostbite could prove deadly since it frequently required amputation to forestall gangrene—an operation that could just as easily lead to gangrene once more in the stump remaining.[10]

While Tolstoy passed a good part of the winter deployed north of the city, the idea that Russian soldiers at Sevastopol, supposedly inured to such weather, did not suffer should be dispelled. If the British died in what remained of their tents and makeshift shanties dug into the ground, the Russians too often found themselves not in city barracks but in ramshackle shelters thrown together from whatever was to hand. The suffering both sides experienced could be measured by the patchwork mélange soldiers wore to face the cold. With their usual sheepskin coats desperately scarce, frontline Russian troops, Totleben complained, wrapped themselves in sacks and matting, and stuffed straw wherever they could inside their uniforms. Back in Britain, as Russell's reports came home, there was a scramble to put together—arguably for the first time ever—care packages of anything that might help the troops stop the cold. Even with the two-to-three-week lag time for delivery, it was help that was most welcome and led soldiers to mix and match *anything* that might ward off the cold. When one officer wrote home to express his gratitude for parcels sent by family and friends, he did it while wearing a uniform that would have never passed muster back in Britain:

> Today is such a cold day I have got on everything I possess; on top of all Susan Blake's cap, (thank her much for it) Katie's and her sister's mitts, the mother's coat, and I don't know whose, (God bless them for them) fluffy bags for my hands, (not while writing tho').

As Raglan's aide-de-camp grimly observed, the men even faced a shortage of blankets because so many had been used to wrap bodies for burial. Losses were simply astounding. The mighty 63rd Regiment of Foot, for instance, which numbered 1,080 men as it embarked in Britain, by winter's end could only muster seven.[11]

Yet even after winter's cold took its toll, summer brought its own toxic charms, almost as if the weather enjoyed toying with the soldiers. Crimea's sun-swept fields were famed for their fruits and wines, about which no traveler from before the war had failed to comment. At the same time, the temperature could be equally unforgiving. In July 1855 it reached 100 degrees in the shade, which cast everything, Totleben wrote, with the "look of death." British troops dug holes in the ground to escape the heat, and deadly cholera gave way to dysentery, which, as noted, took the life of Raglan. Most repellent, of course, was the effect the heat had on the corpses and animal carcasses, including those which were fresh or revealed only when the snows had melted. After the disastrous allied assault on the Russian defenses in June, Henry Clifford, the sword-wielding recipient of the Victoria Cross, wrote to his father that the glaring sun ensured "that the faces of the poor Dead...could not be recognized. Their faces were quite black and many of them had swollen up and burst." In just hours, he added, the bodies "had already begun to decompose and worms and maggots were eating away at the flesh."[12]

Rats, needless to say, feasted on this bounty and grew to absurd sizes, overrunning the armies with no regard for uniform or flag. They were so numerous that the best weapon against them, so it seemed, was humor. As remembered by Mary Seacole, the sutler extraordinaire from Jamaica, they "had the appetites of London aldermen, and were as little dainty as hungry schoolboys." At night, they repeatedly attacked one of her cooks, biting his head and leading him to believe that "the souls of the slain Russian soldiers had entered the bodies of the rats, and made vengeful war upon their late enemies." Only with the help of Pinkie, a cat procured from neighboring troops who "lived in clover" because of the rodents' abundance, was the onslaught abated.[13]

No doubt Pinkie numbered among the few sated creatures serving on either side in Crimea that year. The catastrophic conditions brought by the weather severely hampered what was needed most to keep any army in the field: supplies, especially food. Whatever its reputation as a garden house in the summer, the Crimean peninsula, with its low population density, was incapable of feeding thousands of troops—not to mention providing clothing, ammunition, medicine and other necessities. For the Russians, the main culprit was one of distance and communication lines. The primary source for supplies was the region around Moscow, that is central Russia, which was nearly 1,000 miles away. In real terms, however, that distance could have been twice as far due to the poor conditions of travel, namely the lack of railroads and subpar network of roads in the countryside. To move something over that distance to Sevastopol, whether by wagon, mule or foot, took longer, in fact, than for the allies to deliver supplies and reinforcements to its troops from Paris or London. If the latter could be covered by steamship in just a few weeks, for the Russians it took months and the toll on men or beasts could be prohibitive. Tolstoy noted, for example, that one unit of rifleman marching from St. Petersburg to Crimea had lost over half its strength when it finally arrived over six months later.[14]

On the peninsula itself, which had been in Russian possession for little more than half a century, the roads were even more abysmal and, as described by Totleben, in "primeval condition," resembling more mountain paths that were virtually impassable from fall to spring—that is to say, the period from one *rasputitsa* to the other. This is why food, even when it could be gathered in sufficient quantities to feed the desperate troops, remained untouched and rotted because for a good part of the year there were virtually no means of getting it to them. In turn, the riverways, which generally flow north to south into the Black Sea, could not be used in the winter because they froze solid which meant, for example, that thousands of sheepskin coats, desperately wanted by the exposed troops, were stuck on the Dnieper River, the main artery running south from Kiev, until the spring of 1855 when their need had generally passed.[15]

For the British, as noted, the distance between England and Crimea was not the issue. Instead, it was that between Balaklava, the port of debarkation during the siege, and the army's field camp—in other words, a stretch of approximately six miles. Never before in their history had so short a distance presented so great an obstacle. By the end of November it could take a full day, from morning to night, just to travel one way from the port up to the camp. Wagons broke down and could barely navigate a path with mud so deep that it came up over the wheels; pack animals foundered too when it reached their bellies. When conditions froze, so did the poor beasts, or else they starved for lack of forage. (It was frequently noted how British horses in Crimea lacked tails because they would eat each other's.) Given these conditions, food and clothing piled up in Balaklava, exposed, rotting and undeliverable to the troops, leading George Dallas, a 27-year-old captain in the infantry to write to his family that "we are certainly the worst clad, worst fed, worst housed Army that was ever read of."[16]

When a railroad track was laid between Balaklava and the camp in the spring of 1855, the situation was somewhat relieved. Yet, Russell reported, even when that technology was employed, the army still suffered as supplies and materials continued to run out. Invoking his friend, Charles Dickens, he described the army as orphaned, just like so many "Oliver Twists," abandoned by its "Overseers at home." And just as the title character was denied his second bowl of porridge, so too would many of the soldiers go hungry because of the intransigence of those in charge. (Somewhat presciently, for the novel was published fifteen years before the war, Dickens was spot-on in choosing the name of the fictional town where Oliver was born. Of all places, it was "Mudfog.")[17]

Russell's allusion to the country's favorite writer was not entirely in jest. The army's "overseers" in London were where the problem of supplying the expeditionary force began. Overlapping bureaucracies fought among themselves, pointing fingers and deflecting blame for the shortages of food and warm clothing. Incompetence reigned because the purchase of supplies was operated by the Treasury, not by the military, and thus carried out by civilians who, inexperienced and overwhelmed by demands, could not help but blunder again and again. In January, for example, 4,000 tons of wood designated to build huts on the treeless plateau where the British camp was sited remained aboard ship in Balaklava because no one would take responsibility for unloading them. Boots—no trivial matter in this climate with its sole-sucking mud—often came too small, sometimes even, as many noted, in children's sizes. Even something as comforting (and, arguably, just as necessary) as coffee beans were delivered green and thus immediately thrown out by soldiers since they lacked the equipment to roast them. All of these mishaps and mistakes flew in the face of the Victorian assumption of efficiencies, especially when it came to the manufacture and transporting of goods. Already in April 1854, just weeks out of England and still onboard ship, Russell recognized that outsourcing procurements to private companies might save money, but "the soldiers suffer" because of it. "A powerful maritime nation like ourselves," he reported back, "should take shame" when the cutting of costs claimed lives.[18]

Most maddening of all were the archaic and often inexplicable rules that governed the disbursement, use and consumption of supplies—rules which were generally followed to the letter by the commissariats in charge. To light a fire, for instance, on the treeless plateau outside Sevastopol was no small matter and, soon after the army pitched camp, the land was stripped of all brush. Even the roots were dug out in a desperate attempt to obtain fuel. In order to alleviate the situation, charcoal was sent to Balaklava but it had to remain on the ships because of a rule written back in Britain that permitted its distribution only to soldiers housed in barracks—that is to say, only to those in structures which did not exist in Crimea.

Equally infuriating was another rule governing the issue of greatcoats, the mainstay of any military in the field. No matter how threadbare the British soldiers might be, they received a new one only once every three years which meant, of course, that for many the allotted time skipped them while serving there.

Similar, often fatal, frustrations concerned the issue of rations. Salted meat and biscuit were the never-changing staples of their diet. Any soldier wishing to supplement it with fruit and vegetables was required to buy them on his own—a somewhat impossible task since peasants, farms or markets were nowhere to be found around Sevastopol. The predictable result of this Catch-22 was that scurvy soon appeared. As a final insult, regardless of the item needed and even if it was on hand, requisition forms had to be submitted in triplicate, which led to the predictable point in January when the "army of scriveners" who staffed the supply depots, Russell wryly observed, ran out of the very forms and papers they demanded in the first place.[19]

What, taken together, did all this mean for the average British soldier at the siege? It befell George Macleod, a surgeon with the army there, to paint the portrait of a day in the life of Britain's finest. He was

almost always wet; exposed without cover to the drenching rain and soaking snow, the keen frost and biting wind; standing for days in wet mud; constantly either unnaturally excited or depressed; ever in danger and without hope for a change; their dirty, humid clothes in rags, their bodies covered with loathsome vermin which seem to grow out of their very flesh; no comforts in their wind-pierced tents on the bleak plateau; no fires, unless, weary and foot-sore as they were, they dug beneath the snow-covered sod for wet roots wherewith to kindle a feeble and tantalizing blaze; without food till, after hours of persevering exertion, they managed to half cook their unpalatable ration over their winking fire; huddled into a crowded tent to pass the night in a close, noisome atmosphere, on the oozy ground, covered by the same blanket which protected them in the wet and muddy trenches; longing for the morning, though its early dawn was signaled by the bugle sound which called them to a renewal of that dread task whose severity made them yet again sigh, 'would to God it were night.'

Conditions were so bad, so bizarre and so incomprehensible that many turned, once again, to their beloved Dickens since it seemed only his fiction could help make sense of it all. Having already published before the war, besides *Oliver Twist*, the incomparable trio of *A Christmas Carol*, *David Copperfield* and *Bleak House*, he began serialization of a new novel, *Hard Times*, just when the ships set sail for Crimea. While his attention was on impoverished workers in industrial Britain, the coincidence of that title was too good to pass up. Henry Clifford, for instance, wished that the writer might pay them a visit "and write a book, 'Hard Times' in Crimea." After all, he noted in December, "just what is passing in front of the door of my comfortable little tent, would give him plenty of matter."[20]

Russell certainly had something similar in mind when that same month he sent back a dispatch to the *Times* that dispensed with any humor:

> These are hard truths, but the people of England must hear them. They must know that the wretched beggar who wanders about the streets of London in the rain, leads the life of a prince compared with the British soldiers who are fighting out here for their country, and who, we are complacently assured by the home authorities, are the best appointed army in Europe.

What was so "hard" about his and Clifford's truth was simply that Britain had never witnessed anything like this before. No British army in living memory had ever succumbed to such a fate. The closest, perhaps, was the ill-fated 1809 campaign to the Dutch island of Walcheren when an expeditionary force of 40,000 men—the largest up to that date ever sent by Britain— lost approximately one tenth of their number to malaria without ever engaging their French enemy in any significant battle. Then, however, there had been no one like Russell to describe what had happened, which is why his reports from Crimea, nearly forty years hence, stung the public so deeply and, as we will see in a later chapter, led to the unthinkable: a devastating backlash against the government itself.[21]

The Butchery of Men

Yet for all the disasters that befell soldiers at Sevastopol due to the climate and other conditions, that was not the whole story. Guns, cannon and bayonets also took their toll and on an unprecedented scale. Most lethal of all was the new generation of rifles, known collectively as the "minié" after the bullet's French inventor, which were unmatched in accuracy, distance and rapidity of fire. This rifle became the mainstay of the allied troops, while the Russians, as expected, lagged behind in its issuance. The latter, for the most part, were still armed with the smooth-bore musket (though generally with a percussion cap); the relatively few rifles in the army's possession were given to select units or sharpshooters.

The difference between the rifle and the musket was not just one of terminology. The latter fired a solid lead ball whereas the former fired a conical one, hollowed out at the base, that expanded to meet the rifled grooves of the barrel. And at .577 caliber its impact was devastating. The minié bullet "did not make a practice of stopping half way in a fellow," a British officer casually noted, "some in fact have been seen at 400 yards to go clean thro 3 or 4 Russians and kill them all." When fired in a single, massive volley, the result was not unlike that of the machine gun, and the Russians, unfortunately, were almost always on the receiving end. At their first battle on the Alma River, the allies' concentrated fire decimated the Russian ranks. They "were cut down like corn," one veteran on the Russian side recalled, before their muskets could even come into play—a tremendous disadvantage that stayed with them the entire war.[22]

THE NEW FACE OF WAR

The minié created wounds surgeons had never seen before. It shattered whatever limb it struck, generally smashing the bone (as opposed to breaking it like the musket ball), and those fragments typically rendered the wound inoperable. Along with bits of uniform, mud or debris that were invariably carried with it into the body, infection—almost always fatal if untreated—was virtually certain. Amputation was generally the only recourse. Even then, as one surgeon noted, compound fractures, especially of the femur, were "synonymous with death." Needless to say, those hit in the abdomen or head were as a rule left alone; no treatment could save them.[23]

The killing power of artillery at Sevastopol was also unprecedented. Numbering over 1,000 among the allies, cannon bristled from ramparts, earthworks and the ships of their navies blockading the port. Their range now reached 5,000 yards, more than double that of their Napoleonic predecessors. The standard roundshot was still used and, like before, it killed by plowing through ranks of men. More destructive, though, was the traditional grapeshot, a cluster of fist-sized projectiles that could devastate troops at closer range supplemented by canister, operating in similar fashion though packed with smaller balls. Improved fuses significantly increased the lethality of case shot, which also consisted of a container filled with small balls designed to explode at greater distances and which thus could carry the effect of canister far into enemy fortifications. An officer on the Russian side called the improved shell "the most destructive thing" on the battlefield, capable of killing or maiming two dozen people, especially when exploding in a confined space like an entrenchment. Its cousin, the contact explosive shell, made its debut at the Battle of Sinope in 1853 where, as we have seen, the Russian guns in turn tore out the wooden hulls of Turkish ships. Another version wielded by the Russians on land, a particularly nasty one, discharged 280 balls at a half-pound each (!) in the face of any oncoming soldiers. At least in artillery technology, always an emphasis in the Russian army since Peter the Great, they did not lag behind the allies.[24]

As at any siege, mortars were indispensable for clearing ramparts and raining shot down on the enemy. At night their high-arching trajectories were sometimes fondly recalled for their dazzling "pyrotechnic display," as one British engineer put it. Yet any delight in such star-spangled shows was immediately erased when their shells hit the ground, as the fate of the unfortunate Dmitry Prokopenko could attest. During the Great Bombardment that inaugurated the siege in October, a mortar shell landed in a Russian redoubt, and "he was literally blown apart into little pieces," his superior reported. "Only his boots remained with parts of his legs stuck in them. Almost the entire platform of our cannon was drenched in his blood and intestines. Death was instantaneous but horrible. His remains, as per my instructions, were gathered in a bag and then taken away for burial."[25]

Perhaps the only way gunners might tame the destructive power of enemy cannon was to resort to affectionate, congenial nicknames for their projectiles—a game that was played in the First World War as well. When 13-inch shells came crashing down among them, the British, for instance, would christen them "Whistling Dicks." The Russians, in turn, created an extensive list to draw from, no doubt reflecting the variety of weapons they faced from the allies. Shrapnel came in two tones, "dark" if it contained solid balls; "light" if they were explosive. A howitzer shell, for some reason, was deemed a "mophead," as in a disheveled person, and roundshot a "stallion" since, presumably, it still possessed something a gelding did not. If the shout rang out that "the Moldavian post is coming," gunners knew a hefty shell was on the way after the peculiar squeaking noise a carriage made. An even heavier one was known as an "outta here!" a self-explanatory warning for anyone in its path. The nicknames even extended to bullets. Depending on their whirring sound in the air, they could be "young-uns" or "siggies," as in a cygnet or baby swan. Either way, this game masked the fear soldiers felt under fire by turning death into something humorous and, in theory, harmless. After all, who couldn't handle a "siggy?"[26]

The best protection against Whistling Dicks and the Moldavian post came in the form of fortifications and earthworks built around Sevastopol. Along with the bastions atop the city's domineering heights, there were miles of parallel and perpendicular trenches that crisscrossed in front of it. For the Russians, the signature pieces of their defensive perimeter were the ten bastions that ringed the southern half of the city. Under the skilled direction of Eduard Totleben, a recognized master of engineering who started the war a colonel, the interconnected, multi-layered system was seen as a technological feat in its own right, especially since it had been partly constructed by local women and children and in relative haste once the allies had made clear their intentions to lay siege.

For the allies trenches served as the primary mode of defense, yet the digging of each was a laborious affair because of the hard, rocky ground surrounding Sevastopol. As is often the case in any war, they did not expect the siege to become precisely that—a long, drawn-out duel of bombardments, sorties and waiting with relatively few pitched battles. Neither the French nor British had recently been in a siege of any appreciable length, and the examples from the Peninsular War, like Badajoz in 1812, were of relatively short duration. Moreover, the few veterans of that now distant conflict were by this time, if still serving, senior officers like Raglan and were quite detached from the experience of the rank-and-file soldiers.

If trenches were designed to save lives, they also took a heavy toll on soldiers that can be measured in the misery, wretchedness and anxieties that dominate their letters and diaries. The British generally went on duty for twenty-four hours, having to stand in ankle-deep water with only their coats or a blanket tossed over their shoulders to protect them from the elements. Basic tasks like cooking were near impossible and, unlike the French who enjoyed communal kitchens from which a company of 100 men could draw hot food, each individual British soldier was on his own. With little or no fuel to start a fire, they sometimes ate their meat raw, and even fresh water, despite the frequent rain, was a precious commodity. It was "very scarce and extremely muddy," a sergeant wrote home, so that he never could wash himself or his clothes for weeks on end. Construction of proper latrines seems never to have taken place, at least in the fall and winter months, which left the entire area covered in human waste. The little comfort that might come with self-explanatory "bum bags"—a kind of portable container obtained in Britain— quickly ran out, leaving one soldier to delay the call of nature, his so-called "unmentionables," as long as physically possible until they gave him "the slip," rendering him "almost sans culotte." Needless to say, by spring he could only write that they were "dead tired of trench duty."[27]

As much as physical deprivations, the psychological impact of serving in the trenches scarred the men—a fact present in previous wars but difficult to observe. In Crimea we have at least a clearer record of how siege conditions drove men into heightened states of anxiety and stress. Normally during war, an army on the march rarely engages in battle or even sees the enemy; the chances, in other words, of coming under fire are somewhat low when measured against a soldier's total time in service. At Sevastopol the opposite was true: death was a constant, inescapable presence twenty-four hours a day, no matter if one was on duty like Dmitry Prokopenko or not, given the increased range of artillery and randomness with which its shells fell. Unseen enemy cannon could find their targets anywhere, any time; they were invisible killers that had no regard for rank, branch of service or even civilian status given the large number of the latter who stayed in the city. In a dispatch from February, Russell included a poignant observation on the anonymity of death caused by cannon which, nevertheless, claimed real individuals with real families—not just statistics or numbers in some casualty ledger.

> It is rather an unpleasant reflection, whenever one is discussing the range of a missile, and is perhaps in the act of exclaiming, 'There's a splendid shot,' that it may have carried misery and sorrow into some happy household. The smoke clears away—the men get up—they gather round one who moves not, or who is racked with mortal agony; they bear him away, a mere black speck, and a few shovelsfull of mud mark for a little time the resting-place of the poor soldier, whose wife, or mother, or children, or sisters, are left destitute of all solace, save memory and the sympathy of their country. One such little speck I watched to-day, and saw quietly deposited on the ground inside the trench. Who will let the inmates of that desolate cottage in Picardy, or Gascony, or Anjou, know of their bereavement?

At night, the tension was worse, a Russian officer conceded, because the sounds of birds, small animals, insects, even the wind—harmless during the day—could set a man off. The "first question every morning," a British officer noted, became, "'Well, who was killed last night?'" With nerves constantly on edge, the soldiers' morale plummeted. Sometimes the only solace was, perversely, to make a sport of killing. Henry Clifford could not help laughing, he admitted to his family in a letter, when they could shoot Russians running for cover after defecating. "Anything" was welcome, he wrote, "to break this dreadful state of suffering without result" or, as he added in Italian, "this state of 'Far neinte.'" Needless to say, when the siege ended in September 1855, the most joyous part of it all, he wrote (emphasis in the original), was "*no more Trenches!!!* This alone is a hatful of bliss."[28]

Day of Battle

There were two major battles at Sevastopol that broke the tedium of trench warfare, and they were the reverse images of each other. The first, the Battle of Inkerman in early November 1854, was a Russian breakout attack seeking to lift the siege. The second, coming the next year in June, was a joint British and French assault that sought to break in, take the city and end the siege as well. The one thing they had in common was that both were dreadful failures.

That the Battle of Inkerman would have such an outcome seemed preordained from the beginning. The Russians took the initiative and built up forces on their northern (or left) flank to heavily outnumber the allies. However, the troops making up the assault were totally exhausted, having just arrived the day before from Bessarabia—a march of nearly 500 miles. This hampered their ability to coordinate with the Russians already there and carry out adequate reconnaissance since the unfamiliar terrain was most unconducive to maneuvering. Riven with deep ravines and gullies, overgrown with dense bushes and nearly impenetrable brambles, it became nearly impossible to keep large units together, which was an essential element of Russian tactics.

The time chosen for the attack, early morning before dawn broke, augured ill as well. Any hope for surprise was lost when a heavy fog blanketed the entire area, effectively blinding the soldiers and which only became worse as clouds of smoke from gunfire was added to the mix. Nevertheless, thousands upon thousands of Russians were thrown against the British position from which, Russell wrote as an eyewitness, "the volleys of the minié cleft them like the hand of the Destroying Angel, and they fell like leaves in the autumn." Control of the lead Russian division evaporated as three successive commanders were hit, and it broke down into smaller units, engaging at nearly point-blank range with the British.

Despite facing slaughter, the Russians succeeded in pushing the British back. That, however, only led to the expected counterattack. At this point, Russell continued, the battle turned into "a series of dreadful deeds of daring, of sanguinary hand-to-hand fights, of despairing rallies of desperate assaults."[29] Amid the chaos, Henry Clifford stood out, leading a band of soldiers against the Russians. When one tried to get away, he wrote back home, he "hit him over the back of the neck and laid him dead at my feet"—an act for which, along with taking off the arm of the "Bono Johnny" prisoner relayed before, he received his Victoria Cross (one of the earliest out of 111 issued during the war). When the fog finally lifted, the British line was secure but at the cost of nearly 2,500 casualties out of 7,500 committed or nearly one-tenth of the entire British army in Crimea. (Of the twelve men who charged with Clifford, six died and three were wounded.) For the Russians it was even worse. Exactly how many the Destroying Angel took was never clearly determined but it was at least over 10,000, that is, one quarter to one third of those who fought.

Tolstoy did not see any of the battle since he was temporarily posted to Odessa. But when news came, he was disgusted at his own commanders for allowing such a "horrific murder"[30] to take place. Older men in his unit broke down and cried while the younger ones swore to kill General Dannenberg, the Russian in charge. Back in St. Petersburg a member of the court, Anna Tiutcheva, recorded that when the news came it resulted in "the greatest despair." The defeat hit close to the emperor since his two sons had come to Sevastopol filled with expectations of witnessing a great victory. Instead, they reported back how the city was overwhelmed with casualties for whom there weren't enough doctors, which left women to extract bullets and children to carry food to the troops. Trying to recover something positive, Tiutcheva noted that such tragedies only bring out the true goodness of "our people." It was still quite distressing, however, to all in the capital that this demonstration had to come at the cost of so many lives.[31]

For the British, despite their victory at Inkerman, a cloud descended on their ranks as well. Two of their four divisions had nearly been mauled and the commander of one, General Sir George Cathcart, a veteran of Waterloo, was killed. Worse, the battle drove home a bitter message. If the Russians, though losing, could mount such an attack, then taking the city would be no easy task. As winter was coming, a sobering melancholy set in. "We have nothing to rejoice over, and almost everything to deplore, in the battle of Inkermann," Russell informed his readers. "We have defeated the enemy indeed, but have not advanced one step nearer towards the citadel of Sebastopol."[32]

Nor were the British any closer seven months later when their turn came. In June 1855 they launched a joint assault with the French on two Russian strongholds, the Malakhov and the Great Redan (or Third Bastion), seen as gateways to the city. The first was the French target, without which the taking of the Redan, the goal of the British, was seen as near-impossible. The date chosen was deliberate, 18 June, the fortieth anniversary of the Battle of Waterloo. The idea behind the symbolism was clear. The two former adversaries would come together with the assumption that a victory on that date would continue the line of British successes whereas for the French it would replace their earlier defeat as a date to remember. It did neither, gaining a notoriety all of its own.

The assault devolved into a Somme-like catastrophe, albeit on a smaller scale, for three reasons. First, though the troops gathered in the night, the commotion and noise they caused could not be concealed from the Russians who were poised high in their earthworks just a few hundred yards away. Tipped off, the latter secretly brought up cannon and extra men to sweep down the allied attack lanes at point-blank range, where the superiority of the allies' minié rifle was lost. Second, the preliminary bombardment did little against the Russian entrenchments except to leave the ground in front "scarred," as Russell observed. Finally, the French mistakenly rushed the Malakhov too soon, which forced the British to launch their own attack ahead of schedule and before they were fully prepared lest they leave their allies alone in the field.[33]

Despite these initial setbacks, the allies bravely surged forward across the quarter mile of no man's land, beset with Russian landmines and *chevaux de frise*, wooden stakes fixed upright on a horizontal axis that served as a precursor to barbed wire. They never reached their targets. Russian muskets and cannon loaded with double grapeshot stopped them cold, leaving them stuck in the morning light out in the open. The storming parties that were carrying ladders—essential both to bridge ditches and to scale the heights—were cut down nearly to a man. Caught in the midst of this "slaughter," Timothy Gowing later wrote, their mission was akin to "trying to pull down the moon." Of the 103 men in his company, fourteen made it back, with Gowing counting nine bullet and shrapnel holes in his clothing alone.[34]

If Gowing survived by a miracle, hundreds of his compatriots did not. Casualties for the British numbered nearly 1,500 dead and wounded, which was about a third out of the two brigades committed; the French lost several times more but the actual count was suppressed. Predictably, the anger of the British troops which followed was not directed at the enemy but at their own commanders. Now it was their turn, like Tolstoy's after Inkerman, to cry "murder," a word that "echoed throughout the camp," Russell wrote to his stunned readers. Mishaps and mistakes led to a horrid scene as the allies went out again, this time under white flags, to gather the fallen, their corpses now bloated, black and bursting after just one day under the unrelenting summer sun. Henry Clifford joined them, wanting to help, and promptly vomited several times as the bodies "had already begun to decompose and worms and maggots were eating away the flesh." Bitterness and despair left him grasping for words of comfort to make sense of the horror that lay before them. "This is all part of Honour and Glory I suppose," he wrote home. Yet such words, heard so many times they now bordered on cliché, were inadequate and rang hollow.[35]

A few days later it was reported that some British soldiers, in fact, had held back from the assault, refusing to go "over the top," as it were. This was partly due to their natural fear of getting killed but it also became clear, as George Dallas seethed, that many did not know "what their orders are or were." After months of bloody inconclusiveness, immeasurable suffering and thorough exhaustion, he no doubt shocked his family with the frank conclusion that "we are sick and weary of our Generals, one seems as perfectly incompetent as another." It was "downright madness," another wrote, to launch a frontal assault against defenses that the preliminary bombardment had failed to suppress. Indeed, it was here, under the same white flag, that for the first time—later to be repeated by the Germans in the First World War—British soldiers heard from the Russians that they resembled "Lions commanded by Asses," which was meant as praise, for no one could ignore the bravery of the soldiers who had become victims of a folly orchestrated by their leaders.[36]

Doctors and Hospitals

What happened to those who fell in battle yet were not killed, whether before the Great Redan or in the fog at Inkerman? Their fate, while better than in previous centuries given the relatively advanced standards of medical treatment and the debut of chloroform, can still leave today's reader aghast. Indeed, almost as premonition of what awaited them after a battle, it was commonly reported that many of the Russian wounded preferred to die where they lay rather than be evacuated. Such fatalistic resignation haunted the allies as well but was captured in a different way: in the uncommon number of suicides in the field among the rank and file. The Crimean War was quite modern in yet another way.

This was evident from the first time the two armies clashed at the Battle of Alma in September 1854. The Russians suffered grievously from the impact of the minié rifle and left thousands of wounded behind, unable to remove them in their hasty retreat. There they lay for days, untreated and virtually forgotten, as the British and French had thousands of their own to cope with. Many, of course, died shortly thereafter still lying in the field; others, delirious from pain and thirst, were known to hallucinate that a mother, a friend or even the Queen of England attended them. When days later the Russians came back to the battlefield to collect their wounded, the latter were brought to an aid station but then "thrown on the ground like dogs" and abandoned again, lying in their own filth, with some waiting a full two weeks until a doctor could see them—such was the system in place.[37]

The only bright side for the Russian wounded was if they were lucky enough to be treated by either of two doctors, Nikolai Pirogov, a surgeon who would become Russia's most famous, or Kristian Giubbenet, a professor of medicine. Both favored progressive and humane treatment of battle casualties—something that was still rare in practice. They believed that saving a life depended on speed in diagnosis, which is why Pirogov founded the triage method to separate hopeless cases from those who had a chance yet needed immediate surgery—which is, of course, now standard practice in military hospitals. He was, in fact, already a world celebrity in his profession, being the first surgeon

to use anesthetics on soldiers. In the bloodbath of Crimea, however, both his and Giubbenet's skills, patience and, indeed, sanity
would be sorely tested. As much as they labored on behalf of
their desperate patients, they had to fight equally against the
stupidity, ignorance and indifference of their superiors for whom
the common soldier, the chattel serf, meant virtually nothing.[38]

Giubbenet estimated that after Alma alone each Russian doctor
was responsible for approximately 300 patients. These patients
were not kept under one roof such as in a hospital, but scattered
through several villages in peasants' huts because there was insuf-
ficient space. A doctor, according to his experience, could only
perform a maximum of twenty major operations—generally
defined as a bullet extraction or amputation—a day, which meant
that at best it took six days to treat all of them.

Operations themselves, even on a toe or finger, were quite
dangerous affairs. They could easily prove fatal not just through
shock to the patient but due to sepsis or blood poisoning. And
though the microbes causing sepsis would not be identified
until two decades later, nearly all doctors knew that infection
was the primary killer if a soldier survived the battlefield.
Nevertheless, the proper treatment at this time was in dispute.
Here Pirogov and Giubbenet, along with an enlightened few
among the allies, were opposed to the mainstream medicine
practiced by doctors in Crimea. The majority of the latter,
according to conventional practice, believed that inducing infection—deliberately leaving, for instance, a piece of cloth in the
wound and thereby promoting suppuration—would help purge
it of impurities. Wounds, according to this school of thought
and contrary to the progressives, should therefore remain open
and unsutured—as opposed to cleansed and closed. Needless to
say, this "murky understanding" of blood poisoning, in
Giubbenet's words, led to the deaths of thousands more and
would be corrected only after the war.[39]

Yet to be fair to the medical establishment, the state of knowledge in treating wounds had been fostered in the laboratory and lecture room and was quite divorced from the battlefield conditions that doctors and surgeons in Crimea faced. In the hospitals on either side, no one could escape the freezing cold or blazing sun, the plague of mud and flies, the soul-piercing cries and screams, the horrific smells and piles of limbs, the leaky tents and ramshackle rooms. Amid the exhausted surgeons and a seemingly endless line of wounded, Giubbenet gives us a picture of the operating room (often a charitable term) as one of frightening chaos, with doctors sharing, dropping or taking instruments from each other. There was little control or coordination—the same patient might be unbandaged and bandaged over and over, while others next to him lay untouched. In this, one could say, little had changed since the Napoleonic Wars, with two exceptions: there was a better grasp of infection's ill-effects and anesthesia had finally arrived, the first successful use of which occurred only in 1846 (with ether giving way to the less dangerous chloroform).[40]

Before these two landmarks, the most prized skill a surgeon could have was speed in amputations—something Charles Dickens presciently captured by coining a nickname for them, "sawbones," fifteen years before the war in *The Pickwick Papers*. In ideal conditions and on cadavers (which did not scream or resist), a good surgeon could take off a limb in less than two minutes and sometimes even as little as thirty seconds. Chloroform did not, of course, speed up the process, but it obviously lessened the pain, which was the humane thing to do. An added benefit of using it, as British surgeon George Macleod realized, was that it benefited the wounded who were awaiting treatment by minimizing the screams of those under the knife. Incidentally, Tolstoy himself could attest to this. He took chloroform in 1854 for a non-battle operation on his groin, and only heard the instruments clicking but did not feel any pain—and wrote off the whole thing in one line in his diary.[41]

The war would test the full measure of Dickens's moniker as well as the effectiveness of chloroform, the use of which, unfortunately, was not as common as one might hope. Here the French led all others, using it "as a matter of course" on all their wounded. The Russians, ever short on supply, reserved it for officers and the wealthy, like Tolstoy. The British too were frugal in the use of chloroform—but for different reasons. Though suffering from no shortage of it, some of their surgeons were wary of it, following the lead of Dr. John Hall, the army's chief medical officer in Crimea, who insisted that it was better not to use anesthesia during surgery: "the smart of the knife is a powerful stimulant, and it is much better to hear a man bawl lustily than to see him sink silently into his grave." Not having felt a scalpel himself, Hall could venture such a conclusion, and many British (and Russian) doctors viewed anything new or out-of-the-ordinary with suspicion. Their caution, it should be noted, was not always unfounded. In the era of anesthesia's infancy and for all of its obvious benefits, chloroform itself could kill if given to a patient who was old, had an ailment like a weak heart or received a heavy dosage (a fate not unheard of given the inexperience of most in administering this still experimental drug).[42]

All of this—triage, surgery, convalescence—occurred in hospitals and related facilities which were places the wounded first had to reach if they had any hope of being treated. Yet here too the record was abysmal. For both sides, the poor roads, long distances and shoddy transport that hampered bringing supplies to the men spelled the same difficulties for taking the wounded ones out. Most had to be treated far away. For the Russians, this meant Simferopol, in the heart of Crimea fifty miles from Sevastopol, and then at Perekop, nearly 100 more, where the peninsula joins the mainland in southern Ukraine. The trip took weeks, with the wounded jolting and jerking in wagons, lying in the open night and day, with no bedding and still dressed in the same muddy, blood-soaked and pus-caked rags in which they were found, their only covering a greatcoat.

Their British counterparts suffered similarly as well. That soldiers might be wounded in battle seems almost to have been an afterthought to authorities, who in planning for Crimea, made little or no provisions for their evacuation. Removal from the battlefield was usually done on the backs of comrades or by a makeshift stretcher. If one was lucky, an ambulance borrowed from the French might be available since their army deployed an array of special purpose carts and wagons designed specifically to transport the wounded. For most, however, this was only the first leg of a long journey which generally continued on ships since they were then sent across the Black Sea to Turkey, most of them to Scutari, a small city near Constantinople.

On this trek the wounded were laid alongside the sick who, also awaiting evacuation, suffered primarily from dysentery, typhus and cholera—which constitutes another tragic chapter in the medical treatment of the day. Together, these three diseases were the greatest scourge for soldiers, and the conditions both in and outside of Sevastopol, with thousands jammed into a few square miles, were ideal, needless to say, for such killers to run rampant. The sick who made it to Balaklava, the embarkation point for Scutari, were the lucky ones; cholera, for instance, often proved fatal within hours after the first attacks of vomiting and insidious diarrhea. This, unfortunately, was not a surprise since its effects were already well known to both the British and Russians. In 1848 cholera emptied the capital of St. Petersburg as many fled to escape its ravages, while across the country it claimed around 700,000 people. Six years later, in August 1854, a month before the Battle of Alma, it struck London, killing so many of the poor on its streets that Dickens, long a champion of proper sanitation, charged city authorities with "wholesale murder," especially since, he claimed correctly, it was a "preventible [sic] disease."[43]

Yet to be so fortunate as to survive battle in order to be transported to Scutari was for many a distinction without a difference. The wounded and the sick were simply dumped on the decks of ships, their numbers overwhelming. After Alma, for example, the transport *Kangaroo*, capacity 250, was forced to take on 1,200. Moreover, though the trip across the Black Sea took about a week by sail and two or three days by steam, it could prove equally fatal. A young army doctor detailed what awaited those on board:

> Lying among crowds of other sick and wounded, on bare planks, in torture, lassitude and lethargy, without proper food, medicine or attendance, they were launched on the wintry sea. Their covering was scanty and the roll and plunge of the ship was agony to the fevered and the maimed. In place of the hush, cleanliness and quiet and the silent step which should be around the sick, were sounds such as the poets have feigned for the regions of the damned—groans, screams, entreaties, curses, the strain of the timbers, the trampling of the crews, and the weltering of the waves. The sick flocked in faster than the dead were carried out till the hospitals overflowed, while, still faster flowed the misery-laden ships down the Black Sea as they went on feeding the fishes with their dead.[44]

When they arrived at Scutari, conditions, if one could imagine, got worse. The so-called hospital was an abandoned barracks where "the wards were full; the corridors were lined with men lying on the bare boards because the supply of bags stuffed with straw had given out... The filth became indescribable. The men in the corridors lay on unwashed rotten floors crawling with vermin." This was where Florence Nightingale made her name and became a legend, first volunteering to go to Crimea when reports of the appalling conditions the wounded faced at Alma were published in the *Times*. Arriving in November at Scutari or, as she wrote back, "the Kingdom of Hell," she and her team of nurses waged war not just against the revolting conditions but also against the bureaucratic morass that left most of the soldiers bereft of the most basic items. "There were no pillows, no blankets," it was recorded. "The men lay, with their heads on their boots, wrapped in a blanket or greatcoat stiff with blood and filth which had been their sole covering perhaps for more than a week." Worse, there were only about twenty bedpans for every 1,000 patients, many stricken with diarrhea or dysentery. The latrines, barely serviceable to begin with, quickly became inoperable with the result that in places "there was liquid filth which floated over the floor an inch deep," in which the men's food could also be found, bobbing up and down. By January, with more than one half of the British expeditionary force off the front lines and incapacitated—12,025 versus 11,367 effectives—the mortality rate at Scutari averaged thirty-two per cent of those admitted, reaching a peak the next month at fifty-two per cent.[45]

The Russian wounded had it no better, yet their fate, thanks to Russell, only became known at the end of the fighting when Sevastopol fell in September 1855. As the victorious allied soldiers wandered through the city's burned ruins, he joined them. What he found in one hospital, from which all the doctors had fled, led to one of his longest and most disturbing dispatches:

> Of all the pictures of the horrors of war which have ever been presented to the world, the hospital of Sebastopol presents the most horrible, heart-rending, and revolting...entering one of these doors, I beheld such a sight as few men, thank God, have ever witnessed!... [There were] the rotten and festering corpses of the soldiers, who were left to die in their extreme agony, untended, uncared for, packed as close as they could be stowed, some on the floor, others on wretched trestles and bedsteads, or pallets of straw, sopped and saturated with blood, which oozed and trickled through upon the

floor, mingling with the droppings of corruption... Could that bloody mass of clothing and white bones ever have been a human being, or that burnt black mass of flesh have ever had a human soul?

He went further inside, only to discover worse:

Many lay, yet alive, with maggots crawling about in their wounds. Many, nearly mad by the scene around them, or seeking escape from it in their extremest agony, had rolled away under the beds, and glared out on the heart-stricken spectator—oh! with such looks! Many with legs and arms broken and twisted, the jagged splinters sticking through the raw flesh, implored aid, water, food, or pity, or, deprived of speech by the approach of death, or by dreadful injuries in the head or trunk, pointed to the lethal spot. Many seemed bent alone on making their peace with Heaven.[46]

No one can say for sure how many, including women and children, made their "peace with Heaven" at the siege of Sevastopol. During the course of eleven months, the British Army alone lost over 20,000 soldiers, primarily from illness and exposure; the Russians several times more. Yet what is most striking is that by the end, the soldiers began to speak of their experience as a common one, shared by all who were there regardless of uniform. Their language was virtually interchangeable as Henry Clifford labeled the city and its environs "one large burying ground" that cared not for nationality, rank or class. Modern war turned a corner on that peninsula by creating a place where, at least in this regard, everyone was equal. As a colonel wrote home to Britain, a century before astronomy discovered the concept, Crimea was a black hole where soldiers "come to die."[47]

3

THE MAKING OF LEGENDS

In Crimea the shadow of death was inescapable. It looms over soldiers' private letters and published memoirs, dominates official reports and figures prominently in fiction from the war. The morning query cited earlier of one British captain—"Well, who was killed last night?"—could be, emblazoned on a banner, the one unifying sentiment behind which all could gather, regardless of uniform. For death was the great leveler, claiming not just thousands of rank-and-file soldiers, but also, unprecedentedly, the highest officers in the field. The commanders of both the British and French armies, Lord Raglan and Marshal de Saint-Arnaud, died in Crimea—the first from dysentery following the disastrous assault of 18 June and the second succumbing to cancer shortly after landing on the peninsula. The same was true for the Russians. Both of Sevastopol's commanders, Admirals Vladimir Kornilov and Pavel Nakhimov, were killed in battle, the first during the Great Bombardment and the second by a sniper within days of Raglan's death. For all the armies involved, in short, when it came to death this war exceeded expectations.[1]

To be sure, death in and of itself was nothing new. For what would war be without it? But where Crimea differs from its predecessors is that death arguably became the main event—so much so that it lies at the heart of the two legends by which the war is best remembered in Britain and Russia to this day: the Charge of the Light Brigade and the epic of Sevastopol's defenders. Each country wove near-certain death into an exceptional tale of sacrificial courage that has almost eclipsed the war itself—be it cavalrymen on a suicidal assault or soldiers and civilians standing together as one until the end. Indeed, for both countries the Charge and the story of the City That Never Surrendered have become bedrock chapters in their respective national mythologies.

What is less recognized, however, is the essential role Russell and Tolstoy played in the creation of these legends. Not only were they directly involved in both events, their writing provided the core narrative from which the legends grew. It would not be too much of a stretch, in fact, to argue that if either had not been present—killed, let's say, early on in the siege—then it is likely neither legend would have taken root. Britain would have lost its most valuable eyewitness to that quixotic charge and Russia its most compelling storyteller. Neither, of course, knew it at the time, but when Russell and Tolstoy took up their pens to record the charge and the siege, both would stamp their cultures with images so indelible that they have long outlived the war.

The Heroic Default and the Good Death

With regard to war writing, neither Russell nor Tolstoy was operating in a vacuum. The narrative tradition they were working in—and at the same time against—was one of the strongest in Western culture, with roots going back centuries. In general terms, before Crimea the key purpose behind any representation of war—besides showcasing the pageantry of battle, singing the praises of leaders or demonstrating the valor of soldiers—was to redeem lives lost, to endow death with a higher meaning and, most significantly, to ensure that it was never in vain. Across the centuries, literature, painting and other arts all embraced this imperative with the result that images of battle tended towards a single axis of representation: death for any hero became an obligatory story of martyrdom, of sacrifice for a god, a country or an ideal.

To be sure, not all pictures of war adhered to this convention; nor were people ignorant of what war truly meant, both on the battlefield and, all the more so, for civilians. People knew, in other words, what war was, especially in the modern era with the advent of the printing press and mass circulation of literature, pamphlets and other materials. The seventeenth century stands as a turning point for Europe with the acutely savage, wide-ranging Thirty Years' War and English Civil War. Public, contemporaneous accounts from both include some of the worst war crimes recorded, which anticipate those of the twentieth century. Yet for all of their horror, these depictions were, quantitatively speaking, few in number, and they also tended to be ephemeral propaganda pieces designed to demonize the enemy.[2]

Moreover, such pieces still constituted the exception, produced in isolation and never coalescing into a coherent body or received tradition. Instead, the dominant expression before Crimea was still of a romanticized view of war that did not necessarily sidestep its ravages but allowed for their express mitigation. Perhaps the most famous example was Shakespeare's *Henry V* which, while set in the fifteenth century, was, of course, written and first performed at the turn of the seventeenth. It foregrounds the savagery of war and makes no pretense of hiding the blood shed on the battlefield, yet these revelations are recouped with the king's St. Crispin's Day Speech (Act IV) before the Battle of Agincourt that presents us with some of the most memorable lines to ensure that death in war has a purpose:

> This story shall the good man teach his son;
> And Crispin Crispian shall ne'er go by,
> From this day to the ending of the world,
> But we in it shall be remembered,
> We few, we happy few, we band of brothers.
> For he today that sheds his blood with me
> Shall be my brother; be he ne'er so vile,
> This day shall gentle his condition;
> And gentlemen in England now abed
> Shall think themselves accurs'd they were not here,
> And hold their manhoods cheap whiles any speaks
> That fought with us upon Saint Crispin's day.

Indeed, words like these—repeated across genres and reproducing themselves pictorially on innumerable canvases—had by Shakespeare's time become so expected and so ingrained that one could call it the Heroic Default, unrivaled as the failsafe way any conflict and its attendant losses should be rendered.

In the West, the universally acknowledged origins for the Heroic Default go back even further, all the way, in fact, to Homer's *Iliad*. Its riveting tales of combat and ready-made cast of heroes, enhanced by gripping descriptions and colorful similes, became the standard from which anyone could draw. Indeed, across its twenty-four books death is almost a given, making the *Iliad* something of a go-to guide for its depiction, and, what is more, the epic revels in the gore almost to visceral excess. When, for instance, the Greek hero Diomedes, aided by the goddess Athena, casts his spear at the archer Pandarus, no details are spared:

> With that he hurled and Athena drove the shaft
> And it split the archer's nose between the eyes—

THE MAKING OF LEGENDS

It cracked his glistening teeth, the tough bronze
Cut off his tongue at the roots, smashed his jaw
And the point came ripping out beneath his chin.

Book V, 321–5[3]

Needless to say, Pandarus dies on the spot. Nowhere, however, do such graphic scenes sit in isolation, as if to abandon the reader in shock at what has transpired. They are always preceded, wrapped in or followed by an effusion of rhetoric marking each encounter as a glorious endeavor. There are no deaths due to unseen viruses, hunger or exposure; instead, warriors face off in mortal combat, often exchanging taunts and threats, and then strike until the other falls dead—but almost never without a rousing send-off. When Sarpedon, King of the Lycians and ally of the Trojans, is killed by Patroclus in Book XVI, for example, Homer extends this scene for eight additional lines in order to shower the king with extended similes befitting a hero. He falls not just as a mere mortal but like an "oak," a "towering pine," and "a bull." Across the *Iliad*, whenever death comes for an individual—and it does for nearly 250 named individuals in the epic—it strikes with conspicuous elan. To die in such fashion is, in other words, a key indicator of social status and not available to just any combatant. Sarpedon, after all, is Zeus's son.

Adapting such ideas to war in the age of gunpowder required no special modifications or concessions. Muskets and cannon took the place of spears and arrows but Homer's model remained the internalized norm. It was quite clear that writers and artists preferred its value system, for what else could elevate war to legendary status, turn carnage into something ennobling, make broken bodies whole through the paeans to glory and give mere men immortality as history's champions? One could point to the late eighteenth century as something of a culminating moment in European culture when one of the most famous representations of death appeared. Benjamin West's 1770 painting, *The Death of General Wolfe*, depicted the general expiring under his battleflag surrounded by fellow officers and acolytes as news of his triumph over the French at the Battle of Quebec came to him. This was no ordinary victory—for it ensured British dominance in North America—and West's contribution to the lore of British imperial might was no ordinary one either. Strikingly for its time, the soldiers were shown in contemporary uniforms instead of the expected regalia of the classical age. This dramatic shift turned General Wolfe into a martyr of Homeric proportions, but one who lived in the present day.

This model gained even greater prominence with heroes from the Napoleonic Wars, and West, notably, took the lead again with yet another painting, that of Britain's greatest admiral, Horatio Nelson. Meeting the artist after a showing of *General Wolfe*, Nelson reportedly asked if *he* could be the subject of West's next painting. The artist agreed, even if that pact, eerily enough, would seem to hinge on Nelson's death. The fates did not disappoint, as he was felled by a sniper on board his flagship, *Victory*, during the Battle of Trafalgar in 1805, the triumph which secured Britain's rule over the seas. Bucking historical fact (the admiral died below decks in a cramped, poorly lit cabin), on West's canvas Nelson expires in the open and in a most heroic pose supported by his comrades—just like General Wolfe. That Wolfe and Nelson were both shown, as West clearly intended, like Christ brought down from the Cross into Mary's arms, readily demonstrated how the classical model of martyrdom could just as easily accept Christian tenets through a secularized version of the Pietà.

Homer's influence continued throughout the Napoleonic Wars. His imprint could be felt most readily in Sir William Napier's six-volume *History of the War in the Peninsula*, the most influential British work to come from that period and for many, including Russell, a modern-day bible of how to depict war in prose. One of its more memorable—and exemplary—passages comes with the 1812 siege of Badajoz whose dramatic finish Russell had contrasted, as seen in the previous chapter, with the stalemate at Sevastopol. Here Napier, who was present, holds nothing back; his account reads like a digest of Homeric tropes applied to modern warfare—this time with the British in the role of the victorious Greeks at Troy. Simile, anaphora, paraphrasis and exclamation are Napier's preferred rhetorical weapons. The redcoats advance "like streams of burning lava," and a breach in the fortress walls beckons them "like the mouth of some huge dragon belching forth smoke and flame." And just like the heroes of before, here too valiant officers step forward and fall as martyrs with swords in hand. They were no ordinary men and this was no ordinary ordeal, Napier concludes in words befitting their achievement, for "no age, no nation ever sent forth braver troops to battle than those who stormed Badajoz"— one of whom he singles out as Fitzroy Somerset, the future Lord Raglan.[4]

The ancient bard could just as easily inspire the Russians in their struggle against the same enemy. At the titanic Battle of Borodino in 1812, the single bloodiest day in all the Napoleonic Wars when, outside of Moscow, they turned to face the French invading army, their sacrifice was nothing less, as recorded by one participant, than "Homeric." Others remembered that day as a "feast of death," a bountiful "harvest," that turned their blood into a "regenerative seed" watering the soil.

Truth be told, Russians saw events unfolding in their land as so momentous that analogies extended beyond Homer. When Moscow succumbed to fire—initially blamed on the French—the city's immolation was set against Horace's famous lines that it is "fitting and sweet to die for one's country." Comparisons also paired the Russians with King Leonidas and the Spartans at

Thermopylae with Napoleon in the role of a modern-day Xerxes, the Persian despot leading a huge invading army, a multi-national behemoth that seemingly drew from all corners of the world.[5]

Across Europe, therefore, while the Napoleonic Wars allowed for a greater intensity than ever before—for they were fought, literally, from one end of the continent to the other and across all the world's oceans, thereby engulfing the lives of millions—the Heroic Default did not wane in power. Despite the advent of anti-war tracts at this time decrying the waste, bloodshed and desolation, it still reigned supreme, even shaping the two dominant artistic currents of that time, Sentimentalism and Romanticism, by continuing to endow war with newfound appeal and significance.

In the first, the image of the suffering soldier, with Admiral Nelson as the grand exemplar, became a trope designed to generate compassion in the audience, which was the movement's raison d'être. No matter what befell him, he still suffered for a purpose and his passing was most often couched in the rhetoric of stoic sacrifice for the nation. For the second, the conflict with Napoleon could be reframed as the age's Great Adventure, one which afforded the individual the opportunity to soar to grandiose heights, commensurate with its spirit. In fact, the idea of limning the war in this way served as the title of John Kincaid's best-selling memoir, *Adventures in the Rifle Brigade*, which detailed his campaigns against the French from 1809 in the Peninsula to Waterloo in 1815. As a junior officer he saw it all and wrote it down, including the "putrid carcasses of murdered [Spanish] peasants" and the victims of famine looking like "skeletons who had been permitted to leave their graves." Yet these revelations, when weighed against the whole of his memoir, account for little. Most of his narrative tenor and attention, on the contrary, paints the Peninsular War, including the siege of Badajoz, as a picaresque tale fully of jaunty asides and exploits that showcase British pluck and humor while taking the reader on a tour of an exotic foreign land. Not for nothing does he reference in *Adventures* the two greatest literary examples of such an approach: Don Quixote and Alain-René Lesage's *Gil Blas* from the early eighteenth century.[6] By the time of the Crimean War, the British were thoroughly enamored with both these legacies, that is, the Heroic Default originating with Homer and its recent re-imagining through the irresistible lens of the Napoleonic Wars. Yet, being Victorians, they also romanticized war from another angle, this time with an explicitly Christian take. If Wolfe and Nelson's Pietà were secularized images of Jesus coming down from the Cross, then a more explicit kind of signaling was also available in the emerging idea of the Good Death, that is to say, expiring fully at peace with God. And while this idea originated in domestic life, it quickly found application on the battlefields of Crimea in order to mitigate war's horrors and shield audiences from the true savagery of combat.

For Victorians, the ideal place to die was at home, surrounded by loved ones, where eternal sleep, without suffering and fully confident in God's mercy and love, would be the final reward. Given that in real life no one could know what thoughts came to the dying in their last moments, literature became the ideal venue to promote these expectations. Key examples could be found in two pre-Crimean War novels from 1847, Emily Brontë's *Wuthering Heights* and her sister Charlotte's *Jane Eyre*. However, the pinnacle, unrivaled in its popularity and reach, came even earlier with Charles Dickens's *The Old Curiosity Shop*, a novel which quickly gained international fame and whose depiction of the death of Little Nell caused readers to shed real tears as if she were no mere fiction.

For two chapters Nell's body lies in bed, but in God's hands her passing is more of a peaceful sleep, one that, nevertheless, suggests she is still alive:

> She was dead. No sleep so beautiful and calm, so free from trace of pain, so fair to look upon. She seemed a creature fresh from the hand of God, and waiting for the breath of life; not one who had lived and suffered death... And still her former self lay there, unaltered in its change. Yes. The old fireside had smiled upon that same sweet face; it had passed like a dream through haunts of misery and care... So shall we know the angels in their majesty, after death.

Even Dickens himself could not hold back, writing to the illustrator commissioned to capture this scene that "I am breaking my heart over this story, and cannot bear to finish it." Thousands of others followed suit, including Americans across the ocean who desperately waited for news of what befell their beloved heroine.[7]

Though there was no precedent for its application to war, the idea of the Good Death found a ready home in Crimea because it overlapped with the Heroic Default in one key premise: it imbued death with meaning by asserting that while the body remained, the soul was entering heaven. In fact, one of the most noted soldiers from the war, Captain Hedley Vicars, gained his fame precisely because of how he died or, more accurately, because of what could be made of his death.

Credit for Vicars's posthumous rise as one of the Crimea's first celebrities goes to the evangelist and close acquaintance, Catherine Marsh, who published a best-selling biography of him while the war was still ongoing. For its time it was nearly as popular as Dickens's novel and was printed in the tens of thousands, translated into several languages and was still being distributed by the military up until the beginning of the First World War. This success showed that for the devout Christian the glory of God had as strong an attraction as military glory, and through the Good Death it proved possible to combine the two.

In life Marsh paints Vicars as the perfect Christian soldier, the angel on Earth armed with a sword but never losing God's grace due to his religious bona fides. He is a pillar of nearly unmatched piety whose every waking moment, except when on duty, is spent in prayer, attending the wounded or engaged in other charitable affairs. In all these activities he finds the "deepest happiness" and complements them with a life of self-abnegation, preferring a bed of "stones and leaves" while he shares all his possessions with his fellow soldiers. In death, the same innocent spirit carries over even if now it is steeped in violence. In fact, during the night he was killed—in March 1855, in an otherwise insignificant nighttime sortie—it was reported that he "cut down" two Russians while leading the men of his regiment before he himself was bayoneted several times. Carried back on a stretcher, he bled to death but right at this moment, according to Marsh, he heard a sound. It was "a welcome from the armies of the sky," which rejoiced at his repose. "He had fallen asleep in Jesus, to awake up after His likeness, and be satisfied with it."

While there is no way Marsh could ever have known Vicars's last thoughts, it should be noted that her account of his life was not all fiction. Through his pious living he had already earned renown throughout the army—it being small enough for such news to travel—and when he died his fellow soldiers Henry Clifford and Somerset Calthorpe along with Mary Seacole noted his passing. Even Lord Raglan reported on it in his daily report, singling out Vicars by name. This recognition only paved the way for Marsh to color his life and death through the same hagiographic lens that so many Victorians sought at home when their time came, transforming Vicars into the military ideal of the Good Death. Even if the stretcher had to substitute for Nell's four-poster bed, it was still possible to meet one's maker quietly, without protest or complaint. One could enter heaven from the battlefield, just as much as from the bedroom, if, mutatis mutandis, key protocols were followed. Heaven itself, as Marsh made clear in her parting words, would erase any difference between a peaceful death at home and a violent one in Crimea:

Yes, he has fallen as a soldier and as a Christian... The white robe is now his—the crown of victory—the song that shall never end. Tears may give place to joy. True, it was not amidst kind friends or on downy bed he died. It was in the deadly charge and in the battle's strife. Yet it is all one. He fell as a Christian, nobly doing his duty... Lord, more grace, more grace, that we may follow him as he followed Jesus!

To prove her point, Marsh includes at the end of her account a number of real-life letters of consolation from fellow soldiers sent home to comfort the Vicars family. They are universal in their praise of how he lived as both an exemplary soldier and a Christian, and how that life seamlessly combined the martial imperatives of the former with the pious demands of the latter. In so doing, Vicars represented a new kind of hero for the Victorian age, one fully worthy of those from the past, whether hailing from the siege of Badajoz or that of Troy.[8]

By the time they came to Crimea, Tolstoy and Russell were well versed in the traditions of the Heroic Default and the Good Death. (Dickens was by now not only Russell's close friend but also one of Tolstoy's favorite authors.) Both had already shown their mastery of the two in earlier writings; we recall, for instance, the purple prose animating Russell's reporting on Wellington's funeral in 1852. At the same time, both were fully aware of the artifice behind the conventions—shown most readily in Tolstoy's norm-subverting depiction of the mother's death in *Childhood*, published that same year. This meant that shortly thereafter, when in the midst of the war each writer supplied the narrative core behind the legends of the Light Brigade and the City That Never Surrendered, they did so with enough caveats and twists to upend those very same conventions. And, as will be seen over the next two chapters, that difference—the laying bare of the artifice, the pulling back of the curtains—changed war writing forever.

Anatomy of a Siege

Russians could be excused their surprise when the story with the mild-mannered title, "Sevastopol in December," appeared on the first pages of *The Contemporary*, a progressive journal which, coincidentally, was the first to publish Dickens in Russian including, in that very same issue, the opening section of *Hard Times*. Albeit fictional, this story posed as a real-time report from the battlefield like none other they had ever seen. Readers sitting comfortably in their urban homes and on their estates were not merely invited to go on a tour of a city under siege; they were forcibly pressed into it.[9]

This is done, first of all, by Tolstoy's unusual choice of the second person so as to address the reader directly throughout the story. He then begins the tour in the presumed safety of the rear lines of the city. Yet even here—this being your first time as an eyewitness to war—shock awaits as *you* must step around the decomposing horse that lies in your way while ducking when a shell bursts overhead. It is *you* who turns your head from the manure and human waste fouling the streets and who stops as a camel pulls a cart past, piled to the top with corpses. But watch out too for cannon balls, broken gun carriages and muskets that lie scattered about in the streets. The debris of war hindering your passage also includes soldiers carrying the wounded, sailors checking equipment or other personnel simply milling about indifferent to what is going on around them.

Yet since this is also a city, life goes on as usual. A new day has dawned and the morning rhythms begin. The harbor bells ring; women shout to passersby, selling rolls and hot drinks as a girl jumps from stone to stone, afraid to get her pink dress muddy. A doctor rushes to the hospital, dodging piles of coal and sacks of flour while a soldier splashes icy water on his face and then crosses himself. Others, puffing up clouds of cigarette smoke, gather to share the news. Daily rituals are met as the cold morning mist brushes your face.

The striking feature of Tolstoy's depiction is that everyone and everything co-exists on the same plane of experience. The facts of war meet the facts of urban life as part of a single landscape. Nothing gets privileged, from the soldier rolling a cigarette, a woman hawking her wares, or carrion rotting in a ditch, just as nothing escapes the narrating eye which shifts seamlessly between you and an omniscient one, leveling all and sundry. As mundane as this might seem, it is precisely what Tolstoy strives to convey and results in something new for literature: the intermingled details of life and war carry no symbolic weight; they do not serve a higher purpose or gesture to anything more than what they simply are: a girl, the ringing bells, a cigarette.

Giving no pause for reflection, our guide continues to an obligatory stop on any tour of Sevastopol: the Great Assembly Hall, repurposed as a massive aid station overflowing with the wounded and dead. Bodies torn, bloodied and dismembered; piles of sawed-off limbs; the stench of mortified flesh and human filth—it is all there yet given in the same dispassionate tone. Indeed, in what is likely a first for writing of that time, we have the profile of a woman, albeit fictional, whose leg has been amputated after being shattered by a bomb. Such is the new face of war brought with shocking immediacy and brutal candidness into the parlors and social circles of distant readers. No longer, Tolstoy writes, will it be full of "waving banners, beating drums and generals on prancing horses" but instead "blood, suffering and death." Never before, in fact, had Russian literature delved into the details of bodies broken in war.

The tour, however, is not over. You come back out into the street, gasping for fresh air, and take in the city once more. Shop signs, a funeral procession, a group of men discussing where the best cutlets can be found—all comes back into sight. Yet up ahead looms another obligatory stop: the Fourth Bastion, known as the deadliest place in all of Sevastopol. Here the path narrows and grows muddier as you are inextricably pulled towards it. A few hundred yards and women and children fade from view as you get closer to the frontline. Now it is just soldiers who rush back and forth as cannonballs shriek overhead and bullets strike the earth. Forgotten are the morning sounds that seem to belong to another life. Instinctively you lower your head and then crouch behind parapets and gabions as the path takes a sharp turn—and there it is, the accursed Fourth Bastion, "a certain grave," you have been told, for anyone who dares enter.

You step inside since the invitation, wordlessly extended by a gun crew playing cards and an officer casually rolling a cigarette, cannot be refused; this spot, after all, is the climax of the tour. Yet the soldiers' collective calm is unsettling, contrary to everything you have been led to believe about the frontlines. The commanding officer, for instance, will explain to you the goings-on of his battery, but only if you ask, because no one here needs to boast or has anything to prove. Their mere presence is testament enough to a certain unspoken courage inside each, even though their losses have been frightful. Since the Great Bombardment weeks before, all of their cannon save one have been knocked out and they are all that is left of the bastion's original garrison.

Yet since this is war, such inaction cannot stand and the crew fires the cannon to show you how it's done. To their express delight, its shot seems to kill two in the opposite trench. In response, *he*—the enemy—sends a mortar bomb back, exploding inside the bastion. Its shards tear away part of a sailor's chest and he collapses, eyes full of fear. But as he is lifted onto a stretcher, they begin to shine and he struggles to beg forgiveness from his comrades since he will not return; the wound is fatal. So it happens every day with seven or eight men, the officer explains, yawning as he rolls another cigarette.

With this scene the tour is over but not Tolstoy's story. Something needs to be made of the unconventionality of what the reader has just experienced. From the mundane observations of everyday life to the absence of "prancing horses," it does not feel like a siege or battle given in literature before. Especially striking is the calm acquiescence of the wounded inside the Great Assembly Hall. Facing gruesome amputations or worse, they lie uncomplaining amid the filth and putrefaction. Yet they are not automatons impervious to pain or written off as collective casualties with the sweep of a pen; they are human beings with feeling and emotion. When one dying man, distinguished by his "fairhair" and "puffy face," is asked how he feels as gangrene consumes his flesh, he musters a simple "my insides are on fire"— yielding a fully realized individual down to his southern Russian roots evidenced by the pronunciation of a softer "kh" in place of an expected hard "g" sound. Another who has lost his leg mentions that it didn't really hurt when the cannonball struck; the main thing, he advises with emphasis in the original, "*is not to think about it a lot*" for that is when people feel pain. And nearby lies a woman, quiet but with a feverish flush to her face, also missing her leg, which was blown off when she was "carrying her husband's dinner to him in the bastion." Each has a different tale to tell but given with the same humility throughout and only when asked.

With "Sevastopol in December" Tolstoy crosses a threshold, leaving behind Homeric expectations of warriors scaling the heights of glory. Such failsafe traditions are conspicuously absent. Instead his warriors are simple peasants, conscripted soldiers and sailors, caught up defending a city along with women and children like the little girl jumping from stone to stone who doesn't want to muddy her dress. They know nothing of the greater politics or strategies that have made their city a battle zone but face that reality as if it's simply another mundane feature of their existence. And it is in their quiet acceptance of the situation that the defenders and civilians come alive as individuals—which extends even to their deaths, the depiction of which, as Tolstoy demonstrates, is just a convention of literature, a mere device to be manipulated. In other words, nothing in a war zone—whether people or things—need have symbolic resonance or stand for something greater. The facts of war are also the facts of life, including death and destruction.

Tolstoy overturns expectations even further with another glaring omission: the near complete absence of religion as a reference point for his characters even though, as peasants, they represent arguably the most devout segment of Russian society. In "Sevastopol in December" there is no mention of Jesus or the Cross, and God makes an appearance only through idioms that are as commonplace in his narratives as any other. No peasant in his story, for instance, dies like Dickens's Little Nell or like an "angel in heaven," as Catherine Linton does in *Wuthering Heights*.

This deliberate omission means that none of Tolstoy's characters can experience the Good Death as an explicitly Christian phenomenon—something he was intimately familiar with as a writer in the European, and not just Russian, tradition. Instead, he substitutes a secular alternative. His characters selflessly accept death without complaint and without unduly imposing on others, but with no religious gestures. They sacrifice their lives willingly, in other words, not for a god but for something else—which becomes the real climax of the story and is revealed only at the end.[10]

With the tour over the narrator steps out from behind the curtain, as it were, to summarize all that you, the reader, have witnessed: the men, women and children going about their lives indifferent to the bullets and cannonballs flying around; their conviction, clear to see but never vocalized, that their city will never fall; and a defensive spirit, to which they all contribute and which unites all of them. What is the quiet inner force "lying deep in the soul" of every Russian that sustains them against all odds and in the face of unimaginable anguish? Is it the temptation of "glory," the attraction of "a medal" or the pull of "the cross?" No, he writes, it is "the love for the motherland."

To outsiders these words might seem like a simple propagandistic reflex, a typically "Russian" substitution for God or flag inserted at the end. For Russians themselves, however, such is not the case. Nothing is more evocative of their nation, of their organic connection with the soil that gives them life and to which they all return upon death. Its proper translation is actually "birth-land," coming from the root—*rod*—the first letters of *rodina*, the word signifying that concept. It evokes a pre-Christian past, extending back untold centuries to the idea of a "moist-mother-earth," a divine maternal which nourished and succored its offspring. "Motherland" is thus the ultimate protector—and which readily expanded upon conversion to include Mary, Mother of God—but to which Russians owe their ultimate allegiance and their unquestioning and unremitting love. This fealty need not be vocalized, as Tolstoy suggests, but it is something that all Russians are ready to die for. (Perhaps unique among European nations, Russia also has recourse to the "fatherland," but the two share little between them. The latter is a construct of the modern age, referring to the state, the government and political power and came into widespread use with the advent of the empire in the eighteenth century. The motherland, on the contrary, is essentially timeless and not beholden to the country's political fortunes in any way.)

Evoking the motherland immediately changes the tenor and reach of "Sevastopol in December" and distinguishes it from other accounts of the siege. It reframes the event as a kind of epic, yet written in real time, that rekindles the spirit of 1812 for a new generation and for a new war. Unlike in the fight against

Napoleon, however, the epic's hero is not the romantic individual like Denis Davydov whose cry in 1812, "I am a Russian," rang supreme. Rather it is the Russian people themselves speaking in their own voices as autonomous beings in the flesh and blood. They may not have names but neither are they a collective archetype or abstract, which is something that Russian readers had never encountered before in war writing. And that individuality is secured precisely by their suffering in the most unromantic of places, the suffocatingly repellent hall of horrors in which they lie with their wounds.

The writer Ivan Turgenev claimed to have shed tears of joy when he finished "Sevastopol in December" and he was not alone. Never before in so few words had anyone in Russian literature captured the essence of patriotism so clearly, bringing it down from poetic abstractions and grounding it in the concrete and the real—among the peasants themselves, no less. We know from an earlier letter to his brother that Tolstoy likened the defenders to the Greeks of Homer's time; however, when transferred into fiction that gloss was replaced by a hardened realism. The city's defenders gain heroic status precisely because they are so human, which is why we read at the story's end that they live on not as "legend," the traditional fare of faraway places, but as "fact" in the here and now.[11]

Tolstoy's hand-written original of the story does not survive so it is not clear what, if anything, the censor might have done to it. We do know, however, that "Sevastopol in December" took the capital by storm and a special printing was rushed to Tsar Alexander II, the son of Nicholas, who had ascended the throne just five months before. From the diary of Anna Tiutcheva, a lady-in-waiting for the empress, it is clear that the court had long heard tales of the courageous defenders at Sevastopol, including the women who served alongside the men, but nothing as yet had brought their feat to life in such unerring tones. No

longer would this be the case. The story made such an impression on Alexander that he ordered it translated immediately into
French and published the next month in *Le Nord*, a Belgian
newspaper sponsored by the Russian government. Not only
would this give the story international play, it would also be a
poke in his enemy's eye. On a quieter note, Alexander also alleg-
edly let it be known that the welfare of the young author was
now a concern of the royal court—a gesture of favoritism, so it
turned out, that was short-lived.[12]

A Charge Into Immortality

The origins of the British legend regarding the Charge of the
Light Brigade we know in far greater detail, including the precise
date of its birth. On 25 October 1854 Russell woke to the sound
of cannon following a night filled with suspense. Earlier in the
darkness a spy had crossed over warning of an impending attack
which Raglan's headquarters had casually dismissed. Soldiers on
the ground, however, were more wary and when the dawn broke,
Russell quickly got dressed while an officer nearby exclaimed,
"By Jove, there is something up!"[13]

The attack did come, for the spy was not lying, and in the
engagement that followed, known as the Battle of Balaklava,
occurred the cavalry charge that has been remembered ever since
in one of the most famous of war poems. One could argue that
for Britain Shakespeare's St. Crispin's speech before the Battle of
Agincourt in 1415 is the closest rival to "The Charge of the
Light Brigade," and it was fought, for those inclined to mark
such anniversaries, on the very same day in October over 400
years before. But any potential contest between the two ignores
a salient distinction. Agincourt, with or without Shakespeare,
was destined to stand tall amid the annals of the nation's tri-
umphs. It was, arguably, the finest feat of English arms in the

Middle Ages, the last, most resounding victory during the Hundred Years' War when their outnumbered army, made up primarily of peasants, eviscerated with their longbows the most fearsome warrior of the day, the mounted French knight.

In comparison, by military standards the Light Brigade's charge was the clear opposite. Not only was it a defeat, its impact had no consequence on the battle in which it occurred—not even to speak of the war itself. When the 664 horsemen of the Light Brigade rode against the Russians, the attack the spy had warned about was essentially over and the Russians were in the process of pulling back. Nevertheless, the "gallant six hundred"—110 of whom lost their lives that day—have gained immortality ever since in the pantheon of war heroes.

It is to Alfred, Lord Tennyson that we owe such a distinction. However, it is no exaggeration to say that, without Russell and his eyewitness reporting, no poem or anything lasting would ever have come from that affair. For he is the one who provided the insight, the necessary tenor and the archetypes that captured the poet laureate's imagination and spurred him to take up his pen. This we know not from conjecture, but from Tennyson himself since he duly acknowledged his debt to Russell in a footnote to "The Charge of the Light Brigade" when it first appeared a little more than a month later. Revisiting what happened alongside what Russell wrote, therefore, becomes the first necessary step to uncover why the poem itself has become so iconic.

The Battle of Balaklava, which Russell witnessed firsthand from beginning to end, can be divided into three distinct engagements of which the Charge, as it became known, was the last. After he got dressed, Russell rushed over to the Sapoun Heights where Raglan, the commander-in-chief, stood. From this vantage point, the entire battlefield could be seen, stretching from two valleys, the North and the South, to the port of Balaklava in the distance. The goal of the Russian attack that morning was to cross both valleys, thereby cutting through the rear of the British army, and seize the port through which all British supplies and reinforcements came.

To protect the port, however, the British had mounted only the lightest of defenses: a series of redoubts armed with naval guns pulled off warships and manned by Turks, supported by the 93rd (Highland) Regiment of Foot and a few marines, with a division of cavalry nearby. That division, it should be noted for posterity's sake, was itself divided into the Heavy and Light Brigades which, despite their names, were virtually identical in makeup and armament.

The first phase of the battle was, from Russell's point of view as a reporter, the least compelling. The Russians overran the redoubts, captured the cannon and put the Turks to flight. In the second phase, however, the stakes increased dramatically because now the only thing standing between the Russians and the port were the 93rd Highlanders arrayed on a small hillock in the South Valley. Both brigades of cavalry, while mounted up, stood to the side, uncommitted.

As the Russians pressed their attack and bore down on the Highlanders, the latter never wavered and calmly leveled their rifles at the enemy. Volley after volley resounded into the mass of horsemen and, when the smoke cleared, the line still held but the Russians were in disarray. Taking advantage of this, the Heavy Brigade now joined the fight and counter-attacked, sabering through the Russian horsemen and causing them to fall back to the redoubts which they had captured that morning.

Though it was not even 11 a.m., for all intents and purposes the battle seemed over. The redoubts had fallen but the overall Russian attack on the port of Balaklava had been repulsed. In fact, the Russians had begun retreating and had only paused to take the captured cannon from the redoubts with them. That last move, however, changed everything in the British eyes. It was a direct insult to military honor and there was no way Raglan could let it stand. To allow the enemy to take one's guns from the battlefield was akin to the loss of one's flag. And so he ordered the Light Brigade to take to the field and stop it.

This, needless to say, is where the third phase of the battle began, and it started with controversy. On the one hand, there is the question of Raglan's ambiguously worded orders sent to the Light Brigade and, on the other, the question of who could see what from which point on the battlefield. From the heights where Raglan and Russell were, everything could be seen. On the extreme right was the port of Balaklava, then, moving left, one saw the South Valley and the hillock where the 93rd made its stand and the Heavy Brigade its charge. Then there was a small bump in the land again, what was called the Causeway on which the aforementioned redoubts sat, then the North Valley and, on the far left, the bulk of the Russian forces. The Russian attack, in effect, had been from left to right and had been stopped halfway at the line of redoubts and the captured cannon. Thus, from Raglan's view, he was ordering the Light Brigade to attack the Causeway and retake the redoubts. From the Light Brigade's perspective, however, since it was situated below and more towards the left in the North Valley, the redoubts and their trophy cannon were not visible. In short, the only guns the commander of the Light Brigade could see were the Russian cannon positioned at the end of the North Valley—not the captured ones Raglan had in mind.

To this portrait of clashing perceptions, one must add that of clashing personalities and the infighting between the senior officers involved. It was so acrimonious and so consequential for the fate of the Light Brigade that it became a huge scandal back home and the subject of harsh debate and even investigative commissions that Hollywood and the popular press have greedily drawn upon to the present day.

Four individuals make up the main characters in this drama. First was Raglan, playing the role of the aged grandparent, a

66-year-old veteran of the Napoleonic wars, holding a field command for the first time in Crimea and, as some in the press would have it, commensurately out of touch and in over his head. Below him were Lord Lucan, Lieutenant General of the Cavalry Division that included both brigades, and Lord Cardigan, Major General of the Light Brigade. In personal life the latter two were also brothers-in-law who detested each other, the first marrying the sister of the second over twenty years before. Their mutual hatred was matched, perhaps, only by the lack of respect shown by soldiers under them. Lucan was tagged as "Lord Look-on" for his inaction, whereas Cardigan was known as "the noble yachtsman" because he preferred to spend nights on his private boat in Balaklava harbor (and thus came late to the scene that fateful morning). Finally, subordinate to all three, was Louis Nolan, the fiery, tempestuous young captain known as the best horseman in the army who delivered the order that sent the Light Brigade forward. He would come to play the most outsized role of all, in large part due to the reporting of Russell, his friend, and would serve as both scapegoat for the Charge and its principal martyr since he was the first to die when it began.

Alongside this colorful cast of officers were the soldiers themselves, decked out in parade finery as if anticipating that this would be the swansong of British cavalry. For the last time, so it turned out, each of the brigade's five regiments appeared in battle wearing their best uniforms. There was, for instance, the 11th (Prince Albert's Own) Hussars in high-collared green jackets adorned with gold lace braid, red trousers with gold stripes down the sides, a black fur shako with a large red fold covering the right side, and a black sabretache hanging from the belt. Or the 4th (Queen's Own) Light Dragoons—in which a young Winston Churchill would serve forty years later—with blue jacket and trousers, garish gold sash and piping and a gold-brimmed kepi. Their weapons too, primarily the sword and the lance, were suitably anachronistic and could have belonged to medieval knights. And, almost as if the men were on a pleasure outing, bringing up the rear was the regimental pet, the terrier "Jemmy."

Drawn up in such fashion, the Light Brigade received Raglan's orders, hand-delivered by Nolan who rode down the Sapoun Heights, gallant and alone, in sight of all. Lucan and Cardigan immediately began arguing over their meaning for Raglan had written that the brigade was "to advance rapidly to the front" so as "to prevent the enemy [from] carrying away the guns."[14] But what did "advance" mean in real terms—attack unsupported by infantry or just move forward menacingly—and, for that matter, which "guns," since none could be seen that were being carried away from their vantage point?

Lucan and Cardigan continued bickering until an exasperated Nolan threw out his arm and shouted "there are your guns!" without realizing that his arm was pointing to the Russian cannon down the valley instead of towards those in the captured redoubts on the Causeway. Lucan, enraged that Raglan would have ordered such a suicidal charge against the Russians, nevertheless passed it on to Cardigan who, reluctantly but duty-bound, took his place at the head of the brigade. Thereupon Nolan, one of the prime instigators behind the lords' two disparaging nicknames, asked to stay so he could ride with them—and quickly became the focal point of much attention due to his tiger skin saddle cloth and his self-designed blue uniform sporting various gold and red braids that had reportedly cost a year's salary.

And so the charge began—not in the direction of the redoubts where the captured cannon were, as Raglan had intended, but down the North Valley where, at its end a mile away, were the Russians, no doubt astounded at what was transpiring: an out-numbered cavalry unit advancing to attack a prepared defensive position that was covered by three walls of the valley bristling with Russian guns and muskets. It seems that Nolan, once he realized they were going in the wrong direction, raced to the front to try to correct it but was immediately killed when the first enemy shells landed. Momentum then took over and it was too late for the men of the brigade. They charged the length of the valley—only covering the last meters at full gallop—while continuously fired upon by the Russians from all three sides.

Remarkably, despite these broadsides, the brigade reached the Russian cannon at the end, overran them but, unsupported as it was, could do nothing more but return back up the valley, under fire once again, stopping only when they reached their initial positions. During the seven minutes the charge took, 110 men were killed; 130 were wounded; and fifty eight were taken prisoner, totaling 298 overall casualties or forty-five per cent of the men in the brigade. The worst losses, however, were among the horses; 362 were either killed or destroyed in the field immediately thereafter. Though the precise numbers are still debated, by any count the Light Brigade—which comprised fully one half of the British cavalry in Crimea—ceased to exist as a fighting force. Two notable survivors included Lord Cardigan who, to his credit, rode all the way to the Russian guns and back, and little Jemmy, the terrier who supposedly ran with the troopers the whole way, up and down the valley. Disgraced, Cardigan would stay in Crimea only a month more before setting sail for home on his private yacht never to return, whereas Jemmy received a minor wound in the neck but, unfortunately, would drown four years later in a river in India.[15]

The Story Behind the Legend

Russell sat down that very same evening to write his dispatch by candlelight, with his knee as his desk and his mind, no doubt, still whirring with a myriad thoughts and emotions. During the charge, he never left his position near Raglan on the Sapoun Heights. Immediately after, however, he rode down and circulated among the survivors, several of whom he knew personally. Captain Nolan's mangled body still lay there, his chest ripped apart by shrapnel from an exploding shell which must have deeply affected Russell; they had befriended each other earlier and had shared words just the night before when Nolan lent him his cloak to ward off the nighttime chill. (Russell would later purchase the cloak when the captain's personal effects were put on sale, a common practice then, and kept it for life.) Raglan himself was furious—the armless sleeve of his coat even twitched, Russell observed, when he spoke with Cardigan—while Lucan, whom Russell would later defend, had ridden off. For some inexplicable reason the men themselves were almost forgotten and were kept on the field for hours more without food or, it seemed, much assistance, until dusk when they were allowed to return to camp, accompanied by Russell.

Given these circumstances and the haste with which he wrote his dispatch, his longest to date, we might expect a rambling, chaotic description of the battle. After all, the post was due onboard ship the next day to make the run to Britain. Yet this is where Russell's Victorian education and natural gift for storytelling—the one which made him popular around the campfire—had the opportunity to shine. On the one hand, the three phases of battle easily translated into three acts which, when bookended with an introduction and denouement, lent his dispatch a classical structure. At the same time, as a reporter, he made sure its contents diligently checked off all the boxes: who, what, when, where and why. Finally, while none of its contents was made up, he crafted the dispatch like a tale of suspense written for a reader of fiction.

The dispatch begins by teasing out a central mystery: something terrible, as yet unnamed, has happened:

> If the exhibition of the most brilliant valour, of the excess of courage, and of a daring which would have reflected lustre on the best

days of chivalry can afford full consolation for the disaster of to-day, we can have no reason to regret the melancholy loss which we sustained in a contest with a savage and barbarian enemy.

Disaster, loss, barbarian enemy? The reader is hooked, as these words are not typically used when describing the British at war. The only sure thing, perhaps, is the knowledge, this being Crimea after all, of who the barbarian is. But what have the Russians done? Russell recognizes full well that those at home, as yet, knew no details of the Charge—a point that should be remembered throughout the dispatch—and so adds yet another layer to the puzzle in the second paragraph. What has happened is so serious that he must assert his authority as the reader's trusted on-site eyes and ears. Yet he still retains his prerogative to edit it as he sees fit.

> I shall proceed to describe, to the best of my power, what occurred under my own eyes, and to state the facts which I have heard from men whose veracity is unimpeachable, reserving to myself the exercise of the right of private judgment in making public and suppressing the details of what occurred on this memorable day.

This proposition is nothing short of a paradox. The facts will be forthcoming, as would be expected in any newspaper account; however, certain items will remain concealed based on Russell's own judgment. Which ones and why? Something truly awful must have transpired, one almost hears the reader asking.

Russell baits the reader further by suggesting that the best analogy to understand the battle is that of high drama and describes how he gathered with others on the Sapoun Heights as if "looking on the stage from the boxes of a theatre." This is apt for when the cannons sounded to signal the beginning of the battle, "nearly everyone dismounted and sat down, and not a word was said." As one might expect, the day is pristine and everything literally is picture perfect. "Never did the painter's eye rest on a more beautiful scene than I beheld from the ridge." We also learn that up until now the British cavalry has felt slighted and underused as a siege is not the ideal place for a horseman. These digressions to establish the setting and backstory take pages, delaying the suspense even more.

Now the action is ready to begin. From Russell's perspective the Russians have advanced from left to right, threatening the port of Balaklava, but "we" (the first person is used frequently to establish where the reader's loyalty should lie) have built redoubts on the Causeway against just such a danger. They are manned by Turks, however, who run away before the Russian Cossacks. Here Russell cannot resist using one of his favorite devices, a periphrasis that plays on the stereotype—presumably humorous to him and his readers—of Eastern sloth: they "fled with an agility quite at variance with common-place notions of Oriental deportment on the battle-field." As the Turks fade in the distance under the enemy's lances, the stage is set once again, with a backdrop of the sea "sparkl[ing] freshly in the rays of the morning sun" but now bordered by "ascending volumes of smoke" as the second act begins.

If the first ended in defeat, now it is time for the Russians to meet their match as they prepare to enter the South Valley. The 93rd Highlanders, in kilts and red coats, make up the last defense before Balaklava, on whose fate rests their entire mission in Crimea. If the port falls, the army is doomed. As if knowing the stakes, the Russians pause, eyeing what seems to be an easy conquest. For Russell and the audience up on the Sapoun Heights, "the silence is oppressive" punctuated only by "the champing of bits and the clink of sabres in the valley below." Finally, just as the Highlanders fix bayonets, the Russian Cossacks lunge forward, and Russell pens the immortal lines with emphasis in the original: "The ground flies beneath their horses' feet; gathering speed at every stride, they dash on towards that *thin red streak topped with a line of steel*." Years later, in the hands of others like

Rudyard Kipling, the image will be condensed to a "thin red line," but for now "with breathless suspense every one awaits the bursting of the wave upon the line of Gaelic rock." The Highlanders fire once, but at too great a distance, and then once more. It is the second volley that "carries death and terror into the Russians." They falter and their charge is broken. Up on the heights, the "excited spectators" shout, "Bravo, Highlanders! well done!"

Yet the danger has not passed. Now is the time for the British cavalry of the Heavy Brigade, having finally arrived, to clear the stage of "the dark masses of the Russians." This they do with a fantastic charge, and, like the Highlanders, they are heavily outnumbered but hit the enemy in the flank. In that "terrible moment" the spectators were seized with one thought as the two sides swirl together: "God help them! They are lost!" But "it was a fight of heroes," Russell reassures us, and "as lightning flashes through a cloud," the British cut through their foe and "by sheer steel and sheer courage" put them to flight. All the spectators above, along with the soldiers in the South Valley below, erupted in cheers.

It turns out, however, that their exuberance was premature, and, commensurately, Russell slows his narrative down to return to the mystery at the beginning: "And now occurred the melancholy catastrophe which fills us all with sorrow." He introduces the principal figures, including Lucan and Cardigan, who were involved in the debacle surrounding the order; sets the stakes around the surety of dying if it were to be carried out; and highlights the courage, nevertheless, of those men who were destined to do so. Special attention is thrown on Captain Nolan as a "matchless horseman" and "first-rate swordsman." At this point in the dispatch, the reader has no idea who he is but likely recognizes him as a tragic hero, already presented in the past tense though his fate has not yet been disclosed.

This somber preamble then gives way to Russell's most stirring lines, the kind that obviously captured the hearts of many, including Tennyson, as the action shifts to the North Valley or, as the latter would shortly write, "the valley of Death." With "sabres flashing" the doomed men ride forth, never wavering, to a destiny soon to be known the world over. Anticipating this, Russell compares their achievement with more familiar ones. On the one hand, they rank higher than immortal heroes like Don Quixote, who serves here as a figure of anachronistic gallantry. For they faced deadly cannon, not windmills, as their foe. On the other, they stand just behind "demi-gods" which, needless to say, is praiseworthy in itself since even such deities "could not have done what we had failed to do."

Yet failure it is, as the mystery behind that day is finally revealed. In crafting his account in such dramatic fashion, Russell helped set in motion the particularly British tradition, famously described by George Orwell during the dark days of the Dunkirk evacuations, where in popular imagination defeat has "more appeal than a brilliant victory." After all, gallantry in victory challenges no one. It is when facing the opposite, as the Light Brigade had done, that real courage comes out. Russell, almost foreshadowing Orwell, closes with an extended denouement, highlighting the savagery of the Russians and the advance of the British and French infantry, at long last on the scene having been called up in the morning. This turns the tide of battle since holding onto Balaklava was the British army's sole objective in the first place. Yet the sun of triumph, he writes in his final line, can never rise over "this melancholy day, in which our Light Brigade was annihilated by their own rashness, and by the brutality of a ferocious enemy."[16]

A Legend Comes to Life

On 13 November, nineteen days later, Russell's dispatch ran in the *Times* under the title, "A Cavalry Action at Balaklava," and on 9 December, Tennyson's poem celebrating it appeared in *The Examiner*, a journal that had already made its reputation by publishing some of the biggest names in literature including Byron, Keats, Dickens and Thackeray. In the remarkably short time between those two dates, the poet succeeded in composing one of the most enduring monuments to war and instantiations of the Heroic Default. It begins *in medias res* with lines arrayed in serried ranks, galloping past the reader in pronounced dactylic-trochaic rhythm (hard-soft, hard-soft-soft), as if mimicking the beating hooves of the horses. They describe how the cavalrymen have set off, too late to be recalled.

> Half a league, half a league,
> Half a league onward,
> All in the valley of Death
> Rode the six hundred.
>
> Into the valley of Death
> Rode the six hundred,
> For up came an order which
> Some one had blunder'd.
> 'Forward, the Light Brigade!
> 'Take the guns,' Nolan said.
> Into the valley of Death
> Rode the six hundred.

In the first stanzas Tennyson has already raised the Charge to something extraordinary through the phrase, "the valley of Death," which is a shortened version of Psalm 23: "though I walk through the valley of the shadow of the death, I will fear no evil: for thou art with me." The inaccurate but round number of "six hundred" also shows the need for smooth poetic symmetry, as he admitted in a letter, yet he explicitly does not ignore the controversy behind the whole event. Rather, anticipating Orwell's dictum, it underscores that a mistake has been made; otherwise the poem's message would lose its raison d'être. Moreover,

Tennyson's choice of words reveals that he also drew from the editorial accompanying Russell's dispatch when it was printed in the *Times*. "The British soldier will do his duty," it reads, "even to certain death, and is not paralyzed by feeling that he is the victim of some hideous blunder."[17] Tennyson takes this last point and folds it into the next stanza, the one most famous and most familiar to us.

> 'Forward the Light Brigade!'
> No man was there dismay'd,
> Not tho' the soldier knew
> Some one had blunder'd:
> Theirs not to make reply,
> Theirs not to reason why,
> Theirs but to do and die,
> Into the valley of Death
> Rode the six hundred.

Here, reinforced by a triple rhyme—reply, why, die—is the central point: following orders without question, even until death, is all that a soldier needs to do to serve honorably. His silence, in other words, demonstrates his fidelity to duty even if it also constitutes his one-way, irredeemable ticket to Valhalla. (Interestingly, and as a side note, Tennyson's most cited line—"to do or die"—already circulated as a cliché and was used by Russell in humorous terms to describe landlubber redcoats fighting off seasickness as they embarked from Britain, long before the Battle of Balaklava.)[18]

With the poem's core message now established, the next three stanzas return the reader's attention to the specifics of the charge and the suicidal odds the horsemen faced.

> Cannon to the right of them,
> Cannon to the left of them,
> Cannon in front of them
> Volley'd and thunder'd;

Storm'd at with shot and shell,
Boldly they rode and well,
Into the jaws of Death,
Into the mouth of Hell
Rode the six hundred.

Flash'd all their sabres bare
Flash'd all at once in air
Sabring the gunners there,
Charging an army, while
All the world wonder'd:
Plung'd in the battery smoke,
With many a desperate stroke
The Russian line they broke;
Then they rode back, but not
Not the six hundred.

Cannon to the right of them,
Cannon to the left of them,
Cannon behind them
Volley'd and thunder'd;
Storm'd at with shot and shell,
While horse and hero fell,
Those that had fought so well
Came from the jaws of Death,
Back from the mouth of Hell,
All that was left of them,
Left of six hundred.

The verses repeat themselves, just like the Light Brigade itself going to the end of the valley and back again. But they also show how the outcome of the charge can be turned on its head. The cavalrymen were victorious by carrying out their orders and breaking the Russian line, regardless of the losses incurred and even if, in the end, nothing came of their efforts. This assertion then sets up the final stanza, where the details of the day are reformulated as general imperatives seeking to lock the reader into a predetermined response to the poem as a whole:

When can their glory fade?
O the wild charge they made!
All the world wonder'd.
Honour the charge they made!
Honour the Light Brigade,
Noble six hundred!

Given the haste with which the poem was written, nothing could have foretold the torrent of accolades it unleashed throughout the country. Even Tennyson himself, at least at first, felt some hesitation since he published it only under the initials "A.T." Nevertheless, its smashing success shows how starved Britain was for good news especially during that dreadful winter on foreign soil so far away.

The poem's success also demonstrates—and its enduring popularity proves—how culturally hard-wired an audience can be to accept the Heroic Default. Not only has the Charge alone been the subject of nearly as many books as the war itself, it is the only action by which the war is remembered on screen, beginning with silent pictures. Yet perhaps the most revealing sign of success—and one that affected Tennyson deeply—was how the soldiers in Crimea embraced the poem. Reissued a few months later in a new edition (shorter by one stanza and with Nolan's name absent), it was sent specifically to the troops there and became without question a favorite to recite.

We now know quite a bit more of what happened that day. Not to fault Russell who was caught up personally in the excitement of it all, history tells us that the Turks put up a better fight than they were given credit for, and the 93rd Highlanders were not as outnumbered as it might have seemed. The Heavy Brigade's attack was not as ferocious or decisive as often described, since over the entire day they suffered only about ten killed and unhorsed a few dozen Russians. (The latter's greatcoats were so thick that the slashing effect of a British saber often failed to penetrate.) And, finally, in their charge down the "valley of Death," the Light Brigade faced twenty-six cannon on three sides which together fired about 200 times during the seven and a half minutes it took them to go there and back. The resulting fatalities, which were also due to Russian musket fire, were less than seventeen per cent of the total involved. While that is a high number for any unit in combat, it actually ranks no higher than the losses suffered by other units like in the Battle of Inkerman two weeks later.

While these facts are not meant to undercut the power of the Charge and the Thin Red Line as myth, they lead us back to key points that Russell raises in his otherwise dramatic retelling of that day. Put simply, while the cavalrymen's death was due to a "blunder" at the command level, it can also be attributed to human error of another kind: the failure to recognize that modern warfare might no longer have a place for them beyond scouting and picketing duties. It is clear that this was also running through Russell's mind during his extended discussion of Captain Nolan. After all, in addition to his riding skills, Nolan had written several studies on cavalry tactics that still espoused their decisive value on the battlefield—something, needless to say, which that day proved disastrously wrong. He still believed, Russell informs us in his dispatch, such fantasies that cavalry could break infantry arrayed in square formation (which provided all-round protection against horsemen) or occupy ground defended by enemy cannon. Nolan also "held in contempt" the firepower of grapeshot and canister shells, packed with dozens of murderous iron balls and preferred by cannoneers at close range. Led astray "in their minds," Russell writes, Nolan and others like him tragically proved—by their own deaths in a suicidal charge—how obsolete and wrong-headed this thinking was. Russell even raises the question, albeit indirectly, that maybe it would have been best to leave Nolan and his fellow horsemen in a museum of Napoleonic war remembrances along with their anachronistic uniforms and weapons. Not for nothing does Russell equate them with the quintessence of self-delusional anachronisms: Don Quixote tilting at windmills.

Russell's consideration that the age of cavalry had passed cannot be divorced from his growing premonition, expressed at the same time, that all was not right in Crimea. His Balaklava dispatch was not an isolated piece and those that came immediately after raised doubts about the siege itself. The very next day he concluded another dispatch with words foreshadowing how the siege was headed into a quagmire-like stalemate: "The work in the trenches goes on much as usual. We make very little way, and it is evident this cannot last. The men are worn out." And the day after that came another warning: "Our guns are becoming shaky from repeated firing. We must have more men, and that speedily." On 30 October, just a month into the siege, Russell was already calling into question the effect of the allied bombardments. As the Russians built up their defenses, making Sevastopol even more impregnable than before, he observed that "even if we landed every shell and rocket in the exact spot aimed at, I doubt if we should have had much on which to congratulate ourselves, because the town seems asbestos-like, and utterly incombustible." Indeed, the lack of progress and the continued Russian threat to their rear made him come to a conclusion that would soon become a staple of frustrated British soldiers: "they are besieging us just as much as we are besieging them." Deadlock, malaise and disenchantment were making themselves increasingly known.

Most ominous of all, however, was his observation to readers that, only five days after the Charge, death was making itself known in another way. "The poor creatures are decimated by dysentery, fevers—the typhus particularly—and by diarrhoea, and die in swarms." Here Russell was describing their allies, the Turks. In a few weeks he would be writing the same about the British.

The Russian Troy

Just like Russell's dispatch, the legend of Sevastopol's defense most likely would not have gained iconic status without Tolstoy's story. Its distinctive success lay in the fact that it foregrounded for the first time the travails and trials of individuals—the common soldier, sailor, woman and child—who had been absent from or referenced only in the collective abstract in official reports. In so doing, he made "Sevastopol in December," though fiction, into one of the first modern works of war based on the premise—by now a staple of so many military histories—of telling the story of how a country's "nobodies" become "somebodies" when duty calls.

The setting for his tale, of course, is nothing less than the defense of the motherland, to which Tolstoy would return in *War and Peace* a decade later and with the kind of punch that only a 1,200-page novel could deliver. Yet if the latter employed Napoleon's 1812 invasion as its background, "Sevastopol in December" invokes an even more distant past—in fact, that of Homer himself. When Tolstoy calls Sevastopol's defenders worthy of ancient Greece, there is no need to spell out what other epic siege he has in mind. The situational and symbolic parallels with Troy were too obvious to pass up: foreigners invade from the West, disembark from their ships, and invest a fortress-city on the coast. The grounds of Sevastopol thus become the ultimate modern-day reenactment of that classic plot.

Tolstoy's vision of Sevastopol as a new Troy matched that of other Europeans as well. Victor Hugo, no friend of autocracy, imagined the siege in the same light. Even how it ended nearly a year later—with Sevastopol in ashes—ensured the accuracy of the analogy. For was this not how Troy too met its final fate? A proud city, full of heroes, never-surrendering, fighting to the death— the parallels between the ancient past and present would seem to be irrefutable and showed how Russia too could turn defeat into a moral victory on par with Britain and the Light Brigade. Indeed, on the very day when news arrived in St. Petersburg of the city's fall, it was the Emperor himself who proclaimed that, defiant to the end, it had "never surrendered."[19]

What is more, the fate of Sevastopol rendered as epic remains to this day at the center of Russia's war myth. After all, the siege—any siege—has become such a potent symbol of Russia itself that it arguably serves as its quintessential battle. What better story can there be than one that includes the defense of the motherland; the enemy on all sides; the David versus Goliath odds; the nation as victim of foreign aggression; and the absolute refusal to surrender? Not for nothing, shortly after Crimea the esteemed poet of national-historical themes, Apollon Maikov, equated Russia with a monastery under attack, alone against the world, beset by aggressors coming from all points of the compass. Indeed, in the twentieth century this image gained even more traction with the sieges of Leningrad and Stalingrad and, it should not be forgotten, of Sevastopol once more when in 1942 it withstood the forces of Nazi Germany and its Romanian allies for over eight months. No other type of battle resonates so clearly with the Russian martial spirit which, if one is so inclined, can extend back to the cities which martyred themselves in their desperate, yet ultimately hopeless resistance against the Mongol invaders in the thirteenth century.

Yet like Russell's dispatch, Tolstoy's "Sevastopol in December" offers more to the reader than just a straightforward blueprint for mythic projection. That is to say, as much as it serves as the foundation for city-as-legend epic, at the same time he consciously and consistently breaks tradition in favor of the unusual and unexpected. The basic plot, contrary to the tenets of creative writing, never moves beyond the simple trajectory of the tour from one end of city to the other. Nothing happens out of the ordinary, and the story unfolds as if on a random day chosen from December—yet the historical references in it (to the Great Bombardment, to a new fort being constructed and so forth) are, in fact, a compendium of events that happened over the course of months. The story's structure, therefore, reflects a whole mix of impressions Tolstoy had from his arrival in Sevastopol in November through his time at the Fourth Bastion in April when the story was completed. (That the story was initially titled "A Day and Night in Sevastopol" underscores the loose calendar lying behind it.) This gaming of the story's chronology does not alter, of course, the overall message behind the siege. Rather, it shows how much the supposed ordinariness of the day is part of a deliberate plan on Tolstoy's part to level the events depicted to one plane of reference: from the hospital, to the street, to a café. On this tour, no one scene rises above another.

The same absence of hierarchy applies to the people depicted. Contrary once again to what we would expect from the literature of that time, the social ranking between characters is drawn to the barest of minimums, even down to the well-publicized visit of the Emperor's sons to the Sevastopol battlefield which, while referenced in the story, is remarkably passed off as nothing special. With the exception of the salutation "your Honor"—without which any conversation at that time would have been most unrealistic—characters interact with each other for the most part as individual people, which is a radical proposition for that time, especially in Russia, where the mere act of opening one's mouth would immediately identify oneself, hierarchically speaking, in any given situation. Thus it matters not who lies before us wounded in a bed. In Sevastopol, it can be a woman, soldier, officer or nobleman because in suffering all are equal as human beings.

The irony in all this is something we almost expect from Tolstoy. That which gives the story its bold edge—the leveling of plot and character to the commonplace—is also what makes its epic message stand out. There is no single hero at the center of the city's defenses, as romantic currents would have, no Hector to fight Achilles. Instead, for the first time that role falls to the Russian people as distinct individuals. In other words, Tolstoy achieves the effect of the Heroic Default, a stirring tale of a city under siege, all the while undercutting the traditions of that default narrative. Readers, of course, could and did easily bypass all this; the tears shed by Turgenev and the Emperor were no doubt genuine. Nevertheless, the writer's inner drive, more and more, was pushing him to experiment in this direction, challenging the limits of fiction and the radical idea of not privileging death in heroic colors. For here lay a far greater field to explore, especially as he was surrounded by so much killing.

"A Cavalry Action at Balaklava" and "Sevastopol in December" brought Russell and Tolstoy to a crossroads. On the one hand, their investment in tradition stood firm, allowing them to produce the narrative underpinnings behind the war's two most enduring myths. On the other, they were openly venturing more and more into the new and uncharted. Such equivocation was perhaps to be expected given that it was a time of great transition from the age of romanticism to the age of realism, and from the certainties of the Napoleonic Wars to the doubts of Crimea. Nevertheless, as will be seen in the next chapter, in the space of just weeks, both would unequivocally pivot onto the road of the new and uncharted and leave behind the safe ground of the Heroic Default. In so doing each would hit a breaking point that would cause them to revolutionize what war writing could achieve.

4

THE COMING OF SPRING

By April 1855, the worst had passed. Winter's horrors had lifted and all four armies—Russian, French, British and Turkish—began the siege of Sevastopol once again in earnest. Acute hunger and deprivation no longer crippled the soldiers on either side, and the British troops now enjoyed a relative abundance of warm clothing thanks to the donations from back home and the laying of a rail track from the depots at Balaklava to the front lines. It also carried forward munitions and supplies that allowed the allied cannon, for the most part silent in recent months, to resume their heavy shelling—just as the Russians began to recover and replenish their stocks as well.

The overall mood had also changed—but not necessarily for the better. Spring came as a reminder that neither side held the advantage; the stalemate continued, leaving winter's survivors with little in which to find satisfaction. For the Russians, there was no reasonable chance of defeating the attackers and lifting the siege. Upon the British, a similar malaise had descended. More and more they saw themselves besieged as well. The enemy was not just in front of them on the ramparts of Sevastopol but lurked behind in the rear, fueling the sense of being isolated in a faraway place. "There is one universal feeling of disgust and humiliation amongst us," George Dallas wrote that month. Indeed, finding themselves still stuck "in our corner of the Crimean War," made the whole affair for him "a horrid farce."[1]

At dawn on 19 April, the day before Dallas penned those lines, Russell woke up to join a reconnaissance force made up of Turkish, British and French troops that was more an exercise in multi-national cooperation than a diehard military mission. Led by the Turkish commander in Crimea, Omar Pasha, his counterparts Lord Raglan and General Canrobert rode alongside as observers. Nature blessed them with a "fine and clear" morning, Russell noted, all the more to showcase their uniforms: Turkish infantry in dark blue, British cavalry from the Heavy Brigade in red and grey, and, standing out as ever, the French horsemen of the Chasseurs d'Afrique in powder-blue jackets, white cartouche belts and red pantaloons. Such a colorful entourage, he wrote, "caught the eye like a bed of flowers scattered over the plain."[2]

They proceeded east, past the port of Balaklava and through the valley where the Light Brigade had made its charge five months before. Thanks to Russell's eyewitness dispatch and Tennyson's poem, it was now one of the most famous battlefields in Europe. Yet on this April day there was no smell of gunpowder or smoke in the air, only the "delicate odours" released by the troops as they marched through fields now lush with shrubs in bloom and "a hundred other different citizens of the vegetable kingdom." The sound of cannon was far in the distance as well—nothing compared to the deafening roar that had rocked this area during that battle. Only the horses, it seemed, sensed that something was amiss and began to step gingerly. As the troops continued their march with flowers underfoot, it then became apparent why, and Russell abruptly changed voice.

> The skeleton of an English dragoon, said to be one of the Royals, lay still extended on the plain, with tattered bits of red cloth hanging to the bones of his arms. All the buttons had been cut off the jacket... There was also a Russian skeleton close at hand in ghastly companionship. The small bullet-skull, round as a cannon-ball, had been picked bare all save the scalp, which was still covered with grisly red locks.

Russell drops this on his readers without warning, and the shock surely had some in London spill their morning tea. Here was death in the raw, stripped of any pretense and sense of glory that had attended his reporting on the Light Brigade in October. The details he provided made clear that the bodies had first been picked over by humans (the missing buttons) and then by animals (the bared scalp). Moreover, they had been buried in graves so shallow—if actually buried at all—that they seemed to rise to greet the living. Striking as well was his observance that nationality had lost its significance. British or Russian? It mattered not since flesh decomposes at the same rate—so much so that other species could be added, in his words, to their "ghastly companionship."

> Further on, amid fragments of shells and round shot, the body of another Russian seemed starting out of the grave, which scarcely covered his lower extremities. The half-decayed skeletons of artillery and cavalry horses covered with rotting trappings, harness, and saddles, lay as they fell in the agonies of death, or had crumbled away into a *débris* of bone and skin, and leather straps, cloth, and buckles. From the numerous graves, the uncovered bones of the tenants had started up through the soil, as if to appeal against the haste with which they had been buried.

In a split second, Russell had sprung a deliberate trap on readers, taking them from an innocent outing across an exotic, fertile land to a gruesome outdoor morgue. Many in Britain who lost loved ones that day no doubt gasped, wondering if this was what had become of their husband, son or brother. And those with loved ones still serving might ask, could this soon be their fate?

This was a different Russell, one quite removed from the jaunty character who began his dispatches onboard *Golden Fleece*, cruising through the Mediterranean with the troops, much like a modern-day Jason and the Argonauts, as he was wont to point out in the many classical references peppering his account. That earlier raconteur was chatty and endearing, dazzling readers with the wonders of new technologies, especially the workings of his own ship, launched months before, which represented the height of steam power for its day. By April, however, a new voice had emerged, equally informative but sober, direct and straightforward. While still enamored of periphrasis ("citizens of the vegetable kingdom"), the graphic, unsparing detail that Russell now displayed showed that there would no longer be any self-censorship or suppression of facts.

The new Russell wrote with a confidence unlike before, when he had been unsure of his role as special correspondent; after all, his initial assignment was simply to stay with the army wherever it might go. By now, however, the full responsibility of that remit had become clear. For many in Britain his writing essentially *was* the war. Outside of official communiqués, now quite suspect after a winter of obfuscations, his dispatches were the primary source for them to understand and follow it. When Russell stepped back from the frontlines to take a well-deserved break later that year, Mary Seacole remarked in her memoirs that during his absence in those few weeks "nothing of consequence" happened in Crimea. Her observation was made in jest—but not entirely. In just a few quick months Russell had changed profoundly and grown into what we would now call a seasoned reporter, indeed a celebrity unmatched in authority as the voice of the war. All of which begs the question: what happened?[3]

* * *

The very same day that Russell set out to revisit the battlefield at Balaklava, Tolstoy sat down to catch up on his diary. He was currently posted to the Fourth Bastion, the very epicenter of the allied bombardment and the final destination of the tour presented in his story "Sevastopol in December" which he was finishing up at this time. And while winter had not dampened his earlier patriotic high, feelings of doubt and apprehension now competed with it. For every note of exuberance, such as when he wrote earlier to his favorite aunt about "the funny pleasure" he found in watching people kill each other, now he also lamented that he and his fellow soldiers were but "cannon fodder" in the trenches.

The collision between his simultaneous fascination and repulsion with the trappings of war mirrored a split in his own feelings towards the military: should he stay in it to ensure himself a solid career or embrace wholeheartedly his growing stature as a writer? Earlier in January he had written to the same aunt that he wanted "to do good" in his life. Now that question loomed larger, but after months serving at Sevastopol, it seemed that a military life held out less promise. Which path to choose? Was it time, he confided, "to devote myself fully to a literary one?"[4]

In short, that spring Tolstoy was a bag of contradictions. One section of his diary that increasingly claimed his attention was simply labelled the "facts," and it included both the minor stuff of life casually observed and sometimes events of greater significance—much like the principle undergirding "Sevastopol in December." An entry might, for instance, reflect his colossal gambling losses (a very significant matter) or a nurse who had caught his eye (almost an everyday occurrence). But on 19 April, he also noted that while the shelling had somewhat abated, a boy and girl were killed playing in the street. This he wrote without emotion or comment, almost suggesting that the very definition of what should *not* happen in war—innocent children dying—was now a commonplace feature of his environment. Had he become so inured to death that his earlier, romanticized fascination with it had translated into something else? Was it also merely a "fact" of life at Sevastopol and therefore worthy of inclusion in literature? Tolstoy seemed to think so as he also decided that the topic of his next work would be "a story about a soldier and how he's killed." He would deliver precisely that and, like the first story in the Sevastopol cycle, it too would be a bombshell. But for all the opposite reasons.

* * *

By spring it was clear to both Russell and Tolstoy that the war had descended into such unrelenting violence that the possible ways of rendering it through conventional writing had run their course. The war, in effect, had passed beyond existing norms of expression and the requisite paeans to glory or god. The sheer number of those who lost their lives due to disease, hunger and the elements left an overwhelming numbness that manifested itself in an almost callous indifference to death. Russell, writing shortly after he returned from that tour of the battlefield of Balaklava, captured it best when he described the sights that greeted him on a daily basis:

> I have slept lately in a sunken hut in which a corpse lies buried, with only a few inches of earth between its head and my own. Within a yard and a half of the door of my present abode are the shallow graves of three soldiers, a little earth heaped up loosely over them, mixed with scanty lime, which does not even destroy the rank vegetation that springs out of them. Nearer still is a large mound, supposed to contain the remains of a camel—rather a large supply of

noxious gases; and further away, at the distance of about 180 yards, are the graves of the division, where hundreds of bodies lie lightly covered as close as they can pack. In front of the hut are two mounds, about ten feet distant, containing the buried offal of the butchers; and on the left are the remains of more camels, and of God knows what beside, which emits pestilential odours when the sun shines. This is a nice spot to live in, you will say, and yet I believe it is quite as favourably situated as the tents and huts of many hundreds out here.

The hint of sarcasm at the end only echoed the question both faced. Was the bold, unvarnished truth the only way "to do good" through their writing, as Tolstoy would have it? The pivot he and Russell took would provide the answer.[5]

Ghosts of Winter

For Russell the first major changes in his reporting had become evident already with the onset of winter. His near-daily dispatches came with less frequency, but were also more stark and unsparing as December's freeze swept in, bringing disaster to the troops huddled on the barren steppe outside the city. As might be expected, many were still dressed in summer uniforms, now little more than rags, and grabbed whatever else might shield them from the wind and chill. In "tattered and bepatched garments," with cloth wrap-arounds assuming all shapes and sizes, it became difficult "to tell captains from corporals" as headgear and other insignia denoting rank, so important in a class-obsessed military, also fell prey to the exigencies of survival.

Warm clothing had been sent from Britain but most of it lay at the bottom of the Black Sea in the holds of ships like *Prince*, wrecked in the November hurricane. Or it rotted in the port of Balaklava, lying uncovered in the rain and undeliverable because of the impassability of the lone road leading to their camps. Or, incredibly, because the orders to do so were not issued—leaving Russell at a loss except to state bluntly "we are ruined by etiquette, and by 'service' regulations." So too shoes, not boots, were still the norm despite the snow that was now reaching 2 or 3 feet in depth, and such footwear as it was, predictably, left men worse off at the end of the day. Those who removed their shoes at night found that in the morning their feet had swollen so much that they no longer fit—leaving the men with only one way to get around: "bare-footed hopping," in Russell's reporting.

The shelter that could be had was generally of summer issue as well, that is to say, canvas tents that had long been torn by the wind, resewn haphazardly and then ravaged again. The painfully obvious thing to do, once it became clear that the men would stay beyond the first month, was to build wooden huts but here too the same demons ruled. "Captain Keen"—Russell was now more willing to use names instead of abstract references to press home the direness of it all—"is here [in port] in charge of 4000 tons of wood for hutting, but he cannot get any one to take charge of it, or unload it out of the ships." And such a basic device—the stove—essential not just for life-saving warmth but also for drying clothes (something that simply could not happen outside of an enclosed space) were, we learn, "wretched affairs." Made of "thin sheet-iron," they were just as likely to kill as save—in the treeless steppe, charcoal made the best fuel, but it also produced carbon monoxide. Left lit at night in a tent, something soldiers would understandably do, the stoves, Russell unflinchingly announced, turned into "poison manufactories."

As for provisions, things were no better. Scurvy—the cause and cure long known to all—inevitably reared its head. How could it not, readers back home learned, when the soldiers' principal diet was salted meat and biscuit? To treat it one merely needed fruit and vegetables, but, as Russell passed on, that was inexplicably kept back from them: "I believe there has been only one cargo exclusively of vegetables ever sent up here, and that came in the *Harbinger*, which lay in Balaklava for weeks, till her load of potatoes and onions began to rot and become putrid, so that much of it was unfit for use, and had to be thrown away." The only other source of vegetables became the black market—the inevitable curse of any military endeavor—which was more or less beyond the means of the typical soldier both because of the price and location. Only the fortunate few who could make it to the port of Balaklava had access to it which still meant huge profits for the "adventurers" who illegally used government-chartered ships to secure the delivery of fresh food from Turkey and Bulgaria.[6]

As a result of all these blunders and deprivations, Russell turned to real units and real numbers to impress upon readers of the *Times* how dire the situation truly was. On 30 December, he began charting the decline of the once invincible army. For instance, a contingent of reinforcements for the Scots Fusilier Guards, 150 men, had just arrived in Crimea—which made them most vulnerable since they were not acclimatized to the elements or living conditions. After a few days only twenty of them stood for muster. A little later he reported that the entire regiment, which left Britain numbering 1,562, now had in total only 210 men in the ranks. So too the 46th Regiment of Foot, once of similar strength, could assemble merely forty soldiers, and the 63rd "had only seven men fit for duty yesterday." While back home New Years' celebrations began, Russell welcomed it instead with the grim truth that "our army is rapidly melting away."

What did that loss look like for actual individuals beyond collective tabulations? Russell also provided a dramatic illustration when, for example, he watched a veritable death march of victims to the port of Balaklava:

They formed one of the most ghastly processions that ever poet imagined. Many of these men were all but dead. With closed eyes, open mouths, and ghastly attenuated faces, they were borne along two and two, the thin stream of breath, visible in the frosty air, alone showing they were still alive. One figure was a horror—a corpse, stone dead, strapped upright in its seat, its legs hanging stiffly down, the eyes staring wide open, the teeth set on the protruding tongue, the head and body nodding with frightful mockery of life at each stride of the mule over the broken road. No doubt the man had died on his way down to the harbour. As the apparition passed, the only remarks the soldiers made were such as this,— 'There's one poor fellow out of pain, any way!'

Giving the reader no pause to digest this devastating image, Russell continued:

Another man I saw with the raw flesh and skin hanging from his fingers, the naked bones of which protruded into the cold air, undressed and uncovered. This was a case of frost-bite, I presume. Possibly the hand had been dressed, but the bandages might have dropped off. All the sick in the mule litters seemed alike on the verge of the grave.

For many readers, this portrait of dead or half-living wretches crossed a line into horror and a point of no return. Arguably, however, his most distressing revelation was that virtually all of this suffering was due to the incompetence, lack of foresight and calculated intransigence of fellow countrymen. No one disputed that the climate and conditions in Crimea were hard. However, that fact was well known beforehand, and it was the failure of those inside "the system"—the term had recently been established in the public lexicon—to take this into account that begot such an utter disaster. They had, in a word, betrayed the troops in grotesquely epic fashion. And so as he painted unforgettable images like the one above, Russell never let up on the blame carried by the denizens of bureaucracy, the government contractors and the wardens of the military administration. They were the ones who wrote the rules and regulations which stood in the way of life-saving common sense; they were the ones who enforced them; and they were also the ones who sometimes flouted them out of shameless, selfish greed.[7]

One example of this absurdity reads like a slapstick routine—so much so that Russell includes it verbatim, bringing the reader alongside as witness: "A circumstance occurred in Balaklava to-day which I will state for the calm consideration of the public at home without one single word of comment." He holds to that, introducing the scene without any qualifying adverbs or adjectives:

> The *Charity*, an iron screw steamer, is at present in harbour for the reception of sick British soldiers, who are under the charge of a British medical officer. That officer went on shore to-day and made an application to the officer in charge of the Government stoves for two or three to put on board the ship to warm the men.

The following exchange then ensues, with only the use of "guardian" betraying an irresistible dose of sarcasm:

> 'Three of my men,' said he, 'died last night from choleraic symptoms brought on in their present state from the extreme cold of the ship; and I fear more will follow them from the same cause.'

> 'Oh!' said the guardian of the stoves, 'you must make your requisition in due form, send it up to head-quarters, and get it signed properly, and returned, and then I will let you have the stoves.'

> 'But my men may die meantime.'

> 'I can't help that; I must have the requisition.'

> 'It is my firm belief that there are men now in a dangerous state whom another night will certainly kill.'

> 'I really can do nothing; I must have a requisition properly signed before I can give one of the stoves away.'

'For God's sake, then, *lend* me some; I'll be responsible for their safety.'

'I really can do nothing of the kind.'

'But, consider, this requisition will take time to be filled up and signed, and meantime these poor fellows will go.'

'I cannot help that.'

'I'll be responsible for anything you do.'

'Oh, no, that can't be done!'

The officer from *Charity*—the ship's name itself offers another layer of unintentional irony—then decides to invoke a higher authority, the Principal Medical Officer in charge:

'Will a requisition signed by the P.M.O of this place be of any use?'

'No.'

'Will it answer if he takes on himself the responsibility?'

'Certainly not.'

As these two words from the Cerberus of stoves likely consigned another half dozen men to death, the coup de grâce came in another example given by Russell which one could predict with almost fatal surety: the very paper on which the requisition forms were printed had run out.

Elsewhere Russell could be quite opinionated; how could he not when surrounded with the daily exposure of "the evils in our military system?" Indeed, a sign of how desperate he was to drive home the soldiers' plight was when he switched gears from sober objectivity to a ploy of a more subjective kind, one calculated to hit an British audience hardest: contrasting them with the French. Deployed in the same place and facing the same conditions, not only did their allies enjoy superior stoves, wooden huts, warm clothing, a constant supply of vegetables and better ambulances, they also displayed a generosity of spirit and came to the aid of the suffering British. "But for the kindness of the French in lending us their excellent mule-litters," Russell was compelled to admit more than once, "many of our poor fellows would have died in their tents." This pattern of having to rely on their former enemies for the most basic means of survival, something which he referred to again and again throughout the winter, was "really humiliating to our national pride" but it was the kind of indignity necessary to shock them out of a complacency born of an inbred sense of superiority.[8]

Frustrated by this appalling, senseless death, Russell lost his patience at the end of January and sent back a fiery dispatch. Part of his anger was not just aimed at the military's futile response but, as news swung back from Britain to the camp at Sevastopol, to the disbelief and accusations of slander his reporting had met with there. His outburst was triggered by the recognition that if much of the image of the war at home was transmitted by his pen, then he had the power to manipulate that image according to whatever reason might possess him. In short—and in the starkest of terms—he laid out the stakes: if Britain was so reliant on his reporting, then he might just as easily cover up and ignore the loss of lives; he could, in effect, erase their deaths simply by not reporting them. Perhaps even worse, he could gloss and glorify them, fold them into "the sacrifices we make on the altar of war," or, in our terms, cover them in the ever-resilient, ever-elastic Heroic Default. Yet such maneuvering, he openly stated to his readers in the passage that follows, he could not undertake. What he experienced, what he lived through—"when whole regiments have vanished as if by magic"—put before him a different task:

> According to what I hear from a few people out here, who are eccentric enough to purchase a stray number of the obscurer London journals, I seem to have been honoured by a good deal of abuse from

some of them at home for telling the truth. I really would put on my Claude Lorraine glass, if I could. I would, if I could, clothe skeletons with flesh, breathe life into the occupants of the charnel-house, subvert the succession of the seasons, and restore the legions which have been lost; but I cannot tell lies to 'make things pleasant.' Any statements I have made, I have chapter, and book, and verse, and witness for.[9]

Russell builds to this climax by first gently drawing the reader in with off-putting gestures, though ironic to the hilt: "few people," "eccentric," "stray number," "obscurer" journals. The Claude Lorraine reference he then offers relates to a specially tinted mirror used by painters to view landscapes in reverse; the effect made the view more picaresque and was named after a seventeenth-century landscape master. Such a mirror, later called a Claude Glass or "reflectoscope," became popular in the late eighteenth century and was attributed to Lorrain (a more common spelling), though it seems the artist never used one. The point for Russell was simply that it was an artificial device imposed on reality that made it more beautiful and alluring, that is, more like a landscape "should be" according to convention. In turn, the imaginary power to "clothe skeletons" dips into dark humor since the lack of warm clothing was a precipitating cause of so many fatalities. From there he delivers the punch that helped bring down his nation's government: just as he is not a god who can restore life, neither is he a liar out to comfort readers.

The Storm Breaks

That momentous event—a landmark in the history of journalism—was something Russell never anticipated and likely would not have happened if not for the power wielded by the *Times*. No other newspaper came close to its reach and authority, and it was during the war that its reputation as "the Thunderer" proved truer than ever. Its daily circulation in 1854 was an astounding 55,000, three times greater than that of the next four London papers put together, making it a clear bellwether and driver of public opinion.[10]

Opposition was not always in the paper's blood. Early in the war, the *Times* led the chorus in favor of beating up Russia and offered itself as a forum in which to discuss military strategies and even the best way for women to make mittens for the troops—should one knit or crochet them? (The latter was favored because it was quicker.) Yet as the tone of Russell's reporting went from exuberant to tepid, the paper followed suit. Not only can we follow this change in his published dispatches but also behind the scenes in his private correspondence with the paper's editor, John Delane. From that exchange we learn that Russell, even with his revelations, had to practice a form of self-censorship because he could not risk offending the military establishment too much since he was dependent on them for information.

Russell's position in Crimea was therefore somewhat unusual and this is reflected in his writing. There was no precedent for a journalist to be embedded in the army and no one, including himself, had any idea what to do with him. He was with the army, but not of it (though he had packed a revolver and a saber). He ate and slept alongside its officers and sometimes came under fire, but he also kept his own tent (and servant) and was not issued rations or other provisions. Moreover, he did not have an official commission from the *Times* or carry a press badge— which, of course, did not exist at the time (and would have been of questionable meaning anyway).

We can see how his semi-dependence on the army's good graces impacted his reporting when, for instance, he drew the line on some matters, privately telling Delane of his dilemma when observing X or Y, and his hesitancy in making public such information. It also explains why, when conditions worsened for the troops, he would reveal certain details but tended to conclude with questions instead of direct accusations: who should bear responsibility for what was happening; why wasn't there sufficient foreplanning regarding provisions and clothes; what could be done to better the troops' condition; why were the French handling this so much better?

That gap between his rhetorical questions and the obvious answers was precisely where Delane and his editorial staff stepped in, encouraging Russell in personal letters to "continue as you have done to tell the truth, and as much of it as you can, and leave comment out as may be dangerous to us, who are out of danger." Being in London and free of any concerns for the military, the paper wasted no time in picking up that role and pointing fingers where needed even if, eventually, it was towards those at the very top. Already in late November, after news of the Battles of Balaklava and Inkerman had reached Britain but before that of the destruction wrought by the Great Hurricane, the *Times* raised the specter that "the very flower of our army" might "waste away" for naught. By the next month, as Russell's reports came in, all hell broke loose as the editorial board decried the situation where "Incompetency, lethargy, aristocratic hauteur, official indifference, favour, routine, perverseness, and stupidity reign, revel and riot in the camp before Sevastopol." As a result, it put bluntly, "the noblest army ever sent out from these shores has been sacrificed to the grossest mismanagement."[11]

In addition to the eyewitness evidence contained in Russell's dispatches, the *Times* wielded another weapon: the voices of soldiers serving in Crimea in the form of letters either written directly to the paper or to families who then passed them on to the editors. How the latter published this cache suggests it was part of a plan. Strategically, on the day after Christmas—that is, Boxing Day, when most readers would presumably be at home—

the editorial board released a full broadside of these letters, the first time such a move had ever been made in this kind of public forum. The leading one, by a medical officer dating from late November (all names were removed), was a compendium of all the woes suffered at Sevastopol, both physical and psychological, and reflected a growing recognition in the medical field that not all wounds were visible. The soldiers were ravaged by disease, beaten down by the weather, plagued by transport failures, driven mad by the constant shelling, lacking in vital provisions, appalled at their losses in battle and their inability to capture the city. The only bright spot from this doctor's point of view was the use of chloroform which in his experience had been "most favorable." Otherwise, he wrote in characteristic understatement, "our look-out is rather gloomy."

What then followed, the published words from other soldiers on the frontlines, could not have failed to shock readers in the comfort of their warm London homes:

> "I shall never forget the suffering I endured for five or six days in a miserable, cold tent, with nothing but the ground to rest on and two blankets to cover me."

> "[O]ur troops at Sebastopol are in a dreadful state; 370 died in five days...men actually die of cold and wet in the trenches at night..."

> "[T]he winter has set in with the utmost severity [2 December], and we are neither clothed, nor housed, nor fed for it. We are in tents when off duty, but they are afloat, and we have to lie down in the mud with nothing but a blanket. I need scarcely say the men are dying by hundreds."

> "[New soldiers] frequently die while on duty, and it is but too common to find from six to ten dead from disease, besides those who may be killed by the enemy, which amount to more numbers daily. I fear this letter will put you in bad spirits, for which I am extremely sorry; but, indeed, it is but a faint picture of the sad reality."

Equally hard-hitting was how soldiers viewed the siege itself which, by this time, had only entered its third month:

> "We think and see more of the fearful consequences of this short-handed policy than you at home can fancy; sights I have seen which I never believed could have taken place..."

> "I cannot boast any longer of buoyant hopes and cheerful prospects for the future..."

> "With regard to any prospect of a termination of the siege, there is none..."

> "I am scarcely a shadow of my former self, and that bright star hope, which cheers us under our greatest troubles, is almost extinct within us so far as this world is concerned."

> "I think now the country sees the mistake [of coming here]..."[12]

With this change in tactics, the target of the paper's wrath also shifted. No longer did it blame only the commanders in Crimea such as Lord Raglan, whose head it had long demanded; now it aimed its guns at the government also, painting Prime Minister Lord Aberdeen's coalition as an aristocratic den, aloof, out of touch, inept and, so it seemed, uncaring. This shift was punctuated by the paper's weekly practice, another first, of printing lists of Crimea's dead, including privates who were identified by full name, unit and the cause of death—a distinction once reserved for officers. One such tally, running for four days from 27 to 30 December, focused only on the hospital at Scutari in Turkey—not on Crimea itself. The toll of the dead from that hospital alone over that short period was a staggering 128 or, put another way, a number that far exceeded one fatality per hour, every hour, for those four days. Worse, as the paper noted, virtually all had succumbed to diarrhea or dysentery, that is, deaths that were generally preventable.

Unused to the unrelenting barrage by the *Times* and soon other papers as well, Aberdeen's government failed to act swiftly, which only compounded its image as stonily unmoved by the deaths of its own citizens. This lack of action, bellowed the editorial page, could only lead to one outcome: "the finest army that ever left these shores will soon cease to exist." It was, in fact, too late to do anything to forestall disaster just as, the paper implied, it was too late for the government to resort to its usual rhetorical covers: "no high-sounding names, no Ministerial platitudes, no pretence of loyalty or patriotism shall induce us to feed with human hecatombs the altar of war." Here, once again, the reference was to Homer—but this time only to turn the bard on his head. In Book I of the *Iliad* a hecatomb, the sacrifice of oxen to appease the gods, does its trick and persuades Apollo to put away his deadly arrows which have tormented the Greeks "like a plague." Such luck, of course, was not to happen in Crimea. The continued hemorrhaging of British bodies would appease no god and, so it seemed, the government itself.

Even with these words the *Times* was not finished and hit once again. The devastation in Crimea was not just a distant virus in some foreign land. It reflected as well a cancer at home at the highest level. This turned the war into a mirror of how the country could see itself. The soldiers, representing a wide spectrum of the nation, constituted the body, and were doing the best they could given the circumstances. This was the very definition of "pluck" or perseverance in the face of adversity. But the head, the ruling elite, was not, and was dragging everything down to a depth from which it might not rise. This was nothing short of "national suicide," two words which likely had never appeared together in the history of the paper. Therefore, the only thing that could be done, the *Times* declared, was to "protest, and to warn, and that we will not cease to do."[13]

To be sure, not all members of the Fourth Estate were on the side of the *Times*. In early January one of its main rivals, the *Illustrated London News*, took it to task for serving, no less, "the cause of the enemy." On its front page it singled out the paper's correspondent—without naming Russell—for being "injudicious" by showing only the "dark spots on the sun-like glory" of the army. That indiscretion clearly revealed both his and the paper's lack of "patriotism" that, in so many words, smacked of treason since their primary intent, it seemed, was "to sow disunion" among citizens and "to disgust the nation with the war."[14]

This charge was one of several that helped launch the long history of suspicion between governments and the press during times of war. The *Times*, however, could count on another ally in the public eye, one who, after Queen Victoria, was easily the most popular person in Britain and almost an institution unto himself: Charles Dickens. He had already established himself as a crusader against systemic barriers hampering common sense solutions for urban poverty and poor sanitation. Now he turned his pen on the next biggest killer of his countrymen: the red tape entanglements of government bureaucracy, a term that he coined and popularized precisely at this time.

This subject became the target of satire in his novel *Little Dorrit*, begun during the war and most famously reflected in its chapter on the Circumlocution Office, the place where all well-intentioned plans are crushed by the wheels of bureaucracy. That, however, would not see print until later. During the winter, Dickens aimed for a more immediate impact through his weekly, *Household Words*, and the fairy tale-esque parable, "Prince Bull," which he himself wrote.

In this story Dickens transports the reader to a magical land ruled by a good prince which is "full of treasures," both in terms of resources and citizens. It teems with farmers, engineers, doctors and lawyers, all of whom wish to do good. Yet whenever anything beneficent might come to pass the prince's "tyrannical old godmother"—with the ominous name "Tape" and bedecked in "bright red all over"—descends to gum up the works:

She could stop the fastest thing in the world, change the strongest thing into the weakest, and the most useful into the most useless. To do this, she only had to put her cold hand upon it, and repeat her own name, Tape. Then it withered away.

Needless to say, when Prince Bull sends his army to fight Prince Bear, lord of a "cold and inclement country," along goes the "wicked fairy." There she sets to work making sure all the food, warm clothes, medicines and housing material stay put, never reaching the troops. Her cold hand and one-word curse immobilize all in charge, including the Quartermaster, the Commissariat and the Medical Department. The predictable result? "Soldiers who were sound, fell sick; and the soldiers who were sick, died miserably: and the noble army of Prince Bull perished." Back home, the prince tears out his hair as now all his affairs, both domestic and foreign, are "going to rack and ruin." With Tape always by his side, neither he nor his country lives "happy ever afterwards." Only she does, "chuckling" since no one can escape her reign of "tyranny."[15]

If "Prince Bull" ends on an inconclusive note, such was not the case in real-life London. Perhaps no government could survive the outcry sustained by the biggest guns in the public sphere and the axe fell swiftly on Aberdeen. At the end of January, only one day after a proposal in parliament passed that established a committee of inquiry into the army's handling of Crimea, he resigned and his government collapsed. A Whig, the former Home Secretary, Lord Palmerston, assumed the post of Prime Minister.

Death of a Soldier

At this time, Tolstoy's own doubts over the siege at Sevastopol were growing; after all, the Russian soldiers, though in the city, suffered no less that winter due to failures in provisioning, bureaucratic breakdowns and, of course, the same cold conditions. Yet as a fiction writer not bound to a regular reporting schedule like a correspondent, he did not immediately react but let those feelings percolate inside. Moreover, living in an autocratic, heavily-censored society, he had nowhere near the latitude that Russell had to make them known. Tolstoy could not, in effect, move like his Irish counterpart as a rook on the chessboard, driving forward to his goal. Instead, as would be the case for many Russian writers under such tight control, he would have to maneuver more like a knight—two steps ahead and then a jump to the side.

Fortunately, though, just like Russell at the *Times*, Tolstoy had the steadfast support of his editors at *The Contemporary*. In addition to Nikolai Nekrasov, he enjoyed the backing of another of its editors, Ivan Panaev, who had just turned forty but was already an important name in St. Petersburg. While an author in his own right, one who notably came out in favor of women's emancipation, he also hosted, along with his wife, a literary salon frequented by Ivan Turgenev and a young, pre-imprisonment Fyodor Dostoevsky. And in that capacity, albeit from a long distance, he also became for Tolstoy the key point person in the capital when Nekrasov was away that year.

In the spring of 1855 the support Panaev extended was not just in the pages of his journal. Behind the scenes—precisely when Tolstoy's disenchantment with the war was becoming more manifest—he was pumping the writer with the kind of encouragement that could not fail to go to Tolstoy's head, giving him, in effect, the green light to continue pushing the boundaries of the permissible. "The role you play in our journal," Panaev wrote in a personal letter at the beginning of May, "is so important that its future is connected in no small way with your contributions. Don't keep them from *The Contemporary* or, even more so, from the Russian public which truly loves and values you." These words, notably, were before the manuscript of "Sevastopol in December" landed on Panaev's desk. When that happened two weeks later, he was beside himself, writing in his next letter, "I implore you to send to *The Contemporary* [more] articles like this one. Readers will devour them... We, indeed, all who are the least bit interested in Russian literature, pray for you. May God protect you!"[16]

It is no coincidence that the event that became the basis for Tolstoy's next "article" or story occurred precisely at this time. On the night of 10 May (O.S.), the Russians and the French clashed in the forward trenches on the city's flank, to the right of the Fourth Bastion. For five hours they passed back and forth in savage fighting until the French won control, though at the cost of nearly 5,000 casualties on both sides. Readers of English-language histories of the siege will look in vain for any account of it—the battle has no name—perhaps because it had no consequence. The next morning found the two sides still staring at each other, only with the French a few meters closer. In fact, it was so meaningless that the reader of Tolstoy's diary faces the same void. Nothing of it is recorded even though he was a direct eyewitness to it.

Yet the event obviously stayed in his mind. Perhaps this was because it was so emblematic of the senseless slaughter that the siege had come to represent. In any case, it served as the basis, expressed by him just a month before, for the "story about a soldier and how he's killed." As spring gave way to summer, Tolstoy began to sketch out a prospectus that he first titled "May Tenth." And when *The Contemporary* finally published it, it was clear that the debate once gnawing him inside—to make a career of the military or not—was over. He had chosen to become a writer full-time.[17]

The irony in this—something never far from Tolstoy—is that the story that sealed his decision is really not much of one. That is to say, "Sevastopol in May," the title it finally received, is not much of a story if we assess such things in a conventional story-telling sense. It does not have a developed plot or discernible climax. Its prevailing mood never gets beyond the dull notes of an interminable siege as captured in the first lines stressing the "thousands" of bombs, bullets and shells expended that have resulted in nothing but "thousands" of lives lost and "thousands" of dreams extinguished. From there we get a parade of characters who are flat, underwhelming and, for the most part, unappealing. They consist of Russian officers consumed with jealousy and petty rivalries centering on rank, both in a social and military sense. They are insufferably vain and quintessential "snobs," a word the British satirist Thackeray had coined earlier and which Tolstoy uses here. (At this time Tolstoy was reading his spectacularly popular novel *Vanity Fair*.) The denouement, if that is the word, has these same blowhards, under a flag of truce, trying to show off their (limited) French to the enemy while a ten-year-old boy, wandering the same battlefield, catches fright from a headless corpse.

By violating the conventions of storytelling basics, Tolstoy strips his narrative down to the core components of plot, character and setting, then deliberately "fails" to weave them together into something greater. It's as if we see not the finished painting hanging on the wall but are left instead in the artist's studio amid the brushes, easel and preliminary sketches. In so doing, however, what Tolstoy draws attention to is the craft of combining these elements into a final product, which is the essence of the creative act. How might the raw potential of that night's battle, in other words, be reconstituted as a satisfying war story?

Tolstoy, ever the didact, offers one salient, proven way—only to knock it down. This comes through the character of the petty noble, Baron Pesth, and his experience of combat on that May night. Tolstoy first gives us what this character perceives to have happened in the immediacy of the moment:

Pesth was so frightened that he couldn't really remember how long it lasted, where he had gone or who was who. He just went forward like a drunkard and then suddenly from all sides there flashed the light of a million fires. Something whistled by and there was a huge blast. He yelled and ran somewhere because everyone else was running and yelling. Then he stumbled and fell on something... Then someone took a gun and stuck its bayonet into something soft. '*A moi, camarades! Ah, sacré b... Ah! Dieu!*' someone screamed in a terrible voice. Only then did Pesth realize that he had bayoneted a Frenchman. A cold sweat broke out over his entire body; he was shaking feverishly and threw down his gun.

However, when his comrades ask Pesth afterwards what happened, another language takes over and imposes on him a decidedly different tale:

And Pesth began to tell about how he led the entire company, how the company commander himself was killed, how he had stabbed a Frenchman and that, if not for him, then nothing would have happened and so forth.

With the exception of killing the Frenchman, what Pesth tells us is untrue, distorted, exaggerated or, in a word, a lie. However, he is not lying in the sense of consciously trying to mislead. Tolstoy underscores how Pesth does it *unwillingly*, trapped by the language of his time, its conventionality amplified by the dismissive "and so forth." He knows that what comes out of his mouth is not accurate yet he also knows no other way to communicate his experience. Nothing else is available to him. While his exaggerations would make him, therefore, an easy target for satire and caricature, Tolstoy also emphasizes that Pesth is a victim, an exemplar of how "to get it wrong," as the writer would say. The socially prescribed way to talk about war, the Heroic Default, means that Pesth cannot tell the truth, no matter how much he might want to. His helplessness in trying to bridge the gap between the reality of that nighttime engagement and the flawed language he has to express it, becomes the pivot on which the story turns.

More so than the battle itself, which is inconsequential, or the vanity of the class-obsessed officers, which was a staple of socially conscious fiction then, Tolstoy's challenge to us in "Sevastopol in May" is this disjunction between truth and narrated reality. If the latter, as shaped by tradition, always impedes access to the former, then how can a wordsmith hope to succeed in "getting it right?" Tolstoy might be the first to admit that he does not know, but his dissatisfaction with the current tenets of so-called proper creative writing and its concomitant insistence on round characters and symbolic messaging is on full display here. In fact, it becomes the raison d'être of his story: how to write about war without relying on the usual tropes and approaches.

Tolstoy pursues this quest not just with the episode of Pesth but with the basic building block of all war stories: the representation of death. Can he, the well-read but beginning writer, present it without the romantic gloss of dying on the field of glory? Can battlefield death—*pace* Homer, Napier, and Wolfe; *pace* the Brontë sisters, Catherine Marsh (of Captain Vicars fame) and legions of others—be rendered differently? Perhaps Tolstoy's answer lies in the story's most original passage which, tellingly, is also the longest: the killing of Cavalry Captain Praskukhin, whose life is taken when a piece of shrapnel rips through his chest—exactly as happened to the real-life Louis Nolan, also a captain of cavalry, who delivered the fateful order to the Light Brigade eight months before.

Was Tolstoy playing with his readers? From his diary and surviving letters we cannot know, but the coincidence is worth pointing out since the two deaths, while on the surface strikingly similar, take us down two entirely different paths. Nolan's, of course, is the quintessence of the beautiful battlefield death.

Achilles-like in the superlatives made of him—best horseman, excellent swordsman—he was struck down at age thirty-six in what has become the most famous charge in military history. He, more than anyone else, personifies the gallant 600 of Tennyson's poem and, we recall, is the only figure mentioned by name in its first edition that circulated back to the troops at the beginning of 1855. In a later edition, a more familiar one which is also a verse shorter, Tennyson took his name out. But knowing as we do that Tolstoy spoke with British prisoners, who knows what the latter might have passed on to him since Nolan was such a popular and celebrated figure in the army serving there.

The same cannot be said of Praskukhin, and his creator goes out of his way to make sure we know that. Beginning with his ugly name, which holds true in Russian as well, Tolstoy endows Praskukhin with none of the attributes we might expect to find in a hero. His life is banal to the extreme, he being one of the "snobs" and obsessed with all the affectations of social climbing. What we learn of him instead comes from a remarkable piece of prose which clearly shows Tolstoy's experimental and innovative mind at work. For he draws out the narrative almost in slow-motion as the soon-to-be victim watches the fuse burn down on a shell that has landed at his feet. Playing on the cliché, Praskukhin's life flashes in front of him—or so Tolstoy would have us believe—in that one second before it explodes.

A flood of images rushes upon our non-hero in a jumbled, free-associative way—just like we might expect if we could ever know what happens in the moments before death. Praskukhin first thinks of money he owes to a fellow officer, then about some more debts. These thoughts bring him back to a soiree in the capital where he recalls a song and a woman "in a cap with lilac ribbons" he once loved. Then comes an insult from some-one five years before that he left unanswered. These final thoughts go on as if from a dream, but before Praskukhin can recall anything truly distinctive from his life—or, for that matter, anything that might arouse our sympathy—*ka-boom!*, an explosion goes off. Remarkably, he seems to jump up and run but then stumbles. He can't make a sound because his mouth is unbearably dry yet his chest seems unusually wet. Red fires dance before his eyes and passing soldiers begin to pile stones on him. And then nothing.

In his quest to deflate our expectations further, Tolstoy robs this passage of any suspense. Death comes as a surprise only to Praskukhin himself, since we have been told, a little while before, that he has been killed in the fighting. In other words, since we already know going into this scene its outcome, we are left to focus on how much this character deviates from the qualities of a Nolan-like romantic hero. In this fictional world, where Tolstoy could have just as easily raised him onto such a pedestal, Praskukhin instead is an insignificant, insipid little man whose death brooks no pity or emotional investment on our part. Usually a character's death marks a story's dramatic high point, especially when so much of the narrative centers on him, but Tolstoy denies us that. To rub in how much Praskukhin is not missed either by his comrades or, by implication, us, the next day no one talks or even thinks about him. Indeed, we take leave of him as two soldiers pick up his corpse, its face already turning black and giving off a "foul smell."

Yet this anti-climactic climax holds more significance than just overturning our expectations for a glorified death. By presenting it in the most prosaic, mundane and dull light, Tolstoy turns it into an everyday fact of life at the siege. His outright refusal to be sentimental or wax heroic comes from the same impulse motivating his earlier "Sevastopol in December" when he puts the girl's dress, the screaming cannon shells and the stinking carrion all on the same plane of reference devoid of any emotional pull. And in this tactical maneuvering—the giving of details without any affectation—we can already see, much as Russell was doing for British readers, the hallmark of what would become modern journalism.

In liberating death from the burden of emotion, Tolstoy freed it as a literary trope so that it could accommodate any man, woman or even child. Following this logic, Praskukhin's demise and slippage into near-anonymity is transformative, even groundbreaking in a literary sense. Yes, Tolstoy paints him as a nobody, but that quality is, in its own way, liberating: through particular details, however boring they may be, Praskukhin rises above being a category; he is an individual. In fact, one could almost say that in death he becomes somebody, that is, a person not bound by the dictates of typical war writing, where the field of battle, as the traditional Heroic Default would have it, is a place only for champions and cowards. Praskukhin is neither, since we are explicitly told that he does not run from combat. Ironically, in the dull existence of his small horizons, he is arguably more life-like, more human, than the interchangeable caricatures handed down over centuries.

If all this wasn't enough to cause his editors at *The Contemporary* palpitations—for it was quite daring—how Tolstoy chose to end "Sevastopol in May" nearly sank the manuscript. (He knew he was on dangerous ground and warned Panaev accordingly.) In typical Tolstoyan fashion, the ending is disarmingly simple and revolves around a question that might be asked of any story: who is the hero? The narrator, now somewhat chatty, admits that the list of candidates is short but problematic. Pesth, Praskukhin or any of the other officers named in it are certainly out, and the boy wandering the battlefield is likewise an anonymous minor character. No doubt for Tolstoy the question was spurred by Thackeray's *Vanity Fair* which plays with its own reader through its subtitle, "a novel without a hero." Indeed, Tolstoy's narrator contemplates the same, wondering if a whole Pandora's box might be avoided if the story just ended with no one filling that role. After all, the narrator writes in "Sevastopol in May" that "at this time I've said what I wanted to say" and suggests, by way of analogy, that perhaps it is best not "to spoil the wine by stirring up its contents." Of course, these ruminations are part of the tease, as if Tolstoy, quite the chess aficionado in real life, is playing with us, his hand hovering over the elusive knight. Instead, however, he suddenly picks up the rook and barrels forward with the boldest of assertions in the final line:

> The hero of my story, which I love with all my soul and which I tried to reproduce here in all its beauty—past, present and future— is the truth.

With that one word Tolstoy cast down a gauntlet to the powers that be in Russia. No writer before—let alone at age twenty-seven—had dared to raise it in so garish a manner, especially with the verb "reproduce" (*vosproizvesti*) as if to suggest that the truth is always right there before us but cut off by some artificial barrier, be it linguistic or ideological. In a society where the state had a monopoly on it, at least officially, his claim was nothing short of revolutionary.

This fact was made painfully clear when the story was literally ripped from the presses by the censor after 3,000 copies had already been printed. Panaev was helpless to intercede since he was also away in Moscow at that time and so the manuscript went straight to the desk of the head of the censorship bureau, Mikhail Musin-Pushkin, familiar to us from the scandals surrounding the death of Gogol a few years before. He personally crossed out whole passages, including Tolstoy's lengthy diatribe against the vanities of the aristocracy—over sixty lines—and the details of the boy's after-battle trek across the corpse-strewn field. Out too went references to lice, old coats and dirty blankets, a dialogue in Polish, and any words deemed inappropriate like "swine" or "hell." Needless to say, Musin-Pushkin reserved his greatest wrath for the blasphemous ending. What words he exchanged with Panaev when the latter returned remain unknown; we only have the result. He forced the editor to remove the ending identifying the story's "hero" and substitute the following:

> But we did not begin this war and have not caused this terrible bloodletting. We are only defending our own home, our native land and will defend it to the last drop of blood.

Panaev then balked, as he wrote to Tolstoy, not wanting to publish anything in such a "mutilated" condition. "But if you know [Musin-]Pushkin," he continued, "you can guess what happened next." The head censor insisted that Panaev publish it precisely in its reworked state which made for an unintended ironic twist. Musin-Pushkin's intervention delayed the story's publication until the next month's issue, which meant that its appearance coincided precisely with the fall of Sevastopol.

For us, long removed from the wrath of Musin-Pushkin, the changes he hammered in are telling in a different way. They were so out of place that the mismatch only underscored how ill-fitting the Heroic Default was to Tolstoy's prose. Yet this was the only way, Panaev explained to the writer somewhat graphically, that the censors would allow it: "they don't like it because its hero is *the truth*, and the truth stabs them right in the eye." Given how incongruous Panaev's substitution reads, one might be tempted to ascribe to him an underhanded motive, that is, trying to show up the censors by demonstrating how only patriotic drivel would satisfy them—especially in the cliché-saturated last line. However, the general public could not know the travesty running behind the scenes; they only had the finished product in their hands. Clearly recognizing this, Panaev thus removed from the journal's version any mention of Tolstoy's name or even his customary sign-off, "L.N.T." and published it as "Spring in Sevastopol, 1855." And so it appeared as if an anonymous piece, albeit on the first pages of *The Contemporary*.[18]

Ironically, the intervention by Musin-Pushkin was not only short-lived, it backfired in a salient way, for it helped ensure that Tolstoy would become the writer we now celebrate. The day he learned what happened to his story, he vowed to himself that "My goal is literary glory," defined by him at this time as "the good with which I can do with my writing." And when the story was anthologized the next year as "Sevastopol in May" with his name attached, which is the way it has traditionally come to us, the original ending was restored. By that time, however, the writer was himself back in the capital, having resigned his commission in the military.[19]

Truth and Consequences

Russell also paid a price for telling the truth—albeit in a different way since he was not writing fiction; his pursuit of capturing on paper the reality of the war involved real lives. Therefore, his assertion that British soldiers were dying unnecessarily was insidious to many and was used by detractors to accuse Russell of abetting the enemy. Who else but the Russians, so it ran, could benefit from revealing the conditions of the troops in the field? The blowback he faced in Crimea for his writing came from the top, starting with Lord Raglan, who refused to meet him or grant him an interview. Even if Russell was merely reporting what he saw, the commander wrote back to the Duke of Newcastle, the Secretary of State for War, "the innocency [sic] of his intention does not diminish the evil he inflicts." He even labelled the correspondent a "paid agent of the Emperor of Russia." Newcastle in turn seconded the general, calling Russell's reporting "monstrous"—until he himself resigned because of it at the end of January 1855. Inaugurating a tradition whereby the military would henceforth be suspicious of journalists and the press, Raglan even asked his government if something could be done "to check so pernicious a system" that operated outside official channels.[20]

For the British military it would take until the First World War for Raglan's wish to come true with the issuing of the infamous Field Service Postcard. On it soldiers could only cross out whatever pre-printed phrases did not apply—"I am quite well/I have been sick and am going on well/I have been wounded and hope to be discharged soon"—any other writing or notation would result in its destruction. Fortunately, the Crimean War was too short for such Orwellian methods to be implemented, but that did not stop the ad hominems from falling on Russell. His dispatches were even read by the Queen who was initially furious, calling them "attacks against the army," while her husband, the Prince Consort, dismissed Russell as "one miserable scribbler" and "a vulgar low Irishman." As a sign, however, that the truth could win out, Victoria later changed her mind. After an audience with an officer who came back from Crimea, she pronounced that "Mr. Russell of the *Times*" was right.[21]

Russell's defenders in the military came mainly from the mid-level and lower-ranked officers who were closer to the men and were indignant over their suffering but helpless to do anything. How much he was on target, in fact, can be measured in their private letters written home citing his dispatches. In one, for instance, Major John Strange Jocelyn railed against the Duke of Newcastle for the "deliberate falsehoods" he peddled in the House of Lords and which he had read about in the *Times* as it circulated back to Crimea. He underscored to his family that "everything you read" in Russell's dispatches "is perfectly true" and "not the least exaggerated." In words that no doubt were passed on to friends whose family members were also serving, Jocelyn concluded, "I defy people to exaggerate what this Army has and is undergoing. I assure you men die every night in the trenches."[22]

It was, of course, with the general public that Russell found his greatest support as they waited impatiently back home for his latest dispatch. He stood alone among the other journalists at Sevastopol—discussed in more depth in a later chapter—for no one could match his authority. No one else, in fact, wrote on the war from the very beginning, with the troops boarding ships even before it was declared, to the very end, when he remained in Crimea another three months after the Treaty of Paris was signed in 1856. No one but Russell was an eyewitness to all the decisive moments of the siege, from the Great Bombardment in October and the Battles of Balaklava and Inkerman, through the horrid winter and failed assault of 18 June, to the final attack and fall of the city. No one else lived alongside the soldiers, many of whom became his friends, for the length of time he did, and no one wrote as much as he did on a weekly and often daily basis. When his dispatches were compiled and printed immediately after the war, the bestseller took up two volumes of nearly 1,000 pages of single-spaced fine print.

Finally, one could ask, who else wrote with the skill and dexterity that made Russell's voice so compelling? It was at once friendly, familiar and self-deprecating but also, when the time called, indignant or euphoric. Few besides him showed a willingness to admit mistakes and correct himself, an openness that helped secure readers' trust. Indeed, who else could write as if inviting them to join him by the campfire or so endearingly as if to a family member: "I do not remember if I mentioned to you in my last letter..."; or, amidst a bombardment, "I snatch a few moments to write to you"? Only Russell's prose displayed the passion, consistent energy, anger and devotion to the army, its troops and their overall situation there. Not for nothing did Thackeray, his close friend, ask, "what can any novelist write so interesting as our own correspondent?" No one else except him or a Dickens, it might be said, could capture so vividly the idiocies, injustices and inconsistencies of the war in Crimea.[23]

Of course there was a novelist in Crimea who could do just that—only Thackeray would never read Tolstoy's work, since the satirist died less than a decade after the war, before Tolstoy was translated. Fortunately, though, the latter, even before he became internationally known, was not without his own bastions of domestic support, least of all the increasing number of readers who held his name in high esteem. Just as flattering for Tolstoy—if not more so given his own stilted opinion of himself—was the acclaim he was winning from fellow writers, such as Ivan Turgenev, and from the literary establishment, manifest most readily in the editorial offices of *The Contemporary*.

Writing to Tolstoy just as the mutilated version of "Sevastopol in May" was coming out, Panaev's co-editor, Nikolay Nekrasov offered further words of encouragement, including the most important of all, the "truth." He repeated it throughout his letter, not only as if to take private revenge on the censor Musin-Pushkin, but also to underscore how its excision only showed how vital it was to the country. "The truth is precisely what Russian society needs right now," he wrote to Tolstoy, "and that truth of which so little has remained in Russian literature since the death of Gogol." That this was now Tolstoy's lodestar, almost as if he had inherited it from the previous generation, made his work stand out. "You bring into our literature something entirely new," he continued, looking towards the future, "that takes the most observant people far away in their hopes." Nekrasov's optimism stemmed, on the one hand, from the writer's young age and energy—Tolstoy was also about to send in *Youth*, his third novel, to the journal—and, on the other, from the broader changes awaiting Russia with a new Tsar only six months on the throne. Perhaps the tragedy that befell his second Sevastopol

147

story was a vestige of the past and that "something good," Nekrasov held out his own hope, was on the horizon.[24]

The truth that Tolstoy pursued was close to, but slightly different from the one Russell sought to convey in the *Times*. For the latter, it was more the provenance of basic, undeniable facts: this is what actually happened to our troops versus the falsehoods peddled by others. For the former, truth was more of the moral, ethical kind which is precisely the essence given in Russian by the word *pravda*. This is what many readers sought in fiction, particularly in a censored, autocratic society where there were no public forums like a parliament or newspaper to address issues of the day. Books expressing the "truth" were held as purveyors of justice, decency and fairness; they were the ones that highlighted the humanity of impoverished serfs like Turgenev did in *A Sportsman's Sketches* in 1852 or the depravity of war, like Tolstoy had tried to do in the final passage that was cut from the manuscript of "Sevastopol in May." The key was to do this in an indirect way or in coded terms—a knight's move—which is why Tolstoy got caught. Subtlety, in this as in many other areas of his life, was not his strong suit.

At the same time this truth, the moral one, was for Tolstoy like Russell a literal one. They both challenged the prescriptions of the Heroic Default because for both it constituted a direct assault against what the two had witnessed, experienced and lived during the siege. The obligatory spotlight on a hero, the sacrificial martyrdom, the positive spin on any outcome—all conspired to create a false image of the reality they knew, much like Russell's despised Claude Lorrain glass. Everything such writing traditionally excluded or glossed over was what Tolstoy was trying to supply through his fiction. In his first story, "Sevastopol in December," we see something of that effort in the graphic details he provides, for example, of the hospital visit. All of that, however, was still subordinated to an ending that spoke to a feel-good myth. When he came to the second installment in the series, "Sevastopol in May," nothing of that last part remained. He deliberately stripped away any heroic coating and left readers instead with a different story of the siege, one that eliminated all pretense of drama and hyperbole. In his own way, just like Russell, Tolstoy refused "to clothe his skeletons" to please a conventional readership. That nakedness, as it were, is what the censor sought to cover up.

At the core of Tolstoy's fiction was what we would call an experiential truth. It is a term he would neither recognize nor accept; for him, the truth needed no qualifiers. Yet it was what he was striving for *avant la lettre*. It is not just the province of memoir or real-life reflection, as we might expect; fiction can just as well be a salient vehicle for its transmission. Because this truth rests on lived experience, it can assert itself irrespective of genre as if to say that in war these are the *kinds* of things that can happen and these are the *kinds* of people one bears witness to. Whether or not they exist as carbons in real life is less important. The ultimate gauge of war writing, in other words, is what a reader can take from it no matter if it comes clothed as fiction or non-fiction.

In his Sevastopol stories, Tolstoy was carving out a new approach to recording the experience of battle that would see its fullest expression sixty years later during the First World War with the explosion of autobiographical writing from fellow veterans of the trenches. As will be discussed in more detail in the final chapter, it ran the spectrum from memoir, as in Robert Graves's *Goodbye to All That*, to the novel, as in Erich Maria Remarque's *All Quiet on the Western Front*. Whatever one might call this new genre, Tolstoy would undoubtedly have seen a kinship with these authors. As proof, one might cite another writer, Louis Aragon, also a frontline veteran of the First World War and the co-founder of surrealism. He recalled reading *Sevastopol Stories* in childhood and realized that their depiction of "trench warfare" foretold his own experiences: "No other book gave me a sense of what I would see when I got to the front." Tolstoy, in short, had captured the seeds of what future war—Aragon's own war—would be like. Unfortunately, however, in both his and Russell's case more was to come. The field was not yet fully sown.[25]

5

THE ROAD TO QUAGMIRE

For all the words the war generated—the euphemisms, analogies, the devastating turns of phrase—soldiers were fighting a conflict they could not name. Formal titles certainly existed: the Crimean War, the Eastern War, or, simply, The War. All of these could be heard in both British and Russian variants. Yet none of them captured what kind of war the men were facing. That fell instead to the likes of Russell and Tolstoy, who made it their mission to clarify its new face and to make sense of the unimaginable.

Yet neither writer went to Crimea with the intention of becoming an iconoclast, of laying bare how lies and falsehood insinuated themselves into how the public received—and therefore understood—the war. Both, genuinely so, held the soldiers' welfare as a key motivation behind their work, since they were the war's immediate and most prominent victims. Time and again, Russell was forced to defend his reporting by showing how his revelations helped secure life-saving assistance for those in the field and, in the long-term, systemic changes in the military. Tolstoy, in turn, went out of his way—substantially further than might be expected from a Russian noble—to address the plight of the common soldier. Since he was a junior officer in the army, his opportunities to act were more limited. Nevertheless, during the war he drew up several plans for reform and even proposed producing a journal for the rank-and-file—in essence targeting them as illiterate serfs—that was rejected by the tsar himself. Privately, Tolstoy's anger over their treatment was unstinting, even searing. There was "no army" at Sevastopol, he confessed to himself, "only a horde of oppressed slaves" who suffered egregiously at the hands of their own officers who beat them mercilessly and stole virtually everything from them—clothes, food, provisions—leaving the soldiers only enough so as "not to die of cold or hunger."[1] In short, while neither Russell nor Tolstoy exhibited the character of an angel—the latter's ego, for instance, was borderline excessive when not insufferable—their altruism was not an ex post facto defensive reaction but emerged alongside and within the revolutionary character of their writing.

What made that writing so incisive was not just how it revealed the deceptions surrounding the war but, as an inevitable consequence, how they were inseparable from the portrayal of death. This is what made Crimea different from previous conflicts, and it is important to note that the two were not alone in questioning why so many died and in what circumstances. William Makepeace Thackeray did precisely that in a poem which appeared in October 1854, just three days after the Light Brigade's charge—about which he could have heard nothing as yet. What concerned him at this early date was the fact that the war's fatalities were in no way confined to the battlefield. Already in August cholera had struck the British army in Bulgaria as it was preparing to depart for Crimea, and Russell, present as always, reported back to the "good people of England" how coping with the dead had already led to a gruesome outcome. The easiest way to dispose of the corpses was to throw them into the harbor with weights at their feet. However, many of them, as if in protest, had broken free from their crude anchors and risen back to the surface, bobbing upright alongside the ships in a ghostly, ghastly send-off.

It was revelations such as these that led Thackeray to write "The Due of the Dead" which assumed the voice of one of Russell's readers sitting comfortably by his "peaceful hearth" in London. Upon learning about such calamities from the newspaper, the reader pauses, then asks, how can we mark their sacrifice? Is the usual way of remembering the dead adequate to the conditions and circumstances of this war (which had not yet acquired the moniker "Crimean")?

> Owe we a debt to these brave men,
> Unpaid by aught that's said or sung;
> By leaders from a ready pen,
> Or phrases from a flippant tongue.
>
> The living, England's hand may crown
> With recognition, frank and free;
> With titles, medals and renown;
> The wounded shall our pensioners be.
>
> But they, who meet a soldier's doom—
> Think you, it is enough, good friend,
> To plant the laurel at their tomb,
> And carve their names—and there an end?

This question haunts all sixteen verses of "The Due of the Dead," and the narrator is at a loss to provide an answer. The traditional ways of remembrance, whether in print or in stone, prove inadequate. It is an elegy full of despondency yet, consonant with the Victorian ethos, rendered in stark, mercantile terms. If this is the bill the dead have sent us, Thackeray asks, by what currency can we repay them?[2]

If Thackeray's tenor already displayed questionable enthusiasm for the war, the same could be felt in Russia where, remarkably, similar concerns plagued the tsar himself. As recorded by Anna Tiutcheva, the demeanor of Nicholas I changed dramatically when the allies landed on Russian soil. His once handsome face seemed "lifeless," with "new wrinkles every day." As winter began to set in and the siege entered its third month, he became more "morose," refusing food and unable to sleep, wandering about the palace in his socks. Her diary records a man dying inside, one who has failed in his divine mission to protect Russia and the Slavic world, even refusing purchase of a portrait commissioned from the Hungarian Mihály Zichy that portrayed Nicholas with raised sword, a cross towering alongside him, and grateful Slavs lying beseechingly at his feet. In February, though suffering from the flu, he reviewed troops about to be sent to Crimea in the bitter cold against the advice of his doctors. Afterwards he retired to his bed and never rose again. His final words before dying shortly thereafter were to the defenders of Sevastopol, vowing to pray for them in the next life and taking the blame for failing to rid the land of the foreign enemy.[3]

The convergence of these factors in a conflict increasingly wrapped in falsehoods and marked by diminishing domestic support had a snowball effect. From the fall of Aberdeen's government to the death of the tsar just weeks later, nothing felt right. Like a marauding beast, the war was carving a bloody path through the ranks of British and Russian soldiers. No laurels planted at their tombs, so it seemed, could satiate its rapacious appetite.

The Search for Meaning

In their respective ways Russell and Tolstoy were out in front of their contemporaries in recording the war's staggering impact. The two made their mark not strictly in the aggregate but also on the individual, human level by putting a face or giving a name

to the fallen even if, as with Tolstoy, they were fictionalized prox-
ies. It was almost as if, independent of each other, they were
moving towards a new way or frame to understand the conflict's
toll. This too, initially at least, was not part of either's intention.
Rather, it emerged in both of their cases as a rejection of prevailing norms, that is, consonant with Thackeray, a rejection of
platitudes rolling off "flippant tongues." If the Heroic Default
had run its course, what might take its place?

Where this rebuff was most startling was in Russell's insistence
that the rank-and-file soldiers of the British army could be held
in a different light than before. Prior to the Crimean War they
could be labeled drunkards and criminals—in Wellington's infamous refrain "the scum of the earth"—or be cast as champions
defeating Bonaparte's armies. Never, however, had the warriors
of the world's greatest empire been seen, put simply, as victims.
Yet that sentiment, in large part due to Russell's dispatches in the
Times, was another of the war's unintended outcomes and, what
is more, its roots could be seen even before the siege itself. In his
fifth dispatch, with the army still ensconced in sunny Malta,
Russell had already begun to point out failures in logistical planning and warned of a looming disaster just like that which befell
the Russian army in 1828 when it lost tens of thousands of
men through botched efforts in its previous war with Turkey.
Presumably a more advanced country like Britain, one that prided
itself on modern efficiency and entrepreneurial know-how, could
avoid "a repetition of such horrors." How little did he know that
his exhortations would make him the Cassandra of the expeditionary force.

> Let us have plenty of doctors. Let us have an overwhelming army of
> medical men to combat disease. Let us have a staff—full and
> strong—of young and active and experienced men. Do not let our
> soldiers be killed by antiquated imbecility. Do not hand them over
> to the mercies of ignorant etiquette and effete seniority...

The advice was something any schoolboy could follow: when venturing into new lands, be prepared and do not rely on past practices, especially if they have turned out to be mistaken. Such common sense, however, broke on the shores of military tradition and that, he continued, more than the enemy's "musket or bayonet," was "what we have most to fear." In short, "antiquated imbecility" weighed down by bureaucratic protocol, that is, "ignorant etiquette," would prove to be the army's greatest enemy.[4]

A key sign that a threshold had been crossed was the initiative by newspapers, most prominently the *Times*, during the winter to publish the names of all who died in Crimea, including—for the first time ever—the privates, corporals and sergeants. This, it should be noted, was a striking departure from just months before when the *Times* embraced the more traditional, "good war" stance, replete with all the messaging of noble deaths and so forth. After the Battle of Alma in September, the first engagement between the armies after the British had landed in Crimea, the *Times* saw fit, for example, to publish in its entirety a letter from a general to a father, Delmé Radcliffe, informing him that his son, an officer, had been killed.

My dear Delmé,

I shall wring your heart, and poor Mrs. Radcliffe's, by the sad intelligence I have, alas! to communicate. Your poor dear boy fell yesterday at the head of the company which he commanded (No. 1) while gallantly leading them to the attack of a Russian intrenched battery, heavily armed and most strongly occupied. Never was a more noble feat of arms done than the capture of this battery... God alone can comfort us in these overwhelming calamities, and to His Almighty will let us humbly bow. Your dear boy died instantly, without pain, and lies buried in a deep grave along with his brave comrades, close to the spot where he so nobly died. God bless you, Delmé.

P.S. His wound was in the centre of his breast. He lay on his back, and his body had been untouched and respected. God bless and save him. His face was calm, with almost a smile on it.

How Lieutenant Frederick Radcliffe of the 23rd Regiment of Foot actually died that day can no longer be known, but this notification is an adroit synthesis of clichés from both the Heroic Default and the Good Death—unmatched gallantry, instantaneous death, the hint of a smile—and could serve as a template for hundreds of others addressed to officers' families. What we do know, however, is that the same recognition was not extended to the sixty-one non-commissioned members of his regiment—better known today as the Royal Welch Fusiliers—who fell that day alongside Radcliffe.[5]

That the newspaper could completely shift its stance in so short a time speaks to the feeling of guilt that hung over the nation, as if to atone for the self-inflicted loss of so many. It now held that everyone who served was worthy of recognition even if, tragically, that honor came only with their death. The lists of the fallen became somber rollcalls and stood out on the newspaper's pages because of the voluminous space they took up. Indeed, in a class-obsessed society, this constituted a milestone in putting forth the idea, expressed in its pages in December, that Crimea had become "a people's war."

Russia, lacking newspapers as such, could not move in so open a direction. Nevertheless, a sign that similar sentiments had befallen the country came not only at the highest level in the tsar's demeanor before his death—as if he were resigned to his fate—but also in Tolstoy's own sketch, "How Russian Soldiers Die," begun following the bloodbath of the Battle of Inkerman. Unfortunately, it remained unpublished but, as the title suggests, foregrounded not officers but privates, that is, conscripted peasants, and, what is more, singled out an individual instead of treating soldiers as an abstract, collective unit—just like the

Times was doing in its own way. The soldier in question hails from the simple life, as we might expect, yet is a fully articulated character with distinct speech patterns, a pock-marked face and an earring. His name is Bondarchuk and, as the title also suggests, like Praskukhin from "Sevastopol in May," we know his fate ahead of time.[6]

Bondarchuk does not die like Lt. Radcliffe purportedly did, feeling no pain. Instead, he is shot in the stomach, which proves fatal as with virtually all abdominal wounds. At the same time, for narrative purposes such a wound is ideal, so to speak, since it means his suffering is a prolonged affair. Beginning what would become a typical Tolstoyan trope seen most prominently with the death of peasants, Bondarchuk endures the pain quietly, without undue imposition on others. If this were a straight-forward Christian story, his selfless stoicism would be a perfect entry point for the Good Death, such as Radcliffe supposedly had. However, Tolstoy would have none of that, making sure that Bondarchuk's final words are not a clichéd refrain addressing either glory or god. They constitute a simple remark addressed to his superior that is meaningless in terms of the plot yet, for the reader, unique and quite unexpected: "Your Honor, I bought the stirrups [you wanted]; they're under my bunk. They used up all of the money you gave me."[7]

Almost instinctually, Tolstoy and Russell, supported by their respective editors, recognized that to produce anything of lasting value necessitated grappling with the representation of death. Their continual return to this subject was not, of course, born of some macabre intent but came from their insistence that unless there was a full accounting of the war's victims no writing could ever claim legitimacy or authenticity. It was partly this fact that led Nikolai Nekrasov, the editor of *The Contemporary*, to write to Tolstoy championing his ability to portray, as much as possible, the real experiences of the common soldier—about whom "our literature, as you well know, has expressed nothing but banalities." And it was also this fact that led Russell, in turn, to inform Delane at the *Times* in a personal letter from January that, as the army "melted away almost to a drop of miserable, washed-out, worn-out spiritless wretches," he could not report all the actual details of what he saw. "I cannot tell the truth now—it is too terrible."[8]

It is through their insistence on remapping how death should be understood that Tolstoy and Russell's contribution to understanding modern war can be seen most clearly. For both of them it came down to three principles: who died, how they died and, most importantly, why they died. Regarding the first, they broke new ground by insisting that anyone could be the victim of war, no matter their rank, class or nationality; no longer would there be qualifying considerations for recognition—a condition which was even more in play in the Russian army where typically only a general would be identified by name. In other words, everyone's death was of equal importance; the grim reaper was blind to any socially constructed hierarchies. As for the second, how a victim could die, it was expanded to match the true conditions of Crimea. Dismembered in battle, struck down from cholera or typhus, starving in the field, succumbing to gangrenous rot or by suicide—these were ways of dying that were manifestly distant from anything heroic or uplifting. Moreover, the culprit was not always a bullet, a bayonet or a virus but could just as well be, in Russell's terms, the "antiquated imbecility" of clueless bureaucrats.

Yet it was the third—the "why" of it all—that constituted the most decisive break with the past, because it was new and unfamiliar ground for the nineteenth century. In Crimea the surefire way of explaining wars no longer seemed to apply. If earlier ones more readily fit nationalist sentiments—such as defending against tyrants like Napoleon—any such appeal fell flat at Sevastopol as the siege extended for months. By now the religious dispute in the Holy Land from a few years before, where it all ostensibly began over a set of keys to the Church of the Holy Sepulchre, was of no concern to those in the trenches; indeed, one British historian from the generation coming after the war could only shake his head in contempt: "the question at issue [regarding the Church] seems puerile to the verge of criminal levity."[9] Similarly, the assertion that Russia needed to protect Christians in the Balkans from the Ottoman yoke made no sense if the primary fighting took place in Crimea. Finally, the claim that the nation itself was under existential threat by the West was put to rest by the very scale of invasion. If Napoleon's army forty years before was the largest the world had ever seen, then the allied army invading Crimea was one of the smallest Russia had ever faced and threatened nothing more than a single port that had come into the empire only seventy years before.

The British, in turn, needed an even stronger reason to be there since they were the intruders. Their country certainly faced no danger and whatever back-room reasons Whitehall might have had for declaring war—such as safeguarding communication lines with India—they meant nothing to the average Londoner or farmer from the Midlands. Other claims such as taming the Russian bear or defending liberties from Eastern despotism sounded fine in the abstract but did little to warm the men in the trenches in the winter. For both sides the war became defined more by its exceptional inexplicability than anything else.

How did the average soldier understand his purpose and place at Sevastopol? We only have a limited view. For the British there are letters, memoirs and diaries that, while indispensable, can only constitute a partial picture. From the Russians, unfortunately, we have virtually nothing firsthand, only observations offered by third parties. The attention of the latter was most often drawn to their deep and sincere religiosity—something to be expected in a military where, as noted, priests in cassocks marched in the ranks and gun crews placed icons with candles next to their cannon as protection. Overall, the peasants saw themselves, as described by a Polish officer who later deserted to the allies, as the "Army of the Cross," defending both the tsar, God's emissary on Earth, and Holy Rus, the mystical designation of the motherland hearkening back to the Middle Ages. Consequently, through the centuries nearly every nation they fought belonged to the category either of heretic (Protestant or Catholic) or of heathen (Muslim) since they were the only ones professing the "true faith" of Christian Orthodoxy. This distinction between them and their enemies was nothing new for that spiritual border defined virtually all Russia's foreign conflicts, including in the seventeenth and eighteenth when they fought the Swedes and Poles. In other words, that the foreign enemy was almost always of a different nationality and religion was the best motivating factor for serfs who could not read, had never seen a map and therefore had no other way to understand the difference between themselves and their opponent.[10]

While British troops could be fiercely religious in their own right—as evident in the case of Captain Hedley Vicars—they also absorbed some of the same messaging. Tellingly, though, more of this is seen in after-the-fact reflections where one senses a certain defensiveness in needing to protect the image of the military and its mission in Crimea. For instance, in the memoirs of Timothy Gowing, a sergeant major and career soldier who, we are told, "rarely drank anything stronger than tea or coffee," there is a decided effort to temper any mention of the "terrible sights" found on the battlefield with admiration for what the British army achieved and for the manifest courage it displayed at Sevastopol. No matter the "heart-rending" scenes he witnessed, Gowing assures his reader that throughout the campaign he also observed "that indomitable pluck that will carry a Briton through fire and water." Moreover, he reveals the deep influence of Tennyson by describing the Charge of the Light Brigade, in which he did not participate, as the "noblest feat of arms" and is most confident that "Old England will long honour the memory of the noble six hundred" in perpetuity.[11]

Yet even Gowing, no matter how much he internalized the Heroic Default during a twenty-six-year career in the military, could not resist outbursts of anger when the misconduct of his own bore the blame for hardship. "The whole army was in rags and filth, and half frozen in the trenches in front of the enemy," he wrote, describing the onset of winter. "Not one, but hundreds, were stricken down by starvation; they were only about eight miles from plenty, and yet they were dying of hunger! There were clothing and medical stores in ship-loads, but no organization." It was at this primal level of life and death that soldiers' questions of *why* took hold. For there the stakes were clear and unforgiving, admitting no nuance, equivocation or confusing melange of politics and religion favored by governments to justify the fighting. The latter, often conveyed through pumped-up rhetoric, carried little explanatory weight in soldiers' day-to-day experiences as the body count increased. And it was where those two met, the intersection between death and the need for compensatory meaning, that Russell and Tolstoy focused their sharpest attention.

The Reason Why

For the British, the Charge of the Light Brigade served as an early litmus test to reconcile these two demands. The immense fame it gained thanks to Russell's reporting and Tennyson's verse ensured as much. A non-participant like Gowing, for example, devotes many pages of his memoir to it—far more than he does to Inkerman, a battle of greater consequence. So too did Frances Duberly, who was in the group with Russell observing it from the

Sapoun Heights, feel compelled to comment on the charge at length. In fact, recording one's impression of this famous event seemed almost an expected feature of virtually all accounts of those serving at Sevastopol, regardless of where they might have been and whether or not they even took part in it. The charge, in other words, both for the British army and the readership back home quickly came to signify something much larger than just an engagement involving an under-strength cavalry unit.

How people reacted to the Charge of the Light Brigade reflected prevailing attitudes to the war in its totality and the search for a greater purpose behind its costs. On the one hand, it had all the trimmings of romanticized combat at its most captivating, from the ornate uniforms and weapons of steel to the climactic highpoint of any battle—that is to say, when the cavalry is committed. On the other, it showed how blunder and mistake—some regarded Captain Nolan's interference as a court-martial offense—caused men to die needlessly and in vain. Indeed, Tennyson's signature lines anticipated this dichotomy and sought to erase any questions through silencing the participants: "Theirs not to reason why/Theirs but to do and die." At his insistence, in effect, the horsemen of the Light Brigade are deprived of voice and turned into Heroic Default automatons. Whatever they are commanded to do, they must do, even if it brings on disaster or borders on suicide; purpose is preordained solely in its faithful execution.

The poem's enduring appeal, as evidenced by the enormous response then and its continued resonance today in countless books and on screen, shows the acuity of Tennyson's foresight. If just following orders outweighs and exculpates everything else, then there is no situation or outcome that, in theory, could not support its application. At the same time, however, there were those who saw the charge in the opposite light, like Henry Clifford and George Dallas. Writing home within days after the battle, the former, for instance, labeled it "murder" and the "most useless and shocking sacrifice." Even a member of Raglan's staff, Somerset Calthorpe, concluded after the war that the Light Brigade was "uselessly sacrificed."[12]

More to the point, it turns out that the actual cavalrymen who survived it were also not silent, and it was Russell himself who gave them voice. In fact, they actually did "reason why," and the answer they gave fell quite short of Tennyson's—or Gowing's—expectations. Upon their return, Russell rode down to meet them; after all, he had befriended the now dead Nolan and others in the brigade as well. Yet no words of glory or honor came forth, he observed. Instead, bloodied and exhausted, they milled around, their thoughts and impressions "blurry" but "all spoke in the same way—of the losses of comrades, rank and file and horses." In their eyes, the sacrifice that was soon to become legend meant something else entirely. The dazed survivors offered only one conclusion for the ordeal they had undergone: it was "all for nothing!"[13]

Russell revealed this fact only after the war and with hindsight one can see why. The words spoken at the end of the charge did not fit the paradigm of a noble feat which, as we recall, his dispatch from late October was still trying to paint—before the shock of winter destroyed faith in such facile rhetoric. We recall as well that the first words of that dispatch, composed shortly after he spoke to the riders, included the cryptic assertion of him "reserving" the right to "suppress the details of what occurred this memorable day." It is clear that the survivors' bewilderment was one such detail that he preferred to keep out in order to avoid sowing doubt at home as to the true circumstances of the charge. Russell could not have known at that moment that it would become legend but, consciously or not, the impressions given by his dispatch put it directly on that path.

When combined with the views of eyewitnesses like Clifford, Dallas and Calthorpe, the survivors' words show how a new vocabulary was emerging around a shared event, and it was one quite at odds with prevailing norms. "Murder," "useless sacrifice," "all for nothing" were not categories recognized in military reports. Indeed, as part of the official record describing the battle, Raglan reported back to the Secretary of State for War in fairly positive terms wherein the number of casualties was mitigated by the way in which they died:

> Lord Cardigan charged with the utmost vigour, attacked a battery which was firing upon the advancing squadrons and, having passed beyond it, engaged the Russian Cavalry in its rear... They effected this manoeuvre without haste or confusion; but the loss they have sustained has, I deeply lament, been very severe, in officers, men and horses, only counterbalanced by the brilliancy of the attack, and the gallantry, order and discipline which distinguished it, forming a stark contrast to the conduct of the enemy's cavalry.

The report is a model reflection of Raglan himself. He was ever the bureaucratic staff-writer, having served as Wellington's personal secretary for several years; the expeditionary force to Crimea was, in fact, his first independent command. That most of his previous service was behind a desk showed itself eloquently. His words never move beyond comforting binaries— there is gallantry and discipline on the British side; disorder and chaos on the enemy's—and in no way betray the severity of loss, despite the fact that fully one half of the British cavalry deployed in Crimea was mauled in that single charge, and no replacements would be forthcoming until long into the next year.[14]

What is more, the near-calming effect of Raglan's tone never broaches the true controversy of the event. In other words, it never explains why the men were sent on a suicidal charge. He mentions "some misconception of the instruction," without, of course, admitting that much of the confusion was due to the tortured ambiguity of his very own orders, sent twice to the

Light Brigade. In other words, the very reason why the charge was such a futile mess is washed away by containing it within narrative norms of battle from the command's point of view. There was a charge; it was successful (for they "passed beyond" the Russian artillery); losses were higher than usual; and this last fact, if a culprit is needed, was caused by the heavy concentration of enemy guns. All in all, a battle much like any other.

This, needless to say, was not the experience borne by the troopers themselves and, more to the point, their collective "all for nothing" implicitly pointed fingers back at their own superiors. Indeed, the next event giving rise to similar accusations directed at the army's leadership came shortly thereafter with the onset of winter which no one could escape—only this time, as we have seen, the volume was raised exponentially and cries of "murder" and "useless sacrifice" came on behalf not just of one brigade but of the entire army. This time, however, Russell could no longer mollify them through recourse to a romanticized lens; instead, the accusations spilled out into the open and onto the pages of newspapers back home.

The black hole effect of Crimea showed no signs of abating. Even hospitals, Russell observed, "seem to swallow the sick forever." That sentiment—death without discernible purpose—was by March 1855, when he wrote those lines, a dominant leitmotif in soldiers' letters home, including those from high ranking officers. Colonel John Strange Jocelyn went so far as to come out *against* sending replacements to fill the ranks in Crimea. After all, because of the "total mismanagement in all departments," it was "impossible to do any good with this Army here" and to go through with planned reinforcements would "only [be] sending more Victims to rot and die."[15]

One might assume that the warmer temperatures of spring and the laying of a rail track from Balaklava to the field camp to boost provisions would give rise to optimism. Such was not necessarily the case. Melting snow turned up hundreds of rotting, poorly buried corpses and carcasses right under their feet—to the manifest benefit only of rats and hordes of flies. Rumors of peace, which began to crop up at this time, also had a paradoxically negative effect on many soldiers' morale since it only reinforced a desire *not* to fight so as to avoid the fate of those before who were, in the words of Clifford, "sacrificed without cause." Indeed, the relief spring brought only resurrected the debate of who was better off, they or the Russians, since, as Dallas wrote in April, "we are now ourselves besieged in our corner of the Crimea." For many of the British, the change in seasons did little to dampen the bitterness; there was still, he continued, "one universal feeling of disgust and humiliation amongst us" at the "horrid farce" the war had become. It only needed another shared disaster, another bout of self-inflicted victimization, to burst forth.[16]

That day, 18 June, was not long in coming. As detailed earlier, the Anglo-French assault on the right side of the Russian line, designed to break the siege and timed to coincide with the anniversary of Waterloo, was such a bloody fiasco that it was met with universal contempt across the board. Even for Gowing, the glory-filled rhetoric he once reserved for the Light Brigade had run its course, and he joined Clifford and Dallas in blaming their own generals—with the latter exclaiming that "a more horrid piece of mismanagement never took place." If the allied leaders displayed no more originality than a frontal assault in full daylight against heavily fortified, reinforced Russians, how could they expect the results to be different than before? The soldiers, of course, paid for that arrogance as their bodies lay strewn before the Russian ramparts. Once again, in what had become by now a weary refrain, "all this sacrifice," Jocelyn concluded, was "for nothing—for worse than nothing."[17]

After the June calamity, something unthinkable, but quite telling, happened: British officers began to feign illness so as to escape the hell of Sevastopol, though what truly infected them, Clifford let on, was plain for all to see: it was "from disgust and [being] tired of the long dreary siege." In less charitable terms, leaving one's post under false pretenses bordered on desertion or, at least, that is what rank-and-file soldiers would have been charged with for doing the same. And this was not an isolated case. Clifford, himself a major, called those officers who left "a very great number" and predicted, no doubt from the whispers heard among his peers, that a similarly sized group "will throw up their commissions before winter sets in again." Notably Clifford stayed with his troops, vowing to see out the war to its end or until his "bones [lay] with the many that are under Crimean sod." When Sevastopol finally fell in September 1855, it was not joy that came to him. Writing home, while asking that his letter be kept private, Clifford never felt "more dejected and with a heavier heart"—a telling takeaway from an officer who had been with the army from the first day in Crimea, who had fought at Alma, witnessed the charge of the Light Brigade, won the Victoria Cross at Inkerman, survived the winter, and vomited over the corpses on 18 June. That is how he closed his book on the campaign.[18]

A Never-Ending Conflict

If Russell played an essential role in helping shift the British public's opinion on the war, then in complementary fashion Tolstoy's writing reflected something similar, the only difference being that the latter could not express it so openly. Tolstoy too had once shown enthusiasm for the war, volunteering to serve in Crimea. Yet that exuberance never fully supplanted an inner doubt as to the worth of fighting—a sentiment that had already appeared before the war from his time fighting the Chechens in the Caucasus.

It is not often recognized that Tolstoy's frustration with the siege—clearly evident by "Sevastopol in May"—was inseparable from Russia's simultaneous conflict in the Caucasus which began long before the war with Britain and France. Indeed, dividing his war writing into the Caucasus period and the Crimean one, as scholars are wont to do, is somewhat artificial and derives only from the fact that he served first in the former and then in the latter. To Tolstoy, however, the stories set in either place were written during the same time and came from a shared impulse reflecting his growing dismay with romanticized portraits of war, regardless of where it might be.

While he served in the army, besides "Sevastopol in December" and "Sevastopol in May" Tolstoy published three other war stories of consequence in an intensive burst of activity. Two were set in the Caucasus, "A Raid" and "Woodfelling," and the other, "Sevastopol in August," was the third and final installment in his saga of the siege. Only the very first, "A Raid," was published before the Crimean War, but all five overlap with Tolstoy's combat service and are appropriately reflective of it. Not surprisingly, they also form something of a continuum, almost like variations on a theme. Whatever surface differences might distinguish them—the narrative voice, for instance, ranges from a first-person ingenue ("A Raid") to an old veteran favoring the second-person ("Sevastopol in December")—when they are put together they constitute a single whole in several key areas.

All five stories cover a very short period of time, typically one day or so, during which death and suffering is the focal point. However, the climax or crescendo one expects with such a subject comes to nothing of significance. No character undergoes an epiphany or dramatic change, and, anticipating Anton Chekhov's short stories, the action closes with a then atypical zero-ending. In "A Raid," for example, we read of a unit of soldiers stationed in the Caucasus. They march out on a mission, attack a village and, meeting no resistance, burn it. Their haul? A sack of flour, two chickens and a pot of milk. The cost? On the way back to base, one soldier is killed and another fatally wounded by a vengeful but unseen enemy in the woods. In other words, just another day in the cycle of war.[19]

Any semblance of finality comes in the last of the group, "Sevastopol in August," which, fittingly, covers the final days before the city fell and perhaps is the most "story-like" of the five—if only because it allows for a study in contrasts through the portrayal of two brothers, Mikhail and Vladimir. The first is a veteran officer returning to duty after having been wounded. He knows, therefore, what war is, while the younger brother is the naïve one facing his baptism of fire. As they head into battle their thoughts, though kept to themselves, understandably circle around fear and courage with Mikhail holding to a more realistic, pragmatic view and Vladimir to a more romanticized one. However, any difference between the two is erased by the story's end with both of them dead—as if to say the two most powerful motivations of a soldier are meaningless if he is killed. At first, such cynicism might seem out of place; however, when we learn the details of how each died it seems more fitting. Mikhail, the older veteran, lies mortally wounded and breathes his last, content in his heart—but only because a priest has lied to him that victory is theirs, making his passing a parody of the Good Death. With Vladimir, the circumstances are worse. We get no hint of his final thoughts, only the image of "something lying face down in an overcoat"—not even a "someone," just an article of clothing.[20]

Being fiction, "Sevastopol in August" could have ended on a different note—the two brothers, side by side, fighting to the last on the city's ramparts or something of that heroic nature. Instead, Tolstoy chose a mood more akin to Henry Clifford's just as he had witnessed the final days of the siege. It was also a mood his readers had come to expect. Despondency had begun to link all his war stories regardless of where they were set. Even "Sevastopol in December" and its paean to the city's defenders did not break ranks with the other four with its unsparing details of the siege's effects on soldiers and civilians, including women and children. Crucially for Tolstoy, Crimea and the Caucasus were conterminous conflicts. Both converged on the idea, openly expressed in his diary in late November, that Russia, entangled in two wars without end, was on a collision course with itself. The stories from one, therefore, were written in the shadow of the other. This overlap can even be seen in the potential sixth addition to his series, "How Russian Soldiers Die," discussed before, which remained unpublished. While its similarly mundane plot highlighting the slow death of the peasant Bondarchuk is set in the Caucasus, Tolstoy worked on it in the aftermath of the Battle of Inkerman, fought earlier that same November and for the Russians the bloodiest battle in all Crimea.[21]

The two lines converged most emphatically in "Woodfelling," the third story in his war cycle between "Sevastopol in December" and "Sevastopol in May," where the plot, once again, is deceptively simple. In the Caucasus a detachment is sent out to chop trees—not for firewood but to clear terrain in order to deny the enemy cover (the axe being the equivalent of modern-day Agent Orange). The trees are cut down at the cost of several men receiving wounds, which for one poor soldier turns fatal. From the official point of view, this makes the mission something of a qualified success, if a soldier's life can be measured against felled wood. From the soldiers', however, something different emerges that dramatically upends the story's underlying message—so much so that Tolstoy warned his editor Panaev in a letter accompanying the manuscript that no story had cost him so much effort. It was a clear signal that something more was hidden in it.[22]

One tip-off was that "Woodfelling" was sent to Panaev at roughly the same time as "Sevastopol in May," that is, in the summer of 1855 when Tolstoy was at the siege. In fact, the two were so linked in Tolstoy's mind that his diary tells us the very same day—18 June (O.S.)—he finished "Woodfelling," he also drafted the prospectus of "May," almost as if it were a continuation. Certainly in terms of thematics that would seem to be the case since they both, in their respective war settings, hinge on a relatively actionless plot buffeted by a pointless death and on the pronounced absence of purpose. Moreover, both stories are overshadowed by a conflict seemingly without end. The other tip-off came from inside "Woodfelling" itself and consisted of a single word featured in the soldiers' campfire conversations: *Dargo*. If the name of this Chechen village means nothing to the reader today, to any contemporary familiar with Russia's ongoing campaign in the Caucasus, it could signal only one thing: imperial arrogance and overreach ending in disaster. Taken together, the story's two warning signs give us the closest thing we have yet to a recipe for modern quagmire. Indeed, not for nothing did Tolstoy toy with the title "Alarm" for this story, as if to suggest that we should be prepared for something shocking—which is precisely what he accomplished by inserting that village's name.

What was the historical event behind "Woodfelling?" In 1845 a Russian army marched from its base into the hinterland of Chechnya and to its own destruction. Its target was Dargo, the occasional abode of their arch-enemy, the Chechen leader Imam Shamil. Even now the details are murky, but the outcome of this mission represents a classic case of hubris gone awry, recalling the Emperor Tiberius losing his legions to a German ambush in the deep forests of Teutoburg in 9 CE. When the Russian army set out, it was accompanied by a "galaxy" of luminaries from the capital in order to witness, as the campaign's foremost historian wrote over a century ago, "the final conquest of the Caucasus."

As we might expect, treating war as theater was something the fates would not forgive.

While marching to Dargo, the Russians, laden with excess baggage for the comfort of observers, quickly got mired in the forested mountains as they stretched along a single, narrow road that the Chechens had cleverly bisected with abatis and other debris. Lightning attacks from the cover of surrounding woods split the column into pieces, with the main body eventually stumbling into Dargo, which had been left undefended as bait. Unsure what to do, the Russians just dithered there, ironically like Napoleon in Moscow in 1812. Soon, provisions began to run out, leaving them with only one option: to retreat back through the gauntlet of obstacles (now reinforced with the bodies of their comrades) and deadly fire of partisan snipers. When the remnants of the army finally reached base, nearly forty per cent had become casualties.[23]

In "Woodfelling" references to Dargo loom from the past almost like a ghost. The veterans speak of it in hushed tones, its full significance not clearly given, only the sense that something foreboding happened there years ago. In the meantime, in the story's present, the wounding of a soldier—again a peasant, again fatally in the stomach—allows the reader to draw an uncanny parallel between the two. At the end of the story, the mystery is revealed when the name of Dargo is pronounced out loud and the connection realized: for over a decade the Russians have been fighting the same war in the same place against the same enemy with the same outcome. Death is what ultimately awaits the Russian soldier, be it ten years before when thousands fell in that fateful expedition or now, even if it is just a lone soldier returning from his mission. And to reinforce the dull tread of never-ending conflict, Tolstoy closes "Woodfelling" with two of the Dargo veterans sitting silently in the rain at night, as they wait their turn to go on watch once more.

What is most surprising about "Woodfelling" is not how brazen Tolstoy was in drawing parallels between a disastrous past and a still uncertain present, but that he succeeded. Both "Sevastopol in May" and "Woodfelling" were posted to the censor within a month of each other and whereas the former foundered at the presses and was sent back to be butchered into something anodyne, the latter sailed through with only a few "valuable points" taken out, as Nekrasov wrote to Tolstoy. (The original of "Woodfelling," for instance, had soldiers described as being "driven" like cattle when conscripted; in the redacted version they were just "drafted.")

Why this happened remains a mystery. Our usual inside source, the diary of Aleksandr Nikitenko, the censor who was a closet liberal, tells us nothing about it except to reveal how overworked he and his colleagues were at the bureau. While one might not pity the censor, this might explain how "Woodfelling" slipped through. Many, like Nikitenko, worked at several positions simultaneously which meant that the oversight of manuscripts could be spotty at times. Such, it would seem, was the unpredictability of autocratic regimes when the engines of suppression were never fully in gear. That oversight or overwork essentially allowed for diametrically opposite outcomes to befall Tolstoy's two stories. All we can know is that the editors at *The Contemporary* did not miss the subversive messaging of "Woodfelling" and no doubt wiped their brows in relief when the manuscript was returned to them relatively intact. Indeed, as a credit to Nekrasov and Panaev, they answered Tolstoy's brazenness in their own saucy way. Both "Sevastopol in May" and "Woodfelling" appeared side-by-side in the same September 1855 issue of *The Contemporary*—the first mutilated and without his name; the second with his preferred sign-off of "L.N.T." Only two short poems, one by Nekrasov himself, separated the two.

THE ROAD TO QUAGMIRE

The Bottomless Pit

The travails and successes of Russell and Tolstoy in fighting for their truth, whether the literal or moral-ethical kind, reminds us of the classic showdown between the writer and the state. With hindsight we can draw clear-cut sides of right and wrong, and the former, those armed only with a pen, stand in a favorable light, albeit as underdogs. Arrayed against them are the big guns of the government and military which do not take kindly to having their authority challenged. Yet if the contours of this struggle sound familiar, this was arguably the first time that the contest was explicitly tied to and driven by war. And that fact alone changed the stakes involved.

The linchpin for both Russell and Tolstoy was the challenge caused by a protracted, senseless war, especially one begun by choice and whose stated goals had become muddled on both sides. They were not alone in recognizing this. Nikitenko, again privately to himself, greeted the news of Sevastopol's fall with an attack on the emperor and his reign that put a real face on what Tolstoy could only suggest symbolically in his stories.

> My God, how many victims! What a catastrophe for Russia and humanity! Just a single nod from this madman, drunk with arrogance and absolute power, was enough to wipe off the face of the earth so many in the bloom of their life, to spill so much blood and tears, and to cause so much suffering... What was it all for?

He had no answer, just like Thackeray in "The Due of the Dead." And neither, of course, did Tolstoy or Russell. For all of them—be they at Sevastopol, in London or in St. Petersburg—the well of explanation had run dry.[24]

The barrenness they felt does not mean that answers were not out there. Patriotism, honor and duty or god and the cross could always be called upon to fill that void. The phenomenal success of Tennyson's poem or Vicar's hagiography demonstrates how appealing these concepts were and remain—for they are ageless and not bound to any war. Yet it was precisely because of their default status, their ubiquitous applicability, that for *these* men serving in *this* war they rang so hollow. Showing just how time-worn these notions were was, of course, a primary motive behind Tolstoy and Russell's work, and this effort—the writing against and outside of convention—was what they identified as the "truth." This meant that *their* fight was over language and its impact—which for them, at least, made the Crimean War a war of words more than a war of soldiers.

Yet their battlefield extended beyond exposing how romanticized clichés disguised the reality of death's look, feel and smell. If such conventions derived, consciously or not, from the need to deflect and deceive, then the impact of that rhetoric was potentially far more sinister: it didn't just cover up death, it could cause it. Whether parroting "antiquated imbecilities" or urging men into suicidal actions, words could kill, including, ultimately, those words that made up the storylines that sent men to Crimea in the first place. Both sides were guilty on this count which, when combined with great power arrogance and presumptions of infallibility, made for a most lethal cocktail—the contents of which bear reciting.

From the beginning, in Britain an outpouring of patriotism drowned out how dangerous it might be to send an army to a foreign land despite warnings of its intemperate climate and unforgiving terrain. Alongside expectations of an easy victory over Russia—the "modern Attila" as it was popularly called—such exuberance displaced sober consideration of what provisions, medical supplies and even clothing might be needed to conduct a campaign so far away on the western edges of Asia. Such confidence only grew when the army first fought the Russians at Alma where, despite thousands lost, "no life was unnecessarily exposed," Raglan reported back, and where the battle itself demonstrated "that high courage, that gallant spirit, for which the British soldier is ever distinguished." That sense of invincibility did not diminish at Balaklava, when his orders destroyed a cavalry brigade, or at Inkerman a few weeks later where the death of thousands more was overshadowed by the "brilliant conduct" of so many others who "vied with each other in displaying their gallantry and manifesting their zealous devotion to duty." It could be heard back home as well during the winter in parliamentary debates denying that untold numbers of soldiers were dying over there and, then again that summer, played its hand in launching assaults against impregnable positions timed to coincide with fatuous anniversaries of Napoleonic battles. Finally—and fatally—that sentiment could be summed up by one word, "pluck," that was believed to be an essential component of the British character that would see the soldiers through it all.[25]

Russia, fueled by its own sense of exceptionalism, did not take a back seat to its rival. The claim to defend the motherland "to the last drop of blood" was a comforting cliché commonly heard, and for some, divine intercession could be expected, as in previous victories over foreign invaders from the Mongols to Napoleon. Even Fyodor Dostoevsky, recently released from the tsar's prisons in Siberia, sounded like a court poet when he launched into verse boasting that God had ensured His blessed land and people "could never die." That divine touch also encouraged belief among those in charge that magical thinking could make up for the country's technological backwardness and reduced soldiers to expendable material like bullets or wagon wheels. A favored mantra, for instance, held that the bayonet could vanquish the modern rifle—thereby showing that no one side had a monopoly on imbecility, antiquated or not. Exaltation of a special religious endowment also allowed Russia to claim its role as protector of Orthodox Christians in other sovereign countries or assert that the land of the Caucasus belonged to it as a god-given right. And, to enforce the latter, it could just as well send an army to a village called Dargo, blinded by belief in its own invincibility. Finally—and just as fatally—that sentiment could also be summed up by one word to define the Russian character, *stoikost*, soldiers' legendary ability to withstand anything, that would supposedly see them through it all.[26]

The imperial hubris on display among the great powers during the Crimean War was nothing new. What was, however, was that it was wedded to a war of choice, that is, when words mattered more than ever. As the First World War later demonstrated to the world, if those words become muddled, if the reasons for going to war turn hazy, if the "story" behind it ever changes, things most likely are not going well. To his credit, Emperor Alexander II, just a few months after the death of his father Nicholas, knew all too well the consequences once that occurred. In July 1855 he sent a letter pressing his commander, General Mikhail Gorchakov, to marshal reinforcements for a single, decisive attack instead of frittering them away in the siege's daily grind. Otherwise, he noted from St. Petersburg, a distance of over 1,000 miles, *"as has happened in the past, they will be swallowed up piecemeal by Sevastopol, like a bottomless pit."* With this pronouncement (emphasis in the original), the tsar, as much as anyone else, put his finger on what made the Crimean War the first modern quagmire—before the term was coined.[27]

6

AFTERSHOCKS AND AWAKENINGS

Though in a private letter, the admission from the most powerful person in Russia that Crimea had become a "bottomless pit" constitutes one of those rare moments when it could be said that the government looked in the mirror only to recognize that the cracks in its façade were running so deep that the gulf between its preferred rhetoric and the reality of the fighting around Sevastopol was becoming unbridgeable. The tsar's intense scrutiny over the campaign's progress—first by his father, Nicholas I, and now by himself—also suggested that Sevastopol, despite the relatively small scale of the siege, had come to mean more than a battle over a Black Sea port. It was once again a symbol of the nation at war with the West, something no Russian, let alone the tsar, could ignore.

Alexander's letter reflected how at court—not to speak of society at large—a war weariness had set in only nine months into the siege. Anna Tiutcheva, our gauge of opinion among the elite in St. Petersburg, registered a growing dismay, if not despair, over the war's conduct, with blame increasingly accruing to Alexander himself. Members close to the royal family could see little difference between his actions and those of his father whom Tiutcheva herself had earlier criticized for knowing only how "to play" at soldiers. Indeed, circumstances underscored the disjunction between façade and reality even more by offering an ironic coincidence surrounding the tsar's letter, one knowable now only with hindsight. As it traveled south from the capital to Crimea by imperial post, it crossed paths with Tolstoy's manuscript, "Sevastopol in May," sent two days before, heading north back to St. Petersburg. When the latter reached the city a few days later, the truth it contained set off explosions at the censor's office—as if on cue providing a pungent illustration of the tsar's very own qualms.

Sui generis in so many ways, the Crimean War confounded all of its contemporaries. From the Winter Palace and Whitehall to the frontlines, the one current that stands out was the seeming pointlessness of it all, made all the more alarming by the untold lives it was consuming. If in previous wars despondent voices could be heard, they remained in the distinct minority. Never before had they come to constitute something of a collective impulse or force—soon to be known as public opinion—that could color a nation's disposition and, what is more striking, impact both sides of the conflict. When Henry Clifford decried "the loss of so many lives...thrown away in vain" or George Dallas summed up the entire siege as "a horrid farce," there was little substantive difference from the disgust Nikolai Pirogov felt at the "mediocrity, incompetence, close-mindedness, and depravity" that governed the Russian military. In May 1855, the famed surgeon flipped the prevailing propaganda on its head, writing to his wife that "the Russians [here] are not like those who have sworn to die as one defending the city, but have fallen victim to a kind of chaos of opinions and beliefs from which only one thing is clear: no one understands anything that is going on." The language was virtually interchangeable between the British and the Russians, which only underscored that the tendency to lambast the enemy, typical in most wars, had given way to targeting their own "system" for bungling this one.[1]

This fact was not lost on outside observers. No country had been forced into this war, which spoke volumes when thousands of men were being ground into mud over a city that few—in a trope which would become all too familiar in later wars—could locate on a map, let alone explain the importance of. On this subject at least, Karl Marx and Friedrich Engels proved themselves prophetic and, uncharacteristically, having a sense of humor, when they satirized the whole mess in which the allies found themselves. Safe in London, Marx could sum up the whole affair as a "puny little strife" in which "the French [were] doing nothing and the British helping them as fast as they can." Years later, their opinion had not changed. Engels would still call the war a "colossal comedy of errors," except, of course, no one was laughing.[2]

Why this despondency took hold in Europe so quickly—for nine months, even with the Victorians' obsession with speed, was still quite a short period of time—was also because recent history afforded nothing comparable or analogous. Over the previous 150 years, the continent had been convulsed by major conflicts among the great powers—France, Britain, Prussia, Austria and Russia—that witnessed, alongside epoch-defining battles, numerous sieges as they tried to remake the map of Europe according to dynastic and strategic interests. Yet these conflicts—beginning with the Wars of Spanish and Austrian Succession and then the Seven Years' War—were often set-piece affairs, conducted under strict rules of engagement and capitulation, and generally involved forts, not fortified cities. The loss of life due to these formalities and the weaponry of the time was commensurately low and did little to threaten the domestic social fabric of the warring countries. Those that followed, the wars of the

French Revolution and Napoleon, were, on the other hand, world-shattering and sought to overturn much of the traditional political order. But they too offered little in the way of correspondences or parallels to the war being fought in Crimea, for they were of an incomparable scale and scope with often existential stakes for the participants. The Crimean War, in short, had no precedent in the European mindset.

The Impact of Others

If Tolstoy and Russell were the primary drivers in shaping public opinion over a war that looked nothing like its predecessors, then, it should be noted, they were not alone, especially as it pertained to the allies. Up to seven British papers sent correspondents to Crimea, including *The Daily News, Morning Post, Morning Herald* and the weekly *Illustrated London News*. Moreover, the *Times* had reporters in major cities across Europe such as Paris, Berlin, Vienna and Constantinople. Of these, the last assignment bears special mention because it also covered the hospitals at Scutari, and it was the early reporting from there by Thomas Chenery on the grotesque spectacle awaiting the wounded after the Battle of Alma that prompted Florence Nightingale, back in London, to apply to the Minister of War to be posted there. The French, in turn, were represented by *Le Moniteur* which, however, due to censorship, generally posted only official reports.

Taken together, this was the first time journalists had been sent as a group on assignment to cover an international event. Though none served as long as Russell, they faced all the hardships in the field, and two paid the ultimate price, with one dying of fever and the other killed early on in the fighting in present-day Bulgaria. Given the unknowns of the job, the journalists tended to be quite young and, in family terms, unattached.

Edwin Godkin, for example, of *The Daily News* was twenty-four when he arrived in Crimea, and Chenery twenty-eight. In fact, Russell, in his mid-thirties and already married with children, was the exception.

As a group they also did their job well, with Russell in the lead. Soldiers in the field like Clifford, for instance, wrote to his family telling them to put the most trust in his dispatches since "they are not the least exaggerated, if anything under the mark." Clifford penned this, unknowingly, when the Aberdeen government was in its final days, which perhaps was the truest sign of the impact of the Fourth Estate's work. No doubt the most positive assessment of Russell's role came from Godkin, a fellow Irishman and, after moving to New York, future co-founder and first editor of *The Nation*. He credited Russell with nothing less than "the real beginning of newspaper correspondence" and this for him was the "most important result of the Crimean War." Indeed, the best compliment paid to Russell and his companions in this capacity came, as it were, from their detractors. The British commander who succeeded Raglan after his death called them "the curse of modern armies,"[3] underscoring how from its very birth war journalism has always had a contentious relationship with the military on which it reports.[4]

Another milestone in the war was the advent of photography, inseparable now from the figure of Roger Fenton, even though he was not the only one to work in this medium during the war. In fact, the man initially hired by the War Department to accompany the army drowned in Balaklava Harbor during the Great Hurricane in November, taking all his work with him. Fenton's name, however, was and is the more famous since he was already an acclaimed photographer before the war began. Notably, the debut of his major work was at the Crystal Palace, the unparalleled showcase of Victorian progress, in 1851. In a striking irony of history, Fenton then moved his studio to Russia, where he was one of the first to photograph the tsar's family. When the war broke out, he was back in Britain and from there set out for Crimea, privately financed but with the Queen's blessing. He arrived halfway through the siege in March 1855 and stayed until the end of June.

This breakthrough technology would seem a godsend in recording the war. After all, how better to capture the essence of Russell's dispatches or Tolstoy's stories than with immediate documentation by the camera? Yet any such expectations would remain a dream for quite some time. One simple reason is that photography was still in its infancy; people were required to stand still for up to half a minute, which eliminated spontaneity (and, of course, any battle scenes), and landscape shots needed special light exposure, which limited the time of day at which they could be taken. Moreover, no photography could be done in the summer because of the heat. This is why all of Fenton's pictures of camp life are posed and sometimes misleading, including one of contented British soldiers comfortably dressed in winter clothing—though it was taken in April—and any action shown, such as a famous shot of a wounded soldier being attended to by a nurse, was staged theatre.

Another reason for Fenton's relatively anodyne subject matter is a bit more controversial. Since he traveled under the Queen's auspices (and dedicated many of his portfolios to her), one of his tasks was precisely to counter the descriptions of death and ruination fostered by Russell and others. In this he succeeded; no corpse would ever appear in his lens. Some have argued that Fenton was not out to sanitize the war since he had already purchased his equipment in December, that is, just before revelations of soldiers' conditions came to press. That fact, however, does not exclude the possibility that the directive was given to him before his departure. Either way, to be fair to Fenton and the whole question of what role photography could have played in documenting the Crimean War, it pays to keep in mind that only well into the twentieth century—Matthew Brady's and Alexander Gardner's photos of corpses in the American Civil War notwithstanding—did the gruesomeness of *published* photos come close to the gruesomeness of words describing the same objects.

Where just such an approximation between image and the written word could be found was in the visual arts. Indeed, some illustrators and painters shared a motivation similar to Russell and Tolstoy's and sought to expose the inadequacy of standing tradition while searching for new methods to depict the reality of the war playing out before them. Certain drawings and prints brought out the humanity of common soldiers, notably as victims, freezing and starving, which was a direct challenge to the typical fare of portraiture with its preference for the proud, aristocratic officer astride his mount, foregrounded against a backdrop of a battle scene in miniature. A few, in fact, indulged in satiric caricature to underscore the war's brutality. Most striking in this vein was Joseph Paton's *Commander-in-Chief of British Forces in the Crimea*, an 1855 depiction of a skeletal officer clothed only in epaulettes on his equally skeletal stallion. Wielding a baton labeled "routine," he leads an army made up of dead soldiers, broken cannon and other debris while to the side lie unopened boxes stamped with "MEDICAL STORES IMMEDIATE" and "WINTER CLOTHING CRIMEA."

Obviously inspired by reportage printed in the newspapers, Paton's anti-portrait was scathing for its time—so much so that he refused to publish it. Indeed, it is important to keep in mind that if any work like this catches our attention today, it was, even when made public, distinctly in the minority and often appeared in regional publications of small circulation. Mainstream papers, like the widely read *Illustrated London News*, generally offered little outside the careful parameters that Fenton upheld. During the spring and summer of 1855, for instance, when reports of the war's full horrors were coming out, nothing risqué appeared in its pages. There were handsome pictures of broad battle scenes and bombardments and of micro actions like the loading and firing of cannon, but, despite the fact that the war was *the* topic of the day, they often took a backseat to more docile topics like drawings of fox hunting, new species of birds and plants, the harbor of Nagasaki, the opening of new exhibit rooms in the British Museum and, on 12 May, an eruption of Mount Vesuvius.

Perhaps no greater example of the unbridgeable gap between what was seen and what made it onto film or canvas came from Fenton himself at the beginning of June, shortly before he departed Crimea. Of all places, he took the obligatory trip to the valley near Balaklava, sight of the Light Brigade's charge and already immortalized in Tennyson's poem. What he witnessed, however, and put in a letter, was precisely what Russell had reported on his return to the battlefield in April. No "noble six hundred" were to be found; rather, as Fenton wrote in strikingly similar terms:

> We came upon many skeletons half buried, one was lying as if he had raised himself upon his elbow, the bare skull sticking up with still enough flesh left in the muscles to prevent it falling from the shoulders; another man's feet and hands were out of the ground, the shoes on his feet, and the flesh gone.

A full decade would pass before this kind of imagery—the soldier's skeleton, partially uncovered, rising out of the ground, along with that of his horse—would be visualized in a sketch. Entitled *All that was left of them/left of 600*, this grisly but accurate drawing came not from Fenton but Henry Crealock, then a young infantry captain who arrived at Sevastopol after the charge. Only with this scene, one could arguably say, did the visual match the verbal but with a certain caveat: it was a pen and ink sketch with no color and on a 10½-square-inch piece of paper, kept privately (though his other sketches circulated publicly) and now held by the Royal Collection Trust—but not presently on display.[5]

Here lies the crux of the matter for all visual media from Crimea: the more telling the depiction, the more distant its revelation from the immediacy of the war. This applies to the most famous portrayal of Crimean soldiers in a compassionate, human lens, Elizabeth Thompson Butler's *Calling the Roll* of 1874. Showing exhausted soldiers in greatcoats and bearskins gathering after a battle with no centered heroic figure, it won immediate acclaim and toured the country, attracting many crowds. Its poignancy, however, was already mitigated by the fact that this was the work of the post-war generation (she was only a child during the conflict) and came at a time when paintings of the war, now two decades in the past, still favored its heroic depiction. That *Calling the Roll* remained the exception can be seen, in fact, in her companion piece, *Balaclava* (1876) with its after-the-charge portrait of a dismounted yet defiant cavalryman, or in the work of her countrymen such as Robert Gibb's *The Thin Red Line* (1881) and Richard Woodville's *The Charge of the Light Brigade* (1894). The titles alone suggest how by century's end the disparity between what was accepted in print—virtually all the memoirs and letters detailing the soldiers' experiences had been published—and what was expected on canvas was still quite wide. At least for the time being, the words coming from Crimea were more powerful and revealing than any images. Significantly too, the very titles of the latter suggest *whose* words counted most, that is Russell's, and the impact he still had in shaping the public's understanding of the war in Britain long after it had ended.[6]

On the Russian side there were no war correspondents working alongside Tolstoy since independent newspapers, as we understand them today, did not exist in the empire. However, in large part due to Russia's defeat in the war, the first steps to establish them and the easing (though not lifting) of censorship restrictions would come within the decade after. When that happened, the number of journals exploded, and in their pages veterans engaged in sometimes fierce debates over the reasons for their defeat, centering on command mistakes and the need to reform the military. And while one might assume that the audience interested in this subject would remain small, the very fact that there was a public airing of differences, especially as conducted in the pages of the *Russkii invalid* (The Russian Veteran) and *Voennyi sbornik* (Military Miscellany), meant that the readership could be quite large. It was obvious that the pent-up desire to write, to read and to discuss anything in an open forum about the war was relatively widespread.[7]

Until that time, however, fiction remained the primary vehicle, albeit an indirect one, to express what Tiutcheva called, as if on cue from Tolstoy's story, "the truth, all the truth, and only the truth!" As for the war, no one came close to Tolstoy in probing behind the curtain of the official line, and such a distinction made his voice and literary fiction almost something of a Fifth Estate. As if in recognition of that potential, he hoped to produce from Sevastopol a journal including others' stories aimed at rank-and-file soldiers. (Given literacy rates among the latter, the assumption apparently was that they could be read to the conscripted serfs.) He even went so far as to write a proposal that was passed onto Tsar Nicholas himself, who shot it down immediately. This not only added to Tolstoy's anger and frustration with the military but also underscored the tight constraints under which literature operated: even an idea by a minor noble required the tsar's input before a decision could be made.[8]

Yet not all the blame for Russian literature's tepid contribution to the war—Tolstoy excepted—can be pinned solely on censorship and a hyper-vigilant and hyper-paranoid tsar. Much like in Britain, in Russia the Heroic Default still held sway. When the

editors at *The Contemporary* pressed Tolstoy to serve as an acqui-
sitions agent in-the-field—soliciting stories written by other
soldiers—the results were substandard compared to the master.
In fact, though Tolstoy promised to send in three to four such
pieces a month, not once did he meet that goal. And the only
time he did send one in, as far as can be ascertained, was right
after the success of "Sevastopol in December."

In the issue following Tolstoy's story, there appeared another
with a title recalling its recommender's, "A Sortie at Night in
Sevastopol," accompanied by an editorial note expressing that
"we are grateful to L.N.T. for this article" (the common term by
which the editors referred to short stories.) The author, Arkady
Stolypin, was Tolstoy's friend and fellow artillery officer, which
is about as far as similarities between the two might extend.
Never rising above the standard fare of the day, the story was
little more than a brief vignette extolling the city's "real
heroes"—by now quite a cliché—and a monk who fights alongside them. It offered none of the tension, unusual details or
boundary-pushing tenets that marked Tolstoy's own work and
effectively spelled an end to the latter's role as surrogate editor.
(Stolypin would go on to make his mark in life not in literature
but through his family: he married the daughter of a Russian
general in Crimea—also a distant cousin of Tolstoy's—and their
son, Petr Stolypin, would become Nicholas II's prime minister
and last hope to stave off revolution before his assassination in
1911.) If anything, since Stolypin's story was not republished, its
appearance underscores how much Tolstoy stood out from other
Russians writing about war at this time.

The Passing of the Storm

The war officially ended with the Peace of Paris in March 1856,
precisely two years after Britain had entered it. With the fall of

Sevastopol six months before, however, the fighting between the two rivals had more or less come to an end except for a few desultory affairs elsewhere around the globe. As might be expected from a war whose origins were cloudy, the treaty's provisions were not particularly onerous or game-changing for the defeated Russians. The most notable was the neutralization of the Black Sea, which deprived its navy of all-weather access to water. Yet the ban on its warships there petered out in fifteen years with no recriminations. This abrogation left Robert Morier, the future ambassador to Russia, as noted earlier, to remark that it made the whole affair a "perfectly useless modern war"—contrasting it with the American Civil War, which had at least abolished slavery.[9] As for territorial changes, there were some minor alterations but nothing on any appreciable scale. To this degree the Crimean War had something of a Tolstoyan zero-ending to it, that is, escaping a decisive closure when one might have expected one. When Sevastopol fell in September 1855, Aleksandr Nikitenko could only wonder, "What was it all for?" And when the peace treaty was signed six months later, a participant on the British side could only shrug his shoulders and ask: "who was the loser, who was the victor?"[10]

Upwards of 1,000,000 people died searching for the answers to those questions. For the British, it cost over 20,000 lives, mostly due to disease and exposure. That number, as a percentage of those who served in Crimea, is even higher than the fatalities suffered by the Light Brigade—a consideration generally overlooked by aficionados of the Charge. The French lost thousands more due to the fact that their commitment of forces was several times higher than Britain's and that the second winter spent in Crimea, from 1855 to 1856 when the fighting was over, was unexpectedly tragic for them. For the third allied power, the Turks, lax and non-existent records impede any tally, but most would suggest that their losses were well over 100,000; indeed, their suffering remains an unwritten tale of the war. Finally for Russia, 450,000 stands as the official number but, as one knows from its other wars, the true cost seems to be higher and some put it at 600,000. That there can be no agreement on the conflict's total losses is telling enough, suggesting that when the number is this high, the victor–loser tags are irrelevant. No one came out of it better than before.[11]

Nevertheless, how the Crimean War *did* impact the countries involved could not have been foretold by any treaty's provisions. Its conclusion meant that Europe had turned a corner, one that with hindsight did not portend well. It signaled first and foremost the end of the Concert of Europe, the post-Napoleonic order that had preserved the peace on the continent for nearly forty years after Waterloo. That demise opened the doors once again to inter-state rivalries of which Prussia, for example, took immediate advantage by launching wars against Denmark, Austria and France in the next two decades that resulted in the creation of a united Germany. The post-Crimean age was one in which the cold reality of realpolitik reigned once more and, more ominously, would entangle the great powers in various treaties and diplomatic arrangements that would ultimately implode in 1914.

A different kind of aftershock registered more immediately in both Britain and Russia that, in their respective contexts, represented revolutions in both a political and social sense. The war, in other words, rudely awakened both to the fact that their country's affairs could no longer remain mired in the past. For the former, it shattered the aristocracy's façade of invincibility and presumed infallibility in governing; the general populace would never again bestow its confidence or give it the benefit of the doubt in handling the government's reins. Faith in its unwritten right to run the state died alongside the thousands of soldiers in the winter of 1854. The fall of Aberdeen's government presaged the rise to power of new men, those of business, law and trade, who made their mark ostensibly through their own merits and acumen instead of inherited titles and estates. Reforms were passed ensuring greater participation and tolerations in the conduct of the commonwealth's business. The war, in effect, constituted the final tipping point in determining who would lead from now on. No longer would it be the societal elite of Regency Britain but rather the newly ascendant middle class of the Victorian period.

Moreover, thanks to the reporting of Russell and others, the travails and suffering of the soldiers in Crimea were not entirely in vain. Their newly discovered victimization translated back home to greater compassion and relief for the poor and downtrodden. Never would their lot be an envious one, but the example set by Florence Nightingale and her army of nurses showed what could be done and helped stimulate new efforts to assist the unfortunate. Reflexively as well, in the military the purchase system for officers' promotion was eliminated (though that took some years), removing a major obstacle for advancement based on merit instead of on one's status and family fortune—similar, in theory at least, to what was occurring in the government. In addition, rank and file soldiers now received more pay and shorter enlistment periods, and, following the new spirit of the times, could be officially recognized through a new award, the Victoria Cross, available to any and all for meritorious conduct, no matter the soldier's class or family name.

For Russia, the shockwave was even greater, causing cracks from top to bottom in the once staid façade Tsar Nicholas had done so much to protect and nurture. While the country escaped significant territorial loss, defeat—on the soil of the motherland no less—was profoundly humiliating and wrought significant damage on its reputation and national prestige. What made the loss doubly hurtful, especially when it fell upon Tsar Alexander's reign, was the ironic coincidence that it was his uncle, Alexander

I, who had triumphed over Napoleon in 1812. In other words, if Alexander I had bested Napoleon forty years before, then now, in the contest between both emperors' nephews, Alexander II and Louis Napoleon, the latter had won his revenge.

Moreover, defeat in the war forced Russia to look in the mirror and, put simply, it recoiled at what it saw. Its vaunted army, the largest in the world and in which commanders took such pride for its peacock-precision on the parade ground, turned out to be little more than a stumbling behemoth. While individual soldiers, especially in the lower ranks, could rival, if not outshine, the West in their collective perseverance and stoicism, the military as an institution was backwards, sclerotic and, in many ways, obsolescent—much like the country itself. The fundamental basics of provisioning and equipping troops seemed to be a foreign science to many of its commanders while the army's mobility was antediluvian in the age of the railroad—no small matter, needless to say, for the largest land empire of the modern world. Along with its wind-powered Black Sea fleet resting permanently on the bottom of Sevastopol's harbor, the war also showed up how profoundly behind Russia was in advanced weaponry and industrial-technological potential. For all its pomp and show, in these areas the country ranked a distant second—if not third— behind the other great states of Europe.

Ever since Russia came into being, the primary responsibility of its leaders to their nation was to protect it from foreign aggression. After Crimea, the profound inability of the tsar and state to fulfill this obligation fueled dismay and embarrassment among the intelligentsia and the mercantile class. Anger at the government and its repressive nature and the severe disruption to international trade—all over a pointless war—did little to curb a growing discontentment with the overall state of affairs. When the war ended in 1856, no one could boast of their nation like Denis Davydov did with his rousing cry after 1812: "Now my head rises with pride knowing that I am a Russian."[12] And if anyone was to blame for that, it was the tsar.

As cracks in society threatened to become fissures, the response of the tsar's government was nothing short of remarkable. Instead of tighter repression and control, as might have come with Nicholas, for the first time in Russia's living memory Alexander II took the opposite route to his father: the introduction of substantive liberalizing reform. For instance, the relative easing of censorship and increased granting of print licenses had a tremendous impact on the world of letters—that is to say, the entire gamut of public expression, since there was no other public forum but newspapers and periodicals for political and social commentary, debate and even criticism. (Where such voices might be heard, as in a parliament or congress, would have to wait another fifty years.) Indeed, the number of periodicals the government permitted jumped from 103 in 1854 to 230 by 1860 and to well over 300 by the end of that decade. Printing plants witnessed an even greater explosion in the same period, from 150 at the height of the war to nearly 800.[13]

Regional administrative boards with limited powers, known as the *zemstvo* system, were also instituted, and though restricted to well-off propertied males, they nevertheless resembled the first seeds in the growth of a representative democracy. Similar inroads were made into the archaic judicial system which gave rise to the uniform application of the law (instead of regional variations) and to the jury trial. As in Britain, the military was compelled to put itself under the microscope, which resulted— after the abolition of serfdom—in the institution of a draft-reservist army along the lines of other European nations, and the embrace of modern rifles and other advanced technologies. The next time Alexander II took his army to war in 1877 against a major power—to no surprise, with Turkey once again—it achieved an overwhelming victory, one that erased much of the humiliation of two decades before.

It was the abolition of serfdom that was the most sweeping and revolutionary of the reforms Alexander introduced. Coming in 1861, two years before Abraham Lincoln's Emancipation Proclamation, it was not done for humanitarian purposes, though the impulse was there, even among serf owners. In fact, we need look no further than Tolstoy himself who, uncharacteristically for a nobleman of the time, attempted even before the war to alleviate their plight, especially through the education of children. By the time he entered military service, that impulse fed tendrils of rage surrounding the incessant abuse and mistreatment serfs endured as soldiers. They made up "no army," we recall his words from the previous chapter, "only a horde of oppressed slaves."

To this end, in the winter of 1855 he began drafting "A Project for Reforming the Army." The emotion that lay behind it, however, belied its anodyne title:

> By virtue of my oath and still more because of my conscience as a human being I cannot be silent about an evil, which occurs right before my eyes and clearly is the cause behind the deaths of millions of people and the death of this country's strength, dignity and honor.
>
> Birth and education put me above those with whom I have served, but I have had the opportunity to study this evil down to its dirtiest and most pernicious details. It was never hidden from me, indeed, it believed me a compatriot and I helped it through my silence and inactivity. But today, when this evil has reached the heights where tens of thousands suffer and where it threatens to destroy the country, I have decided, as much as I can, to act against it with my pen, my word and with all my strength.[14]

Tolstoy never got to the reforms that might solve these problems and, thankfully for his career, never sent his project to the tsar; it remained unpublished among his private papers during his lifetime yet it shows where his heart was. That he even contemplated sending such an inflammatory document testifies to the degree of his fury that, for now, channeled itself into "Sevastopol in May" and "Woodfelling" and later, into his full-fledged, selfless devotion to helping the peasantry who, despite liberation, still wallowed in poverty.

The humanitarian ideas of Tolstoy and others notwithstanding, the primary impetus for the tsar in abolishing serfdom was to stave off popular unrest and to dampen the flames of mutiny that flared during the war as villages were hit with successive and unprecedented quotas for conscripts. An offshoot of abolition was the transition to the aforementioned reservist system which, by limiting service to just a few years, drastically improved the operations of the army.

In any case, Tsar Alexander's motives for overturning the country's socio-demographic base were quite clear as he himself memorably declared that it would be "vastly better" if liberation came "from above than from below." Fate, it should be noted, held otherwise. Freeing the serfs did earn him the popular sobriquet of "the Liberator," but it also earned him the undying enmity of a new generation of revolutionaries who espoused violence as a means to achieve far greater reforms. One such cell succeeded in assassinating the Liberator in 1881—the first time the Russian people and not the nobility took the life of their tsar. In a roundabout way, one could say that perhaps Alexander was the last victim of the Crimean War.[15]

Yet whatever the political and social upheavals wrought by the Crimean War, it led to another that transcended the circumstances of any one country and has continued to the present day: a revolution in how we write about, record and thus understand war. Little could have prepared participants for its acute lethality, made all the more shocking given its compression in time and space. Combined with world-altering advancements in communications and mobility, it shattered all previous norms and marked a true "before" and "after" moment in history. Without precedent or comparison, the Crimean War challenged existing vocabularies and mindsets and overturned standards that had been nurtured for centuries. In a Europe that was itself changing almost exponentially on so many fronts, the acute distance between the past and the present left a void that was beyond the comprehension of many.

This is where Russell and Tolstoy made their mark. If modern war was born when the medium and mode for writing about it changed irrevocably, then their essential role cannot be overestimated. Wasted lives, rotting corpses, blunders and atrocities—human conflict had always included its share of such violence as every veteran, survivor and eyewitness knew. Thanks to Russell and Tolstoy, however, this fact entered the public domain, permanently. They sought to bridge the gap between actual battlefield experience and the anodyne versions preferred by many—most emphatically through the Heroic Default—and if judged only by the tremendous impact of their work, for their time they were largely successful. In their respective attempts to find a language adequate to the war, they brought home to readers a new one in all its sights, sounds and smells. By breaking the conventions of the expected and the acceptable—and paying the price for such transgressions—they, more than any others, redefined how it could be understood, especially when soon after the war the demarcation between "British" and "Russian" lost any functional valency and it became known as just "the soldiers' war." Suffering and death, in other words, were the same, regardless of uniform.

As this book has tried to show, Russell and Tolstoy led the way not just in revealing the war's true devastation in such raw detail, but also in exposing and making public the complicity, intentional or not, of higher-ups in that regard. In so doing, they shattered the cult of the hero warrior which had long reigned in previous wars and did so most conspicuously by showing how death, literally and figuratively, was the sine qua non of war. No matter the outcome, whether victory or defeat, dead soldiers were its only constant.

In showcasing this point, the two writers undercut both the earlier idea of death as a martyr's final act, as defined most famously, perhaps, by Benjamin West's painting *Death of General Wolfe* from 1770, and the more contemporary, Victorian idea of turning death into an abstract statistic as if payment due on a military transaction. Instead, their dispatches and stories made death something simpler yet more raw—it became the appalling waste of an individual's life—but at the same time played up the decisive point that no matter how seemingly unimportant that individual might be; he or she was a human being nevertheless. Whether taken by bullets, hunger, cholera or dysentery, that person was just as worthy of the sentiments expended on the likes of Wolfe.

To be sure, before the Crimean War we can find empathetic glances at the fate of the common soldier. In Joseph Wright's popular painting, *The Dead Soldier*, completed twenty years after West's, we see a woman with an infant grieving over a fallen redcoat, name unknown, face unseen and with battle in the distant background. Yet this was the exception until Russell and Tolstoy brought it to the Western world's nearly undivided attention. Only with the Crimean War would the brief foretaste offered by Wright come into its own as a permanent challenge to the Heroic Default and, in the hands of Tolstoy and Russell, reshape our understanding of war, especially in its ability to claim anyone, including civilians, as its victims.

Key to their dismantling of the Heroic Default was the insistence on the "Truth" as their guiding light. While today this might sound trite, then it was quite revolutionary, particularly in

Tolstoy's case where the Russian state had long assumed a monopoly on its expression. By foregrounding the Truth, their writing, whether in the form of fiction or reportage, inherently implied that what dominated before was a fount of deception and distortion aimed at comforting the public and serving the government's needs.

That the two writers came to this understanding was not a foregone conclusion. It could almost be said that they stumbled onto this path, inadvertently and unintentionally. One can see this, for instance, in Russell's caveats and hesitations over the Light Brigade's charge: glorious affair or needless slaughter. Similarly, in "Sevastopol in December," Tolstoy's first story from the siege, we see him wavering between an epic emphasizing the city's heroic defense and a cold, detailed revelation of its indiscriminate toll on the city's inhabitants. For both writers, however, such equivocation had disappeared by spring when their voices, independent of each other, crystallized into bitter dissent and the calling out of their respective governments' predilection for falsehood and obfuscation. And in that process—and unbeknownst to them—together they raised the two pillars of modern war writing: the insistence on an experiential truth and the rendering of detail, no matter how appalling or seemingly trivial, without emotion or sentiment. Never again would Homer-like affectations be the default.

Russell and Tolstoy thus constituted, for their time, the two most important names on a curve along which the Western world was trending. War was entering a phase of revolutionary modernization where the results of one decade were overturned by the next in a technological leapfrog that used to take centuries. That trend, to be sure, was only for the worse: greater destruction, greater loss of life—all of which profoundly altered the impact of any war undertaken by a state so possessed of this technology. (In just a few decades both empires would be using machine guns against peoples armed with hand weapons and obsolete muskets.) In showcasing the intersection between death and lies they became the progenitors of a parallel discursive revolution in which the representation of war tried to keep pace with the nightmares the next century would bring.

The Crimean War also launched their names into the rarified—and newly emerging—world of international celebrity. In journalism Russell reigned supreme for the next fifty years as *the* reporter of iconic renown. He was eventually knighted and feted by leaders as both the first and most famous war correspondent. While this appellation was not entirely accurate and Russell himself did not favor it, no one was going to split hairs. Writing in 1907, the year of his death, E.L. Godkin, who had once reported alongside him from Sevastopol, believed that the Crimean War's most significant result were the dispatches of "Billy Russell" because they led to a "real awakening" both for "the British Army and the people." That this awakening was a rude one—what Godkin calls "the troubling of the waters"—was precisely the point for it made him a "power before which generals began to quail." Indeed, Crimea was only the beginning for Russell. Years later he continued to stir the waters, reporting onsite for the *Times* on the American Civil War (where he incurred the wrath of the U.S. government for detailing the defeats of the Union Army in its first years), the Indian Mutiny (as the British press then called it), the Franco-Prussian War and other luminary events that impacted Europe in the second half of the nineteenth century.[16]

For Tolstoy, with the appearance of *War and Peace* and *Anna Karenina* within two decades after the war, few living writers could rival him in world literature. The reach and impact of his name only continued to the end of the century with his potent writings against all governments, organized religion, capital punishment, poverty and a host of other issues that for many turned him into a martyr persecuted by the Russian state and excommunicated by the Church. His radical progressiveness—or whatever term might be appropriate since it did not extend, however, to fighting for gender equity—hardened as well around an uncompromising pacifism, extending back to the Crimean War which he later came to see as "a pitiful mistake." His political and social exceptionalism was too much for recognition by the newly formed Nobel Committee on Literature, though he was eligible for its award until his death in 1910. But it did ensure that his estate outside of Moscow would become a site for international pilgrimages and that thousands of enamored readers would write to him as a great sage and teacher. Surveying his legacy five years before the writer's death, Petr Kropotkin, the famous anarchist, bestowed the same laurels Godkin had on Russell for what Tolstoy accomplished during the Crimean War. His *Sevastopol Stories*, which Kropotkin had read repeatedly as a teenager when they first came out, constituted nothing less than "a new departure in war literature the world over."[17]

From Crimea to the First World War

The sons of Crimean War veterans were spared the likes of what their fathers experienced. In Russia and Britain they looked back on the war as a calamitous folly but without the bitter rhetoric that once animated both sides. As if anticipating that turn, in 1856 Russell wrote to his wife in one of his last letters from Crimea, just a few months after the Treaty of Paris, that the "Ruskis" are "kindly, well-disposed, clever and warmly attached to friends and country... In many respects they more resemble us than any people in the world and I think we ought never to have been enemies."[18] By century's end that prediction had, for the most part, come true; for the post-war generation to see each other as existential foes would have been so out of place as to seem risible. Even the Great Game, the extension of Britain's and Russia's imperial rivalries into Central Asia that petered out by the beginning of the twentieth century, witnessed none of the fury that had coursed through the public during the war.

Perhaps the surest sign that any ill will between the two countries had long since ended came on the sixtieth anniversary of its outbreak. In 1913 the first feature film made in Russia was dedicated to the siege of Sevastopol, and while it dutifully played up the myth of the city never surrendering, its final scenes cut to the present time to honor on screen the actual veterans of the war, aged and be-medaled, but from the British and French armies as well—like a family reunited. Similarly in Britain by that time—with the exception of the legend of the Light Brigade and related portraiture—the war's memory was retained in ways that offered the least provocation, having devolved into the naming of streets, pubs and, for the unfortunate few, children: "Alma" for girls; "Sebastopol" for boys.[19]

For the grandsons of the Crimean generation, however, such was not the case. That past—enshrined in the horror of trench warfare—came back to haunt them to an unfathomable degree in the First World War. This conflict overshadowed its predecessor in a most decisive way: it wed the devastation of quagmire with that of a total war, one impacting all of society as never before. The sheer scale of loss suffered from 1914–18 is still jaw-dropping, reaching approximately 20,000,000 dead, including civilians. What this meant in real terms can be seen, for example, in the family of Henry Clifford, VC recipient at the Battle of Inkerman, whose letters have been frequently cited here. Not only did his son, a general, lose his life in the First World War, but so did *six* of his nine grandsons. Clifford himself was fortunate enough, one could say, to have passed away before that conflagration and so did not witness his family's devastation. But, as a fitting sign of the continuity between Crimea and that war, one of the surviving grandsons chose to publish Clifford's letters only after 1918 as a wakeup call to the world.

It comes as little surprise, therefore, that the literature coming from the First World War followed in the steps first laid by Russell and Tolstoy. If in Crimea the butcher's bill could still serve as a metaphor, in 1914 it was literalized—and normalized—as the machine gun and artillery shell, the two greatest killers, pulverized soldiers into bodily fragments, ripping off limbs, heads, torsos and private parts, and rendered them into faceless, anonymous corpses, indifferent to rank, nationality or class. Indeed, the obliteration of Victorian propriety in the trenches of Flanders also swept away the last conventions limiting what narrative could express.

The literary result of this destruction, pummeling Europe for years instead of months as at Sevastopol, are now classics of war literature—a somewhat dubious distinction. Best known, perhaps, is Erich Maria Remarque's *All Quiet on the Western Front* which has given us indelible images of war at its worst: an exploding shell leaving "lumps of flesh and smoking splinters"; a soldier's hands hanging in barbed wire, sliced off at the wrists with one pivot of a machine gun. Here too are the pitiful clichés of bodies blown into trees; of a headless corpse still running around with blood spurting from its neck; or of rats grown to the size of cats feeding on human bodies. Given its unprecedented readership and critical reception, the novel quickly became the bible of modern warfare. No wonder the Nazis burned it in 1933 and, ten years later, beheaded the author's sister expressly for the sins of her pacifist sibling. (Remarque had emigrated shortly before the Nazis consolidated power.)

True to the adage that total war impacted all of society, the sufferings of civilians received the same tragic airing in its literature, only now in greater detail. If in "Sevastopol in May" Tolstoy showcased a 10-year-old boy wandering across the battlefield, traumatized by a headless corpse, in the memoirs of Ellen La Motte, an American volunteer nurse in French service, for instance, we have another ten-year-old boy, only this time he himself is a casualty, having been struck in the abdomen by shrapnel. With such a wound, La Motte lets us know, his future is preordained: "The child would die without an operation, or he would die during the operation, or he would die after the operation." And so he does, following the third variant—the only question the hospital personnel are left to answer is how much the boy's cries will annoy the other wounded.

La Motte's episodic vignettes, first published in 1916 and then not again until nearly twenty years later because of their contents and, most likely too, because they were written by a woman, demonstrate how the Victorian idea of the Good Death, first challenged in Crimea, had become a ludicrous pipe dream. Virtually no one in her hospital faces it with quiet, stoic gallantry. The only competition that stands out is to determine whose passing is worse, whether judged by sound (the wailing and weeping) or smell (perforated bladder versus faecal fistula versus gas gangrene). Here too we catch hints of Tolstoy and the ghost of Praskukhin, whose vapid life flashes before his eyes before the shell explodes in "Sevastopol in May." In La Motte's vignettes that role is reprised by a French soldier, Roland, suffering from gangrene, of whom "no one was fond... He meant nothing to anyone else there. He was a dying man, in a field hospital, that was all." Whether or not La Motte read Tolstoy (she was born twenty years after the Crimean War and thus represents the in-between generation), the underlying premise for both is the same. If previously only heroes died in war—and therefore everyone who died was eligible for such an honorific—from this point forth it is the Praskukhins, the Rolands and the unnamed children who fill its ranks.[20]

The very first page of La Motte's memoir makes short work both of the Good Death and the Heroic Default by showcasing the failed suicide of a soldier: holding a revolver in his mouth, he succeeds only in blowing out his eye. This shocking scene set the stage for what would become a systematic takedown of both paradigms by countless veterans, including some of the most famous. In *A Farewell to Arms*, Ernest Hemingway's narrator lambasts "abstract words such as glory, honor, [and] courage" when used to described the dead. Likewise, in Robert Graves's *Goodbye to All That*, Tennyson's theirs-is-but-to-do-and-die refrain is already a cliché. Another British poet, Roland Leighton, shortly before his death in 1915, gave perhaps the most emphatic rejection when he wrote to his fiancé from the frontlines after she sent him a collection of traditional, spirit-rousing war verse:

> Let him who thinks that War is a glorious golden thing, who loves to roll forth stirring words of exhortation, invoking Honour and Praise and Love of Country with as thoughtless and fervid a faith as inspired the priests of Baal to call on their own slumbering deity, let him look at a little pile of sodden grey rags that cover half a skull and a shin bone and what might have been its ribs, or at this skeleton lying on its side, resting half-crouching as it fell, supported on one arm, perfect but that it is headless, and with tattered clothing still draped around it; and let him realise how grand & glorious a thing it is to have distilled all Youth and Joy and Life into a foetid heap of hideous putrescence. Who is there who has known and seen who can say that Victory is worth the death of even one of these?[21]

Yet it was not just the horrific ways in which soldiers died that spelled the end of the Heroic Default and similar romantic glosses on war; what they saw and felt when they were alive contributed to it as well. Henri Barbusse, the famous novelist who in his forties served as a private and later became an anti-war activist, took a page from Tolstoy in his eye-opening auto-biographical novel, *Under Fire*. In the opening pages we are treated to a tour like in "Sevastopol in December" with special attention paid, once again, to the scent of a battlefield:

> You can see a maze of long ditches in which the last remnants of night linger. This is the trench. The bottom of it is carpeted with a viscous layer that clings noisily to the foot at every step and smells foul around each dugout because of the night's urine. The holes themselves, if you lean over them as you pass, smell like a whiff of bad breath.

Later, in passages reminiscent of Russell's discovery of corpses on the field of Balaclava six months after the battle and the Light Brigade's charge, here the first-person narrator describes what has become of his dead comrades. They come nothing close to a band of brothers united in glory, as we might have hoped. Instead, they are just bodies, rendered in the most prosaic terms as rigor mortis has set in:

> Barque is rigid and seems extended. His arms are stuck to his sides, his chest has collapsed, his belly has sunk into a bowl. With his head raised on a pile of mud he watches over the top of his feet those who approach from the left with his darkened face, smudged by the viscous stain of hair that has fallen across it, thickly encrusted with black blood, and his scalded eyes, looking bloodshot and as though cooked. Eudore, by contrast, looks very small and his little face is completely white, so white that it could be a clown's face made up with flour; it is heart-rending to see it there, like a circle of white paper in the grey and bluish tangle of corpses.

As the narrator retraces his steps over the battlefield—and comes across more and more corpses in similar poses—his parting words sound, once again, like Tolstoy's. These dead men are "lost" to both place and time and cast away into a world in which the "truth," now according to Barbusse a "holy word," cannot penetrate.[22]

Similarly, only with the First World War do we finally learn the full repertoire of actions soldiers may engage in. If Tolstoy's soldiers did the things that, in print at least, soldiers were not supposed to "do" like spit, roll cigarettes and have lice, then Barbusse, along with Remarque, expanded their "allowable" activities to include: making games of killing lice; mutilating corpses; committing suicide; suffering wounds in the testicles; saying "fuck," "prick" or "shit"; offering matter-of-fact instructions on how best to kill; masturbating; dreaming of women's legs, then buttocks, then genitalia and then having spontaneous, casual sex—with the enemy. They also fart, defecate collectively as a supreme bonding moment, and soil their pants out of fear. All of these dirty details, the base nature of their existence, de-heroicize soldiers, but they also affirm, as some of the basic building blocks of life, that they could no longer serve in literature as mere vehicles for patriotic messaging.

Yet as much as the veterans of the First World War continued along the path set by Russell and Tolstoy, they too hit a firewall but of a different kind. If Russell and Tolstoy had struggled to find a language adequate to their war, now came the recognition that nothing could ever fully convey the devastation of the battlefield. Vernon Bartlett, a wounded British soldier, began his memoirs with the simple caveat: "the words to describe war do not exist." In similar fashion an aging yet still quite observant Henry James declared just months before he passed away in 1915 that "the war has used up words." Indeed, the world paid for ignoring his Cassandra-like prescience. The very day war was declared in Britain he predicted that it would plunge into an "abyss of blood and darkness." What is most telling is that word became one of the most commonly repeated metaphors to describe the bottomless chasm into which words, meanings and lives disappeared. Repeated across the trenches by various combatants, *l'abîme, der Abgrund,* in French and German respectively, the abyss became a shared calling card for those at a loss to comprehend the new face of modern war. It figures prominently, for example, in Barbusse's *Under Fire* and again, most notably as well, in Remarque's *All Quiet on the Western Front*, through the tribulations of its protagonist, Paul Bäumer.[23]

Remarque, more than any other, delves into the full ramifications of the abyss metaphor. It looms over the novel as Paul contemplates the void of devastation brought on by the war. Pursuing this notion to its logical end, he experiences another mind-twisting jolt: the realization that at the bottom of his own *Abgrund* "words hold the horror of the world." In what way? Language, beyond merely shocking us with the dirty details of trench warfare, can lead us into a dead end from which there is no escape. If, on the one hand, it can only gesture towards but never adequately render images of "men living with their skulls blown open," then we must judge it impotent or, at least, lacking necessary force, to convey reality. Yet, on the other hand—and this is Remarque's more striking point—it can simultaneously be supremely powerful by driving us to act against our own consciences.

What leads Paul to his abyss is the revelation that the Russian prisoners he is guarding are, in reality, not the enemy but human beings. But mere words or, in this case a command, have made them that. Mere words are to blame for empowering one human over another, for causing so much suffering. ("*Ein Befehl hat diese stillen Gestalten zu unsern Feinden gemacht; ein Befehl könnte sie in unsere Freunde verwandeln.*") Extending the logic further, Paul and his comrades realize that, in fact, mere words made the war. If only twenty, thirty leaders of the various nations had said "no" at its beginning, his friend muses, then "all of Europe would be at peace." After all, he continues, in France "the majority of men are laborers, workmen or poor clerks. Now just why would a French blacksmith want to attack us? No, it is merely the rulers." In short, the impotence, the emptiness of words that the war has exposed, makes them seductively attractive at the same time. And who wields this power? Who has the ability to attach the label of "enemy" to anyone and consign them to death? Only society's "rulers," regardless of time or place.[24]

Paul cannot fully confront the implications of this realization since he dies at the novel's end. We, however, as readers are forced to do so. The last page of the novel, after informing us he is killed by a sniper, shifts from his first-person narrative to third-person—in other words, the language of the military bulletin in which the report of the day reads "All quiet on the Western front." (Literally in German, "nothing new on the Western front.") These words, if anything, put into play the whole game that has doomed his generation. They strip Paul's death of any meaning; it is literally a non-event. In the eyes of officialese—the preferred language of rulers everywhere—it does not happen or, more accurately, does not matter. The default paradigm, the only language the army knows and employs, cannot see, register or care about the fate of a single soldier. It knows no word for death except when couched in the rhetoric of sacrifice, heroism or martyrdom.

At the bottom of Paul's abyss is the recognition that language could determine all when it comes to life and death. One can be erased by language—the soul-draining emptiness of "nothing new"—or, following the rules of this semantic game, one can embrace existence only through some kind of falsification. Trapped between the two in this existential quandary, Paul retreats from the edge of his abyss by clinging to the lie. If words are mere chameleons or constitute a shape-shifting force able to turn humans into "enemies" (or "allies" for that matter), then he will openly play that game. He tries to comfort, for example, a comrade's mother with words that her son died instantaneously (instead of a tortured, gangrenous demise) just like he consciously deceives his own mother by telling her that things aren't "so bad" at the front. Paul surrenders to language's seemingly all-powerful grip by acknowledging words are empty shells that can be filled with anything and placed anywhere.

It is not difficult to accept Paul's decision. Open recognition that deception was the preferred—and expected—mode of discourse was yet another way the First World War qualitatively outstripped Crimea. Lies became the open and approved method for dealing with war's realities—like the ironic distancing detailed by Paul Fussell in *The Great War and Modern Memory* as a means to confront the war's horrors. During Robert Graves's first night in the trenches he discovers a telltale suicide—boot off, toe near trigger guard—which his superior casually waves away: "don't forget to write his next-of-kin. Usual sort of letter; tell them he died a soldier's death, anything you like." Similarly, Charles Montague, an over-forty volunteer who in 1914 dyed his hair black to pass for a younger man, describes in *Disenchantment* how soldiers succumbed to "the duty of lying." What Tolstoy had tagged as soldiers' hyperbole and what Russell decried as "clothing skeletons" to make things pleasant for readers in Britain—that was now the norm.[25]

Yet the First World War did more than normalize the lie as the default coping mechanism; it forced that generation to absorb the full ramifications of making such a step. No longer was deception just employed for self-aggrandizement; no longer did it spin the horror of the trenches merely so as to protect those at home from the reality of battlefield violence. Its tentacles not only covered up death; they caused it. If Russell had first probed this by criticizing his government's conscious embrace of deception to mask the suffering of its own soldiers, now the monster revealed its true colors.

In Britain, this role fell to no less a figure than Rudyard Kipling, born in 1865 and the poet most famous for promoting the "thin red line" mythos in support of British imperialism. When his own son, Jack, was killed at Loos in 1915, the personal devastation he felt forced him to walk back his jingoism and call Tennyson's bluff.

AFTERSHOCKS AND AWAKENINGS

If any question why we died,
Tell them, because our fathers lied.

This couplet, appearing in his *Epitaphs of War*, could barely capture the crushing sense of guilt Kipling bore. Jack was posted to the front, against the wishes of his mother, only because his father had pulled the necessary strings for the military to overlook his poor eyesight, a condition that normally would disqualify one from military service. It would not do, however, for the son of Britain's Nobel Laureate and preeminent voice behind its militant imperialism to sit out the affair while thousands of others marched off to fight. Indeed, Kipling senior had taken the lead in bashing the Germans in the war's first year; it was he, in fact, who is credited with pasting them as "Huns" and whipping up their alleged atrocities and bestial acts as they rampaged through Belgium and northern France. If anyone, in short, was guilty of pushing the lies that condemned millions like Jack to their deaths, then Rudyard Kipling, a "father" born between Crimea and the Great War, stood in the front ranks.

The literature of the First World War followed in the footsteps of Russell and Tolstoy in one other consequential way. On the one hand, like Russell's dispatches, it claimed the authority and legitimacy of an eyewitness-survivor account, but, on the other, it also employed the narrative and creative liberties enjoyed by Tolstoy—all of which made it something like a hybrid genre at the intersection of both orientations. Whether called the autobiographical novel or the fictionalized memoir, it ran the spectrum from the highly subjective and pseudo-fictional to a more constrained, reportage-like treatment. Either way, the writers who produced it rank among some of the finest of their age. Whether it be Graves for Britain, Remarque for Germany, Barbusse for France, Emilio Lussu for Italy or Hemingway for America, the war was their defining moment and the work produced from it constitutes their defining mark. Unfortunately, the other great powers—the Russian, Ottoman and Austro-Hungarian empires—have left us no one of their caliber. The first, because the revolution and civil war that came on the heels of the war overwhelmed all that stood before; the second dissolved, leaving a secularized Turkish nation bent on washing its hands of any imperial past; as for the third, the Austro-Hungarian state fragmented into so many national independence movements that no single voice could speak for its fate. (Somewhat fittingly, the only work to come from its disintegration that still garners deserved attention is the upside-down comic absurdity of *The Good Soldier Švejk* by the Czech writer, Jaroslav Hašek.)

These hybrid works proved to be the optimal vehicle for pushing the bounds of war representation even further than Russell or Tolstoy could for their time. But what they share with their predecessors is a passion for the truth to combat the lies and falsehoods that flooded their lives during the war, and this pursuit, much like we see in Tolstoy's stories, was for an experiential truth rather than an ontological one. That is to say, fictionalizing certain aspects of one's experiences in no way mitigated or interfered with the transmission of a compelling truthful essence. Indeed, veterans like Louis Aragon—who singled out Tolstoy's accomplishment in doing this—noted that leavening the raw material of combat with novelistic techniques conveyed more accurately what it was like to serve in the trenches because only through the dynamics of active, open storytelling—rather than the dry articulation of facts—could one arrive at something resembling what it was all *like* in a verisimilitudinous sense.

One important difference, however, between Crimea and the First World War was of sheer quantity. Instead of a lone figure like Tolstoy plying the waters, now this drive extended to a whole generation of writers who were swept away by the war. There was also more of a lag time for this second generation of writers to produce their work. With the exception of Barbusse's *Under Fire*, published remarkably in 1916, the significant accounts all appeared at least a decade after the war—sufficient time for its traumatic shock to lessen but also for memories as to the precise nature of conversations and events to fade or blur. In Lussu's case, writing in 1936 after a twenty-year "period of imposed rest," he preferred the term "personal recollections" to describe that which fell between "a novel or a history." This designation, perhaps more than any other, plays up the hybrid nature of these works and why, in their drive to capture a certain no-holds barred representation of the conflict, they forewent the straight-jacket of a strict autobiographical approach. Indeed, that Remarque's hero dies on the final page suggests as much in the most obvious way.[26]

Another difference is that works from the First World War tend to cover years instead of just a few days, like Tolstoy or Russell's accounts. Nevertheless, the principles of their composition still share something with their Crimean predecessors. With the exception (usually) of a definitive beginning and end, the interior of a given narrative from the First World War tends to evade chronological or even logical order. They are constructed of vignettes and scenes that are seemingly interchangeable and depict the kinds of things that occur—whether tragic, humorous, boring or idiotic—both in combat and at rest. Their apparent haphazard appearance is an artifice, of course, mimicking the random, unpredictable rhythm of events in war. The effect is much like taking one of Tolstoy's days and duplicating it through months and seasons with capturing the dull repetition of army life being a primary objective. Even death, presumably the most dramatic event in one's life, thus becomes "nothing new," as the title of Remarque's novel would have it.

Yet what the short story or daily report from Crimea could not fully develop was the chasm between life on the front lines and that of the readers back home. What for Tolstoy could only be implied through the guise of a battlefield tour and for Russell could only be suggested through analogies with life in London, became a key structural opposition, for instance, in Remarque's *All Quiet on the Western Front* and Barbusse's *Under Fire*. What we learn from the latter works is that life in the trenches was pared down to the core elements of human existence: food, water, sex, blood, survival. Anything not directly tied or germane to one of these is irrelevant or passes unrecognized. Sturdy boots trump any university degree; furniture is useful only for kindling; newspapers for toilet paper or, perhaps for the one luxury to be had, for rolling cigarettes. When Paul returns home on leave—something British soldiers in Crimea could only dream about and which for Russians, as serfs, was simply unimaginable—his book-lined shelves stare at him, offering nothing of value anymore. His beloved poets and philosophers, whose works he once cherished and cradled, have become mute to him. "Words, words, words," he laments, as these prior examples shape-shift into supreme impotence, "do not reach me." They are windows onto a past forever gone; true value for him now only comes in the form of something like a garden tool and how it can be turned into an instrument to kill.

It is this bitter truth—of language, of emptiness, of the slipperiness of meaning—that stares up at him from the bottom of his abyss. And though he may ultimately pull back in horror and return to the comforting yet false world of lies and deception, where everyone dies according to the Heroic Default, the brief glimpse of this truth may be the only positive lesson to be had from the apocalyptic carnage of those years. Notably Remarque, who of course survived the war, has Paul pass this on to us in the opening chapter of the novel when he and his company face their first bombardment. It wipes out a good share of them even before they can see the enemy, and yet it "showed us our mis-

take" in following the tyrannical dictates of the words and com-
mands rulers wield over them. In dying, though, there is one
cold comfort. Because of what the bombardment has wrought,
"we distinguished the false from the true, we had suddenly
learned to see." It takes the rest of the novel to bring us, the
reader, to that terrible insight.[27]

CONCLUSION

For all the unprecedented things the Crimean War wrought, it was, in a profound sense, bound firmly to the distant past. If the *Iliad* constitutes the ground zero of war literature in the West and is the progenitor of the Heroic Default, then, in one of history's early ironic twists, it also describes a war that is the first quagmire. For it opens with the Greeks in a foreign land mired in the tenth year of a siege—with the only result being that they have died "in droves" before the walls of Troy. What King Agamemnon declares to his troops would sound eerily familiar to those at Sevastopol:

> Our work drags on, unfinished as always, hopeless—
> The labor of war that brought us here to Troy.

Book II, 161–2

Conditions inside the city for their enemy are no better. The overall mood is one of disappointment, disenchantment and anger, and the only sign of victory seems to be simple survival, with "each man praying to flee death and the grind of war." Indeed, from the *Iliad* it seems that all the words of modern quagmire were already circulating then, three millennia before Crimea, including what has become its signature line, repeated

217

in its first books as a catch-all refrain for both sides, Greek or Trojan: there is "no end in sight."[1]

If these allusions make the Crimean War an essential link in the chain from the Homeric past to the troubled present, its lineage did not end with the First World War. For the matrix defining it—a war of choice becoming stalemate, the tyranny of the lie, the unforgiveable losses, the absence of a fulfilling victory—has found the twentieth and twenty-first centuries most accommodating. The next generation of quagmires following that conflict—best exemplified by the United States in Vietnam and Soviet Union in Afghanistan—degraded these four points further while introducing a few new ones as well.

These last two wars share striking parallels that, if abstracted to the category of quagmire, allow for an uncanny pairing. Both, notably, were preceded by their nation's greatest military triumph, victory in the Second World War, in which each could extol its sense of exceptionalism on a global stage. These laurels brewed up a cocktail both countries imbibed willingly but whose ingredients proved nearly fatal: a superpower, smitten by its own arrogance and sense of infallibility, invades a so-called Third World country enmeshed in its own civil war. Caught in unfamiliar terrain, ignorant of the local languages, cultures and histories, and tied to a Second World War mentality that brute military force can solve political problems, both founder, taking casualties neither can sustain except by cover-up and deception. The result, on the one hand, is a near-genocide inflicted on the native population and, on the other, a punishing defeat for each superpower with colossal repercussions back home. For America it nearly broke the country; for the Soviet Union it helped precipitate its collapse, making both quagmires veritable graveyards of exceptionalism.

That these conflicts could pull civilian populations into their vortex of lies and destruction became the most disturbing fact of the next generation of quagmires. Indeed, their most memorable events could in no way be mythologized or made into legend like the Charge of the Light Brigade for they consisted of mass shootings, the intentional killing of children, the burning of villages, the gang rapes and mutilation of corpses. Atrocity and war crimes became the calling cards of these new quagmires wherein the ostensible "good guys," the armies of the superpowers, committed the kinds of acts previously reserved for history's extreme villains like the Nazis or the Mongols.

In capturing the raw details of Vietnam and Afghanistan, the visuals of camera, film and television caught up with and, in certain ways, overtook the written word. At the same time, journalism's debt to the likes of William Howard Russell was never lost. One of Vietnam's most famous correspondents, Michael Herr, a force behind New Journalism and who later contributed to the films *Apocalypse Now* and *Full Metal Jacket*, captured like no other those aspects of the war that came to define its legacy as one of a crazed bloodbath. His position was remarkably similar to his Irish predecessor—an embedded journalist who could also travel anywhere with the military and, in turn, was heavily criticized by high-ranking officers for his writing. Indeed, when it came time to publish his reportage as a book collection, Herr honored his predecessor by titling it *Dispatches*.

At a personal level, soldiers' recognition of how quagmires have scarred them inside escalated prodigiously after Crimea. If the First World War normalized the lie and victimization of soldiers, then Vietnam and Afghanistan conjured something qualitatively worse: an all-encompassing sense of betrayal of soldiers in all three phases of the war—going in, serving there and coming home. No other theme links more strongly the accounts of Americans and Soviets than this one, which also explains why the traumas of these two wars have still not healed.

First was the betrayal behind being sent. Soldiers were fed with delusions or outright lies about domino theories in

Southeast Asia or American-Chinese mercenaries taking over
Afghanistan. This directly impacted the second, the betrayal felt
while serving there. Were the Americans, for instance, fighting
communists, Vietnamese nationalists, Russian and Chinese prox-
ies, terrorists or some combination thereof? Neither could Soviet
leaders agree on who they faced in Afghanistan as they cycled
through various options: insurgents, counter-revolutionaries,
foreign mercenaries, religious fanatics, terrorists (always a convenient catch-all) or, most chillingly, just the Afghan "people."
Moreover, this semantic slippage was compounded with another
sort of betrayal while fighting there, whether it be the acute
racism in the American army or, for the Soviets, the pitiful
equipment and provisions with which they were issued and the
widespread violent bullying, or *dedovshchina*, that greeted all conscripts into the army. And then came betrayal once more when
the veterans of both wars returned home neglected, abandoned
or ignored. In the Soviet Union that final indignity extended
even to the dead—casualty lists were officially suppressed and
inscriptions on headstones were dictated beforehand by the state
to eliminate any indication of cause or place of death.

Throughout Vietnam and Afghanistan, the lessons learned
from Crimea and the fields of Flanders crystallized again but in
sharper relief. As paradigmatic wars of choice, the story for both
superpowers going in had to be concise and compelling for the
public back home; after all, the latter had to be convinced of the
need for intervention in a country few, once again, could locate
on a map. The Soviet Union first held that there was essentially
no war in Afghanistan; its soldiers were only aiding the civilian
population by building schools, hospitals, bridges and the like.
Then when the flow of coffins home became impossible to deny,
the government reframed the conflict into a just war to defend
innocent neighbors from foreign mercenaries. Yet when the latter never materialized, the state resorted to the old standby, the

Heroic Default, and turned the war into the noble struggle of Soviet soldiers against so-called terrorists. That story lasted until it was officially denounced as a criminal enterprise during the death throes and collapse of the Soviet Union.

If quagmire is marked by the absence of a consistent or believable story, then that vacuum carries over past its endpoint. When the superpower exits, generally leaving things on the ground more mucked up than before, what does it say of the soldiers who fell in the intervening years? If the end result, in other words, is worse than the beginning situation, what recourse does a government have but to reach for some kind of Tennyson-like closure? The anytime, anywhere, death-is-noble message of his verses—as long as the soldiers "did their duty"—becomes the necessary last resort. Otherwise, soldiers' deaths in quagmire truly are in vain, which is a conclusion no state or military can countenance. That zero-sum, either-or truism too often, however, leads to the prolonging of the very same conflict—as if to say, we can't leave now because it would render pointless those who died before. The result of this logic, tragically enough, is an endless loop of fatalities until someone or some crisis forces the superpower to pull out.

What links the quagmires of the twentieth century, from the First World War to the Soviet-Afghan War, is the Lie, the foundational stone first uncovered by Russell and Tolstoy. From it, just like a biblical plague, flows everything described above. Even its lesser derivatives—deception, cover-up, obfuscation, distortion—are equally culpable when marshaled into its service. One of the more remarkable documents to surface after the breakup of the Soviet Union was an official list of talking points disseminated to its embassies to help them explain to foreign audiences why, in its words, the Red Army "entered" Afghanistan. If there ever was a smoking gun akin to the Pentagon Papers for Vietnam, then this was it. Some of the lies are small-bore; others are outright howlers. The Soviet Union, one diktat reads, "does not have any connection to the changes in leadership in Afghanistan"—except that its commandoes killed the president in a coup the night of the invasion. Indeed, another shines as a supreme example of unintentional irony: Soviet troops were being sent there to protect the Afghan people "from foreign aggression" when, of course, the actual aggressors were staring right back at them in the mirror.[2]

This blueprint of mendacity encapsulates how all ultimately circles back to the foundational lie. Rhetoric surrounding the stalemate, the never-ending light in the tunnel, the trenches and the jungle thus become more of its symptoms, treatable but failing to get at the root cause. With documents such as these, it is easier than ever to acknowledge the one constant emanating from war: truth really is its first casualty. Origins unknown, but dating back in some form to classical times, this maxim became widely accepted among the public during the First World War—for obvious reasons.

In this century, which began with the Americans invading Afghanistan and then Iraq, the road to quagmire has now become so tread-worn and predictable that it has occasioned a depressingly complacent acceptance. In the aptly titled *Generation Kill*, Evan Wright, an embedded journalist riding with American marines as they raced to Baghdad in 2003, quietly observed that these troops, aficionados of shooter video games and what they term "war porn" (violent action on screen), expected to be lied to. Even before getting to Iraq, they were already "predisposed toward the idea that the Big Lie is as central to American government as taxation."[3]

After the official announcement of the U.S. withdrawal from Afghanistan in 2021, twenty years after it entered, there was the usual handwringing over what that meant for the thousands of Americans—not to speak of the Afghans—who had died up until that point. Were their lives lost in vain since by the war's end conditions on the ground were no less encouraging than at its start? It is noteworthy that after its conclusion came the inevitable bombshell: the U.S. government had ordered its own internal review, documenting how it had lied again and again during the war. Big ones, little ones—the whole gamut of falsehoods, fabrications and ludicrous additions were then published for all to see. (The more the Taliban attacked, ran the upside-down logic of one talking point, the more it showed how much the U.S. was succeeding, since it demonstrated their desperation.) However, following the war's conclusion and with the admission of this betrayal, there was no outcry, no push for congressional hearings, no call for outside investigations. No one, it seems, was surprised and no one, as of this writing, seems to care. It's as if a quagmire fatigue has descended on the country as a whole. There was even a subgroup formed to study "Lessons Learned" from the two-decade ordeal. What was discovered, not surprisingly, was that the Afghan War was infected through and through with shifting story lines, a manifest absence of clear purpose, confusion over the enemy's identity and intentions, and deep corruption. In short, there was nothing new to learn, at least nothing that couldn't have been learned from Crimea in 1854.[4]

The same would apply once again to Russia, which at the time of this writing has invaded its sovereign neighbor, Ukraine, on a "Big Lie" of such magnitude that it collapsed even before the tanks rolled. The story that Ukraine was a hotbed of neo-Nazis with genocidal aims against its own Russian-speaking population was so preposterous that days into the war, the Russian government's propaganda machine went into overdrive, spitting out so many different—and often contradictory—rationales that they quickly dissolved into air. Since then its only recourse has been a predictable one: falling back onto Heroic Default overtures—soldiers doing their sacred duty by defending the motherland—with a specifically nationalist inflection. In other words, Fortress Russia standing alone as an island amid foreign aggressors, an image with which we are intimately familiar thanks to Sevastopol.

This conflict again gives us the standard recipe for quagmire: a war of choice yields to a bloody, chaotic stalemate beset with gross falsehoods and constantly changing story lines. What remains to be seen is the nature of the blowback that Russia will suffer after inflicting upon Ukraine and its people crimes against humanity with genocidal implications. On this final note, it pays to remember that in its modern history Russia has already fought in four quagmires, starting, of course, with Crimea. That was followed by the Russo-Japanese War of 1905, the First World War and then the Soviet-Afghan War. All four constituted major defeats for Russia which resulted in colossal, sometimes catastrophic change at home. What came of the first and fourth we already know. The second culminated in the Revolution of 1905 which, in turn, was a dress rehearsal for the Bolshevik Revolution which was precipitated by the third. It remains to be seen whether this latest quagmire—one in which Russia has embroiled itself voluntarily—will end with blowback on a similar scale.

NOTES

INTRODUCTION

1. Tiutchev, 518.
2. Dallas 185; Massie, 197; Feigenbaum, 15.
3. Marx, "Poland's European Mission," 106.
4. Tiutcheva, 168.
5. Wemyss, 215. On losses, see Edgerton, 5; Ponting, 389, estimates 650,000 of which ¾ were Russian but focuses primarily on the Siege of Sevastopol itself and therefore woefully underestimates Turkish losses.
6. Ackroyd, *Dominion*, 196.

1. CALL TO ARMS

1. Houghton, 39; Nikitenko, 362.
2. Gates, 60; Dawson, 254.
3. Hood, 138; Houghton, 40.
4. Tiutcheva, 168.
5. Davydov, 91; Glinka, 472, 399.
6. "Russian Soldiers," 101; Hodasevich, 51.
7. Duffy, 80, 177.
8. Ershov, 341; Hodasevich, 24.
9. Tolstoy, *PSS*, XLVI, 102.
10. Nikitenko, 548–51.
11. Hankinson, 34.
12. Morley, 81.
13. *Times*, 19 October 1852, 1.

14. Russell, *The Great War*, 3.

15. Tolstoy, *PSS* LXIX, 270.

2. THE NEW FACE OF WAR

 1. Seaton, 75.

 2. Reid, 102.

 3. Clifford, 91; Berg, 23.

 4. De Quincey, 369–97.

 5. Russell, *The War* I, 351.

 6. Ibid., 290.

 7. Totleben I, 179; Calthorpe, 189, 359; Russell, *The War* I, 356.

 8. Russell, *The War* I, 265–6.

 9. Gowing, 64; Duberly, 118.

10. Calthorpe, 215.

11. Totleben II, 768; Dallas, 78; Calthorpe, 205; Russell, *The War* I, 319.

12. Totleben, I, 179; Reid, 103; Clifford, 227.

13. Seacole, 115–6.

14. Tolstoy, *PSS* XLVII, 47.

15. Totleben, I, 155; II, 774.

16. Dallas, 71.

17. Russell, *The War* I, 431.

18. Ibid., 298, 30; see also Calthorpe, 202; Dallas, 71.

19. Lawson, 128–30; Russell, *The War* I, 298–9.

20. Macleod, 41–2; Dallas, 164; Clifford, 124.

21. Russell, *The War* I, 280.

22. Strachan, 41; Hodasevich, 70.

23. Macleod, 254, 251.

24. Hodasevich, 155; Ershov, 347.

25. Porter, 70; Babenchikov, 335.

26. Russell, *The War* I, 237, Ershov, 346, 361; Berg, 180–1, 59.

27. Massie, 133; Clifford, 208–9.

28. Russell, *The War* I, 358; Babenchikov, 360–1; Dallas, 180; Russell, *The War* I, 317; Clifford, 210–11, 140, 265–6.

29. Russell, The War I, 253.

30. Tolstoy, PSS XLVII, 27.

31. Tiutcheva, 183–4.
32. Russell, *The War* I, 247. According to conventions of the time, in English (contrary to Russian), Inkerman was often spelled with two "n's" and Sevastopol with a "b" instead of a "v".
33. Russell, *The War* I, 497.
34. Gowing, 87, 91.
35. Russell, *The War* I, 498; Clifford, 227–8.
36. Dallas, 148–9; Airlie, 306, 311.
37. Giubbennet, 3.
38. Pirogov, 17. See also Helmstadter, 251ff.
39. Giubbenet, 3, 35–6, 67.
40. Ibid., 40, 67.
41. Macleod, 126; Tolstoy, *PSS* XLVII, 13.
42. Gabriel and Metz, 175; Lawson, 13; Naumova, 387. See also Helmstadter, 23–6.
43. Ackroyd, *Dickens* 709. Trying to understand what caused cholera, however, stood at the crux of the problem. Dickens, along with many of his contemporaries, attributed it to miasma or bad air that rose from the fetid slums, cesspools and dung pits that fouled all major cities. Such places, to be sure, were the source of the disease but not the cause, which occurred when water supplies mixed with raw sewage, particularly human waste. Only a few recognized that by boiling water one could eliminate contamination but that practice and the realization that the disease was caused by microbes would catch on in the mainstream only years later.
44. Massie, 154; Shepherd, 167.
45. Woodham-Smith, *Florence Nightingale*, 113–14; Nightingale, 36; Macleod, 78; Shepherd II, ix. See also Helmstadter, 61–76.
46. Russell, *The War* II, 181–2. On Turkish hospitals, see Helmstadter, 193–200.
47. Clifford, 214; Massie, 136.

3. THE MAKING OF LEGENDS

1. Dallas, 180.
2. See, for example, Donagan, 312ff.

3. All references to the *Iliad* are from the Robert Fagles translation.
4. Napier, IV, 422, 430, 433.
5. See, for example, Glinka, 394–491.
6. Kincaid, 42–3. On Sentimentalism, Romanticism and their connection to the Napoleonic Wars, see Watson; and Ramsey.
7. Dickens, *The Old Curiosity Shop*, 538–9; Hartley, 74.
8. Airlie, 85; Marsh, 226, 205.
9. All references to "Sevastopol in December" from Tolstoy, *PSS* IV, 3–17.
10. Brontë, 128.
11. Tolstoy, *PSS* LIX, 281.
12. Tiutcheva, 184.
13. All references to the Battle of Balaklava are from Russell, The War I, 222–234.
14. Adkin, 127.
15. The *Times*, 13 November, 1854, 6.
16. Adkin, 217.
17. Orwell, 143.
18. Russell, *The War* I, 4.
19. See, for example, his letters "La Guerre d'Orient" (29 November 1854); "Sixieme Anniversaire du 24 Fevrier 1848" (24 February 24 1855); "Lettre a Louis Bonaparte" (8 April 1855) in Hugo, *Actes et Paroles, v 2: Pendant l'exil 1852–1870*. For the Russian embrace of Hugo's comparison, see "The Russian Troy." For the emperor's words, see Tiutcheva, 254.

4. THE COMING OF SPRING

1. Dallas, 113–4.
2. Russell, *The War* I, 420-423.
3. Tolstoy, *PSS* XLVII, 41.
4. Seacole, 162.
5. Russell, *The War* I, 436.
6. Ibid., 304, 343.
7. Ibid., 319.
8. Ibid., 307, 304.
9. Ibid., 324–5.
10. Desmond, 177.

11. Hankinson, 84; *Times*, 23 December 1854, 9.

12. *Times*, 26 December 1854, 9.

13. *Times*, 25 January 1855, 6.

14. *Illustrated London News*, 6 January 1855, 1.

15. Dickens, "Prince Bull," 49–51.

16. Tsialovskii, 220.

17. All references to "Sevastopol in May" from Tolstoy, *PSS* IV, 18–59.

18. Tolstoy, *PSS* LIX, 328–30.

19. Tolstoy, *PSS* XLVII, 60.

20. Atkins, 192.

21. Atkins, 192; Hankinson, 54, 83, 99, 101.

22. Airlie, 170.

23. Russell, *The War* I, 337, 218; Thackeray, *The Letters*, 403.

24. Nekrasov, *PSS* X, 241.

25. Tkachev, 270.

5. THE ROAD TO QUAGMIRE

1. Tolstoy, *PSS* IV, 286.

2. Russell, *The Great War*, 143–4; Thackeray, "Due of the Dead," 124.

3. Tiutcheva, 188–9, 199.

4. Russell, *The War* I, 15.

5. *Times*, 17 October 17 1854, 8. The letter is dated 21 September.

6. Tolstoy, *PSS* V, 232–6.

7. Ibid., 236.

8. Nekrasov, 241; Atkins, 184–5.

9. Marriott, 224.

10. Ershov, 341; Hodasevich, 24.

11. Gowing, 34, 37.

12. Clifford, 72; Dallas, 42; Calthorpe, 121.

13. Russell, *The Great War*, 159. On the Charge in more detail see Adkin; Woodham-Smith, *The Reason Why*; Brighton, *Hell Riders*.

14. Grehan 70–1.

15. Russell, *The War* I, 374; Airlie, 199.

16. Clifford, 206; Dallas, 113–4.

17. Dallas, 148; Airlie, 307.

18. Clifford, 234, 261.
19. Tolstoy, *PSS* III, 15–39.
20. All references to "Sevastopol in August" from Tolstoy, IV, 60–119.
21. Tolstoy, *PSS* XLVII, 31.
22. Tolstoy, *PSS* III, 40–74; 319.
23. Baddeley, 391
24. Nikitenko, 626.
25. Grehan, 57–8; 83.
26. *Sevastopol' v nyneshnem sostoianii*, 13; Tkachev, 11–12.
27. "Imperator Aleksandr Nikolaevich," 208. Emphasis in the original. Interestingly, Russell did use the word "quagmire" when referring to Crimea but in the literal sense, referring to the ruthlessness of its muddy conditions.

6. AFTERSHOCKS AND AWAKENINGS

1. Clifford, 261; Dallas, 113; Pirogov, 112.
2. Marx, "That Bore of a War," 337; Engels, 45.
3. Hankinson, 92.
4. Clifford, 152.
5. Lalumia, 259.
6. On the literary and artistic legacy of the war in Britain, see also Markovits.
7. Ruud, 95.
8. Tiutcheva, 343. Her entry, from 9 March 1856, the year when "Sevastopol in May" was reissued in its corrected form with precisely that hero restored leads one to wonder if the scandal behind the story had reached the imperial court.
9. Wemyss, 215. Morier wrote this observation in a letter dated 1870.
10. Nikitenko, 626; Ponting, 329.
11. Figes, 488–9.
12. Davydov, 91.
13. Ruud, 254–7.
14. Tolstoy, *PSS* IV, 285–6.
15. Curtiss, 564.
16. Ogden, 102.

17. Kropotkin, 120.
18. Hankinson, 108.
19. Hankinson, 108.
20. La Motte, 29, 27.
21. Hemingway, 161; Hynes, 112. This is not to say that veterans could not take anything noble from this war; *Storm of Steel*, Ernst Jünger's graphic, no holds-barred account of Germans fighting and dying for, in his eyes, a worthy cause still earned a sizeable readership. However, this merger of the new violence with the traditions of the past was the notable exception.
21. Barbusse, 209–10, 237.
22. Bartlett, 1; Walker, 144; Lubbock, 384.
23. Remarque, 194, 205.
24. Graves, 106; Montague Ch. VII.
25. Lussu, vii.
26. Remarque, 13.

CONCLUSION

1. *Iliad*, II, 477; I, 60.
2. "Sekretnye dokumenty," 10.
3. Wright, 6.
4. Special Inspector General for Afghanistan Reconstruction, "What We Need to Learn: Lessons from Twenty Years of Aghanistan Reconstruction," August 2021. https://www.sigar.mil/pdf/lessons-learned/SIGAR-21–46-LL.pdf

BIBLIOGRAPHY

Ackroyd, Peter. *Dickens* (New York: HarperCollins, 1990).

Ackroyd, Peter. *Dominion: The History of England from the Battle of Waterloo to Victoria's Diamond Jubilee* (New York: St. Martin's Press, 2018).

Adkin, Mark. *The Charge: the Real Reason the Light Brigade Was Lost* (London: Pen & Sword, 1996).

Atkins, J. B. *The Life of Sir William Howard Russell, the First Special Correspondent*, Vol. I (London: John Murray, 1911).

Airlie, Mabell, Countess of Airlie. *With the Guards We Shall Go: A Guardsman's Letters in the Crimea, 1854–1855* (London: Hodder and Stoughton, 1933).

Babenchikov, V. P. "Den' i noch' v Sevastopole," *Voennyi sbornik* 8 (1875): 315–64.

Baddeley, John. *The Russian Conquest of the Caucasus* (London: Longman & Green, 1908).

Barbusse, Henri. *Under Fire*. Trans. Robin Buss (New York: Penguin, 2004).

Bartlett, Vernon. *Mud and Khaki: Sketches from Flanders and France* (Alpha, 2020).

Berg, Nikolai. *Zapiski ob osade Sevastopolia* (Moscow: Kuchkovo pole, 2016).

Brighton, Terry. *Hell Riders: The Truth About the Charge of the Light Brigade* (New York: Henry Holt, 2004).

Brontë, Emily. *Wuthering Heights* (New York: Norton, 2019).

BIBLIOGRAPHY

Calthorpe, Somerset. *Letters from Headquarters* (London: John Murray, 1858).

Clifford, Henry. *Henry Clifford VC. His Letters and Sketches from the Crimea* (New York: Dutton & Co., 1956).

Curtiss, John. *Russia's Crimean War* (Durham, NC: Duke UP, 1979).

Dallas, George. *Eyewitness in the Crimea: The Crimean War Letters of Lt. Colonel George Frederick Dallas* (London: Greenhill Books, 2001).

Davydov, Denis. *Voennye zapiski* (Moscow: Voennoe izd., 1982).

Dawson, Anthony. *The Siege of Sevastopol* (Yorkshire: Frontline Books, 2017).

De Quincey, Thomas. *The Collected Writings of Thomas De Quincey*, Vol. VIII (New York: AMS Press, 1890).

Desmond, Robert. *The Information Process: World News Reporting to the Twentieth Century* (Iowa City: U of Iowa P, 1978).

Dickens, Charles. *The Old Curiosity Shop* (New York: Knopf, 1995).

———, "Prince Bull." *Household Words* (17 February 1855): 49–51.

Donagan, Barbara. *War in England, 1642–1649* (Oxford: Oxford UP, 2008).

Duffy, Christopher. *Russia's Military Way to the West* (Boston: Routledge, 1981).

Edgerton, Robert. *Death or Glory: The Legacy of the Crimean War* (Boulder, CO: Westview Press 1999).

Engels, Friedrich. "The Foreign Policy of Russian Czarism." In *The Russian Menace to Europe*, ed. Bert Hoselitz (Glencoe, IL: 1952): 25–55.

Ershov, Andrei. "Sevastopol'skie vospominaniia artilleriiskogo ofitsera." In *Voina za Krym v rasskazakh i memuarakh* (Moscow: Olma, 2015): 392–420.

Feigenbaum, Anna. *Tear Gas: From the Battlefields of World War I to the Streets of Today* (New York: Verso, 2017).

Figes, Orlando. *The Crimean War: A History* (New York: Picador, 2010).

Gates, David. *Warfare in the Nineteenth Century* (New York: Palgrave, 2001).

Giubbennet, Kh. *Ocherk meditsinksoi i gospital'noi chasti russkikh voisk v Krymu, 1854–1856* (St. Petersburg: Nekhliudov, 1870).

Glinka, Sergei. "Iz Zapisok o 1812 gode." In *1812 god v russkoi poezii i*

BIBLIOGRAPHY

vospominaniiakh sovremennikov, ed. N. N. Akopova (Moscow: Pravda, 1987): 394–491.

Gowing, Timothy. *Voice from the Ranks* (London: Folio Society, 1954).

Graves, Robert. *Goodbye to All That* (New York: Knopf, 2018).

Grehan, John and Martin Mace. *British Battles of the Crimean Wars, 1854–1856* (Barnsley: Pen & Sword, 2014).

Hankinson, Alan. *Man of Wars: William Howard Russell of the Times* (London: Heinemann, 1982).

Hartley, Jenny. *The Selected Letters of Charles Dickens* (Oxford: Oxford UP, 2012).

Helmstadter, Carol. *Beyond Nightingale: Nursing on the Crimean War Battlefields* (Manchester: Manchester UP, 2020).

Hemingway, Ernest. *A Farewell to Arms* (New York: Scribner, 1929; 2012).

Hodasevich, R. A. *A Voice from within the Walls of Sebastopol* (London: John Murray, 1856).

Homer. *The Iliad*. Trans. Robert Fagles (New York: Penguin, 2008).

Hood, E. P. *The Age and Its Architects* (London: Partridge and Oakley, 1852).

Houghton, Walter E. *The Victorian Frame of Mind, 1830–1870* (New Haven: Yale UP, 1985).

Hugo, Victor. *Actes et Paroles, v 2: Pendant l'exil 1852–1870* www.gutenberg.org (accessed 12 August 2023).

Hynes, Samuel. *A War Imagined: The First World War and English Culture* (New York: Atheneum, 1991).

"Imperator Aleksandr Nikolaevich v epoku voiny 1855-ogo goda." *Russkaia starina*, 39 (1883): 195–220.

Kincaid, John. *The Complete Kincaid of the Rifles [Comprising Adventures in the Rifle Brigade and Random Shots from a Rifleman]* (Leonaur, 2011).

Kropotkin, Petr. *Russian Literature: Ideals and Realities* (New York: Black Rose, 1991).

Lalumia, Matthew. *Realism and Politics in Victorian Art of the Crimean War* (Ann Arbor, MI: UMI Research Press, 1984).

La Motte, Ellen. *The Backwash of War* (Champaign, IL: Book Jungle).

Lawson, George. *Surgeon in the Crimea* (London: Military Book Society, 1968).

BIBLIOGRAPHY

Lubbock, Percy. *The Letters of Henry James*. Vol II (New York: Charles Scribner's Sons, 1920).

Lussu, Emilio. *A Soldier on the Southern Front*. Trans. Gregory Conti (New York: Random House, 2014).

Macleod, George. *Notes on the Surgery of the War in Crimea* (London: John Churchill, 1862).

Markovits, Stefanie. *The Crimean War in the British Imagination* (Cambridge: Cambridge UP, 2009).

Marriott, J. A. R. *The Eastern Question* (New York: Oxford UP, 1940).

Marsh, Catherine. *Memorials of Captain Hedley Vicars* (London: James Nisbet & Co., 1856).

Marx, Karl. "Poland's European Mission." In *The Russian Menace to Europe*, ed. Bert Hoselitz (Glencoe, IL: 1952): 104–8.

Marx, Karl. "That Bore of a War." In Karl Marx and Frederick Engels. *Collected Works*. Vol XIII (New York: International Publishers, 1980): 334–9.

Massie, Alastair. *The National Army Museum Book of the Crimean War* (London: Pan Macmillan, 2005).

Montague, Charles Edward. *Disenchantment* (London: Chatto & Windus, 1922).

Morley, John. *Death, Heaven and the Victorians* (Pittsburgh: U of Pittsburgh P, 1971).

Napier, William. *History of the War in the Peninsula*, Vol IV (Cambridge: Cambridge UP, 2011).

Naumova, Iulia. "Ranenie, bolezn' i smert' v povsednevnosti russkikh voisk v krymskuiu voinu," *Russkii sbornik* (7) 2009: 367–402.

Nekrasov, Nikolai. *Polnoe sobranie sochinenii i pisem*. Vol X (Moscow: Gosizdat khudozestvennoi literatury, 1952).

Nightingale, Florence. *I Have Done My Duty: Florence Nightingale in the Crimean War 1854–1856*, ed. Sue M. Goldie (Iowa City: U of Iowa P, 1987).

Nikitenko, Aleksandr Vasilevich. *Zapiski i dnevnik* (Moscow: Zakharov, 2005).

Ogden, Rollo. *Life and Letters of Edwin Lawrence Godkin* (New York: MacMillan & Co., 1907).

BIBLIOGRAPHY

Orwell, George. "The Lion and the Unicorn." In *Essays* (New York: Penguin, 1994): 138–87.

Pirogov, Nikolai. *Sevastopol'skie pis'ma, 1854–1855* (St. Petersburg: Stasiulevich, 1899).

Ponting, Clive. *The Crimean War: The Truth Behind the Myth* (London: Pimlico, 2005).

Porter, Whitworth. *Life in the Trenches Before Sebastopol* (London: Longman, Brown, Green, 1856).

Ramsey, Neil. *The Military Memoir and Romantic Literary Culture, 1780–1835* (Aldershot: Ashgate, 2011).

Reid, Douglas. *The Crimean War Letters of Dr. Douglas A. Reid* (Knoxville: U of Tennessee P, 1968).

Remarque, Erich Maria. *All Quiet on the Western Front*. Trans. A. W. Wheen (New York: Fawcett Crest, 1958).

Russell, William Howard. *The Great War with Russia* (London: George Routledge & Sons, 1895).

———, *The War: Landing at Gallipoli to the Death of Lord Raglan*, Vol I.; *From the Death of Lord Raglan to the Evacuation of Crimea*, Vol II (London: George Routledge & Co., 1855–6).

"Russian Soldiers," *Army and Navy Chronicle* 11(7), 13 August 1840: 101.

"The Russian Troy," https://sales.vgtrk.com/en/catalog/history/14689/?sphrase_id=19701 [Accessed 3 March 2023]

Ruud, Charles. *Fighting Words: Imperial Censorship and the Russian Press, 1804–1906* (Toronto: U of Toronto Press, 2009).

Seacole, Mary. *The Wonderful Adventures of Mrs. Seacole in Many Lands* (New York: Oxford UP, 1998).

Seaton, Albert. *The Crimean War: a Russian Chronicle* (London: Batsford Ltd, 1977).

"Sekretnye dokumenty iz osobykh papok: Afganistan." *Voprosy istorii* 3 (1993): 3–33.

Sevastopol' v nyneshnem sostoianii (Moscow: Aleksandr Semen, 1855).

Shepherd, John. *The Crimean Doctors: A History of the British Medical Services in the Crimean War* Vol. II (Liverpool: Liverpool UP, 1991).

Special Inspector General for Afghanistan Reconstruction, "What We Need to Learn: Lessons from Twenty Years of Afghanistan Reconstruction," August, 2021. https://www.sigar.mil/pdf/lessonslearned/ SIGAR-21-46-LL.pdf (accessed 14 December 2021).

Strachan, Hew. *From Waterloo to Balaclava: Tactics, Technology and the British Army, 1815–1854* (New York: Cambridge UP, 1985).

Thackeray, William Makepeace. "Due of the Dead." In *The New Oxford Book of War Poetry*, ed. Jon Stallworthy (Oxford: Oxford UP, 2014), 124. Originally published in *Punch* vol. xxvii (July–December 1854), 173.

———, *The Letters and Private Papers of William Makepeace Thackeray*, ed. Gordon Ray (Cambridge, MA: Harvard UP, 1945–1946).

Tiutchev, Fyodor. "Iz pisem F.I. Tiutcheva," *Russkii arkhiv*, 1899 (Bk. 2): 505–20.

Tiutcheva, A. F. *Vospominaniia* (Moscow: Zakharov, 2004).

Tkachev, Aleksandr. *Podporuchik Sevastopol'skii* (Moscow: Russkii mir, 2013).

Tolstoy, Lev. *Polnoe sobranie sochinenii*, ed. V. G. Chertkov (Moscow: Gosizdat khudozhestvennoi literatury, 1928–1958).

Totleben, Eduard. *Opisanie oborony Sevastopolia*, Vol. I (Moscow: Principium, 2017).

Tsialovskii, M. A. "Perepiska L. N. Tolstogo s I. I. Panaevym," *Krasnaia nov* 9 (1928): 219–230.

Walker, Pierre. *Henry James on Culture: Collected Essays on Politics and the American Social Scene* (Lincoln, NE: U of Nebraska P, 1999).

Watson, J. R. *Romanticism and War: A Study of British Romantic Period Writers and the Napoleonic Wars* (New York: Palgrave MacMillan, 2003).

Wemyss, Rosslyn, ed. *Memoirs and Letters of Sir Robert Morier*, Vol. II (London: E. Arnold, 1911).

Woodham-Smith, Cecil. *Florence Nightingale, 1820–1910* (New York: McGraw-Hill, 1951).

———, *The Reason Why* (New York: McGraw-Hill, 1954).

Wright, Evan. *Generation Kill* (New York: G.P. Putnam's Sons, 2004).

INDEX

INDEX

INDEX

INDEX

INDEX

INDEX

INDEX

writer and the state, 175

Russia

  autocracy, 15, 19

  casualties, 191

  censorship, 31–2, 188

  cholera, 67

  conflict with Turkey, 7–8

  defeat and post-Crimean age, 193–7

  as the "gendarme of Europe", 17, 19

  Great Exhibition (1851), 17–19

  literacy rates, 16

  and Napoleonic Wars, 20

  newspapers, lack of, 157

  Orthodox Christian nation, 6, 8

  rail road, 16, 48

Russian army

  Alma, Battle of (Sep 1854), 9, 37, 52, 63, 64, 68, 156

  loss of soldiers, 155

  Nicholas's army, size of, 26

  purpose and place at Sevastopol, 160–1

  serfdom, abolition of, 194–5

  soldier's life, 23–6

  superstitions, 25

  See also Sevastopol, siege of; Tolstoy, Lev

Russian Cossacks, 99

Russian guns, 53–4

Russian literature, 30–1

Russkii invalid, 188

Russo-Japanese War (1905), 224

Russophobia, 8–9

de Saint-Arnaud, Marshal, 71

Sapoun Heights, 91–2, 94, 98, 163

Scotland, 16

Scots Fusilier Guards, 121

Scutari, 67, 68, 69, 130, 183

Seacole, Mary, 116–17

serfdom, abolition of, 194–5

Sevastopol, battles at, 58–62

Sevastopol, siege of, 4, 9–10, 13–14, 25, 26, 36, 40–52

  Aberdeen's government, failure of, 130–1

  Alma, Battle of (Sep 1854), 9, 37, 52, 63, 64, 68, 156

  death march of victims, 121–2

  defenders of, 72, 83–90, 108–11, 154

  fall of Sevastopol, 168, 189–90

  Great Bombardment, 9, 38, 54, 85

  guns, cannon and bayonets impacts, 52–7

  Inkerman, Battle of, 9, 38, 58–60, 61, 171, 177

  kindness of the French, 124–5

  provisions, 120–1

  Sevastopol as a new Troy, 108–11

  "Sevastopol in August", 169, 170–1

  "Sevastopol in December", 83–90, 108–11, 117, 140–1, 148–9, 169, 189, 199, 206

  "Sevastopol in May", 135–45, 147, 149, 169, 171, 172, 174, 180, 196, 203–4

INDEX

CW00501236

THE
NATURE
OF THE
GAME

A STICK SIDE NOVEL

AMY AISLIN

TITLES BY
AMY AISLIN

Beta read by Jill Wexler at LesCourt Author Services
Edited by Brenda Chin
Copy editing by Boho Edits
Proofread by Between the Lines Editing
Cover art by Natasha Snow Designs
Interior design and formatting by Champagne Book Design

AUTHOR'S NOTE

The Nature of the Game takes place several months after the final chapter (but before the epilogue) of the first book in the series, *On the Ice*. If I've done my job right, *The Nature of the Game* should stand on its own, but I hope you'll check out *On the Ice* too. Thank you for reading!

ONE

AUGUST 2009—PRESENT DAY

DAN GREYSON STOOD ON THE SIDEWALK AT BAY and Richmond in downtown Toronto's sticky late-summer heat and swallowed hard. On the other side of the door of the bookstore across the street waited his biggest regret. Two of his biggest regrets, actually.

At least he'd started to make amends with one. The other . . .

The other involved broken hearts and broken promises. Was there any mending that?

The part of him that didn't enjoy confrontation—or people in general—wanted to hide out in the pub down the street, maybe order a full Irish breakfast. The big brother part of him knew he'd never do that—he'd promised he'd be here.

There was a line of people that started inside the bookstore and trailed out the door, all the way down the street. His brother's boyfriend's book launch was a huge success, and it hadn't officially started yet.

Dan checked his watch. Only a few minutes until the launch.

Taking a deep breath in through his nose, he released it through his mouth. He'd dressed up for the occasion in a blue checkered collared shirt tucked into a pair of fitted black pants. It was too hot for his outfit, and the crush of bodies at this intersection made the humid air seethe and push against him. If he didn't get inside soon, he'd sweat through his shirt.

The next time the lights turned green, Dan crossed the street with a dozen other people. Toronto reminded him a lot of New York City but with fewer people. Smelled like NYC too—car exhaust, BO, sewer water, and cigarette smoke with an undercurrent of some kind of spice from one of the nearby restaurants.

He didn't realize his hands were clenched into fists until he reached for the bookstore's door handle.

"Excuse me, sir." A woman with a headset and a clipboard blocked his entrance. "If you're here for the signing, you need to head to the back of the line."

"No, I'm . . . I should be on the guest list. Dan Greyson."

"Oh, right." She marked something on her clipboard. "Mitch said to expect you right about now. Go on in."

Dan couldn't help the burble of laughter that rose in his throat. He and Mitch, his younger brother, had a bad habit of arriving at a scheduled event at the last possible second.

Inside the bookstore, it was cool and bright, crowded and noisy. There were a few browsing customers, but most people stood in a line that extended from the back of the store, wound around bookshelves and displays, down the center aisle, and out the front door.

Man, there were a lot of people in here. So many people in a large space made it feel tiny. Throat constricting, Dan opened the top button of his shirt and wiped sweat off his brow.

Mitch had told him that the signing station would be near the back, next to the employee lunchroom, so Dan headed there.

He didn't find Mitch, the first of his two biggest regrets, but he found his dad and Mitch's best friend. They stood off to the side with a group of tall and fit guys Dan recognized as Alex's teammates.

Alex Dean, Mitch's boyfriend, played professional hockey for Tampa Bay's NHL team.

And it was just Dan's bad luck that the second of his two biggest regrets, Ashton Yager, also played hockey for Tampa. Dan, in full stalker fashion, had continued to follow Ash's career after . . . Well, after.

But not once in the past six years had he thought he'd ever actually run into the guy again. He'd wanted to, sure. Dreamed about it often. But he wasn't fanciful enough to think that he'd willed Ash back into his life. Their being in the same place at the same time today had everything to do with Mitch and Alex: Mitch being Dan's brother and Alex being on the same team as Ash.

They were bound to run into each other at some point.

Ashton Yager had been Dan's first everything when it came to men. Before Ash—and after—he'd dated strictly women. Before, because he hadn't known he was bisexual until he met Ash. And after, because he'd yet to meet a man who affected him as much as Ash had. And, truthfully, the thought of being with someone other than Ash, of having what he'd had with Ash but with someone else, man or woman, had hurt too much. He hadn't had the kind of intimacy and trust he'd had with Ash with anyone else since.

Six years was a long time to yearn for someone, which probably made Dan utterly pathetic, especially since Ash hadn't sat around yearning for him in return. No, Ash had gotten married. Then divorced, although Dan couldn't find the reason why online. And since his divorce four years ago, Ash had been linked to more than one woman.

So yeah. Dan needed to get over it. Maybe if he faced Ash head on and apologized for what he'd done six years ago, he finally would. Apologizing to Mitch had put them on the right path. Why wouldn't it be the same with Ash?

But maybe not just yet. He took the easy way out and avoided the crowd of hockey players altogether, heading instead for his dad.

"Hey." His dad clapped him on the back. "I was starting to wonder if you'd make it on time."

Dan checked his watch. "Just. Seems Alex is late, though."

"He's nervous," Alex's mom said from his dad's other side, her French-Canadian accent a musical lilt. "He's in the lunchroom." She tilted her head in that direction. "Mitch is talking to him now."

"Alex is nervous?" Dan asked. "Doesn't seem like him."

His dad shrugged his huge shoulders. "Happens to the best of us."

Dan shifted slightly, putting his back to the pack of hockey players. He hadn't spotted Ash yet, but Ash was definitely in there somewhere. Dan knew from both Mitch and Alex that Ashton Yager was Alex's best friend on the team. There was no way he'd miss Alex's book launch.

"How'd your meeting go this morning?" Dan asked his dad.

"Good." His dad leaned against the bookshelf behind him, a section of self-help books obscured by his huge bulk. "You should see this printer they were trying to sell us."

By *us*, he meant Westlake Waterless Printing, the company they both worked for, of which Dan's mother was CEO. The company, started years ago by his great-grandfather on his mother's side, was the biggest environmentally friendly print company in the United States. Dan listened as his dad talked about the new printer he'd gone to see and all of its snazzy new features. Apparently, there was only one of its kind in North America, and if Westlake Waterless Printing bought one, it'd give them an edge and allow them to print more boutique-type products.

Except it cost $3.5 million dollars.

"It cost *how much*?" Dan goggled at his dad. "Jesus, Dad. And you want us to buy it?"

"Not necessarily. I was doing Shawn in purchasing a favor by checking it out. It'll be up to him to discuss with his operators and print programmers."

"Can we afford a $3.5 million-dollar piece of equipment?"

"Beats me. You're the financial analyst."

A job Dan didn't hate as much as he thought he would, but he didn't exactly enjoy it either. Although he had a feeling that the reason he was so apathetic toward it had more to do with his mother than with the job itself. Simply the thought of working for and with her for the rest of his life made him sweat.

"How did your meeting go?"

Dan grunted. "It was fine. They were trying to sell us a new analytical tool we don't need." He sighed. "Look at us, working on a Saturday."

"Yeah. Listen." His dad cleared his throat and straightened, squaring his shoulders. "I told your brother earlier but didn't have a chance to tell you. I found a place in Burlington."

Dan's heart sunk. "You were serious about moving to Vermont?" Not that he didn't want his dad to live closer to Mitch, who attended college in Vermont, or for Mitch to have more access to their dad. But if he moved to Vermont, it'd leave Dan all alone in Manhattan with no family except their mother, and Dan's relationship with her had moved a level past strained a long time ago.

"With your mother and I divorcing, I don't feel comfortable living in the house anymore or working out of the same office. The move to Vermont, transferring to the office in Burlington . . ." His dad's smile was small, but it was pleased. "I think it'll be good for me."

Dan thought so too, but—

"What about you?"

"Huh?" Dan blinked at his dad. "What about me?"

"You ever think about moving? Transferring offices? Westlake's got twenty satellite offices you could work out of."

"I've thought about it more and more lately, to be honest, but . . ." He scuffed the heel of his loafer against the carpeted floor.

"But?"

"I don't know. I'm comfortable there."

His dad grinned and squeezed his shoulder. "Get out of your comfort zone and live a little, kiddo. Pick one of the satellite offices and try it out for a couple of weeks."

"I can do that?" Dan asked.

"Why not? Talk to Grace in HR. She'll make it happen."

Question was, did Dan want it to happen? He liked the city. His condo, as well as the office, were both in Manhattan, and everything he needed was within walking distance. He might not be a people person, but everyone ignored everyone else in New York anyway, so he might as well have been on his own island.

Trying a new office wouldn't be so bad, though, one in a big city. Westlake had an office in Chicago. San Francisco. Denver. Nashville.

Tampa.

Don't even go there.

Alex's publicist, a tiny blonde with a huge attitude,

marched past them and stopped in front of the employee lunchroom door. Mitch must've seen her coming from the other side of the glass window; he stepped out, had a short conversation with her, then slipped back into the room. The publicist headed back to her post next to the table set up as Alex's signing station. She didn't look happy.

The table was adorned with a white tablecloth, an assortment of pens, and a dozen copies of Alex's new book, *No Guts, No Glory*, which Alex described as the dark side of professional sports. Next to the table was a stand holding a poster with the book's cover, short quotes from reviewers praising the book, and a picture of Alex's face.

Hovering nearby were what Dan could only assume were reporters and bloggers, weighed down with cameras and notepads.

Finally, Alex came out of the lunchroom. Dressed in fitted black suit pants and a light-blue shirt paired with a forest-green tie that made his green eyes pop, Alex appeared anything but nervous. In fact, his expression went from confident and determined to shocked mixed with pleasure as his teammates let out a roar of cheers and applause.

Dan jerked, cold sweat breaking out on the back of his neck. The thundering of the crowd was too much, too loud. Surrounded by people on all sides, hidden in the bookstore's stacks, there was no exit, no exit, no exit. It was like being trapped in a closed box. He stepped back with a muttered, "Excuse me," when he bumped into someone, and—

"Dan?"

—blindly found his way around bookshelves, vision growing fuzzy, until finally he reached the store's front where the bank of floor-to-ceiling windows looking onto the outside world finally allowed him to breathe.

For fuck's sake. Who'd have thought he'd get hit with a

dose of claustrophobia in a damn bookstore?

"Of all the bookstores in all the world," a voice said, "you happen to walk into mine."

Dan whirled, pulse skyrocketing, and there he was— Ashton Yager, in the flesh. Or in a lovely charcoal-gray tailored suit with a lavender shirt and shiny black loafers, as it were.

Dan's knees turned to water. He was unable to blink. Unable to breathe. He was swimming in regret and lost opportunities, and it kept him frozen in place.

"Yours?" he managed to croak.

Lips twisting wryly, Ash hitched up one shoulder in a half shrug. "You don't know that it isn't."

"That's . . . true."

Dan might've purposely avoided seeking Ash out since he arrived, avoided looking too closely at the hockey players for fear that he'd spot Ash's six-four bulk and huge shoulders and be unable to do anything but stare, but he'd been prepared to see him. Had been psyching himself up since Alex had invited him to this book launch weeks ago. And yet, the butterflies on crack that erupted in his stomach were still a surprise.

Who was he kidding? He was so not prepared, and he was sure the expression on his face conveyed everything he was feeling, starting from his hesitancy to the joy that made him light-headed and made his fingers tingle.

Though that could've been the claustrophobia talking.

The look on Ash's handsome face, however . . . Stupefaction, anger, confusion. Maybe a hint of pleasure? And a whole lot of *what the fuck are you doing here?*

Ash had started going prematurely gray a few years ago and now, at twenty-seven years old, he had a full head of gunmetal gray hair. But his eyebrows were still the chocolate brown Dan remembered, and they rose high up his forehead as Dan watched him try to add up one and one to arrive at two. Because from Ash's perspective, one and one was adding up to a giant *what the fuck*.

Dan stepped toward him, pulled in by those eyes of his, an unremarkable shade of medium brown with unique tawny-colored marbled undertones that only became apparent in close range. *Extra* close range.

Ash crossed his arms over his chest, biceps and shoulders making the material of his suit jacket stretch taut. He was as big as he'd been six years ago. Except for his lower half, which actually appeared bigger, if that was possible. The NHL had clearly been good to him.

"What are you doing here?" Ash asked. By the tone of his voice, he might've asked Dan why he'd poisoned the water supply.

Not an auspicious start.

Dan threw his shoulders back. "Mitch is my brother."

"Your . . ." Comprehension dawned, Ash's eyes going wide. He gave a tragic-sounding chuckle. "I never put that together."

"Why would you? Greyson's a pretty common last name." Rallying, Dan rubbed his chest over his slowing heart rate, intent on . . . something. Getting Ash not to look at him like he was something vile underneath his shoes? "You look good, Ash."

Ash cocked his head. "And you look like you're about to pass out. Can I buy you a coffee?" He gestured at the bookstore's coffee shop a dozen steps away.

Dan really should head back to Mitch. He was here to support him after all. Well, he was here to support Mitch's boyfriend, which was basically the same thing. But it was so stuffy over there, too many people packed into a small area.

The coffee shop, on the other hand, was currently empty.

"That'd be great. Thanks, Ash."

Ash grunted and led the way into the coffee shop. "Don't thank me. I don't want an ambulance showing up at Alex's book launch."

Fuck him. He shouldn't have said that. It was mean. True, but mean.

Standing in line at the coffee shop, Ashton Yager caught himself turning to where Dan sat alone at a table for four next to the window—and abruptly straightened.

God forbid Dan catch him looking. He didn't want Dan to think he cared.

By the expression on his face, Dan had been expecting to see him. At one point, he'd appeared almost afraid, as if he expected Ash to stride over and pop him in the nose.

Please. Ash almost scoffed. First, he kept his fighting for the ice. Second, he had no reason to punch Dan. What was done was done. It'd happened and he'd moved on. He'd had six years to move on, in fact. He hadn't sat around pining for Dan that whole time like a lovesick sixteen-year-old, despite his ex-wife often accusing him of having the maturity of a teenager. Her verbal abuse was only one of the many reasons they'd divorced, not the least of which being that she'd cheated on him.

"Yo, Yager." Fingers snapped in his face. "You in, or what?"

"Huh?" Ash faced Carlie, who'd joined him in line a minute ago. "In for what?"

"I was talking to one of the guys from the Toronto team earlier. Staples?" Carlie—Tampa's goalie—bent to peer into a display case of pastries. "He wants to set up a friendly game tomorrow night, for those of us who are still here."

That some of the guys on the Toronto team had shown up today to support Alex was all kinds of awesome.

"You in?" Carlie repeated.

"Fuck yes." Anything to take his mind off Dan.

Dan, who should be in New York City where Ash had left him. Or more like where Dan had left *him*.

Man, they had a complicated past. Or maybe not so complicated when Ash thought about it.

How was he supposed to act right now? He didn't want Dan to think he was happy to see him, because he wasn't, so he couldn't smile at him. And he didn't want Dan to think he was angry with him—Ash had moved past that a long time ago—so he couldn't scowl either. And avoidance never helped anyone.

If only Ash could get a handle on what he was feeling, that might help. Because, although he wasn't happy to see Dan, there was a tiny kernel of pleasure he didn't want to admit to, despite the fact Dan had broken his heart. And okay yeah, maybe there was some old anger and hurt, which just made him resentful that he wasn't quite as over it as he'd thought. Add some amazement that this was actually happening, both of them in the same city for the same event, and a little bit of anxiety and nervousness thrown into the pot with the lingering confusion and shock and a whole truckload of attraction . . .

Overwhelmed. He was overwhelmed as fuck and coffee wasn't going to help the knot in his belly.

Conflicted too. Seriously, how was he supposed to act in the presence of the ex-boyfriend who'd left him at the altar?

Okay, not *altar* altar. Not really. But Dan had left him at the airport with nothing but an *I'm sorry, I can't* text minutes before their flight to Syracuse, where Ash had been playing in the AHL for Tampa's affiliate, where they'd co-signed a lease for an apartment, and where Dan had secured an apprenticeship with a local woodworker outside the city who specialized in small household items.

They might as well have been married.

Maybe he was a little angrier than he'd thought. But he didn't want Dan to know that. Didn't want Dan to think that he felt anything for him at all.

Pleasant, yet distant. He could be pleasant, yet distant, couldn't he? Sure. Maybe. It was probably all in the eyebrows.

It was so unfair that Dan was just as good looking as ever. Same curly blond hair falling in every direction. Same eyes the color of light maple syrup. Same lithe runner's build. Same sleek and fashionable men's fashion magazine outfit. The light layer of blond scruff on his face was new, but overall? On the outside, he was the same.

Ash should've known. Back in February when he'd met Mitch for the first time, when Mitch had looked so damn familiar . . . Not in a we've-met-before kind of way. More in a you-look-like-the-brother/cousin/relative-of-someone-I-know kind of way. It was the eyes: light brown. It was the smile: wide and genuine. It was the hair: curly and fucking adorable, although whereas Mitch's was brown, Dan's was a medium shade of blond.

But he'd never, not once, connected Mitch *Greyson*—his teammate and best friend's boyfriend—to Dan *Greyson*—his own ex. Maybe he should have, but like Dan had said, it was a pretty common last name.

"The guys'll have extra skates, sticks, and gear for us at the rink."

Ash tore his gaze off Dan. "For what?"

"The game with the guys from the Toronto team to-morrow?" Carlie's eyes narrowed. As Tampa's goalie, he no-ticed everything on the ice. And off it.

Ash tried not to squirm.

"Are you okay?"

"Fantastic!" Overselling it a bit, but whatever. Ash moved forward in line. "Which rink?"

The change of subject wasn't lost on Carlie, but he went with it anyway. "Staples'll text me the address."

"Who's still around tomorrow anyway?"

"Other than you, me, and Dean? Greer, Masterson, Delaney. Mooney, I think. Everybody else flies back to Tampa tomorrow afternoon, after brunch at Dean's mom's."

Brunch. At Alex Dean's mom's house out in the sub-urbs. Which meant Mitch would be there.

Ergo, Dan would be there.

Fuck his life.

Speaking of the bastard . . .

Dan's face had regained some color, and the sweat on his upper lip had dried. His composure had returned too, and he sat in his chair, back straight, one ankle crossed over the other knee, and could be getting ready for an early lunch meeting if Ash didn't know better.

Ash's stomach flipped and folded as their eyes met across the coffee shop.

Carlie nudged him. "You know that guy?"

"Huh? Who? Oh. No. I mean . . ." Ash stuffed his hands in his pockets and pretended to eye the coffee selection. "Yeah, that's, uh, Mitch's brother."

"Cool." Another nudge. "Your turn, dude."

A minute later, two coffees in hand, Ash waited for Carlie to be served. Carlie was the buffer between him and

Dan. Carlie wasn't allowed to leave.

Reaching across the table, Ash held Dan's coffee out.

"Thank you."

Their fingers brushed, shooting warmth up Ash's arm, zinging into his chest. Dan smiled tightly, eyes meeting Ash's before cutting away.

Goddamnit, why did Dan have to affect him so much?

"Mitch's brother, right?" Carlie held out a hand. "I'm Evan Carlson. Everyone calls me Carlie."

"Dan."

Oh, and look, here was Mitch, plopping himself into the chair between Ash and Dan, hugging Alex's book to his chest like he'd eat and sleep with the thing for the rest of his life. He dusted some crumbs off the table, then went to set his book down. He seemed to think better of it for some reason, because he changed his mind and set it on his lap instead.

Ash reached for it. "Can I see that?"

Mitch twisted away, scowling. "No. Get your own."

"Seriously?" Ash forced a chuckle, determined to ignore how much Dan's presence was making him twitchy. Good thing the AC was blasting, otherwise Ash's damp back would've been patchy with sweat spots. "I can't even look at it?"

"There's a zillion more copies in there." Mitch waved in the direction of the bookstore. "Get your own."

"I'm surprised you left Alex's side." Alex and Mitch tended to be disgustingly glued to each other's hips.

"He's fine. Busy signing autographs." Mitch stroked the book on his lap. "The line-up's still out the door, so we'll be here for a while. I'll bring him a snack in a bit."

"Was he nervous?" Carlie asked.

Mitch's grin was sappy as hell. "Yeah. But he's good

now. Just needed to get out there and stop thinking."

Honestly, how Alex and Mitch's relationship hadn't been discovered by reporters yet was a mystery. They were keeping it a secret from everyone except close friends and family, and yet, in public, they were constantly brushing hands, standing too close, and staring at each other with starry eyes and lovesick grins.

Worst kept secret *ever*.

"A few of us are playing a friendly game with some of the guys from the Toronto team tomorrow," Ash told Mitch, a left-winger on his college's hockey team. "Wanna play?"

Mitch's mouth dropped open. "Are you serious? Because if this is a joke, it's a really mean one."

"Dude, I don't joke about hockey. Carlie, tell him."

"You joke about hockey all the time." Carlie crossed his arms. "Like that one the other day about the fans."

Ash grinned. "Yeah. That was a good one."

Mitch side-eyed him. "I don't think I want to know."

"Sure you do. Why does a hockey team never sweat?" Ash paused for dramatic effect and drum rolled on the table. "Because they have too many fans!"

"That's not funny," Mitch said while Carlie rolled his eyes, and Dan . . . Dan let out a choked sound Ash chose to interpret as a laugh.

"It was a little bit funny," Ash insisted.

Mitch punched him in the shoulder. "Were you serious about tomorrow or not?"

"Okay, *that* I wouldn't joke about. Of course I was serious."

Mitch's smile was so big his cheeks must've hurt. "I gotta tell Alex!" He disappeared into the store with his precious book.

Carlie sipped his coffee and made a face. "This isn't

what I ordered. I'll be right back." He disappeared to the back of the line.

Leaving Ash alone with Dan. Like he knew the two of them needed to talk. Which was impossible. Ash had never told anyone about them except his parents, and Dan . . .

Dan hadn't told anyone while they'd been together, not even Mitch, even though they'd always been close. On the day they were meant to fly to Syracuse, the plan had been for Dan to tell his parents—at the last minute so they couldn't stop him or attempt to talk him out of it—that he was dropping out of Columbia, where he was studying business and accounting, to move to Syracuse. They'd both known that Dan's mom would be the hard sell, that his dad would support him in anything, but Dan had been determined. Determined and confident and *excited* for their future together.

And then that stupid *I'm sorry, I can't* text that had told Ash nothing. Ash had always assumed that Dan's mom had somehow talked him out of going with him.

Or maybe Dan simply hadn't been as serious about them as Ash had.

Sitting across from Dan now, all of the old hurt came back as if Dan had left him at the airport yesterday, not six years ago. The devastation. The aching sense of loss. The confusion that had left him grasping at nothing. The realization that Dan didn't want him enough. The bigger realization that even though, for him, Dan had been the one; to Dan, Ash had just been a summer fling. Some guy he'd met who was working in Manhattan over the summer before he headed back to his AHL team in Syracuse in August. It had hurt like nothing before or since. His divorce, while anything but amicable, hadn't hurt as much.

He didn't let any of that show on his face, or in his

posture, keeping his shoulders relaxed and his expression smooth. Pleasant, yet distant. Even his eyebrows were cooperating.

Dan had folded his shirtsleeves back, exposing fore-arms dusted with blond hairs that he rested on the table, hands cupped around his mug. They were nice forearms too, graceful and gently tanned. Taken together with his build, they told Ash without words that Dan still jogged every morning.

Ash took a deep breath, ignoring the dullness in his chest.

Dan cleared his throat and rubbed his forehead—a nervous tick he clearly hadn't gotten rid of. "Hey."

"Hey."

Dan attempted a smile. It was a pale imitation to the one Ash remembered.

Ash checked his watch. How long would this book launch last, and when could he leave?

"How've you been?" Dan asked.

Fuck, even his voice was the same. It threw Ash back to the day they'd met. Stuck in that elevator, he'd known that he wanted Dan as a friend. But he'd never expected, could never have predicted, what they'd become to each other. "Good," he answered. "You?"

Dan was nodding. "Good."

Look at them, having a conversation like mature adults. An awkward one, but still. No, not awkward. A pleasant yet distant one.

"Are you going to Alex's for brunch tomorrow?" Dan asked.

"Yeah. All of the guys from the team are."

"That's a lot of mouths to feed."

Ash loosed real, unexpected laughter. "Yeah. I don't

think Alex's mom knows what she's in for."

Dan's smile was more real this time, punching Ash right in the solar plexus.

"Listen." Dan cleared his throat again. "Do you want to get out of here? Go somewhere more private to talk?"

"We don't have anything to talk about."

"I want to explain." Dan leaned his elbows on the table. "About—"

Ash held up a hand. "Don't. I don't want to hear it."

"But—"

"Six years ago I would've begged for an explanation." *Had* begged for an explanation—via text, email, and phone, all of which had gone ignored. "But now?" He shrugged. Now he was done with it. Now he was on the final year of his NHL contract, and he was still waiting for his club to offer him a new one—something that should've happened already—which meant keeping his head down and playing the best hockey he could. And getting involved with Dan again was *not* keeping his head down. "I don't want it. What happened, happened. It's done. It's over. I don't need to hear excuses. I'll be right back. Need a refill." He rose, full mug in hand. He needed to breathe, just for a minute. Needed a second without the scent of Dan's cologne clogging his nostrils.

Why did he have to be as fucking earnest and good looking as he ever was?

Joining Carlie in line, he glanced back at Dan and found Mitch there, gesturing toward the bookstore. Dan hesitated, eyes snagging on Ash, his lips downturned, seeming to seek some sort of guidance. He blinked once and the question was gone from his face, and he followed Mitch into the bookstore.

It was probably for the best.

TWO

MAY 2003—SIX YEARS AGO

THE ELEVATOR WAS EMPTY. THANK GOD.

Dan stepped inside, pressed the button for the ground floor, and slumped against the mirrored rear wall, tugging at his tie.

Twenty years old and he was already wearing a tie. It was suffocating.

A portent of the future?

He sighed and rubbed his forehead. God, he hoped not.

The elevator stopped on the fourteenth floor and someone got in. Dan ignored them, too focused on his own misery. Seriously, this day. You'd think he wasn't going into his third summer working at the head office of his mother's company. He'd screwed up one thing after another, and the day was only half over.

"That's a lot of sighing you're doing over there."

"What?" He glanced over at his elevator companion, a tall guy—like, seriously tall—and huge to boot, with brown hair the color of milk chocolate and eyes to match. The guy was about Dan's age with a charmer of a smile and a messenger bag slung over a strong shoulder.

"I said you were doing a lot of sighing," the guy said. "Bad day?"

"Understatement."

And it got worse as the elevator shuddered, groaned, and stalled.

Oh god.

All of a sudden, Dan was six years old, visiting cousins in California with his dad. A playground, crawling through a plastic tube that led from one section of the jungle gym to another. Earthquake. Small, yet enough to cause the jungle gym to shudder, groan, and come toppling down on top of him.

He'd later learned that he'd been trapped in the plastic tube for less than an hour. At the time, it had felt endless. No window. No way out. Not enough room to sit up or lie down, so he'd been curled in the fetal position as he banged against the plastic, begging to be let out. Begging for his dad.

Small enclosures made him sweat. Elevators were usually fine—the mirrored walls made the small space appear larger than it actually was. But elevators were most certainly not fine when they were stalled between two floors, the red numbers above the floor selection buttons flickering between eleven and ten. Were they high enough that they'd die if the cables snapped and they went plunging down, down, down, past the ground floor and into the parking levels?

He folded in half and stuck his head between his legs. "We're going to die here."

"Don't be so dramatic," his elevator companion said.

There was the sound of a click, and then a tinny female voice said, "Maintenance. How can I help you?"

"Yeah, my friend and I are stuck in the elevator between floors ten and eleven."

"Can you tell me which elevator?"

"Uh, one of the main ones, but I don't know the number. The last one on the east side."

"Six," Dan wheezed.

"Six," the guy repeated. "You might want to send help fast. I think my friend's about to hyperventilate."

"I've never," Dan huffed, "hyperventilated—" Huff. "—in my life." He unfolded himself slightly, propping himself up with his hands on his knees.

"Uh-huh."

"Can you tell me your names, sir?"

"I'm Ashton Yager. My friend is . . ." Dan's companion—Ashton—bent and snagged Dan's eyes with his own. "Dude, what's your name?"

"Dan Greyson."

"We should have you guys out of there in a jiffy!"

"A jiffy, huh?" Ashton stared at the elevator speaker, clearly unconvinced. "A jiffy like ten minutes? Or a jiffy like an hour?"

"Hmm, well, we're looking into it on our end. Looks to be a simple malfunction, so maybe . . . a couple of hours?"

"How is that a jiffy?"

"How is that simple?" Dan countered.

Ashton grinned at him, seemingly delighted about something.

"Is there anybody in the building we should contact for you?" the tinny voice asked. Considering their situation, she was much too chipper.

"Nope." Ashton popped the *p.*

"Could you let Greta Westlake know I might be late for our meeting after lunch?" Dan rose to his full height and rubbed his forehead. "She's with Westlake Waterless Printing, eighteenth floor."

"Will do! Hang tight, boys."

Hang tight. Right.

"Hang tight," Ashton repeated, letting go of the speaker button. "Where does she expect us to go?"

Amusement sparked in Dan, distracting him from his current circumstances. If he was stuck in an elevator for two hours, at least he had company. He held out a hand. "Dan."

"Ash."

They shook quickly, then Ash sat on the floor, back against the wall, long—really long—legs out in front of him. Dan mirrored his pose on the other side of the elevator, trying not to move too fast and jar the car. What if one small movement was enough to send them falling?

"So." Ash crossed one ankle over the other. His legs were so long they almost reached Dan's side of the car. "What do you do at Westlake Waterless Printing?"

"I'm an intern in the finance department. What do you do in the building?"

"I'm spending the summer working at Goal. Sort of. If the mostly salary-free kind of work can be considered work. I get a stipend. Is that the same thing?"

"You lost me."

"I've got this friend who was supposed to help out at Goal for the summer—"

"The non-profit on the fourteenth floor?" Dan jerked a thumb upward. Goal helped fund sports programs for underprivileged kids.

"Mm-hmm. Except he—my friend—had to bail at the last minute. Family emergency. So here I am."

Working on a stipend, apparently. "What will you be doing there?"

"Mostly coaching hockey summer camps at their recreational facility. Until then, just helping out with after-school programs, and . . ." He scratched his chin. "Other stuff, I guess. I don't really know yet. It's my first week. Mostly admin stuff and meeting people." Ash's turn to jerk a thumb upward, presumably also at the fourteenth floor.

"You play? Hockey, I mean."

"Yeah. For the AHL team in Syracuse."

That explained why the guy was enormous, and also why he could—possibly, maybe—live on a stipend. How much did AHL players make, anyway? "That was nice of you to take your friend's place."

"I was gonna head home for the summer now that the season's over, but . . ." Ash shrugged. "This way I get to help kids, you know?"

"Where's home?"

"Tampa."

"I went to Florida in August once," Dan said. "Told myself I'd never go back in the summer ever again."

Ash laughed, and the sound did something unexpected to Dan's insides. "Yeah, it does get pretty hot in the summer. It's not so bad here, though."

"This is nothing. May in the city is actually pretty nice. Wait until July. You'll be wishing for a swimming pool."

"Or the beach."

"Or that. Will it be fun, do you think? Working with a bunch of kids for the whole summer?"

"Are you kidding? It's gonna be great! I did it a couple summers ago and it was awesome."

Abruptly, Dan was wildly jealous. Not because he wanted to coach kids—he was much better with numbers than people—but because Ash said it with joy in his voice. Dan couldn't remember ever speaking of his double major in business and accounting with joy.

"You hungry?" Ash dug into his messenger bag and pulled out a protein bar. "I've got extra."

"God, yes. Thank you. I was on my way to lunch when this—" He waved a hand around. "—happened."

"Speaking of lunch," Ash said as he ripped open his own bar, "are there any decent places to eat around here? I haven't gotten a lunch break all week, but I'm hoping to explore the area a bit more next week."

"When did you start your internship?"

"Monday."

"And you're already so busy that you're skipping lunch?"

Ash swallowed his mouthful and said, "I usually work out in the gym in the basement on my lunch break."

Dan bit into his bar. "Ugh." Forcing himself to swallow, he glared at the offending bar masquerading as food. "This is disgusting."

Ash toasted him with his own bar. "But filling."

"Seriously, what did you give me?" Dan read the ingredients. "I can't even pronounce half of these."

"It's probably best we don't know what they are."

"There's got to be side effects to eating too many of them, though." He carefully wrapped the rest and handed it back to Ash.

"You sure?"

"I had escargot once," Dan said and pointed at the bar. "That's worse."

"Escargot, huh? Sounds fancy. The fanciest food I've ever had was mini hamburgers at a benefit I was at last year. A bunch of us went out to a pub after for real food."

"Speaking of real food, there's a dozen places to eat around here. If you can get away for lunch one day next week, I'll take you to my favorite pizza place."

"Yeah? Sweet!" Ash finished off his bar, placed Dan's unfinished one into a pocket of his messenger bag, and came back out with a deck of cards, "Crazy Eights?"

Why did he have cards on him? And what else was in that Mary Poppins bag?

Ash waved the deck. "Wanna play?"

Dan scooted forward and sat cross-legged in the middle of the elevator, making it sway gently. He swallowed hard, ignoring the jump in his belly, and removed a handful of coins from his pocket. "Let's make it interesting."

"Ooh." Ash rubbed his hands together and mimicked Dan's posture, his huge bulk rocking the car more than Dan ever could. Dan spread his arms wide, hands flat against opposite sides of the elevator, as if he could stop its shaking by somehow stabilizing it.

"Sorry," Ash said. "But you know we're not going to plunge to our deaths, right?"

"You don't know that."

"Actually, I do. There's more than one cable holding up this elevator, and any one of them alone could hold this thing up. We're fine."

"How do you know?"

"My dad's an engineer. I used to be afraid of elevators too until he told me that."

The information didn't help slow Dan's heartbeat at all.

Ash held the cards out to him. "Shuffle?"

Dan shuffled.

THREE

IT WAS STUFFY AND CROWDED IN ALEX'S MOM'S townhouse in the Toronto suburb of Oakville. The air conditioning was off to prevent the cool air from escaping out the back doors, which were thrown open to the patio to accommodate everyone here, most of whom were hockey players. Very large hockey players. They spilled into every part of the house and out into the backyard.

Dan was way overdressed. Growing up in his mom's world in the Hamptons, Sunday brunch meant dressing your best. Mitch had taken one look at his dark-blue, short-sleeved button up tucked into a pair of slim white pants and said, "Mom's not here, you know."

You could take the man out of the Hamptons, but you couldn't take the Hamptons out of the man.

Even his dad had dressed down. But he was originally from California, and now that he was getting divorced, he no longer had to conform to Greta Westlake's standards.

Dan shook his head to rid himself of thoughts of his mom. Lingering in a corner of the living room, he tried to find someone he knew that he could talk to or something to do to pass the time. The handful of people he knew were either mid-conversation with someone he didn't know, or helping Toni, Alex's mom, set out all the food. Toni had already turned down his offer to help, shooing him out of the kitchen, leaving him restless and desperate for something to occupy his time. He wasn't used to idleness. For the past six years, every second of every day had been planned to the nth as a way to keep his mind and hands busy. He'd needed something else to do with his hands when he gave up woodworking, and something to occupy his mind when he'd pushed both Mitch and Ash away.

He thought longingly of his LEGO and 3D puzzle collections at home, and of the new seven thousand-plus-piece Millennium Falcon waiting to be built, and wished fervently to be in his own apartment in Manhattan, surrounded by the familiar, with tiny puzzle pieces spread out in front of him.

He'd spotted Ash outside earlier, sitting in a folding chair that looked like it was about to crumble underneath his bulk. He was dressed casually in khaki shorts and a gray T-shirt that matched his hair, chatting with a couple of his teammates and cradling a mug of coffee to his wide chest.

If Dan was a little jealous of that mug, it was no one's business but his own.

"Food's ready!" came Toni's voice from the kitchen, and fifteen hockey players raced for the buffet spread out on the kitchen table.

Mitch found Dan a moment later, still hanging out by himself in the living room, where pictures of Alex at different ages sat atop the mantlepiece. Alex in peewee hockey; Alex in a birthday hat with the number seven on it; Alex playing street hockey in an alley; Alex in a hockey uniform, standing next to an older gentleman with flyaway silver hair.

"That's Alex's Grandpa Forest," Mitch said, standing next to Dan.

"He passed away recently, didn't he?"

Mitch's small smile was sad. "Yeah."

"Were they close?"

"Extremely."

"Did you get to meet him?"

"Yeah." Mitch's smile was more genuine this time. "He was great. A bit of a kook. Alex was his whole world." He sat on the arm of the couch, his attention shifting to Dan. "Are you okay? You seem a bit off today. Yesterday too."

Dan forced his lips upward. "I'm fine. Just have a lot on my mind."

Mitch cocked his head, brown curls flopping everywhere. "Anything you want to talk about?"

Dan peeked out the living room window. Outside, Ash now sat on a different chair, one that made up part of a semicircle of chairs occupied by his teammates, a plate of food in his lap. Dan's heart kicked against his ribs, and he turned away. "Nothing to talk about." He sat on the coffee table and gave Mitch's knee a gentle shove. "How are you? Ready to head back to Vermont in a few days?"

Tomorrow morning, Mitch and Alex were scheduled to fly back to Tampa, where Mitch had lived with Alex in Alex's condo for the summer, working at a nearby café. The day after that, Mitch was flying to Vermont for his junior year of college.

"Yes," Mitch said with a sigh. "And no. I miss school, and I miss the team, and I miss hockey, but . . . I don't want to leave Alex. I just spent four months living with him, and after Tuesday, I won't see him until October. I miss him already and I haven't even left yet. How fucked up is that?"

"It's not fucked up at all."

Dan rubbed his chest, thrown back six years to when Ash had taken a week off from Goal to fly home to visit his mom in Tampa. They'd already been living out of each other's pockets by then, and Dan had been bummed that he hadn't been given the vacation time to go with Ash. They'd spent the night before Ash's flight at Dan's apartment, wrapped around each other. Dan had barely slept that night, memorizing Ash's every feature. Every dip and curve of his face. The way he breathed. The way he smelled.

Pathetic. He'd been so pathetic, getting weepy over a week's separation. Hell, he was getting weepy now, but it had less to do with the week apart and more to do with that feeling Mitch described, of missing someone while still in their presence. He wanted that again, that unity with someone else, that feeling of being part of a whole. Someone to miss when they went away.

His eyes went to the window again. "Mitch, do you believe in second chances?"

"Of course." Mitch nudged Dan's knee with his bare foot. "You and I wouldn't be here otherwise."

And there it was, that familiar punch to the throat whenever he thought about how he'd treated Mitch the past six years.

On the day Dan had been meant to fly to Syracuse with Ash, where they'd been ready to start their lives together, he'd been packed and ready to go, ready to start living his life outside of his mother's purview, confident in his future. In *their* future. He'd known she'd put up a fight when he told her that he was dropping out of Columbia to pursue woodworking. He'd always been good at building things and couldn't wait to start making a living making small, personal items like jewelry boxes, toy sets, games, and his favorite—sun catchers.

He hadn't known his mother would blackmail him into staying.

"If you don't complete your degree and come work for me," she'd said, her tone indifferent as she sat behind her large desk in her office, perfectly coiffed and radiating a coldness Dan had never understood, "I'll take Mitch's college tuition away."

She used his own brother against him. Mitch, fourteen years old at the time, had already been a hockey prodigy, and he'd wanted a college degree in kinesiology, something he could fall back on once he retired from sports.

And Dan had been his biggest supporter.

What else could he do? What choice did he have? Of course he'd stayed. He wasn't going to ruin Mitch's future by going after his own.

The old fury at what she'd done came roaring back, threatening to choke him. She'd taken not just Mitch from him that day, but Ash too. And she hadn't even known about Ash. Dan had known better than to tell her, instead making the move to Syracuse all about him and his desire to live his own life.

But what *he'd* done . . . That was worse. Pushing Mitch away, pushing him from his life, out of anger at something that wasn't remotely Mitch's fault, but also out of fear. Fear that their mother would make good on her threat if she saw how close they still were. Irrational maybe, but the anxiety had been a real thing for a long time.

And if his mom could use Mitch against him, she wouldn't hesitate to use Ash as well once she found out about him. So Dan had pushed him away too, even though he was kind and big-hearted and fearless and everything Dan had ever wanted.

He'd patched things up with Mitch, but they were family. Things with Ash would always be strained, especially since Ash didn't want to hear anything he had to say. And why would he after Dan left him at the airport with nothing but a text?

What was so wrong about wanting to live his own life? Why did his mother want her claws in him so badly that she'd blackmailed him into staying?

More, why had he caved so easily? Hadn't sought help, hadn't searched for another solution. Just let her manipulate him into doing what she wanted.

He'd tried so hard to have everything he wanted. Go big or go home, right?

Instead, he'd gone big and failed epically.

"Hey." Mitch slid off the arm and onto the couch. "I didn't mean to make you feel bad. Sure you don't want to talk about what's bothering you?"

Dan wanted to unload everything about Ash onto Mitch, but—

"There's nothing to talk about. We should get in line for food."

"Dan—"

"It's nothing. Really." He shot Mitch a smile. Mitch's brows were pulled together, and he looked so concerned that Dan searched for something to appease him. Something he *could* talk about. "I'm just glad to be here. Glad we're in each other's lives again. If you hadn't fainted from exhaustion in March and Dad hadn't found out about Mom taking your tuition away . . ."

"We wouldn't be here," Mitch finished for him.

Yeah. Because their mother was just that wicked. She'd taken Mitch's tuition away when she'd found out he was studying kinesiology in college—not business or accounting or something else that would benefit the family business in some way, like she'd expected. To make matters worse, she'd never told Dan about it, and he'd gone years thinking Mitch had been allowed to do what he wanted, while he himself hadn't been. There'd been so much anger directed at his mother, but he'd also been so damn proud that Mitch was following his dreams.

Until he'd found out about everything—about their mother denying Mitch his tuition. About Mitch keeping it a secret from their dad because he didn't want to strain their parents' relationship more than it already was. About Mitch working two jobs to make ends meet, barely able to afford food, working himself to exhaustion until he passed out after a game.

Which, it turned out, had been a blessing in disguise, forcing truths from secrets and bringing them back into each other's lives.

That Dan's sacrifices had been for nothing grated so much it made him sick to his stomach. He'd given up *everything* he'd loved—woodworking, Mitch, Ash. All of it for nothing.

"I've been thinking of making some changes," he told Mitch.

"How do you mean?"

"I've been struggling at the office recently," he admitted. "Not with the job, but with working under the same roof as Mom. I was thinking of working out of the Burlington office for a bit, see if I like it. Maybe transfer there if I do."

"Really?" Mitch surged forward and squeezed Dan's shoulders. "Dude, that'd be so awesome! You'll like Vermont, and Burlington's really cool. It feels more like a small town than a city, it's super outdoorsy and pretty, and there's great little coffee shops and restaurants. The Church Street Marketplace is the best, and I could come visit on Sundays since I don't work at the long-term care facility anymore."

It sounded like Mitch was trying to convince him. Dan had to laugh. "So I guess you're not opposed to the idea."

Mitch looked positively insulted.

"Guys." Alex appeared in the doorway. He was huge— as big as Ash—and broad and bearded and so completely opposite to the kind of person Dan had expected his brother to fall for. But they were so well matched that, now that Dan had spent time with them together, he couldn't imagine Mitch with anyone else.

"The line's gone," Alex said. "You might want to get some food now before the horde descends for seconds."

"Come on." Mitch dragged Dan to the doorway by the arm, where he let him go to grasp Alex's hand in his own. Apparently, the guys from Alex's team who were here today were ones who knew about their relationship.

Dan grabbed a plate and served himself a couple slices of French toast, a handful of strips of crispy bacon, sausages, and a pile of scrambled eggs.

"Don't forget your protein," Alex said.

Dan glanced up to tell him he already had a bunch on his plate, only to find Alex's unimpressed gaze on Mitch's plate, loaded with French toast, pancakes, a mini muffin, and a croissant.

"Oh, don't you worry." Mitch poured maple syrup—the real stuff—onto his food. "I'm going there next."

"Gonna leave some of that for the rest of us?"

Mitch threw Alex a cheeky grin and handed the syrup over. He leaned against Alex's side as he reached across him for the bacon, adding several slices to his heap of food.

Envy, pure and heavy, hit Dan in the heart, squeezing his ribs. Not jealousy; he could never be jealous of Mitch's relationship with Alex. But he envied them the easy familiarity and casual touches.

He leaned sideways, peering around Alex and through the open back door. In the late morning sunshine, Ash sat with his friends, laughing, his gray hair haloed atop his head.

Ash didn't want anything to do with him, yet Dan wasn't sure he was ready to shut the door on that part of his life for good.

Dan came out of the house behind Mitch and Alex, and Ash almost choked on his coffee.

Fuck, Dan looked edible in that blue shirt and fitted white pants. Anger might've chafed at Ash's insides, but he could appreciate a good-looking man. And Dan was definitely that.

And then some.

Pretty, some might've called him. Which he was. Dressed the way he was, with his curls perfectly coiffed and frizz-free, and with that air of Hamptons I've-got-it-and-you-don't that guarded a vulnerable core, he was perfectly put together. The you-can't-touch-me was ten times louder than it used to be.

Ash knew better and hated himself for caring about him, even just a little.

Dan sat on a chair close to the deck, Mitch and Alex next to him. Until Alex was called away by his mom, and Mitch was lured into a conversation with one of Alex's old college friends. Leaving Dan alone . . . and lonely. He ate his breakfast with single-minded focus, as if the food would disappear if he didn't inhale it. His shoulders were straight, and he held himself stiffly, not out of a desire to be left alone, but rather to protect himself.

Ash sighed and didn't think twice. He'd do it for anybody else.

"Hey."

Pausing with his fork halfway to his mouth, Dan's eyes tracked him as he took the chair to Dan's right, placing his plate on his lap and his coffee mug in the grass by his feet. "Hi?"

He still looked like Ash was about to deck him. It would've been funny if it weren't so sad.

"Enjoying the brunch?" Man, lamest small talk ever. But pleasant, yet distant, right?

Dan blinked at him. "Yes?"

"Gonna stop answering me in questions?"

Dan's lips twitched.

"Have you tried the croissants? Toni made them from scratch." Seriously, they'd be talking about the weather next.

"Uh, no. Not yet."

Silence descended between them, tense and awkward. Ash bit into a piece of bacon drenched in maple syrup, a habit he'd acquired after one too many breakfasts with Mitch and Alex over the summer. Actually, now that he thought about it, it was a minor miracle that he hadn't run into Dan at Alex's condo sometime during the past few months Mitch had been living with Alex. He knew from Mitch that Dan had visited more than once. It was pure dumb luck that Ash had missed his visit each time. And sheer stupidity that he hadn't linked Mitch Greyson to Dan Greyson. Or was it? Had Mitch ever mentioned his brother by name? Had *Dan* mentioned Mitch by name back then? Either way, Ash couldn't remember. It was entirely possible the connection had been there, dangling in front of his face, but that he purposely hadn't seen it. Self-protection at its best.

Dan cleared his throat. "Listen—"

"Don't," Ash interrupted, knowing exactly where he

was going. "I told you yesterday—I don't want to hear it."

"But—"

Ash stared him down.

"Seriously?" Dan's eyes narrowed, his face settling into tense lines. "We're never going to talk about it?"

"Why should we? It's not going to change anything."

"So, what then? We just let bygones be bygones and carry onward?"

"Yeah." Ash bit into another piece of bacon. *Crunch, crunch, crunch.* "Why not?"

"Problems don't get solved by ignoring them."

"We don't have a problem, thus there's nothing to ignore. Or solve." *Crunch, crunch, crunch* sounded like *lies, lies, lies* in his head. He thrust his chin in Mitch's direction, sitting on Dan's other side. He was still chatting with Alex's friend, as well as Cody, his best friend, who'd appeared from somewhere and was glaring holes into the side of Dan's head. "Cody doesn't seem to like you much."

Dan grunted, slicing off a small bite of French toast with his fork. "He's still mad at me for what I did to Mitch." He sounded resigned to that fact.

"What did you do to Mitch?" *And was it worse than what you did to me?*

Dan popped his forkful of French toast into his mouth, eyeing Ash over his fork. *None of your business*, his expression said.

Yeah, okay. That was fair. They weren't friends anymore and never would be. Why had Ash even come over here?

He ate some more maple syrup-drenched bacon. Man, this was good. Real maple syrup was the nectar of the gods. God bless Mitch for coming into his life and introducing him to it. He was never eating that fake crap again. Jemima was no aunt of his.

"Congratulations."

He almost didn't hear Dan over the crunch of bacon in his mouth. "For?"

"Making it to the NHL." Dan's smile was surprisingly sweet, making him look like the twenty-year-old Ash had known. Against his better judgment, Ash's heart softened toward him. "You made your dreams come true."

"I suppose I did. How about you? You must be making a mint off your woodworking business."

The smile fell off Dan's face. Ash nearly kicked himself for being the cause of his sudden turn from happy to . . . resigned? Sad? He couldn't tell.

"I, uh . . ." Dan swallowed hard and poked at the crumbs on his nearly empty plate. "I gave up woodworking a few years ago."

"You—What? Why? But you're so talented."

Dan had left Ash, done something to Mitch that had left Mitch's best friend still angry with him, *and* given up the one thing that he'd once told Ash made life at college bearable? His pride and joy and the thing that gave him purpose? Damn it. Ash *did* want to know what had happened six years ago for Dan to push away everything that meant anything to him.

But would it change anything between them?

No. He wanted to know to satisfy his own curiosity more than out of any obligation to clear the air between them.

Dan shrugged and averted his gaze. "It wasn't working out."

Yeah, there was definitely more to that story.

"I'm sorry to hear that. Really," he added when Dan's expression turned skeptical. "Your pieces were beautiful."

Their gazes caught and held, and for a moment, a very

brief second, Ash was six years younger and falling in love for the first time. The only time. The stomach-fluttering, pulse-racing, heart-hammering, weak-kneed kind of love he hadn't felt before or since.

And in that tiny brief second, he almost reached out to Dan, almost wrapped Dan's slimmer frame into his arms.

But he wasn't going there again. Wasn't going to let Dan reel him in with his adorable hair and charming smile. Although that charming smile had been in serious limited quantity over the past couple of days. In fact, Ash was almost certain he'd only seen it a couple of times, and it had lacked the spark it used to have.

Dan had never been the life of the party, never been outgoing or especially social, preferring his own company or that of his closest friends and family, but he'd been confident and happy and he'd known what he'd wanted.

What had happened to that guy to turn him into this shell of who he'd been?

Don't ask, don't ask, don't ask.

"Are you okay?" *You weren't supposed to ask!*

Dan picked at invisible lint on his pants, then set his plate underneath his chair before picking up his water glass from where it sat at his feet. Took a sip.

Stalling for time.

"You're the second person to ask me that today," he finally said, head turned toward Mitch.

Ash raised an eyebrow. If Mitch had noticed something was up with Dan—Mitch, who was usually too busy, too focused on what came next, to notice the little things—then something was definitely wrong. Dan's shoulders were stiff to the point of breaking. One brisk wind and *crack!* He'd break apart, right down the middle.

"Do you want to take a walk?"

Ash almost regretted the words, but Dan's entire body sagged with relief.

They stood, snagging Mitch's attention. "Where're you going?"

"I'm gonna show Dan the neighborhood."

"Yeah? Go to the burger place. They have the best butterscotch milkshakes!"

"That sounds pretty good, actually," Dan said as they went through the house and out the front door.

The burger place on Lakeshore, one street north of Toni's, was in what was considered Oakville's downtown. It was quaint, if one liked quaint. Ash was more or less indifferent about it. He wasn't picky about where he lived. As long he had a roof over his head, indoor plumbing, a California king, and a fridge with space to store enough food for a small country—or a hockey team—he was good. Oakville was as good as anywhere, although he wasn't convinced he could brave its winters. He'd lived through minus forty-degree weather in Syracuse and it had been hell. Or maybe the opposite of hell? A frozen hell.

He snorted at his oxymoron.

"What?" Dan asked.

They sat across from each other at a small table for two on the restaurant's front patio, which was itty-bitty. Honestly, Ash's shoulders took up half the space. Not to mention that it took up half the sidewalk. He and Dan might as well've been seated in the middle of the pedestrians.

It was a cloudless day, with a dry wind that broke yesterday's humidity. Not that Ash would've minded. He was born and raised in Florida—he could handle the heat. Dan's forehead was dotted with sweat, though.

Dan was looser, relaxed, a real smile on his face. The weight of the world—or whatever was bothering him—gone for the moment.

"Nothing," Ash replied, easing back in his seat. "Just making bad jokes in my head."

"Worse than yesterday's hockey fans?"

Ash released a huff of laughter. "So much worse."

"Tell me."

"Nah, that one was lame. I'll tell you another one, though. Why is the hockey rink hot after a game?"

Dan was already grinning at him, anticipating the joke. "Why?"

"Because all the fans have left!"

Laughter shook Dan's frame, creating tiny lines at the corner of his eyes that hadn't been there six years ago. "That's not funny."

"Made you laugh, though. Couldn't have been that bad."

"Maybe I'm an easy sell."

"Or you're lacking fun in your life."

"That's . . . a distinct possibility."

A buzzing sounded. Ash fished his cell phone out of his pocket and blanked the screen when he saw who it was.

"Do you need to get that?" Dan pushed his chair back. "I can give you some privacy."

Ash returned the phone to his pocket. "Don't worry about it. Nothing urgent. Just my agent."

"Your . . .?" Dan's eyebrows shot up. "Is that really a call you should be rejecting?"

"He'll still be at his desk tomorrow morning. The guy never sleeps. Besides, I don't work on vacation."

"Is this a vacation?"

"A mini one. How about you?"

"Well, I worked yesterday, so I wouldn't exactly call this a vacation."

THE NATURE OF THE GAME | 41

"I guess they're keeping you busy at the printer? Assuming you still work there."

Dan's face clouded, but before he could answer, a second buzz sounded. Dan this time.

"Mitch wants us to bring him back a butterscotch milkshake." He frowned at Ash. "Are they really as good as he says?"

"We're about to find out," Ash said, jerking his head in the direction of their server weaving her way between tables toward them, a tall glass filled with a golden frozen concoction in each hand.

"Jesus," he said after taking his first sip. "It's like sugar wrapped in sugar and infused with flavor."

Across from him, Dan's groan was scandalous. "Oh my god." He took a second sip. "This is amazing! It's heaven on Earth infused with sunshine and rainbows."

Ash laughed.

"You gonna finish yours?" Dan reached for Ash's glass despite his own nearly full one.

"Hey!" Ash hugged his milkshake to his chest. "Hands off, thief."

"You just said you didn't like it."

"I said it tasted like sugar straight from the Powerpuff Girls' asses, not that I didn't like it."

Dan chuckled and stirred his straw through his drink. "I missed your sense of humor."

"Dan—"

"Sorry, sorry." He raised a hand, placating. "You don't want to talk about it, I know. So let's talk about something else. Tell me something that's happened in the past six years."

Ash sipped his milkshake, hiding a wince at the sugariness that made his teeth hurt. What was he supposed to tell Dan? He didn't want to give Dan any part of himself. Didn't want to leave Dan an opening that he could later use to eviscerate him with. He'd been there, done that, had the heartless text to prove it.

He should get that made into a T-shirt. And then wear it everyday to remind himself why milkshakes with Dan were a bad idea.

His phone buzzed again, and he used the excuse this time to take a breather, a minute away from Dan's sad, pleading eyes. Pleading for what, Ash had no idea. But whatever it was, Ash wasn't going to give it to him.

He waved his phone. "I've gotta take this one. Excuse me a sec." Heading for a quiet corner of the restaurant, near the restrooms in the back, he answered the call with a glance over his shoulder at Dan, sitting slumped over the table, the weight of whatever was bothering him squarely on his shoulders once again. Even his enthusiasm over the milkshake was gone, deadened by what had been between them. "Hey, Scott."

"Ash! Finally." His agent's voice in his ear was loud. Scott didn't have an indoor voice. "I'm about to forward you the revised contract for the Select Yogurt commercials their marketing department wants to shoot in November. I'll need your thoughts on it by Tuesday, end of day."

Ash sighed and stared at a truly atrocious painting of a pear floating on a leaf. The hell was it supposed to represent?

"Ash?"

"Hm? No, I heard you. Tuesday's fine. Anything about the contract from my club yet?

"I'm still working on it."

The pear wasn't just floating on a leaf; it was melting into it. The hell was wrong with this restaurant?

"Ash?"

"Huh? Yeah, I'm here. Thanks, Scott. Keep me posted on that, and I'll read over the yogurt contract on the flight home tomorrow morning and get back to you on Tuesday."

"You do that."

They hung up, and Ash turned away from the creepy painting, sucking in a lungful of oxygen as he prepared himself to face Dan.

Only to find Dan standing at their table, tucking what looked like a receipt into his pocket. Their milkshakes had been transferred into to-go cups.

"Going somewhere?"

Dan startled. "Oh. Hi."

Had he been about to leave without saying anything? Ash scoffed. "Typical. Running off without so much as a goodbye."

Back stiffening, Dan straightened to his full five-ten height, eyes spitting fire. If that narrow-eyed expression woke something up inside Ash that had been buried for a long time, well . . .

He was only human.

"I wasn't *running*." The *you asshole* was implied. "I was making a strategic exit."

Ash opened his mouth. Closed it again. "How is that different?"

"Because I wasn't going to leave until you came back."

"Something wrong with my company?" Ash crossed his arms.

"No," Dan said, and his breathy laugh was bitter. "But there's obviously something wrong with mine."

They were attracting attention. Ash felt eyes on him from both the customers and passersby on the sidewalk. All he needed was to be recognized and have someone post a recording of his argument with Dan online.

If you could call what they were doing an "argument." Ash grabbed his milkshake and motioned for Dan to precede him out. He remembered seeing a small alleyway next to the restaurant, and he steered Dan there with a hand on his lower back.

"I'm sorry," Dan said as soon as they were alone.

"I don't—"

"You don't want to hear it." Dan's jaw ticked. "I know. But that's not what I'm sorry about."

"What else is there?"

"You hate me, I get that. I'm sorry I made you uncomfortable back there."

Ash scowled. "I don't *hate* you." He realized the scowl might say differently and smoothed out his features. Pleasant, yet distant. Too bad his eyebrows weren't cooperating this time. "And you didn't make me uncomfortable." What he *did* do was make Ash relive a period of his life he thought he'd set aside. Gotten over. Earmarked as *It was fun but it didn't work out.*

It annoyed him more than anything, mostly. Especially since, sometimes, usually in the middle of the night, Dan turned into *the one that got away*

"Sure you don't," Dan said, sarcasm dripping off his tongue. "Thank you for getting me out of the brunch. I needed to breathe. But . . ." His smile was so sad it might as well've been upside down. "This is all we need to see of each other. You don't have to put up with me anymore."

Ash's arms fell to his sides, Dan's words making him feel like he'd accidentally revealed that Santa Claus wasn't real. "Your brother and my best friend are in a committed relationship. I'm pretty sure we'll see each other again."

"Don't sound so thrilled by it."

"What do you want me to say, Dan?" Figuring some

honesty might not hurt, he said, "This isn't easy for me."

"And you think it's easy for me?"

"You're the one who walked!"

"I didn't have a fucking choice!"

"You—What?"

"Oh, but you don't want to hear about it." Dan's arms flailed, face a thunderstorm about to go off, body coiled to spring.

"Dan—"

"You know what the worst part is?" Quiet now, he closed his eyes and took a deep breath. "It's not that you hate me. I hate myself enough for the both of us. It's that everything I did was for nothing. I lost the two people who meant the most to me . . . for nothing." The last two words were harshly whispered, and when Dan's eyes opened—his light brown eyes that Ash had stared into so many times, that had stared back at him with love and friendship—they were soft and so full of regret that Ash found himself reaching for him. "Give this to Mitch, will you?" Dan handed Ash his milkshake and backed away. "I need to take a walk."

Before Ash could utter a word, Dan was swallowed up by the crowd.

It smelled crisp and cold and clean at the ice rink the Toronto team had rented out for this friendly match. Not the kind of clean that smelled like laundry detergent or Windex, but the kind that brought to mind Ash's childhood at the neighborhood rec center. He'd spent more time there than at his own home while growing up.

Ash took a deep breath and held it, savoring his favorite smell in the world. It didn't matter where he played—every arena smelled the same, with an underlying aroma of buttered popcorn and beer.

"Yager, you're on the wrong side." Alex poked him in the back of the knees with his hockey stick.

Ash pivoted on his borrowed skates. "Are we on opposite teams?"

Nine Toronto players had shown up for the game. Added to the Florida contingent, plus Mitch, they made an uneven seventeen, and rather than play Toronto versus Tampa, they'd intermingled.

"Yup," Alex said. "Too bad we don't have an extra player."

Ash scanned the stands but didn't see the face he both wanted and didn't want to see among the few spectators peppering the bleachers. There was Mitch's dad, Alex's mom, a few WAGs—wives and girlfriends. He cleared his throat. "Where's Dan? He could've been our extra player."

"At the airport. He flies home tonight."

Oh. Oh, *wow*. The stomach-sinking disappointment that flashed through him at the news was wholly unexpected and potent enough to buckle his knees.

What was *wrong* with him?

He shoved thoughts of Dan aside and focused on the here and now. "Who's refereeing?"

Alex gestured. "Cody."

To Ash's right, Mitch was poking the whistle in Cody's mouth. "How many people do you think have used this?"

Cody blew the whistle in Mitch's face. "I don't care. It's mine now."

"Hey, college boy!" one of the Toronto players called to Mitch. "You ready to play in the big leagues?"

"College boy." Mitch skated up to Alex and Ash, decked out in borrowed gear like the rest of the Florida guys, toothy grin making him look delirious and slightly unhinged. "That's me!"

"You on my team?" Ash asked him.

"Yup!"

Ash skated away and pointed his stick at Alex. "College boy and I are going to kick your ass."

"We'll see about that," Alex said. "I've got more men on my team."

"Oh, I see how it is." Mitch skated circles around Alex. "You need an extra player to win."

Alex pushed him away with his stick to Mitch's back. "Get on your own side of the ice, brat."

The game wasn't exactly ferocious. A bunch of guys who'd seen little—if any—ice time in at least a couple of months. Sunday night. Summer heat outside. It made them lethargic.

It was competitive, though. Mitch scored the first goal, a surprise to everyone except Alex and Ash, and Alex grinned at his boyfriend as if he'd just found the cure for cancer or invented a transporter or found out how to keep cling wrap from clinging to everything except the thing you wanted it to.

"College boy has some skill," Carlie said from where he was in net for Ash's team.

"That he does." One of the Toronto guys—Staples, the one who'd organized this game—eyed Mitch. "You want to go pro after college?"

"That's the plan!"

Ten minutes later, Alex stopped Mitch from scoring a second goal. "I hate you."

Alex waggled his eyebrows at him. "That wasn't what you said last night."

Ash couldn't help a surprised laugh. First, he'd never

heard Alex make a sex joke. And second, did they not care that the Toronto guys were *right there?* Seriously. Worst kept secret in the history of secret relationships.

What would he do if he fell in love with a guy while still in the NHL? Keep it a secret from the public until he retired, like Alex and Mitch? Come out? Was there some middle ground he hadn't thought of?

Not that it mattered anyway. He hadn't been in a serious relationship since his divorce, preferring instead to date casually as the mood struck. The last woman he'd dated had ended up falling for one of his teammates. Not that he'd been crushed or anything, but it had still been a blow to the good ol' ego. And it hadn't made him all that eager to jump back on that bandwagon. Besides, its wheels were broken and constantly veered him off course.

What the correct course was, he wasn't sure yet.

A whistle blew. "Hooking! Two minutes in the penalty box!" Cody yelled, pointing at Greer.

"What? I didn't do anything."

"Take it up with your coach."

Greer looked around as if their coach had flown here for this game, all the way from Florida. "He's not here."

"That's right!" Cody cackled. "I'm the king of the arena. Penalty box! Two minutes!"

"It's a community rink. There is no penalty box."

Cody huffed and waved a hand at the bleachers. "Just take a seat, will you?"

Grumbling, Greer did so.

Greer's penalty evened out the teams, and it lit a fire under the collective asses of the opposite team. Ash found himself having to wrestle the puck away from them more than once. The whistle blew with alarming frequency, trash talk ran wild, and Mitch grinned through it all like he'd been granted every wish he'd ever had.

They played for an hour, and after tying at 1-1, the Toronto guys took them out to a pub nearby for wings and Guinness.

"I'm innocent," Greer told Cody once they'd been seated. "Your eyes were playing tricks on you."

"Please. Give me some credit." Cody rolled said eyes. "I might not play, but I've been watching Mitch play since we were kids. I think I know a thing or two about hockey."

Ash was about to dive into their conversation when Staples said, "Your boyfriend has some mad skills."

Whipping his head around, Ash caught Alex with a stupid and sappy smile on his face as he looked at Mitch, who was too busy digging his license out of his wallet for the waiter to pay them any attention.

"Yeah," Alex said on a sigh.

"Dude." Ash couldn't help himself. "Do you have any sense of self-preservation?"

Alex shrugged and scratched his cheek. "It's just Staples."

"How do you know you can trust him?"

"Hey!" Staples said across from him. "I don't judge."

"Besides, it's not like I told Kinsey," Alex said, naming one of the guys on their team.

Ash grunted. "Kinsey's an asshole."

"That's what I'm saying."

"Hey!" Mitch punched Ash's arm. "What did you do to my brother, Yager?"

Man, Mitch had *no* idea what a loaded question that was. "Uh, what?"

"He didn't come back to Toni's until after everyone left and he was all . . ." Mitch waved a hand.

"All what?"

"Like . . ." Searching for a word, he looked to Alex.

"Taciturn."

"I was gonna say quiet, but that works too. What happened?"

"We had milkshakes," Ash said.

"And?"

Ash shrugged, shoulders brushing against Carlie's on his other side. These tables were tiny, and trying to cram seventeen hockey players into them meant sharing elbow space. "And nothing. He said he needed to take a walk." Not a lie, but not the whole story either.

Mitch slumped in his seat, drumming his fingers on the tabletop. "But why?"

Ash shrugged again. "Why didn't you ask him?"

"I did."

"And?"

"He said he needed to think."

"Give him some space to figure it out," Alex said, sitting back as their server reached around him to set their drinks on the table.

"But I want to help."

"Well, you and your brother both have the same bad habit of not asking for help when you need it, so you might just have to let him be."

"That's . . . okay yeah, that's true." Mitch smacked the table. "All the more reason for me to help!"

"Maybe he doesn't want your help," Ash piped in. He grabbed a handful of pretzels from the basket on the table and popped one in his mouth. Tried to anyway. It got stuck on his hand and ended up in his lap. All this talk of Dan was making his hands sweat and the man wasn't even here.

"Yeah," Alex said. "Maybe he wants to figure it out on his own." He winked at Mitch. "Like someone else I know."

Sighing, Mitch rested his forearms on the table and leaned forward, the fingers of one hand reaching toward Alex. "I just want him to be okay. I don't think he has been since . . ."

Since what? Ash mentally sent the question Mitch's way. *Since what? Finish the sentence!* Not that it was any of his business, and he wouldn't find out today anyway—Mitch changed the topic and started a friendly debate with Staples. But the fact that Dan had done something to Mitch—according to what he'd said yesterday, anyway—had Ash wondering if what Dan had done to *him* was related.

And he'd thought he didn't want to know. Ash stuffed another pretzel in his mouth. Turned out his curiosity was stronger than he'd thought.

FOUR

"**W**HEN YOU SAID YOU WERE TAKING ME TO your favorite pizza place, I expected an actual restaurant."

Ash inspected the food truck from the back of a long line. Considering they'd walked almost four blocks for it, it had better be the best pizza in existence.

"Trust me," Dan said when Ash voiced his thoughts. "You'll never be able to eat pizza from anywhere else again."

The food truck was a bright candy-apple red, with a red awning over the order window that extended out two feet. Across the front of the awning, *Frankie Joe's Pizza Truck* was written in white block letters. Underneath the order window was a wide rectangular shelf inset into the truck that held a dozen different beverage options, and next to it was a menu in a thick black frame.

Something bumped the top of Ash's head, and he glanced up to find the umbrella hovering mere centimeters above him.

"Sorry," Dan said, lifting it up higher.

"Here, let me hold it." Ash took it out of Dan's hands. "I'm taller, so it's easier."

"Rub it in that I'm short."

"You're not short. Just short*er*."

At five foot ten, Ash wouldn't call Dan short. But Ash was six foot four, so anyone who couldn't meet him eye to eye—which was most people—was short to him.

"You're right, you are short," he amended.

Dan only laughed. He moved closer to Ash, stepping out of the way of a crowd edging by him. Ash repositioned the umbrella so it covered him better.

When they'd met, Dan had been pale and wan, wide-eyed at every small movement of the elevator car. It'd taken over an hour to get rescued, and Dan had spent the first ten minutes of his freedom sitting on the lip of the fountain in front of their office building, just breathing. He didn't handle small spaces well, he'd said, as Ash sat with him and they'd squinted at pedestrians hustling by in the midday sun.

Today he was alert, settled in his own skin, dressed in black dress pants, a white dress shirt paired with a black-and-white polka dot tie, with a light-green V-neck sweater to complete the outfit. He looked every inch the New York City businessman. Ash, in comparison, in his jeans and T-shirt topped with a fitted shirt, sleeves rolled up to the elbows, looked like he belonged in a college classroom.

"What kind of pizza should I get?" he asked. They moved forward in line, the rain *plop, plop, plopping* onto the top of the umbrella. It was cozy underneath it. Not un-comfortably so. Dan's body was warm against his where it brushed against his left side. He was slim and fit with a swimmer's body—or a runner. His light brown eyes were bright and his curly hair was made even curlier by the damp weather. Curly bordering on frizzy. Cute.

"You a meat eater?" Dan asked.

Ash shot him a disbelieving side-eyed glance he hoped conveyed *Are you freakin' kidding me?*

Dan grinned. "How about spicy foods?"

A second disbelieving glance.

"Then the hot chicken, definitely. Spiced chicken, hot

peppers, hot sauce."

Ash might've drooled. "You're speaking my language."

"I'll have to make you my Thai chicken curry one day. I learned the recipe from one of my friends at Columbia. She's an international student from Thailand, so it's the real deal."

"Columbia." Ash whistled lowly, impressed. "Fancy."

Dan's thin-lipped smile didn't reach his eyes. "Yeah. Hey, we're up."

Don't talk about school. Got it. Ash wasn't stupid—he could read body language.

Ash ordered a slice of the hot chicken, Dan got four cheese, and they added on a basket of fries *and* a basket of mozzarella sticks—because they were growing boys and needed it—plus a soft drink each to wash everything down. It was wet everywhere, and the rain was still coming down. Not in sheets, but steadily. They found a bench tucked under a tree just beginning to sprout spring leaves that was a tiny bit less wet than everything else. They perched on the very edge, juggling trays and baskets of food.

Sitting underneath the umbrella, the raindrops cast gentle shadows across Dan's face, making him appear ethereal and soft. Something tilted in Ash's chest, making the world fuzzy and sweet.

"Here." Dan tore his slice in half—tried to, anyway, cheese getting everywhere—and handed it to Ash. "So you can try another flavor."

"Nice. Thanks, man." Ash held his slice out to Dan. "Take some of this."

Their pizzas divided and shared, Ash finally took a bite of the hot chicken. "Oh, man," he said, umbrella in one hand, pizza in the other. "You were right. My mouth is on fire. It's awesome."

"See why it's my favorite pizza place?"

"You've ruined me for all other pizzas."

"Mission accomplished, then."

"The day I moved to Syracuse," Ash said around a french fry, "I was so tired after two days of driving that I couldn't be bothered to cook dinner. Didn't have much in the way of groceries anyway, and I couldn't find my pans, so I ordered from this pizza place around the corner. I was so hungry that I'd eaten half the pie before I realized it was disgusting."

Dan chuckled and dipped a mozzarella stick into a small container of marinara sauce. "And here I thought you couldn't mess up pizza."

"You'd be surprised. Tasted like cardboard run over by a muddy tire."

Dan's shoulders shook with laughter. Ash liked his smile, the way it thinned his bottom lip, highlighted his cheekbones, and wrinkled his nose.

"I tried making a cauliflower crust for pizza once," Ash said, because he wanted to see Dan smile more, "but I must've done something wrong because the crust came out limp and mushy."

"I tried making one too! And it turned out the same way. Maybe we were using the same recipe."

"Well, they do say cauliflower crust is hard to make."

Dan ate a fry. "Who's they?"

"Everyone who's a better cook than us?"

"We should tag team it," Dan suggested. "Maybe with two of us, we won't fuck it up."

"That's the best idea I've heard all day. How about this Saturday?"

"Sold." They fist-bumped under the umbrella handle, and when their eyes met, attraction flared to life in Ash's sternum.

FIVE

THE BUILDING DAN HAD ONCE USED AS A WORKSHOP in the backyard of his childhood home in the Hamptons was incredibly dusty. Way dustier than he'd left it. That being said, he hadn't stepped inside the space in six years. Dust thick enough to swallow was to be expected.

Having missed the scent of wood and varnish, he sucked in a breath . . .

And promptly coughed on a lungful of dust. Jesus.

Setting aside his newly purchased materials, he surveyed the room.

Honestly? He was having trouble believing his mother hadn't turned it into something else.

There were a handful of elegant buildings on the property. A pool house. A mother-in-law cottage. A shed for gardening tools. A second shed for storing patio furniture in the winter. A third for sporting and outdoor equipment, like Mitch's damaged or too-small hockey equipment, a handful of old crazy carpets, skis, bicycles, and a skateboard from Mitch's elementary school days. A two-car garage that was never used; there was a four-car garage attached to the house. And Dan's sixteen- by twenty-four-foot workshop with twelve-foot high vaulted ceilings.

It was stifling, the heat oppressive. He tried the window fan. Out of commission, unsurprisingly. The windows were unexpectedly clear of spiderwebs, so he opened one up. Then he headed for the double doors at the far end, opening them to the covered porch, letting in the summer evening breeze.

He'd missed his workshop. A space that had been all his ever since his dad had it built for him in his freshman year of high school. His tools, his ideas, his projects.

The small size of the workshop had never impeded his workflow. The vaulted ceiling and double doors made maneuvering materials easy, and the covered porch extended his work area when he worked with long stock. There were two aisles lengthwise and three widthwise, allowing easy access to the tools that hung on pegs on the walls. The radial-arm saw, jointer, bandsaw, and sander were all on wheeled bases in case they needed to be moved. A cluttered corner made efficient use of the precious wall space—carving tools and chisels in a cabinet on the right; stains, paints, and varnishes in a cabinet on the left; pull-out boxes containing screws, nails, bolts, and hinges; and sanders, drillers, and other accessories tucked into wood compartments bolted to the wall. Racks built into another section of the wall stored sheet goods and boards. Underneath, a portion of the wall swung out, revealing yet more storage for sheet goods.

Dan went over to the desk in the back left corner of what he'd once considered his office, and as he sat in the old leather chair, a cloud of dust billowed around him. Waving it away, he picked up the sketch pad lying on the desk, open to a drawing of a sun-shaped sun catcher with a stained glass center. The last idea he'd drawn during what he'd come to think of as The Summer of Ash. It had also been the last time he'd entered this building.

Also on the desk were drawing pencils, a reference

book about different types of wood, a printed sheet of paper listing local glass workers, and an empty water jug and plastic cup, all sitting there as if waiting for him to come back and pick up where he'd left off.

"Six years late," he said to the dust and wood and tools. But at least he was here.

If Mitch could take back his life, so could Dan.

To be fair, though, Mitch had never had to take back his life. He'd known what he wanted for a long time, had set himself achievable goals, and then powered through them with the force of an elephant stampede. And with about as much grace. But he'd done it. And he'd done most of it on his own too.

Dan flopped back in his chair, early evening sun streaming through the windows, highlighting clusters of dust and previously invisible dust bunnies in the corners. He needed to channel Mitch's ambition and determination, his fearlessness and grit, and stampede through his own damn goals.

Except . . . He wasn't sure what those were. He'd spent so long doing what other people told him to, and it had become habit to go with the flow rather than make his own decisions.

Columbia University: his mother's preferred choice of colleges for him to attend.

Business and accounting: his mother's chosen majors.

His old college apartment in Herald Square: one of a handful of apartments owned by Westlake Waterless Printing for visiting board members or other high value stakeholders.

Westlake Waterless Printing: his mother's company.

The last decision he'd made for himself was six years ago, and look how that had turned out. All he knew for sure right now was that he wanted Ash back in his life, and for more than the infrequent occasions where they *might* run into each other thanks to Mitch and Alex. How did he do that when they lived in different states, and when Ash didn't want to bring up their past?

To be determined.

And he wanted to build things again. He missed working with his hands, creating something from nothing, the sense of satisfaction that came with completing a piece. Most of all he missed the headspace he entered and lived in while working with wood. That quiet place that made his problems seem insignificant. The silence that allowed him to see clearly. To breathe. To center himself.

Standing, he went over to the front of his workshop and hauled his new materials to the workbench in the center.

"Why do you still work for Westlake if you hate your job?" Mitch had asked him when he'd finally returned to Toni's after wandering around aimlessly for an hour after leaving Ash at the burger place.

"I don't hate my job," he'd countered. He wasn't the math genius Mitch was, but he was nevertheless gifted with numbers. Numbers made sense. One plus one always equaled two. The answer to a problem was either correct or it wasn't. There was no gray area, no guesswork, no frills.

"You don't exactly like it either, though," Mitch had said.

"No, but it's . . . comfortable."

"Comfortable?" Mitch had scoffed. "That's not a reason to stay."

It wasn't. But Dan wasn't about to quit his job without a fallback plan. And without a fallback plan—even an inkling of one—quitting his job seemed very far away.

"I would've quit right away and burned bridges on my

way out," Mitch had added.

That might've been true, but it wasn't who Dan was. Quitting wouldn't inconvenience his mom; she was at the top of the food chain. It would, however, inconvenience Dan's boss and the rest of their team. If Dan suddenly upped and left without giving a two weeks' notice, his work would fall on the shoulders of the already overworked junior analysts. That wasn't fair to anyone.

The vibration of the electric hand saw traveled into his hand and up his arm, the *whir, whir, whir* of it cutting through wood filling his small workshop. Wood shavings and chips flew in every direction, landing on the floor, striking the wall opposite, pinging against his safety glasses, settling on his cheeks and lips. He'd only cut through one sheet of wood and already his jeans and T-shirt, topped with a thick, multi-pocketed leather apron, were a mess.

He did an awful foot shuffle happy dance and grinned at nothing.

A delicate throat cleared near the open double doors, nearly ruining his good mood. His mother stood on the porch in a breezy fuchsia top with a beaded collar tucked into a pair of flowy white pants. Her brown hair was knotted into some kind of complicated twist thing at the base of her skull, and her flats were studded with rhinestones.

Greta Westlake was never anything except perfectly put together.

She took a delicate step inside, tentative, as if stepping on glass. Dan got a little thrill knowing her pristine outfit was about to become a little less shiny. Okay, he got a big thrill. Yes, he was that petty.

Lacing her hands together, she stood just over the threshold, lips pressed in a tight line. "I didn't expect to see you tonight," she said. "How was your trip? Visiting friends, was it?"

"Uh-huh." So he'd lied about the purpose of his trip, so what? She didn't know about Mitch and Alex, and Mitch wanted to keep it that way. "It was good, thanks." He made a mark on his sheet with a pencil.

"I hope your first day back to work after a vacation wasn't too stressful."

She said that like he hadn't spent many a working week-end since he'd started interning straight out of high school.

"It was fine," he said. If by *fine* he meant *distracted*. By Ash. By how he'd left things between them yesterday morn-ing. And six years ago. That was twice he'd walked away now. He wouldn't blame Ash if the man never spoke to him again, but he hoped that wouldn't be the case.

Except he didn't even have Ash's phone number, so what was the point in hoping for anything?

His mother cleared her throat again. Bent over his workbench, Dan glanced up with a quirked eyebrow. "Something I can help you with?"

She rubbed the thumb and index finger of one hand together like she'd touched something rotten. "Grace in HR mentioned that you put in for a transfer to the Burlington, Vermont, office."

"It's not a transfer." He tucked his pencil behind his ear and dug into his apron for a measuring tape. "I'll just be working out of there for a couple of weeks."

"Is there something wrong with the Manhattan office that's making you run all the way to Vermont?"

Run. Ash had accused him of running too.

"Not at all." The windows across from him gave him a direct line of sight to the house, a big, ugly, gothic mon-strosity. Just looking at it made his throat clog with the des-peration to leave. He should get blinds for that window.

Pursing her lips, his mother tucked an errant strand of hair back into her knotted twist thing. "You're still angry with me."

"That surprises you?" Anger was much too tame a word for what he felt. He wasn't sure there was a word out there for the emotion that was so far beyond *anger* that Dan couldn't see the way back.

"I was only doing what I thought was best for you and your brother."

Dan's knuckles whitened on the measuring tape. "No, you were doing what was best for you."

"That's not true."

"No? Then tell me how blackmailing me was supposed to help anyone? If you were trying to alienate both your sons, then congratulations. You succeeded."

Her eyes flashed. "Mitch was never supposed to find out about our deal. We agreed."

Mitch was never supposed to find out. Which made Dan what? The expendable son? "You broke our deal when you took his tuition away even though I did what you asked. I had every right to tell him. I should've told him years ago."

His mother took another careful step into the room. The lines bracketing her eyes and mouth were more pronounced than he remembered.

"It was my grandfather's dream that the company remain in the family," she said quietly, almost dreamily, her gaze distant and . . . Dan would've said yearning. It was possibly the softest he'd ever seen her look.

"So you've said." Many times since he was a kid.

Her gaze went unfocused for a second. Then her spine firmed and her hands jerked into fists. "When do you leave for Vermont?"

Dan considered calling her on the change of topic but

couldn't be bothered. He wanted to get back to making stuff. "Two weeks from now."

"And after that? You'll return here?"

"I don't know. Maybe I'll try another one of our offices." He'd try them all if he had to, until he found the one he liked best. Anything to get him out of Manhattan.

"Should I assume you're heading to Burlington because it's the office nearest your brother?" No hint of remorse, of compassion, in her eyes.

"You can assume whatever you want," he said. Coldness enveloped him, seized him, but it melted away as she nodded and left his workshop. Through the window, Dan watched her stride purposefully toward the house, head high and shoulders back.

Maybe, by moving three hundred miles away to another state, he might finally be able to breathe.

SIX

THE TRY OUT CENTER FOR YOUTH WAS A SQUAT, square, one-story building in downtown Tampa. Affiliated with Ash's NHL organization, the center relied primarily on donations and volunteers to keep the place running. Ash had been volunteering here for years, as had many of his teammates.

Try Out was a fully functional facility providing sport and recreational programs to underprivileged and at-risk kids. There was an ice rink, a swimming pool, a large gym that could be divided into thirds, a small workout room, an art classroom, a music room, and a lounge that sold soft drinks and candy out of vending machines. Despite the crap pay, most of the staff were here because they wanted to make a difference.

Ash had never needed a place like Try Out. His dad was an engineer; his mom, a lawyer. Growing up, he'd been lucky and had never wanted for anything. He could understand, though, how people like Alex Dean—whose dad left when he was a kid, leaving his mom alone to make ends meet—would benefit from a center like this.

Peeling paint curled from the walls; the benches of the workout equipment were ripped, revealing the foam padding; the sports equipment was dirty and nicked and smelly; some of the musical instruments were out of tune; the art room had water marks from last year's burst pipe;

and the couch in the lounge smelled vaguely of curry. No matter its state, to the kids who came here every day, it was a refuge, a hangout, and a learning establishment all rolled into one.

The neighborhood rec center Ash had spent most of his youth in was similar except for one glaring difference: whereas Ash's old stomping ground was shiny and polished and sparkly and politely declared *We cater to money*, Try Out screamed *DONATE NOW!*

Most afternoons there were half a dozen classes going on and a dozen kids completing homework in the lounge. On the days that Ash or one of his teammates showed up, the kids dropped their homework like moldy potatoes, commandeered half the ice rink—which, most days, was open for free skate since the center had yet to find a skating instructor or hockey coach—and held themselves a scrimmage. Those nights were also ones where reporters and bloggers tended to show up, because NHL players giving back to their community was good publicity.

It annoyed the fuck out of Ash—these kids deserved to have fun without a lens scrutinizing their every action—yet he understood that it was also good publicity for a center that desperately needed funding.

Who said he couldn't be annoyed and grateful at the same time? As Mitch would've said, he was annoyful.

Ash snickered to himself as his players passed the puck back and forth. They were technically in overtime, and man, were they making it count.

"Two more minutes!" he shouted.

"Aw, come on, Coach."

"Yeah, Coach. We're having fun."

"You think I can't see what you're doing?" Ash did the universal *I'm watching you* sign: two fingers pointed to his own eyes, then to his team. "Prolonging the inevitable so you don't have to finish your math?"

"I don't know what you're talking about, Coach."

"Yeah, we finished our homework already."

"We did math first, 'cause it's the worst. Hey, that rhymes!"

Ash hopped up to sit on the wall. "Do you know how many times I could've scored on Grant? He leaves his left side wide open."

"What?" Grant turned his head toward him. "I do?"

The puck sailed past him.

"Hey! No fair, I wasn't paying attention."

"Not my problem, dirtbag."

"Assface."

"Fucktard."

As insults went, they could use some work.

"Butthead."

"Faggot."

"Whoa!" Ash jerked to attention and hopped off the wall, holding up a hand to halt the retreat off the ice. "I don't *ever* want to hear that word again."

Ten pairs of eyes suddenly found the ice very interesting.

"Next person who says it is banned from the ice for the rest of the year."

He expected pushback. To his surprise, he got nods and a few mumbled "Okay, Coach," and "Sorry, Coach" as the kids filed off the ice. Grant trailed them, neck and face crimson, jaw working, shoulders curled inward. Ash held a hand out to him as he passed by but didn't touch—he'd seen some of these kids cower from a friendly hug.

"You okay?"

"Fine." Head bent, Grant stalked past.

Sighing, Ash headed into the lobby, where he found

Teri, the center's director, manning the front desk. Somewhere in her forties with sun-kissed Florida skin and blonde hair cut in what Ash would call a boy cut but that he'd once heard referenced to as a pixie cut, Teri reminded him of a no-nonsense principal who was cool yet stern.

"Hey, Ash. I didn't know you were here. That explains why the lounge was empty."

"Yeah, we just played a friendly game." He left out the not-so-friendly *faggot*. "Listen, I wanted to talk to you about the ice skates. I noticed some of the ones the kids were wearing are starting to fall apart. Are new ones in the budget this fiscal?"

Teri blew out a breath that ruffled her bangs. "Nope. Are they that bad?"

"They could be worse."

"Why do I feel like you're hedging?"

Because he totally was. "If I gave you a check, would you use it to buy new skates?"

"Honestly, I'd probably use it to pay bills and my staff."

Ash had heard about the difficulties of balancing costs too many times from Teri. Donors wanted their contributions to go toward programs, but those programs couldn't be run without incurring administrative costs—air conditioning and lighting and rent and taxes and salaries. Annual reports were apparently a charity's worst nightmare.

"Bills and salaries are important too." He rapped his knuckles on the countertop. "I'll bring in a check next time I come in."

"You're an angel, Ash. I swear, your team is keeping this place running."

"That's the idea. I'll see you next week."

He was steps away from the door when a tentative "Mr. Ash?" reached his ears.

Turning, he found Grant hovering behind him, a ratty backpack slung carelessly over one shoulder. Behind Grant, Teri was typing away at the computer, and behind *her* was one of the writers for one of the more popular sports blogs, *Sport Check,* her heels *click clacking* loudly on the tiled floor. She paused near the front desk and fished through her car-sized purse.

"It's just Ash, Grant." He was Coach during games and Ash the rest of the time. The kids had come up with that themselves and it never failed to make him smile.

Grant's nod was stiff. "I just wanted to say thanks for what you did back there." He waved toward the rink.

"I'm sorry it happened in the first place. Hopefully it won't happen again, but let me know if it does."

"I don't think it will." Grant smiled shyly. "I think you put the fear of God into them."

Ash chuckled.

Grant bit his lip, then blurted, "I get teased like that at school sometimes. That word . . . it's actually one of the nicer ones they use."

Jesus. Ash's stomach dropped.

"It's not always easy to ignore it."

"That how you got the shiner?"

Shrugging, Grant kicked his toes against the floor, little *squeak squeak squeak*s harsh in the quiet lobby. "Sometimes fighting is the only way to get them to stop."

"I've found that if you're comfortable in your own skin, the slurs get easier to tolerate. If you believe in yourself, nobody can take that away from you." Was it him or did he sound like a trite greeting card?

Head cocking, Grant's eyes narrowed. "I don't under . . . Are you . . .? Wait, are you saying you're gay too?"

The reporter, having finally found her keys, froze.

"No," Ash said.

"Oh." The kid's shoulders slumped.

And Ash had a choice here: take the easy way or brave the hard way. The decision should've been difficult. Not only that, but there was no one in his life right now to come out for—*don't think about Dan.* But how many kids like Grant were out there, bullied at school for who they were? How many kids were out there excelling in sports but afraid to go pro because of the traditional homophobia in professional sports? Would he himself have felt more comfortable acting on his attraction to men if he had someone in professional sports to look up to while growing up?

Maybe.

In the end, the decision took less than a second to make.

"I'm bisexual."

The reporter dropped her keys.

Grant stood straighter.

Teri's mouth hung open.

On his way to his car, Ash pulled out his cell phone and called his team's senior manager of media relations. "I think I may have done something stupid."

He didn't have time to think about it, though.

"The Category 1 hurricane currently over the western Caribbean Sea has shifted direction due to a high pressure system over Bermuda and is now tracking northwestward into the Gulf of Mexico," said the weather lady. Ash sat on a barstool in his kitchen and gaped at the television. "Strong winds on Great Swan Island threaten to turn the storm into a Category 3 hurricane by late tomorrow afternoon.

Experts say it will have reached Category 5 status by the time it makes landfall in Western Florida later this week. Evacuation orders have been issued for the following counties . . ."

"Jesus." He'd kept an eye on the storm since it'd developed, just like every other Floridian in its path, watching it go from a tropical storm to a Category 1 hurricane. And now this.

His pending coming out temporarily relegated to the back burner—there were much bigger things to deal with—he found his phone and dialed his mom.

When was the last time Tampa Bay saw a major hurricane? Not in Ash's lifetime, although he'd survived a handful of tropical storms.

"Hi, sweetie!"

"Hey, Mom. Have you been watching the news?" He headed over to the floor-to-ceiling doors that opened up onto his patio. Outside, the sky was a cloudless blue. Hard to imagine a hurricane was headed their way.

"No, why? Did you receive an award? Did I miss it? Why didn't you tell me?"

Ash chuckled. That was his mom: his number one fan. "No, but someday maybe."

"It'll happen one day soon."

"Don't I know it? I'm a good player." Better than good, which was why it didn't make sense that they were two weeks into September, two games into the preseason, and his club hadn't offered him a new contract yet. And he'd played like an asshole at training camp last weekend too. The good kind of asshole. Yes, that was a thing. "But no, that's not why I'm calling. Hillsborough County is under mandatory evacuation."

"The storm?"

"The storm is going to be a Category 5 hurricane by the time it reaches us."

"Category 5?"

"Can you head to Aunt Georgia's?"

Aunt Georgia lived in Tallahassee, and according to a quick Google search on his laptop, the hurricane wouldn't reach that far north.

"Sammy and I can leave tomorrow morning." Sammy was her Pomeranian. "But what about my apartment?"

"Pretty sure you live in one of the reinforced buildings, but I'll come by after you leave and board the windows up from the inside, just in case." He'd need to board up his own place too. At least his mom was on the tenth floor of a high rise. Ash looked out at his white-stoned patio, stone fire pit encircled by a stone bench, iron patio furniture, and outdoor cooking area, complete with oven, stove, sink, and BBQ, and called himself ten times the fool for buying a ground floor condo. He fully expected to return to find his home in ruins. At least his building's storage unit was on the sixth floor in a windowless room. Anything he stored there would survive the hurricane as long as the storm surge didn't reach that high.

Did his insurance cover hurricane damage?

"What about your game this Thursday?" his mom asked.

He rubbed a hand over his face. His third preseason game would have to be rescheduled; there wasn't any way around it. "I haven't thought that far. I'm sure there's a plan." A plan that was most likely outlined in the player documentation he'd received when he'd first joined the team. The club's version of an employee handbook. If only he knew what he'd done with his copy.

"What about Laura?"

Ash scowled at the mention of his ex-wife. "What about her?"

"Who's going to board up her apartment?"

How was that Ash's problem? "Her boyfriend?"

"She's single." He could just picture his mom waving a hand in dismissal.

"Okay?"

"Maybe you could offer to help?"

"You want me to offer help to the woman who cheated on me? Mom, Laura and I haven't spoken since the divorce." Four years ago, to be exact. "She has other people in her life who can help her. And who says she needs help, anyway?"

"Could you please just give her a call, make sure she doesn't need anything?"

"No. Why is Laura my problem all of a sudden?" Harsh maybe, but he didn't particularly care.

"Do it for your mother?"

Ash leaned his forehead against the countertop and sighed. "I hate when you play the mom card. It's not fair."

"I don't know what makes you think life's fair. You certainly didn't get that from me."

They were both divorced and single. "Life certainly seems to have it in for us."

His mom scoffed. "Pah! I don't know what you're talking about. I quite enjoy my life. In fact, I recently joined a singles travel group. They vacation together twice a year. I'm going to Las Vegas with them in October."

A *singles* group? Ash shuddered. Ew. "That's more information than I ever wanted to know about you."

"It's not *that* kind of group."

"Uh-huh. When did you start talking to Laura again, anyway?"

"I haven't, not really. We bumped into each other at the

grocery store a couple weeks ago and had a bit of a chat."

A bit of a chat with his mom could last several hours.

They hung up shortly after, Ash agreeing—with much reluctance born out of lingering anger and resentment—to call Laura.

But first he called Alex.

"We have to *evacuate?* How does one evacuate a whole city?"

"It's not just the city," Ash corrected, logging onto his email. "It's eight different counties."

"Jesus."

"Yeah, that's what I said."

"The club's probably got a contingency plan for something like this, right?" The sound of papers rustling reached Ash's ears. "Hang on, I've got the papers here somewhere."

"At least you know where your player's handbook is."

"You can thank Mitch for that. He organized my files over the summer."

Ash couldn't think of anything more boring. Except maybe *Star Wars: Episode I.* "Why?"

"Because he's Mitch and disorganization makes him crazy. Oh, here we go. Page 211." It sounded as if he was reading off a table of contents. "Honestly, I can't believe there's that many pages in this thing."

"Hey, wait." At the top of Ash's unread emails was one from Heather Arnold, the club's business operations manager. "Check your emails. There's a message from Heather."

A message announcing that the club had secured a private jet to transport players and their families—including significant others, kids, and pets, as well as parents, siblings, cousins, aunts, uncles, grandparents, and anyone else who fell under the heading *family*, including cousins twice removed—to Nashville, where the club had also secured rooms at a hotel, *and* organized a friendly game with the Nashville team on Friday afternoon. Their Thursday evening game would be rescheduled to a later date.

"Do we have to go?" Alex asked after a pause where they both read over the email.

"You can't stay here. That's suicide." Ash hoped there was enough of *you dummy* in his tone for Alex to grasp how stupid an idea it was to remain in the city.

"No, I know that." Alex's tone certainly had enough of *I'm not stupid, you asshole* for Ash to grasp *that*. "I mean, can I organize my own transport and go elsewhere?"

"Oh. I don't see why—"

"Here it is," Alex interrupted. "Scroll down to the bottom of Heather's email. 'Please let me know by Tuesday at noon if you would like a spot on the plane, and for how many,'" he read. "'If you've arranged your own transportation out of the city, please send me the information, ie: flight number or anticipated driving route, as well as the address of where you'll be staying.'"

Tap, tap, tap as Alex typed on his keyboard.

"What are you doing?" Ash asked absentmindedly, mulling over his various options. He could go to his Aunt Georgia's with his mom, he supposed, but Aunt Georgia smelled like mothballs and lemon-scented furniture polish and preferred the company of her beast of a cat rather than that of actual humans.

"Searching for flights to—"

"Burlington," they finished together.

Ash rolled his eyes. "Of course you are."

"What are you going to do?"

What *was* he going to do? Aunt Georgia was officially out, mothballs and all. And as much appeal as a friendly game with the Nashville team held, he didn't really want to spend a handful of days with his teammates and their families. He loved the guys—most of them anyway, no names mentioned, cough cough, Kinsey, cough cough—but he saw them enough as it was.

He could go to his dad's in New York City, but the city held too many memories he wasn't in the mood to revisit.

"Can I come with you? I've never been to Vermont in the fall." Or ever. Semantics.

"It's not technically fall yet," Alex pointed out. "I found a flight that leaves Wednesday afternoon. I'll book it for both of us if you're sure you want to come with me."

"I'm in."

That'd leave Ash the rest of today, all day tomorrow, and Wednesday morning to hurricane-proof his condo and his mom's apartment. It'd have to do. They had to get out ahead of the storm that was coming Friday morning whether they wanted it to or not.

"You'll have to find a place to stay, though," Alex was saying. "Unless you want to sleep on Mitch and Cody's couch." Mitch and Cody attended Glen Hill College in Glen Hill, Vermont, about an hour southeast of Burlington, as Ash understood it.

"Will it fit me?" he asked.

"Not unless you want your feet hanging over the end."

"Can you send me a list of hotels?"

"In Glen Hill?" Alex's voice *dripped* disbelief. Ash could've caught it in his hands had they been in the same room. "There aren't any hotels in Glen Hill, but there's at least half a dozen B&B's. I'll send you the name of the one my mom stayed at when she used to visit me."

Alex had studied at Glen Hill College too before graduating and starting his career on Ash's team. It was how Alex and Mitch had met—Alex had been speaking at a lecture series at the school last fall, and Mitch had been in the audience.

Next on Ash's list of phone calls? Laura, she of the *I didn't mean to sleep with him.*

"So, what?" he'd asked her when she'd told him about the extracurricular activities she'd participated in while he was out of town for away games. "You tripped over his dreamy eyes, your underwear got caught on his man hands, and your vagina accidentally landed on his dick?"

"Why do you have to be so brash?" Her brown eyes had flashed fire. Fire that had initially attracted him to her. They'd argued about *everything,* and it had been so completely contrary to what he'd had with Dan, whose brush off had still smarted several months later when he'd met Laura, that it had been welcome, and more than that, wanted. He'd wanted to fight. He'd wanted to argue. He'd wanted someone who would fight back.

He'd wanted someone who would fight for him, but apparently that wasn't in the cards.

Ash thumped his forehead against the countertop once, twice, three times. Fuck Laura for showing up at the same grocery store as his mom. Fuck his mom for guilting him into this.

Actually no, not fuck his mom. She was, in truth, the best mom ever and was only looking out for someone she thought needed help. He was the sap who'd fallen for her do-it-for-your-mother trap.

So fuck him for being a good son. There.

"Just do it, you stupid asshole." He could rep for Nike's evil alter ego.

"Ash?" Laura's voice was smooth, holding a hint of uncertainty as she answered.

For no reason he could explain, Ash had expected to

get her voicemail. He'd thought he was still angry with her, but hearing her voice after so many years made him realize that all he felt for her was . . . a whole lot of nothing. No anger. No resentment. No sense of betrayal or abandonment or failure. The emotional wounds she'd caused still lingered, might always linger, but his feelings for the cause of those wounds had disappeared.

Huh.

Must mean he was growing as a person.

Or that running into Dan had put his feelings for Laura into perspective. Because he definitely didn't feel a whole lot of nothing for Dan. What he felt was a whole lot of something, although he still didn't know quite what that was.

"Is everything okay?" she asked.

"Yeah." Ash rubbed his eyes. He might feel nothing for her, but that didn't mean he was especially excited to talk to her. He'd rather poke his eye out with a used hockey stick. "Just wondering if you need any help boarding up your apartment before you leave?"

"Am I going somewhere?"

Which was how he found himself explaining, for the third time, about the evacuation. Was nobody paying attention to the news?

"Well, shit. I have concert tickets for this Friday. Guess that's getting canceled," she grumbled. "I'll see if I can find a flight to Syracuse, I guess. Visit my parents." They'd met in Syracuse when Ash had still been playing for the AHL team there, gotten married, and moved to Tampa shortly after when he'd been sent up to the NHL, where they'd divorced not long after that.

"That's great," Ash said. *But it wasn't what I asked.* "Do you need help or not?"

"Well, since you offered so graciously . . ." He didn't need to see her eye roll to know there was one.

He waited her out, refusing to be baited.

"I could use the help, yes." Said with so much reluctance, he almost rescinded the offer. "Thank you." So grudging.

The laugh tickling the back of his throat was so unexpected he almost let it loose. "I'll be there Wednesday morning."

"Where are you evacuating to?"

"Vermont."

"Why?" He could picture her button nose wrinkling. "What's in Vermont?"

None of your business. "Trees."

"Trees. Really? You don't have to be sarcastic about it."

"Who's being sarcastic? There are trees in Vermont. Look it up." Still sitting within reach of his laptop, he did exactly that to ensure there were actually trees in Vermont, and—hey! Look at that. There was even a fall foliage season that typically started in mid-September. Maybe he'd get to see the leaves change colors. Cool.

"Wouldn't it make more sense to go to your dad's? There's probably way more to do in NYC than in Vermont."

Now he wanted to go to Vermont for entirely different reasons. "I like Vermont," he said, even though he'd never been.

"Okay." She said it like *You're an idiot*, but he let it bounce off him. The only opinions he cared about were his parents', his coaches, and his teammates. "I'll see you Wednesday, then?"

"Yup. Early. Sevenish. I'm flying out that afternoon."

"You could come tomorrow."

"I still need to fix up my place and my mom's."

"I see. I'm third on your list."

"Did you expect any different?"

She was no doubt seething. Ask him if he cared. He wasn't doing this for her.

"Of course not," she said, voice mocking. "I've always been third on your list, right below your parents and hockey. I'd actually insert your teammates into third and place myself below them."

That was true and something they'd argued about ferociously when they'd been together, but that he'd denied at the time.

He rubbed his eyes. "I'm not getting into it again with you, Laura. I'll see you Wednesday morning. Let me know if you change your mind."

Hanging up, he stored his laptop away and got started on hauling his patio furniture and any loose pieces of backyard decor—potted plants, decorative rocks, the fugly gnome his mom had a particular affinity for—to the sixth floor.

SEVEN

HE'D FORGOTTEN HOW MUCH BEING IN LAURA'S presence made him itch, like hundreds of hornets buzzing under his skin.

Laura had an apartment on the second floor of a semi-detached house. One window in her bedroom, one in the small office, one over the kitchen sink, a circular stained glass piece in the bathroom, and two rectangular tall ones in the living room.

It took Ash an hour to board them up, and before he knew it, he was ready to head home to finish packing. He'd be in Vermont by late afternoon, where he'd spend the next few days trying not to watch the news and hoping he had a home to come back to by the time the storm passed.

Overly dramatic, maybe. Turned out the hurricane was more likely to be a Category 4 by the time it reached landfall, not 5 as previously predicted, but that was still a lot of wind and water.

Reason number 597 not to watch the news? His coming-out article.

Yeah. His *coming-out article*.

Somehow, his team's senior manager of media relations, Rachel, had convinced the *Sport Check* reporter not to go public with Ash's bisexuality. Instead, he had a phone interview scheduled with her for tomorrow afternoon.

"This way you can control the narrative," Rachel had said this morning before going through a list of the most likely questions he'd be asked and then coaching him on his responses.

Control the narrative. What kind of bullshit was that? In his experience, reporters did whatever they wanted. Nobody said his words wouldn't be taken out of context, no matter how hard he tried to "control the narrative."

"That's true," Rachel had said when he'd voiced his concerns. "That's why you and I are going to work with Kristin"—that was the *Sport Check* reporter—"and *Sport Check* directly. This way we can get in front of it. By the time the article releases on Monday morning, there won't be anything in it we haven't already approved."

What it all boiled down to was that in five days' time, he was going to be the subject of *a lot* of conversations. And not all of them good. Basically, he was going to be a walking, talking bug under a microscope.

Coming out to Grant in front of a reporter was possibly the stupidest thing he'd ever done in his life. In less than a week, he was going to be the only NHL player ever to come out as bisexual. And here he was, still waiting to be offered that new contract. Would his club even want him after that? To say his agent was annoyed with him was putting it mildly.

He tossed his tools and extra planks of plywood into the trunk of his SUV so forcefully they left a mark on the back of the leather seat. "Fucking hell."

"Thanks for the help," Laura said from the sidewalk. The wind was picking up, sending her long brown hair flying, although the sky was still a clear cerulean. "Did you get your place done?"

"Yup. Mom's too."

He'd spent most of Monday afternoon into almost dawn Tuesday transferring everything from patio furniture to books to paperwork to electronics to framed photographs and other items he was attached to—like trophies he'd won over the years, a signed Wayne Gretzky jersey, the puck from his first goal in the NHL, and a handful of sun catchers he hadn't realized he'd still owned—into storage. Furniture had been shoved as far into the middle of his apartment as he could manage and covered in plastic tarps. Hopefully that'd be enough to save it.

"Good. Well." Laura paused and surveyed her home.

Ash slammed the trunk closed and leaned against the car. Waiting. Any second now, he'd hear it. Hell, he was surprised it'd taken this long.

Laura's mouth opened and three . . . two . . . one . . . "I'm surprised you bothered to help me at all."

There it was.

"You can thank my mom. Otherwise, I wouldn't have even thought of it," he said, just to watch her brown eyes spit flames. And because, apparently, he was a spiteful asshole. Considering he was working off six hours of sleep over the past forty-eight hours, he could live with that.

Laura's laugh was hard. "Of course. Anything for your mom, but I don't rate a second thought."

It was an effort not to roll his eyes. "Had you found out about the evacuation first, would you have thought of me for even a second?"

Squinting against the sun, Laura gathered up her hair, twisted it, and tucked it down the back of her T-shirt. "I suppose not."

Ash contemplated her for a second and said, "How've you been?"

"Do you really want to know?"

"I asked, didn't I?"

There. That. Fighting with him. For a long time after they'd started dating, he'd thought it'd equated to fighting *for* him. Something Dan hadn't done that had attracted Ash to Laura. Not that he and Dan hadn't argued, but where his relationship with Laura had been like attacking a hockey drill they didn't understand from opposite sides, he and Dan had been a pair of defensemen who'd been skating together for years. In sync. In tune. Able to read each other's body language. Able to finish each other's sentences. Hearts beating for one thing.

Each other.

His phone beeped in his pocket and he pulled it out, eyebrows winging up when he saw who it was.

Speak of the damn devil.

I heard about the hurricane coming your way. Are you okay? Did you get out?

Then a second text: *Oh, BTW, this is Dan.*

How had Dan gotten his phone number? It was different than the one he'd had while living in Syracuse.

I'm fine, Ash sent back. *Flying out this afternoon.* And because he didn't want to seem like a jerk who didn't appreciate the concern—which, honestly, he wasn't sure whether he *did* appreciate it or not—he added, *Thanks for thinking of me.*

I'm always thinking of you.

Ash's mouth dropped open and something suspiciously like butterflies erupted in his belly.

OMG I DIDN'T MEAN TO SEND THAT!

"Who are you talking to?" Laura stood on her tippy toes, attempting to peek at his phone.

He blanked the screen. "No one."

"Then why are you grinning like an idiot?"

"I'll admit to being an idiot," Ash said, wiping what was most definitely not an idiot smile off his face.

"No argument here."

"But I wasn't smiling."

"Uh-huh. Who is she?"

"There is no *she*." He rounded the SUV and slipped his large frame into the driver's seat.

"He, then," Laura said through the open window.

"No *he* either." If there was ever a *he* in his life again, it wouldn't be Dan, no matter how fluttery his stupid text made him.

"If you say so." She tapped on the windowsill. "Thanks again for the windows. Have a safe flight."

"You too."

He was pulling out his phone before she was halfway up the outside stairs to her apartment and re-reading Dan's last two texts.

I'm always thinking of you.

OMG I DIDN'T MEAN TO SEND THAT!

Didn't mean to send it because he didn't mean it? But then why would he type it out? There was a series of new texts after that last one.

Can we pretend I didn't send that?

Just delete it and pretend you never saw it. Which is probably what you'll do anyway. So good.

Sorry.

I didn't mean to make you uncomfortable.

Ash wasn't uncomfortable, though he'd be hard pressed to name what he was feeling. He kept reading.

I'm glad you're getting out safe. Take care.

Something in that "Take care" sounded oddly . . . final. Ash didn't like that, so he scrolled up a bit and re-read his favorite message. *I'm always thinking of you.*

And drove home with a grin on his face.

EIGHT

"**W**OW." MITCH WHISTLED LOW AS DAN parked his rental car in front of Sleepy Hollow B&B in Glen Hill, Vermont, where Mitch attended college. "This is where you're staying for the weekend?"

"Looks cozy," Dan said.

The bed and breakfast was a three-story mansion complete with a turret and a wraparound porch. Painted yellow with green shutters and maroon trim, the Queen Anne Revival style home appeared to be lovingly maintained. It was surrounded by tall trees and nestled on a quiet side street off Glen Hill's Main Street.

"I didn't know this place was here," Mitch said, stepping out of the car.

Dan followed suit, then grabbed his suitcase from the backseat. "You don't know your own community?"

"I've never come down this street. Never needed to."

Inside, it was cozy and inviting. The main entrance was done in dark wood and pale yellow. A grandfather clock dominated the space, along with framed yellowed photographs and a chandelier. To the right was a large, elegant living room in white and pale pink. To the left was a wooden welcome desk sitting squat next to a carpeted staircase leading to the second floor. Dead ahead, Dan spotted the dining room with a single table large enough to seat a dozen people, and beyond that, a door that led, presumably, to the kitchen.

"Hello." A woman in her sixties with wire-framed glasses perched on her nose emerged from the dining room. "Checking in?"

"Yes, ma'am. Daniel Greyson."

She removed a notebook from a drawer in the welcome desk and flipped it open. "I have a reservation here for one guest." It came out as more of a question as she peered at Mitch over her glasses.

"Oh, I'm not staying," Mitch said. "Just tagging along while he checks in."

"Ah."

She introduced herself as Marion, the owner of Sleepy Hollow B&B along with her husband, and efficiently checked Dan in before giving him a key attached to a wooden postcard-sized placard that read *Tara*.

"Tara's the honeymoon suite," Marion announced as Dan hefted his suitcase. "It's lovely. King-sized bed, en suite bathroom with an oversized shower, bright seating area, and a hot tub." She sounded like she was reciting her website word for word. "Up the stairs and to the right," she said, with instructions to fill out the breakfast order card in his room by six tonight and hang it on his doorknob.

"Too bad I don't have anyone to share a honeymoon suite with," Dan muttered as he headed up the curving staircase.

"Except your own hand," Mitch said, cackling at his own joke.

"You're even more crass than you were as a teenager."

"More experience under my belt, more jokes to pull from."

"Does Alex know you're an adult with the humor of a fifteen-year-old?"

"Yup." Mitch grinned. "Loves me anyway."

"Says something about his intelligence level, doesn't it?"

"Hey!"

Throwing Mitch an unapologetic smirk over his shoulder, Dan crested the top of the stairs onto the second level. To the left, a long hallway led to a handful of rooms. Dan went right and found the door to his room immediately on his left. Past his door was a small landing with a pool table, and a window seat with the window curtains thrown open to the early evening sun.

The Tara room was decorated in shades of purple and gray—lavender bedspread patterned with gray flowers, dark purple accent pillows, purple-and-gray wallpaper, pale purple lounge chairs with steel-colored throw pillows. Even the soft-sided hot tub tucked between the windows was gray.

"This room is in the tower!" He hadn't realized when booking it.

After thoroughly exploring the room, and ignoring Mitch's uttered "Alex and I need a shower that big," they headed out. Directly across from Tara was a staircase leading up to the third floor.

"Let's go see," Mitch said, shouldering past Dan.

The third floor only had two rooms, but to the right of the staircase was a small den with half a dozen cozy chairs, a love seat, and—score! A bookcase ran along an entire wall and the bottom half was filled with board games and—even better—3D puzzles and LEGO sets.

Mitch eyed it all and said, "Who comes to Glen Hill to play games?"

"Who comes to Glen Hill at all?"

He got the finger for his snark. "You're here, aren't you?"

That was fair.

"Come on." Mitch headed back downstairs. "Let's get dinner."

"I have to fill out my breakfast card first."

Once that was done, they left Sleepy Hollow B&B behind after getting the side door code from Marion; the front door was locked between 8 p.m. and 8 a.m.

"Where are we eating?" Dan asked. They turned the corner into tiny downtown Glen Hill.

"Mama Jean's."

"The infamous pizza joint I've heard so much about?"

Mitch knocked his shoulder into Dan's. "Thought it was time you tried it." He side-eyed Dan for a second. "It's cool that you came to visit this weekend."

"Yeah?" Secretly pleased, Dan smiled at his feet. "It's why I chose Burlington to work out of for a couple of weeks. Wanted to be closer to you for a bit."

"You've spent a whole work week working out of the Westlake office there. How do you like it so far?"

"It's . . . different than what I'm used to. Less frantic, more social. Did you know that every Monday someone brings in homemade breakfast?"

"I'd work in a place like that."

They shared a chuckle over Mitch's love of anything drenched in maple syrup.

"But what will you do after your two weeks are up?" Mitch asked, stepping out of the way of a woman pushing a stroller. "Go back to New York?"

"Not New York," Dan said firmly. "But beyond that, I haven't thought much about it."

"It's not like you not to have a plan."

"I'm trying to live my life a little less structured these days," Dan said wryly.

Mama Jean's smelled like pizza dough and tomato

sauce, and despite the early evening hour, Dan's stomach rumbled. The lighting was bright and every table had an old school white-and-red checkered tablecloth, with cutlery wrapped in thick napkins. It was half full, mostly with college students, some studying while they ate, others in groups of friends.

He followed Mitch to a booth near the back corner. Mitch grabbed two of the four napkin-wrapped cutlery bundles and moved them off to the side.

Dan raised an eyebrow. "Cody and Alex not coming?"

"Cody's working," Mitch said, grabbing a menu from between the salt and pepper shaker set in the middle of the table. "And Alex is visiting some friends today with Yager."

Dan reared back, attention pulled from his own menu. "With who?"

"Yager," Mitch repeated absentmindedly. "He came with Alex to escape the hurricane."

"Oh." Yes, that *was* his heart kicking into overdrive, thank you very much.

Something in his tone caught Mitch's interest. His eyes narrowed on Dan, too intent for Dan's tastes. "Something happen between you two when you went for milkshakes?"

"No," Dan said, too fast if the way Mitch cocked his head was any indication. "No, no. I was just wondering why he didn't—" *go to his dad's instead*. Except Mitch didn't know Dan and Ash knew each other from a previous life. There was no reason for Dan to know that Ash's dad lived in New York.

He should tell Mitch about their past.

But what was the point?

"Why what?" Mitch said.

"Why he didn't head somewhere more interesting than Glen Hill."

Shrugging, Mitch set the menu down. "I didn't ask. You have his number. Ask him."

Dan had begged Ash's number off Mitch earlier this week when he'd heard about the hurricane on the news, under the guise of needing to ask Ash a question about something they'd talked about over milkshakes.

"Where's he staying?"

"One of the B&Bs. Don't know which one, though." Mitch slipped out of the booth. "Did you decide what you want? I'll go order."

Dan scanned the menu and chose a pie at random, then handed Mitch a fifty.

Mitch waved it away. "I don't—"

"Don't argue with me." Dan pressed it into Mitch's hand. "Older brothers are allowed to spoil younger brothers." Especially when the older one was trying to make up for lost time.

"Thank you." Mitch gently cuffed his shoulder before heading for the order counter.

Releasing a long breath, Dan slumped into the cushioned booth and rubbed his forehead.

Ash was *here*. What were the chances?

He pulled out his phone and contemplated a text to Ash. Something along the lines of *Heard you're in Glen Hill. I am too. Want to grab a coffee?*

Definitely something other than *I'm always thinking of you*. Part of him wanted to ignore the fact that Ash was here altogether so he didn't have to face his embarrassment. Didn't have to face how crushed he'd been when Ash hadn't answered that text.

He still couldn't believe he'd sent those words to Ash.

At the office, whenever he received an email that made him see red, he hit Forward—leaving the sender field blank—and typed out a reply that would've had HR's ears bugging out of their heads if they ever read it. Something that went against all propriety and that he'd only ever send if he didn't care about office politics. Which was never. It was enough to get his thoughts out before deleting the email.

That was what he'd done after Ash's *Thanks for thinking of me* text. Hit Forward . . .

And then written what was in his heart.

I'm always thinking of you.

But he'd never meant for Ash to have those words.

Turned out he'd hit Reply by accident, and his thumb had slipped over Send, and before he knew it, he'd exposed himself to someone who would never accept his heart again, even if he gave it to him on a twenty-four-karat gold platter.

Suddenly bone tired, Dan put his phone away. He could shout his apology from the rooftops, shout about how he'd never forgotten Ash, shout about his desire to be in Ash's life again, shout about how he'd always loved him . . .

It wouldn't change a thing.

After a night out with Alex and his old college friends on what was probably the last Friday night out Ash would have for a while without having a lens on his back—yes, he was in doom and gloom mode, thank you very much—the silence of the bed and breakfast was both jarring and welcome. Dinner at the home of Alex's friends had successfully taken his mind off what was happening back home and on Monday's pending article, but now that he was alone again, the worry wormed its way in.

His mom had once told him that it was pointless to

worry about things he couldn't change. Good advice, but it wasn't so easy to shut off.

He headed up to the second floor and contemplated a game of pool, but the *crack* of balls likely wouldn't be appreciated at this time of night. Besides, playing alone was no fun, so he headed up to third floor, where his room, Claire, was located. It'd been the only room left when he'd called to inquire about a reservation, and while it was perfectly lovely, it was right under the turret roof. The *sloped* turret roof. He couldn't count the number of times he'd conked his head, and he'd only been here two days.

Heading left at the top of the stairs on the third floor, he paused outside his room when the sound of . . . something . . . a small clicking . . . reached his ears. Curiosity had him backtracking to the small sitting area Marion had called the reading nook. Unsurprisingly, at almost midnight, it was empty.

Empty save for one brown-eyed man with floppy, curly hair wearing loose sweatpants and a threadbare sweatshirt with the logo of Ash's old AHL team on the front. A sweatshirt Ash hadn't seen in six years. Worn by a man he hadn't expected to see again so soon.

I'm always thinking of you.

There had to be a reason Dan had hung on to that sweatshirt this whole time.

Ash noted the LEGO pieces strewn around Dan where he sat on the carpet in the middle of the room, as well as the completed LEGO sets—three of them—and their discarded boxes. It looked like he'd already completed a six-hundred-piece train station, a four-hundred-piece princess castle, a one-hundred-piece storm trooper, and was currently a quarter of the way through a Jedi starfighter.

"Of all the B&Bs in all the towns in all the world," Ash

drawled, stepping into the room, "we both booked this one."

Dan blinked at him. Blinked again, cheeks pinking.

It was a good look for him. He resembled a little kid, sitting there cross-legged surrounded by toys.

"You're staying here?"

"Yeah." Ash sat across from him. "What are the chances, huh? What are you doing?"

"Building LEGO sets."

"Why? And why these? What kind of interplanetary colony are you trying to build? And can I name it?"

Dan chuckled and slotted a couple of pieces together. "Sure. What would you call it?"

Ash contemplated the train station, the princess castle, the storm trooper, and the fighter jet. It made sense, in a way. The fighter jet would need a place to dock: the train station. And the castle needed guards: the storm trooper.

"Sparklepants Space Station."

Dan's laughter lit his eyes. "And what are the rules at Sparklepants Space Station?"

"No gum chewing," Ash said, eliciting a strangled sound from Dan. "Always use punctuation in emails. No getting on the subway and then stopping right in front of the fucking door. No smoking. No using the word *literally*. Ever."

"No clipping nails at the office."

"Ew. People do that?"

Dan nodded. "I've seen it on the subway too."

"Ugh." Ash shuddered and turned the instruction booklet toward himself. "Speaking of subways—no pole hugging. And no listening to music through speakers. Use your fucking headphones."

"Do we need a subway, though?" Dan asked. "Considering we have a starfighter, you'd think our colony would have something a bit more sophisticated than a subway system."

Ash snapped his fingers. "A public transporter system."

"Excellent," Dan said. "The world of the future—cutting commuting time by hours."

"That should be our colony's slogan."

Dan chuckled. "Any more rules?"

"No stopping suddenly in the middle of the sidewalk."

"Seriously." Dan consulted something in the booklet and gathered a few pieces. "Move over."

"No online shipping charges."

Dan laughed outright at that. "No copying people on an email message without explaining why they're being copied."

"I get the sense you feel strongly about that one."

"I don't have time to read through twelve emails to find that one that might explain what you need from me."

The princess castle came complete with a horse and carriage. Ash plopped the prince and princess figurines inside it while Dan kept working on his starfighter. The single lamp Dan had lit cast shadows across his face.

This was nice. Companionable. Serene. Dan got a little furrow between his eyebrows while he worked, and he muttered to himself when he read the instructions. Ash couldn't help but smile at him when he wasn't looking.

And that sweatshirt . . . Ash didn't remember leaving it behind, but seeing it on Dan . . .

It made his chest constrict.

"When did you take up LEGOing?" he asked.

Dan was biting his lip. He glanced from the pieces in his hand to the instruction booklet and back again. "I don't think you can make it a verb like that."

"I can make it so."

A true smile from Dan. "Okay, Captain Picard."

"Are you here visiting Mitch for the weekend?" Ash asked. He picked up one of the train cars and spun its tiny wheels.

"Yeah. I'm heading back to Burlington on Monday morning."

That gave Ash pause. "Burlington? Not New York?"

"I'm working out of the Burlington office for a couple of weeks."

"How come?"

"I'm thinking of transferring there."

Not what he'd expected. "Really? Something wrong with the New York office?"

Dan eyed him critically for a moment, and that *look*. Ash recognized it as Dan's should-I-or-shouldn't-I look. "If I explain, then I'll inevitably have to go into detail about the thing you don't want to talk about, so . . ."

So the ball was in Ash's court.

What did Dan's potential transfer have to do with Ash?

"Do you like the Burlington office?" he asked instead of what he really wanted to know.

"I thought I'd like it better, to be honest. Not that I *don't* like it, but I find myself missing the fast pace of the New York office. New York in general, really. There's always something to do there, whereas Burlington sort of falls asleep after ten."

"Maybe you need to try an office in a bigger city. Doesn't Westlake have one in Chicago? Houston?"

"Yeah," Dan said on a sigh.

"Not interested in those?"

Dan shrugged. "Not really, though I couldn't tell you why. They don't . . . feel right, if that makes sense."

"Not really," Ash said. "I'm at the whim of my club." At

this point, it was becoming less and less likely that he'd be offered a new contract. What team wanted to be the center of a media circus? Management was probably patting it-self on the back for not offering him one sooner. Now they could quietly let him go without any fuss.

"That's the nature of your job, though, right?" Dan said. "The general manager, or team owner, or whoever says, 'Yager, you've been traded to Arizona,' and you say, 'How fast can I get there?'"

Ash smiled at Dan's summary. "Pretty much."

"That doesn't bother you?"

Shrugging, Ash put the train back. "It's like you said—it's the nature of the job."

"I don't think I'd like having that choice taken from me."

"It's hard, for sure," Ash agreed. "It's hard for the play-ers who have to pick up and head sometimes hundreds of miles to their new team as soon as possible, often without the chance to say goodbye. And it's hard for spouses or partners. They're the ones who have to pick up the pieces: pack up, sell the house, pull the kids out of school."

"What was it like when you went from Syracuse to Tampa?"

Ash stretched out on his back and let Dan finish his LEGO set. "It was bittersweet, right? Exciting because I was going from the AHL to the NHL. The big leagues, you know? And Florida's home. I was glad to be getting out of the cold. But the guys on my team in Syracuse were my family, and I barely had time to say goodbye before I left. So in a way, it's defeating too.

"It was worse for Laura, I think." He didn't fail to notice how Dan stiffened at the mention of his ex-wife. "Her en-tire life was in Syracuse—friends, family, work."

Laura had dropped everything to move to Tampa with him, something he'd needed after Dan had left him, although he still sometimes felt guilty for dragging her to Florida only to ask for a divorce less than a year later. But Laura was right about him loving hockey more than her, so while there was some guilt, there was no regret. In hindsight, it'd been a rebound relationship. At the time, it had seemed like everything he'd needed.

Dan cleared his throat, shoulders stiff, and reached behind him to grab another LEGO box off the shelf—a trio of law enforcement personnel—upending the pieces onto the carpet. "How'd you guys meet?"

"How everyone meets—in a bar."

"Wasn't how we met."

"Yeah, and look how that turned out."

Silence. Silence so thick and fraught with everything unsaid between them that the tension crawled along his skin, prickling like ants.

Ash sat up, sighing. "I'm sorry." He rubbed the bridge of his nose. "I've been on edge the past couple of days."

Nothing from Dan. Ash looked over to find him staring at Sparklepants Space Station. The stricken expression on his face—devastation and realization, like he'd just figured something out that left him pale—bit Ash in the gut and he reached for Dan's hand.

Dan sucked in a breath and jerked away.

"Sorry—"

"No, I'm sorry," Dan interrupted. "I forgot for a second that you don't want to talk about it."

Yeah, but that didn't mean Ash had to be an ass.

"I'm going to clean up and head to bed." Dan packed up the pieces of his yet to be assembled law enforcement personnel, putting them back in the box.

"I can help."

"No." Dan smiled tightly at the carpet, not even looking at Ash. "I got it, thanks."

"Okay, well . . . goodnight."

"'Night."

Ash's feet took him to his room, but his conscience took him back to Dan before he could insert the key into the lock.

He'd known people who paced as they thought—himself included. Not Dan. Dan went eerily still, staring into nothing. The only part of him that moved were his eyes as his brain went from thought to thought to thought. Ash stopped in the entrance to the reading nook, trying not to make a sound. Dan sat where Ash had left him, shoulders rounded, empty stare on Sparklepants Space Station. His entire body seemed about to cave, crumpling into a defeated sag.

They'd been having a good time, hanging out like they used to. And Ash had shit all over that.

He didn't know what to say, what to do to make things better between them. And was it really his responsibility to? Again he went to his room. Again his conscience stopped him. Turning, he—

"Jesus!"

—jumped about a foot and rammed his hip into the doorknob.

"Don't scare a guy like that! What's wrong with you?"

Dan pressed his lips together, but it didn't stop them from twitching into a smile. "Sorry."

Ash rubbed his chest over his thundering heart. "Give a guy a heart attack, why don't you?"

"Please. You're more in shape than you've ever been."

"Not in shape enough to withstand death by sneak attack."

Dan crossed his arms. "If I was attacking, you'd know it."

Ash gave him a droll look. "When have you ever attacked anything?"

"I attacked a disaster of a spreadsheet once. With vigor. You should've seen those pivot tables. How do you mess that up?"

Ash hadn't had much occasion to use spreadsheets and didn't know what a pivot table was, but it must've been important. He smiled at Dan's earnestness and rubbed his sore hip.

"Sorry," Dan muttered.

"You said that already."

"I meant about everything else."

Instantly, Ash went rigid. "Dan—"

"I know you don't want to hear it, but shut up and listen for a second, okay?"

Rendered mute from surprise, Ash could only stand there and listen as Dan went on.

"I'm *sorry*," he breathed, grave and sorrowful. "I'm sorry that I hurt you. I'm sorry that I wasn't—" Cutting himself off, he sucked in a harsh breath. "You know, I spent the past six years wondering if I could've done things differently."

What things?

"And the truth is, yes, I could have. But at the time, I couldn't see a way out of the corner I'd been put in."

What corner? What was he talking about? The thing he hadn't had a choice in that he'd briefly mentioned last month over milkshakes?

"I'm sorry that my decision ended up hurting you. I never wanted that, I never—" His curls bounced everywhere when he shook his head. "I lost the two best parts of my life that day, and ever since I've been trying to figure out how I let myself be so easily manipulated. Best I can figure is that I was scared."

With every uttered word, Ash's chest squeezed painfully tight. He swallowed hard past all the questions he didn't know how to ask. "Scared of me?"

"No." It was said on a soft laugh full of disbelief. "I could never be afraid of you, Ash. You made me feel like I could fly." Dan's voice trailed off into a whisper.

Ash's eyes closed against the pain on Dan's face.

"I was scared I couldn't protect you."

His eyes flew open. "From what?"

Dan looked so small standing there in Ash's old sweatshirt, the logo more faded than not, that Ash took a step toward him.

But Dan just smiled thinly. "Doesn't matter. Not anymore."

"Dan—"

"Thanks for listening." He stepped away, hugging his arms to himself. "'Night, Ash." He headed back to the little reading nook.

No. Just no.

"Dan."

He stopped but didn't turn around, shoulders so stiff Ash wanted to smooth the tension out of them.

"You still jog every morning, right?" he asked.

Dan turned halfway at that, lips pinched. "Yeah."

"Want company tomorrow?"

NINE

"**I** DON'T GET IT." DAN POKED AT THE MUSHY lump on the baking sheet with a fork. "What did we do wrong?"

Next to him, Ash choked on the bite he'd tasted. "Ugh." He shuddered and gagged. Grabbing his water glass off the counter, he downed it in two swallows.

"But we followed the recipe." To a freakin' T.

"God, I can still taste it." Ash refilled his glass from the kitchen sink.

"How hard can it be to make cauliflower pizza crust?"

"It's stuck in my throat." Ash gargled, spitting his mouthful into the sink.

"Listen to this." Dan scrolled down the screen of his laptop to the comments section at the bottom of the recipe. "'This is the easiest recipe I've ever made! My kids loved it.'"

"Kids have no taste."

"'Cauliflower crust is hard to make,'" Dan continued, "'but this one turned out great.'"

"What kind of diet do these people have that they think this—" Ash waved a hand at the cooling crust. "—is good?"

Dan scratched his head as he read over the recipe. "We messed up somewhere."

"Or everybody else is messed up," Ash muttered.

"Maybe we didn't squeeze enough water out of the

cooked cauliflower."

"There was no water left, trust me."

"Obviously we did something wrong."

"Obviously everybody else is wrong," Ash grumbled.

Chuckling, Dan closed the laptop. "I have frozen pizza in the freezer."

"Sold. As long as it doesn't have a cauliflower crust."

"I don't think they make frozen pizza with cauliflower crust." He took a box out of the freezer. "Pepperoni, mushrooms, and green peppers okay?"

"Better than," Ash said, scraping the cauliflower mush off the baking sheet and into the garbage. It fell in with a loud *plop*.

Dan turned the oven on. "I can't believe you tried it."

"One of us had to, and by the look on your face, you'd rather eat dirt."

"That's not inaccurate."

"Can't we make some of that spicy chicken Thai thing you were telling me about the other day?"

"I wish." Pizza in the oven, Dan set the timer on the microwave. "I think I'm missing some of the spices, and I don't have any chicken."

"Bummer."

"Come by next Saturday," he offered. "We can make it then."

"Awesome." Ash found a sponge and started washing the pan.

He took up a lot of space in Dan's studio apartment in Herald Square, but it didn't make the tiny home feel smaller. Instead, Ash livened up the space with his presence, made Dan want to spend more time here . . . as long as Ash was here.

Which was a squirrelly kind of thought. He'd never

craved another man's presence before, and certainly not after knowing them only two weeks.

The apartment really was minuscule. Not that Dan needed more than this. The front door led directly into an exposed brick kitchen, with a handful of white cabinets, a fridge, an oven, and the smallest microwave he could find sitting squat on his limited counter space. A small, square table with room for four was usually a mess of papers, textbooks, notebooks, and binders, but as it was summer vacation, he'd stored everything on the tall shelf opposite his bedroom. At the back of the kitchen was a blue couch he never used and was seriously considering getting rid of. Through a set of closed curtains on the right was his en suite bedroom.

He didn't entertain here. Not often. Mitch visited on occasion, when he was in the city, and Dan had made his dad dinner a few times. Other than that—and a handful of hookups—he preferred to meet his college buddies elsewhere just to get out of the claustrophobic space.

Ash was so tall and wide that his head nearly reached the top of the cabinets, and his shoulders took up the entire space at the sink between the wall and the fridge. And yet, somehow, Dan was less claustrophobic with him here, not more.

"Shove over a second," Dan said, scooting in next to Ash at the sink, where the man was scraping off bits of gross cauliflower that had burned onto the pan, and reached around him for the plates in the cabinet. A zing shot up his side where they touched, goosebumps chilling his skin where their arms brushed, so potent that he jerked and almost dropped the plates.

"Easy." Ash placed a wet palm against his back, steadying him.

"Sorry," Dan choked out. "Lost my balance."

Ash only grunted and finished washing the pan, clearly not as affected by their proximity as Dan. That was fine, though. Great, in fact. It'd make things less awkward. Not that things were awkward now. Except they sort of were since Dan was just standing here, holding a pair of plates to his chest, and staring at Ash's profile like an idiot.

Or like a formerly straight guy who'd just realized he was attracted to men.

Not the greatest realization to have while alone in an apartment with the guy he was attracted to.

Ash caught him staring as he placed the finally clean pan into the drying rack. "What's up? Forget how to set a table?"

That made Dan scowl playfully. "Ha ha." He removed some cutlery from a drawer, then moved to the table. Unearthing a couple of placements from underneath a stack of books on his shelf, he finished setting the table, adding a couple of wineglasses to finish it off.

"Fancy," Ash said, wiping his hands on a dish towel.

"Frozen pizza deserves fancy." Dan pulled out his only bottle of wine, one his dad had left behind last time he visited, but hesitated before uncorking it. "Do you want beer instead?" Ash seemed more like a beer guy.

"Wine is good." Ash's eyes narrowed on him. "Are you legal?"

Dan grinned. "Nope. I'm a few months away. My dad tends to leave stuff behind when he visits."

"Your dad promotes underage drinking? Can he be my dad?"

"Speaking of dads," Dan said through a laugh. "You live with yours, right?" Something Ash had mentioned at lunch the other day at Dan's favorite food truck when they'd been deciding where to attempt their cauliflower pizza crust experiment. "What's that like?"

"Weird." Ash leaned back against the counter while Dan uncorked and poured the wine. "My parents divorced when I was nine, and I lived with my mom growing up. Living with my dad now is like meeting a new side of him."

Dan handed Ash a glass of wine. "How so?"

"I've visited him every year since he moved here, but visiting was more like hanging out with a big brother. He'd take me to do touristy things and to ball games. But now he's being a dad. *Where are you going? Who are you going with? What time will you be back?*"

"Is that a bad thing?" Dan asked, taking a seat at the table.

Ash shook his head. "Not bad. Just different. Like he forgets I'm twenty-one and have been living on my own since I was eighteen."

"Did you consider renting your own place?"

"In this city?" Ash snorted a laugh. "I didn't even bother trying." He glanced around. "I do like your place, though."

"It's minuscule," Dan countered, secretly pleased.

"It's cozy."

"That's one way of putting it."

"You don't like small spaces," Ash observed.

"Oh, did our time in the elevator give it away?"

Ash was grinning as he sat across from Dan. "Little bit."

"Small spaces don't bother me if they have an exit," Dan said, nodding at his front door.

"Elevators have exits."

"Not when they're stuck between floors. Jiffy, my ass."

"You don't consider an hour and a half to be a jiffy?"

"That's not even a jiff."

Throwing his head back, Ash laughed loudly, exposing

the long line of his throat and the small patch of brown hair on the underside of his jaw that he'd missed while shaving this morning. Heat flared in Dan's gut, and his swallow of wine went down the wrong hole.

"You okay?" Ash's large hand slapped Dan's back once, twice, jerking Dan forward.

Fuck, who knew learning he was bisexual would kill him?

Also? Choking on wine really fucking hurt.

"Here." Ash replaced the wine glass in Dan's hand with a water glass as Dan continued to choke. "Drink this."

Dan obeyed, taking tiny sips between coughing fits. "Sorry," he wheezed past his constricted throat.

"Don't apologize," Ash said. The timer went off and he started rooting through drawers until he found the oven mitts. "I choked on my own saliva during a game once. I still get made fun of for it."

Dan couldn't do anything but laugh.

TEN

SEPTEMBER 2009—PRESENT DAY

DAN WAITED ON THE SLEEPY HOLLOW B&B'S FRONT porch, shuffling from one foot to the other to keep warm. The morning was cool and dewy, not yet warmed by the sun that was rising in the east. He rubbed his bare arms and paced the length of the porch.

It was quiet outside, everyone cooped up in their beds this early on a Saturday morning, the sun barely peeking above rooftops. It was mid-September, but the leaves hadn't started to turn yet and everything was lush and green. Birds sang, squirrels ran to and fro, wind gently stirred the leaves in the trees, and it smelled like the roses in Marion's garden.

Pretty. It was all very pretty and charming. The type of neighborhood a couple raised two-point-five kids and a dog in. Maybe he'd spent too much time living in a big city because it didn't appeal to him other than for occasional visits.

A woman jogged past with a chocolate lab on a leash. She spotted Dan and smiled and waved. Dan waved back.

That wouldn't happen in New York, and Dan liked it that way. The anonymity of a big city. The freedom to disappear in a crowd.

He was giving Ash two more minutes, and then he was going on his jog without him.

Why did Ash want to come with him, anyway? To get his daily cardio workout in? To reconnect with Dan?

Pity? Definitely pity.

You made me feel like I could fly.

First he told Ash that he was always thinking about him, and then *that*? Obviously he had no sense of self-preservation. He was laying his heart out at Ash's feet, handing it to him on a platter layered with their past. But Ash didn't want it. Didn't want him. Not anymore.

Or did he? The more Dan bared his soul, the more Ash seemed to soften toward him. Maybe if he kept being honest, they could at least be friends again, even if they were never anything else.

It was freeing, in a way, to speak his mind. He'd spent the past six years bottling everything up. Heartache for what he'd done to Ash. Sorrow for what he'd done to Mitch. Outrage at his mother. Frustration at his own helplessness. An older brother's pride at Mitch's success—getting into college and excelling at hockey. Absolute *fury* when he'd discovered his mother had taken his sacrifices and disregarded them like they meant *nothing*.

Defeat. Pure and heavy and confining *defeat* that sat heavy on his shoulders, on his soul. So heavy that he still threatened to sink under its weight. To buckle underneath the pressure. To fall apart at everything he'd done and hadn't done. What he'd said and hadn't said.

He leaned his hands on the porch railing, head hanging forward, chin to his chest. Sometimes he didn't know how to deal with it all.

The door opened behind him. "Are we doing this, or what?" Ash's voice boomed out into the silent morning.

Dan sucked in a deep breath and made a conscious effort to loosen his shoulders from where they hovered around his ears.

Ash mimicked his position on his right. "Are you okay?"

Honesty. Ash reacted to honesty. "No." Dan gazed out into the distance, not really seeing the white gingerbread style house with red trim across the street.

"Want to talk about it?"

That Ash would ask . . . It made Dan smile. "I wouldn't know where to start."

"The beginning."

The beginning. But the beginning was six years ago, and for Dan to talk about it would mean going places Ash didn't want to hear about.

He straightened, shaking out the kinks in his wrists, and looked Ash up and down. Black running shorts hugged his huge thighs and a gray T-shirt outlined his wide shoulders. The phrase *good enough to eat* was wholly accurate when it came to Ashton Yager.

"I'd rather run," he said. "Ready?"

"Yeah." Ash's gaze was assessing as he handed Dan one of the water bottles he must've pilfered from the kitchen. "You've been to Glen Hill before. Where to?"

They ran along the sleepy side streets, passing a couple other joggers, a pair of cyclists, a handful of dog walkers. Dan normally jogged through Central Park when he was home, and the last week in Burlington he'd taken to jogging along the waterfront. But Glen Hill didn't have a waterfront or anything resembling a Central Park. What it did have was, unsurprisingly, many hills and lots of trees. And also a small creek that meandered the length of the town. Dan led them into the forest at the edge of town, down a dirt path, and onto the rocky shore of the creek, their heels kicking up rocks behind them as they ran.

"What do you make of Glen Hill so far?" Dan asked between breaths.

"Huh?" Ash said distractedly, forehead pinched tight.

"Glen Hill? Honestly, I'm not sure."

"What was your first impression?"

"Too quiet."

Dan huffed out a brief chuckle. The only sound in this part of Glen Hill was the creek trickling over rocks in the water, the melody of singing birds, and their own steady breathing and repetitive footsteps against the rocks. "Yeah, that was my first impression too. Pretty, though."

"But boring."

"I think it's an outdoor enthusiast's state."

"You could say that about every state, though," Ash pointed out.

"Could you? Even, like, Arkansas?"

"Huh." They hopped over a rotting tree trunk in their path. "Don't think I've ever been to Arkansas."

"Do they have a hockey team?" Dan asked. Everything he knew about hockey came from watching Mitch's games, and everything he knew about the NHL came from following Ash's career the past few years.

"Possibly an ECHL team, but don't quote me on that," Ash said.

"You never played in the ECHL, right?"

"Nah." Ash grinned. "Drafted out of the Major Juniors by Tampa and sent to their AHL team in Syracuse."

"You've been with the same club for a long time then."

"Yeah, I've been lucky."

They rounded a bend and the creek widened, encroaching onto their jogging route. Up ahead, a set of steep stairs made out of large boulders led back up into the forest. They went that way, emerging onto a trail made of dirt and gravel. It smelled earthy and fresh and slightly damp even though it hadn't rained since before Dan had arrived yesterday.

The rumble of a car engine and tires on asphalt reached Dan's ears.

"Sounds like Glen Hill's waking up," Ash said.

"Finally. It's not *that* early. Manhattan would've been up hours ago."

"Tampa too."

They emerged onto a side street, breathing hard, sweat trickling down their necks. Dan had warmed considerably and he paused to drink some water.

"I have a confession," he said once he'd chugged half the bottle. "I don't know where we are." He'd never been up this way, always turning back when the creek widened.

"Really? Lost in Glen Hill?" Ash appeared thrilled by the idea. "Well, it's the size of a bird's nest, so it can't be that hard to find our way back to the B&B."

There was really only one way to go: up the street.

"Lost in Glen Hill," Ash mused as they jogged, the *slap, slap, slap* of their running shoes hitting the sidewalk. "And yet you can find your way around Manhattan, no problem."

"I've lived in Manhattan for eight years. I've been to Glen Hill all of four times, and the first two I stayed in Montpelier. Last time I stayed at a B&B. Actually . . ." Dan's steps slowed until he came to a stop in front of a pale blue house with dark blue shutters. "This one. Okay, I know where I am now. What are your thoughts on coffee?"

Ash's eyes lit up.

From here, downtown Glen Hill was easy to get to: one block north and then a left.

"Glen Hill Café," Ash read off the front of the coffee shop Dan took them to. "Original."

"Don't knock it." Dan held the door open and waved Ash inside. "The café in Tampa that Mitch and Cody worked at over the summer was called Oceanside. That's not any better than Glen Hill Café."

"True."

They got in the line up and waited their turn, Ash perusing the menu behind the counter. It smelled strongly of coffee with an underlying aroma of breakfast pastries. Muffins, bagels, Danishes, and scones filled the glass display case.

Sweat cooled on Dan's skin and cold air swept over him, the air conditioning on too high for the crisp morning temperature. He shivered and bounced in place.

"We had to create a business plan for a mock business when I was in college," he said, digging a twenty-dollar bill out of his pocket, "and I called my woodworking shop Greyson's Woodworking."

The side-eyed glance Ash shot him was unimpressed.

"Shut up," Dan grumbled. "I was twenty-one."

"What would you call it now?"

"Oh, look! It's our turn."

Ignoring Ash's soft chuckle, Dan stepped up to the counter and ordered for himself, then waved at Ash. "And whatever he wants."

Taking their coffees to go, they headed back out into the morning sunshine, aiming themselves for the Sleepy Hollow B&B. It was still early and the only places that were open were the café, a breakfast place a few doors down, a veterinary clinic across the street, and a second café on the other end of downtown.

Ash nudged Dan's elbow. "Tell me."

"Tell you what?"

"What would you call your shop now?"

Dan huffed. "I don't have anything better, which you know perfectly well, fuck you very much."

Ash laughed and dodged around a woman and her

terrier. "I'll come up with something."

"Oh really? Like what?"

"Let me think about it and get back to you."

"Don't hurt yourself."

Ash shoved him gently, and the friendly gesture made Dan laugh. Made him hope that they were on the road to being friends again. To being who they once were to each other.

The Glen Hill College student arena was packed for the Glen Hill College Mountaineers' first hockey game of the season. Ash sat between Alex and Dan, with Cody and a couple of Alex's old college buddies behind them.

Ash adjusted the baseball hat he wore. Alex wore one too, an attempt to not get recognized and take the focus away from the Mountaineers.

The arena wasn't as large as an NHL ice rink, but for a school the size of Glen Hill College—tiny—it nevertheless appeared to hold a capacity of at least a thousand. Ash munched on his buttered popcorn, and despite college hockey not being quite as exciting as professional hockey, he still enjoyed watching the game and taking in the atmosphere full of cheering fans. And Mitch? Mitch had more talent in his pinky finger than the rest of the guys on his team combined.

Okay, maybe Ash was biased—Mitch was his friend, and his best friend's boyfriend. There was a handful of other guys on the team who were equally as talented. But Mitch . . . There was something about the way he played that didn't just scream *talent* in big, bold, neon letters, but also *determination* and *persistence* and *commitment*. He was lightning fast, had great footwork, amazing reflexes, and an uncanny ability to anticipate where the puck was going to be.

"How is he doing that with his feet?"

"Figure skating," Alex and Dan said together. They grinned at each other across Ash, and Alex said, "Jinx!" making Dan laugh loudly.

The sound . . . It shouldn't have done something so basic as make Ash's stomach bounce. He was twenty-seven, not seventeen. He didn't get nervous anymore, and he certainly didn't get crushes. Especially not on men who'd broken his heart. But there his stomach was, bouncing away in fluttery excitement like it was a fucking bouncy ball trapped in a box, making him jittery and . . . and . . . and *flustered*, of all things. Dan was making him flustered just by laughing.

Nothing good could come of this.

He was jerked out of his thoughts when Dan stood suddenly, dropping his own bag of popcorn to the sticky floor. "Mitch!"

A whistle blew, play stopped, and Mitch picked himself up off the ice. Ash had missed what happened, but he could put the pieces together: Mitch had been tripped and . . . was being sent to the penalty box? What the hell?

"What the fuck was that?" Dan yelled.

"How is that a penalty?" Cody shouted from behind Ash.

Dan was fairly vibrating. "You don't give the victim a penalty—"

Cody wasn't any better. "Something's wrong with your eyesight—"

Booing. Lots of booing.

"Are you stupid—"

"Who's paying this ref—"

"Were you even *watching*—"

"The other guy gets the penalty, you asshole—"

"Touch my brother again and I'm coming down there!"

Ash's eyebrows were up to his hairline as Dan and Cody continued to shout and swear, the crowd went absolutely crazy, and Mitch's coach had a word with the referee. He'd never been to a college hockey game before, but maybe he should go to more. This was awesome.

Dan and Cody, who still weren't getting along, high fived over Ash's head.

Hockey had a way of bringing people together.

Cody slapped the back of Alex's shoulder. "Where's your indignation?"

Or maybe not.

"I think you two—" Alex waved a finger between Dan and Cody. "—have enough for all of us."

Dan sat, biting his lip. "I hope he's okay. That looked like a hard fall."

"He's fine," Alex said. "Probably more upset that he didn't see it coming than over any bruising he might have."

Dan didn't look convinced, and Ash's hand was halfway to his thigh for a reassuring squeeze before he realized what he was doing and yanked his arm back.

No. No, no. None of that. Fluttery, bouncy stomach or no, he was *not* Dan's caretaker.

He offered Dan some of his own popcorn.

Damn it, what had he *just* said?

"Thanks." Dan took a handful, then glanced between his feet. "I lost most of mine."

"I noticed. Hey, question for you: why did you get claustrophobic at Alex's signing but not here?"

"Hm." Dan munched on popcorn. "I think it has to do with the arena being bigger. At the bookstore, I was stuck between bookshelves and people and I couldn't see the way out." He shrugged. "I can't always predict what will trigger me. What's okay once might not be okay next time."

"Humans are contradictory creatures."

"That's for damn sure."

It took several minutes for everything to get sorted, and not much happened during that time. Members of each team huddled around their respective coaches, doubtlessly discussing plays for the two likely scenarios: either Mitch would stay in the penalty box or he'd be replaced by the other guy. Hell, who knew? Maybe both players would get the penalty.

Mitch sat in the box, and Ash could see him growing more and more restless the longer nothing happened.

"He looks like he's about to bust out of there," Ash said.

"Yeah." Dan ate more of Ash's popcorn. "He's never been good at sitting still."

Alex was busy having a conversation with his friends and Cody behind them, so Ash said, "I'm surprised I never met him when I was in New York."

"He was fourteen at the time," Dan said. "He didn't spend much time in the city, and then he went to development camp for a few weeks in . . ." He made a noise in the back of his throat and cocked his head as he thought. "Quebec City? Winnipeg? Somewhere in Canada that summer, I think. I really wanted him to meet you." A smile thrown in Ash's direction. "He would've loved to pick the brain of a professional hockey player."

Ash almost asked then. Almost. About what Dan had done to Mitch, that thing he'd alluded to at brunch last month that had Cody so angry with him. But Dan was smiling and happy and having a good time, and Ash wasn't about to shit on him again. And right now, surrounded by friends who didn't know about their past?

Probably not the best time.

They'd had breakfast together this morning at the B&B, all domesticated-like, Dan trading half his Belgian waffle for Ash's eggs Benedict on a croissant. They hadn't even had to talk about it. Just split their meals in half and forked it over onto the other's plate, exactly like they used to do.

Almost as if six years hadn't gone by. It was an odd feeling, falling into old patterns as if no time at all had passed.

It took five minutes for play to resume, and when it did, Mitch was let out of the penalty box and the guy from the other team who'd tripped him went in. Which was what should've happened in the first place. Who were these college hockey refs?

Within the first thirty seconds of the power play, a kid named Yano sent the puck Mitch's way. And Mitch, knowing when to take advantage and having the on-ice vision that he did, skated toward the net like he'd die if he didn't, maneuvering around the other team's players as if they were standing still.

Pressure on Ash's arm made him look down. Dan had a hand clamped on him, knuckles white; the other was poised near his head, fisted, ready to throw up in a cheer if Mitch made the goal.

Which he did seconds later, with a sweet backhand shot that flew right past the defensemen, putting the puck right where mama kept the cookies. His message was clear: payback's a bitch.

Dan flew out of his seat, his whoop of laughter so carefree and joyous, all Ash could do was grin at him.

This was bad. Very, very bad.

Two in the morning. Ash stared up at the ceiling of his room at the B&B. His eyes had adjusted to the dark hours ago, and he noted every striation on the ceiling. He was pretty sure a spider had made itself a home where the wall met the ceiling above the window, but he didn't care enough to get up and check. Let the little bugger live there. At least its home was undamaged.

Ash couldn't say the same for himself.

It was his own stupid fault he couldn't sleep. He'd purposefully avoided the news since leaving Florida and had deleted the weather app on his smartphone. His room at the B&B didn't have a television, thank god for small miracles. But they'd gone to Mitch and Cody's after the game tonight—after Mitch's team had won—and Cody had turned on the television to set up a game of Mario Kart . . . and Ash had caught a glimpse of the weather report.

The good news was that the hurricane had been downgraded to a Category 2 by the time it made landfall early Friday morning, and then had been further downgraded to a Category 1 as it made its way over central Florida. His mom's place would be fine; she lived in a reinforced condo tower. His own home would *probably* be fine. It was concrete, had storm shutters, and he'd placed extra reinforcements over them. He was relatively certain it'd still be standing when he went back.

It was the storm surge he was worried about.

At least he was further inland, so maybe it wouldn't be so bad. But what about Pinellas County? And downtown Tampa? What about Alex's apartment? He was in the Channel District, so close to Ybor Channel that he might as well be on the fucking thing.

The hurricane had already passed over Tampa and was now on its way to the Atlantic Ocean, but the airport had taken some damage and there weren't any flights going in or out. He and Alex would be needed back in Tampa at some point soon, and it looked like they might have to rent a car to get there. However, according to the weather report, many of the roads were impassable—debris, downed trees and electrical lines—and could take a week to reopen.

Ash hadn't heard from any of his team's operations people yet, but he had a feeling their canceled game would be rescheduled for sometime next week in their rivals' city, or possibly at a neutral site.

Speaking of his team, he'd finally manned up and called his head coach this morning to explain what was happening with the *Sport Check* article. The conversation went something like this:

Coach Ness: "Why are you telling me something I already know?"

Ash: "Oh. Um. I guess Rachel told you?"

Coach Ness: "Uh-huh."

Ash: "I wanted to apologize for the shitstorm that's about to come down on the organization."

Coach Ness: "Son, if you think this is going to be a shitstorm, you haven't lived long enough."

Whatever that meant.

Coach Ness: "Besides, once game three gets rescheduled, everyone will go back to analyzing what it means for us this season that Taylor didn't score a single goal in the last six games last season."

That . . . was probably true.

And that was that. Coach Ness was about as worried as he'd be had a fly landed on his arm.

Ash wasn't sure what to do about that. Coach's cavalier attitude was both immensely comforting and mildly frustrating.

Why was Ash the only one dreading Monday?

At least Alex understood.

"You're doing what?" His face had paled—actually paled—when Ash drew him aside before Mitch's game. "Are you crazy?"

"I just . . . You should've seen Grant's eyes, man. He looked like a baby animal that knew it only had a few more seconds to live."

"That's the most morbid thing you've ever said." Alex had sighed. "I can't even say I wouldn't have done the same thing under those circumstances. I don't envy you. Do the rest of the guys know?"

"Texted them before leaving the B&B."

"What'd they say?"

"Variations on *good luck* and *I wouldn't want to be you* and *I got your back, dude* and *wait, you're still on the team, right*?"

"So basically they didn't care."

"Nope."

Rolling over, Ash exhaled into his pillow. His brain wouldn't shut off, and he was not only wide-awake, but bored to boot. And kind of hungry. He could go for a run, expend some energy, down a bowl of cereal when he got back, then pass out.

Good plan. But he didn't want to go for a run by himself in the dark. It was creepy.

Throwing on running shorts, a T-shirt, and a hoodie, he went down a flight of stairs barefoot and knocked softly on Dan's door.

Tap, tap.

Nothing. Not even the sound of bedsprings squeaking as the room's occupant got up to answer the door.

Ash knocked again, louder.

Tap, tap, tap.

Still nothing. Ash debated going back to his room and trying to sleep, but he'd tried for almost three hours to no avail and was tired of his own thoughts.

He knocked again.

Tap, tap, tap, tap, tap, tap, tap, tap, tap, tap, tap, tap, tap, taptaptaptaptaptaptaptaptaptaptap—

The door flung open. "What?"

Ash grinned at Dan, the kick in the gut at the sight of him still unwanted, but not unexpected. He wore a bright red onesie of all things. It even had footies. Ash swallowed a giggle—Dan already had murder in his eyes.

"It's two in the fucking morning," Dan growled, curls a mess, eyes squinting against the hallway light.

"Come for a run with me."

"No." By the tone of Dan's voice, Ash suspected he really meant *No, I will not go for a run with you in the middle of the night, you asshole, are you crazy?*

"Please?"

Dan flung the door closed.

Ash caught it before it slammed in his face and entered Dan's darkened room, only to find his potential jogging companion crawling back into bed. His very large, very long, very comfy-looking bed.

"Dude, you got a California king." Ash shut the door behind him, plunging the room further into darkness. The only light came from the bathroom, the door of which was halfway closed. "Mine's just a double, and my feet hang over the end."

"Swell," Dan said, already under the covers.

Ash lay down on the other side of the bed.

"What are you doing?" Dan asked.

"I'm bored."

"How is that my problem?"

"You're here, I'm here . . ."

"That doesn't answer my question." Dan rolled onto his side, facing Ash, eyes closed and blankets up to his chin. "Unless you're here for a booty call, in which case I could be persuaded."

Surely he was half asleep and hadn't meant to say it, but either way, Dan's words sent heat through Ash's veins. The space between them went taught, crackling with life and energy.

Where would they be right now if they'd stayed together?

A dangerous thought, that.

He poked Dan in the nose.

One eye slitted open.

"I'm hungry," Ash declared.

The other eye opened. "I could eat."

Dan followed him upstairs to his room so he could throw on a pair of sweats over his running shorts. And socks. It was chilly at night in the B&B. No wonder Dan was wearing a onesie.

Dan was still knuckling the sleep out of his eyes when they reached the kitchen. Ash turned the lights on, making Dan groan and wince.

Opening the large refrigerator, Ash scanned its contents. It was packed to the fullest but he wasn't sure what they could eat without leaving the owners short on something. "What should we have?"

"Anything but cauliflower pizza."

Ash snorted a chuckle that turned into a full belly laugh. He couldn't say why he'd gone to Dan in the first place, but he was glad that he had.

Nothing in the fridge appealed, so he rooted through

cupboards, then the pantry until he found—

"Mm, yum." He held up a package of chocolate chips.

"Ooh, nice find."

They divided and conquered, Ash gathering the dry ingredients, Dan the wet ones. It was as familiar as it'd ever been between them. That disgusting cauliflower pizza hadn't been the only thing they'd cooked together, and the ease with which they danced around each other as they gathered ingredients was like déjà vu mixed with a blast from the past sprinkled with a dash of how-did-this-happen.

Unsettling. He might as well have been dropped into Dan's tiny kitchen in Herald Square.

"You know," he said, "if you added little Christmas trees to your onesie, you'd look like a Christmas decoration."

Dan retrieved the carton of eggs and the butter from the fridge. "Mitch got this for me as a birthday present a couple years ago."

"As a gag gift?"

"Doubt it." Now he was going through cupboards on the other side of the kitchen. "Mitch is a pretty good gift giver. He must've known I'd love something like this. As soon as fall hits, my feet get cold. Ah ha!" A little bottle of vanilla joined the eggs and butter on the island. "He got me a clamp kit for Christmas last year, and I haven't had the heart to tell him that I gave up woodworking a long time ago."

"Why did you give it up?" Ash asked, double-checking the recipe on the back of the chocolate chip package. Brown sugar, white sugar, baking soda, flour. He found them all in the same cupboard. Awesome.

"It wasn't—"

"Working out," Ash finished for him. "Yeah, you said that last time I asked. But *why* wasn't it working out?"

"I . . ." Dan found mixing bowls, a wooden spoon, and various sizes of measuring cups and spoons. "After you—" He took a deep breath. "After I—" He inspected the measuring cups, maybe checking their capacity, but didn't seem to really see them; he laid them all out in front of him and then stacked them inside each other again. "Woodworking felt like . . ."

Ash stole one of the measuring cups and measured out the flour. "Like a chore?"

"No. Never that. It was an escape from everything."

What is everything? Ash wanted to ask but instead said, "Why give it up, then?"

Dan measured out the wet ingredients into a separate mixing bowl. "I felt like I didn't deserve it."

"What?" Ash's head snapped toward Dan at that. What kind of bullshit was this? "What are you talking about?"

"I hurt people," Dan said, suddenly finding the mixing bowl super interesting. "I felt like I didn't deserve to be happy."

"That's an extremely fatalistic attitude." *Felt like,* Dan had said. "How do you feel now?"

Dan's mouth opened, and Ash could read it all over his face, how he was seconds away from changing the subject. Disappointment swept over him, surprisingly thick for someone who claimed he didn't want anything to do with the man in front of him.

Lies. He wanted everything to do with Dan, this Dan, who was so different and yet exactly the same as the Dan Ash had met six years ago.

But Ash knew he'd never trust Dan with his heart again.

Dan reached for the egg carton. "I feel like I'm going to make some changes in my life."

Surprised by the candor, Ash said, "Like what?"

"Well, for starters, I want to get back into woodworking again. But I'm sort of . . . directionless at the moment, half living in New York, half not. I need a workshop to make things, and until I settle down, that's . . ." He waved a hand. "Up in the air." Pushing his bowl of mixed wet ingredients toward Ash, he then took the dirty dishes to the sink. "I feel bad using the chocolate chips without asking Marion."

"There's six more packages in the cupboard," Ash told him, adding Dan's wet ingredients to his dry ones. "But if it makes you feel better, I'll go out first thing and buy a replacement."

Dan smiled at him over his shoulder. "You'll be the only one up first thing on a Sunday morning."

"Will I? You don't run on Sundays anymore?"

"Nope. It's my sleep-in day."

"But we have to work off these cookies."

"Maybe you do." Dan turned off the water and dried his hands on a dish towel. "Not me. I'm not reporting for duty."

"I'm not reporting for *duty*." Ash finished mixing everything and found a baking tray.

"It's sort of like that, isn't it, though? Ashton Yager reporting for duty, Coach. What plays are we practicing today and how many games can I expect to play this season?"

The chuckle took Ash by surprise. "Shut up and help me with this. Besides, it's more like, Ashton Yager reporting for duty, Coach. Whose ass can I kiss to stay on this team?"

"Stay on the—What?" Dan's brow furrowed as he carefully placed a ball of dough onto the baking tray. "Are you being traded?"

"No. At least, I don't think so. My contract's up at the end of this season, and I haven't heard anything from the club about a new one yet."

And I might never since the entire world will know about

my sexuality in less than thirty-six hours. He didn't tell Dan that, though he wasn't sure why he held back.

"There's still time, though, right?" Dan said. "The season's barely started."

"Yeah. Except usually these kinds of things happen before the season starts, so it doesn't distract the player from the game." *Usually*, but not always. Could be he was worrying for nothing. He was a damn good defenseman, and as far as he could tell, there wasn't any reason for them not to keep him. He didn't cause trouble (Monday's article notwithstanding), didn't talk back, took his job seriously, and always gave 150 percent of himself to the game. "It's frustrating. Like giving your number to someone in a bar and waiting impatiently for them to call."

"Can other teams call in the meantime?"

Ash smirked at Dan's attempt at word play and spooned out more dough. "Not until the season's over and my contract's up."

"Hockey politics are complicated."

"That's not even the worst of it."

Sitting across from each other at the island, they continued to spoon small balls of dough onto the tray. Although it wasn't long before Ash realized he was way faster than Dan.

Because Dan was busy eating raw dough.

"That's disgusting."

Caught in the act, Dan's eyes widened. With the hood of his onesie covering his head, he resembled a teenager stealing from his mom's wallet.

"I didn't do it," he said.

Ash mock scowled and pointed at the baking tray with his spoon.

Reluctantly, Dan plopped his piece of dough onto it.

Once the tray was full and the bowl empty, Ash placed

the tray into the preheated oven, set the timer, and passed the bowl and spoons to Dan for him to wash.

"Why are you up in the middle of the night, anyway?" Dan asked.

"Couldn't sleep." Ash rubbed his hands over his face. His eyes were gritty. He could probably sleep now, but he found himself unwilling to leave Dan's presence, no matter how much his heart told him to run far, far away. "Kept thinking about what I'll return home to in a few days." Among other things.

"When do you head back?"

Ash shrugged. "Not sure yet."

"This your first hurricane?"

"Believe it or not, yeah." He leaned his elbows on the island. "And I thought Syracuse was bad with its minus forty degree winters and snow up to my eyeballs."

Dan finished the dishes and retook his seat. "I'd take snow over hurricanes any day."

"Ditto."

"Besides, snow means skiing. And snowboarding. Skating."

"Sledding."

Dan's gaze became distant. "I haven't done that since I was a teenager. Last I remember of it is taking Mitch when he was ten or so. There was this great hill by our house that was perfect."

"I've never been sledding in my life. I spent my winters fishing with my dad until he moved to New York."

"How is he?" Dan asked, the question jarring Ash for some reason. It shouldn't have—Dan and Ash's dad had always gotten along. Ash had just assumed that by leaving him at the airport, Dan had forgotten not just about him, but about his dad too.

As was becoming increasingly clear, there was more to Dan's story than Ash had thought. Much more.

Ash just wasn't ready to hear about it.

Not yet.

Maybe not ever. But definitely not yet.

The cookies eventually came out of the oven, and Dan made fun of him for burning his tongue.

"Did you eat that right off of the pan?" Dan's expression said *Are you stupid?* as Ash choked and fanned his mouth. "Idiot."

Twenty minutes later, only crumbs remained. Dan was rubbing his eyes, and Ash was finally tired enough and distracted enough that he could sleep now. He washed and dried the baking tray and put it back where he'd found it, steps dragging. "Thank you," he said and brushed a crumb off the corner of Dan's mouth. Dan sucked in a sharp breath, eyes darkening. Ash swallowed hard. "For hanging out with me in the middle of the night."

"It was worth it." Dan's smile was soft. "Even without the cookies."

Warmth shot through Ash, unnerving yet thrilling, shooting tingles into his heart, beating rabbit-fast. He couldn't bring himself to step away from Dan, to pull his arm back. His fingers swept over Dan's prickly jaw and into the curly blond hair above his ear, as soft and silky as he remembered.

Dan exhaled shakily, and warm air caressed the skin of Ash's wrist. His gaze dropped to Ash's mouth.

Ash backed away with a gasp. He cleared his throat. "We should go to bed."

Blinking, Dan looked like he was coming out of a trance. "Yeah." His voice was hoarse. "Bed. Yeah."

They kept their steps light on the stairs, staying quiet.

Three in the morning and nobody stirred in the B&B except them.

"Think you can sleep now?" Dan asked, voice intimately soft in the hallway outside his room. The dim wall sconce made his eyes shine.

"Yeah. I'm beat. Good night, Dan." Ash headed for the stairs to the third floor. "Enjoy your king-sized bed."

"There's room enough for two. If you want to share."

Pausing on the steps, Ash's hands clenched on the railing, tension arcing between them. Burying the instinct—the *desire*—to stay, he meant to turn Dan down—

But Dan's posture was stiff and unyielding, braced for impact. Braced for Ash to reject him.

And Ash couldn't do it. Didn't want to, if he was being honest, even though he should.

"Okay."

ELEVEN

IT WAS A COUPLE OF WEEKS BEFORE THEY COULD make Dan's Thai chicken curry. Dan had a family thing one weekend, and then Ash had to fly to Syracuse for some PR stuff with his team the week after. So although they met for lunch a couple times a week, Dan still found his thoughts straying to Ash more often than not.

After an extensive Google search, it became clear that discovering one's sexual orientation later in life was not unusual. Not that Dan considered himself *later in life* at the ripe old age of twenty, but didn't most people figure it out in their teenage years, or before? Not according to the internet.

So yeah. Not unusual. And freaking out about it? Apparently, that was also a thing.

Not that Dan was freaking out about being attracted to his own gender. He was merely . . . confused. Why hadn't he discovered it sooner? Had he been attracted to men before but ignored it? Repressed it? Misinterpreted it as admiration for talent or physique or lifestyle? Mitch had come out to Dan as gay when he was eleven, and yet it had never crossed Dan's mind that he might be the same.

Well, not the same. Bisexuality wasn't the same as being gay.

So, okay. He was bisexual. According to the internet, anyway. Although there were some forums that said labels weren't needed.

Dan liked labels, though.

Bisexual it was.

Why had it taken Ash for him to figure it out? Did it really matter?

Part of him thought he should've been worried about being attracted to men. Or perhaps freaking out more. Or anxious about coming out. But . . . Mitch. Mitch was gay, had never freaked out about it, and was one hundred percent okay with who he was. And he was the most important person in Dan's life. He could've been attracted to three-headed Martians and Dan would've loved him anyway. Therefore, if Dan was fine with Mitch being gay, then he should, theoretically, be fine with himself being bisexual.

And he realized, with some amazement, that he was. A little bit of anxiety, sure. But mostly the knowledge settled over him as if he'd always known. And maybe he had.

His cell phone rang and he flipped it open. *Ashton Yager* flashed in the small display screen.

How had he known Dan was thinking about him?

"Hey, Ash."

"Hey, are you still coming over?"

"Yeah, why? Oh, shit." Dan caught a glimpse of the time in the bottom corner of his desktop computer. "I'm late. I'm so sorry. I got caught up in work. I'm leaving now."

"Are you . . . at the office?"

"Um, yes?" The empty, silent, dark office that would've been creepy had Dan never spent a weekend here before, trying to catch up on work.

"Dude." Ash's tone held confusion bordering on derision. "It's six thirty. On Saturday night."

"You work Saturday nights," Dan mumbled as he saved his work.

"That's the nature of the game. That's different. Get out of there. Right now."

"I'm going, I'm going," Dan said through a chuckle, heading for the kitchen where he'd stashed the groceries he'd purchased earlier. "I'll see you in about a half hour."

It was more like forty minutes later by the time he knocked on Ash's door. His armpits were sweating, and it had nothing to do with the summer heat.

"Hey!" The door flung open and Ash stood in the doorway. He was so huge his shoulders took up the entire space.

Dan gulped. "Hey."

"Let me take some of these." Ash unburdened Dan's arms of a couple of the grocery bags and waved him inside. "Did you buy out the grocery store?"

"I brought all the ingredients."

"I can see that." Ash pulled a small bag of sugar from one of the bags. "I do own sugar, you know."

Dan shrugged and deposited his own bags on the kitchen counter. "Just in case."

"We also have vegetable oil. But not most of this other stuff." Bell peppers, a bottle of fish sauce, a can of coconut milk, and shallots joined the vegetable oil and sugar on the counter. Dan unpacked his own bag, adding more ingredients to the mix.

"Okay," Ash said, examining it all, hands on hips. "Where do we start?"

They divided up the chopping and measuring, spreading it out on the kitchen island, which was bigger than Dan's tiny kitchen alone.

"Thanks for suggesting we do this here." Dan cut the chicken breasts into strips. "You were right—we definitely wouldn't have had enough space at my place."

"That's for sure. Pretty sure I take up the entire space at

your counter."

"Damn." Dan paused as he suddenly remembered. "I forgot beer."

"Dude. Give me some credit."

Ash's dad's apartment was spacious. It was essentially a long, rectangular room that opened into a combined sitting/dining area. Behind it was the kitchen, and then a narrow hallway led to what Dan assumed were a couple of bedrooms and a bathroom. It wasn't decorated in any particular shade; the couches didn't match the chair, the curtains looked like they'd been flown in from the eighties, the living room carpet was a faded pale pink, and the kitchen dishes were all mismatched.

It appealed to a certain part of Dan that had grown up in his mother's carefully organized world. When he voiced his thoughts to Ash, Ash smirked and said, "You mean you haven't always lived in that tiny apartment?"

"I grew up in the Hamptons, in a hideous mansion that's been in my family since before I was born."

"'Hideous' and 'mansion' seem like an oxymoron."

"It's a big, dark, gothic-looking thing. Reflects my mother's personality perfectly."

"Ouch." Ash dug into a cupboard for a pan. "I take it you two don't get along?"

"If by *getting along* you mean frigid conversations over family dinner, then sure. We get along."

"Don't you work for her?"

"Yeah. Add frigid conversations over spreadsheets too."

"I'm sorry." Ash gathered all of the chopped and measured ingredients and laid them out next to the stove. "Did something happen to make your relationship that way?"

"No." Dan dumped the cut chicken into the pan. "She's always been cold, almost like she didn't want children and only had them for appearances' sake. She's very contained, very proper. Obsessed with how other people see her, and by extension us—her family—as well as the business. She's not as cold with me as she is with my brother, though. Something about his desire to go pro doesn't sit well with her."

Ash turned the burner on under the pan. "Is that why you went into the family business? Do you have instructions for this?"

"Yeah. In my back pocket." Dan turned his back on Ash to wash his hands in the sink.

Fingers deftly slid into his pocket and plucked out the folded instructions. Gasping at the contact, Dan held still for a moment, dick twitching in his pants. Jesus, what a time for an erection. In front of a guy who could knock him out with one punch. Not that he'd gotten any homophobic vibes from Ash, but still. Better to play it safe.

Although, if he were looking for further evidence that he was attracted to Ash, well . . . here it was. Metaphorically waving its hand hello.

So not the time for bad sex jokes.

"No," he said, answering Ash's question as he dried his hands. "I joined the family business because . . . Actually, it was always assumed that I would, which is why I'm taking business and accounting in college."

"There's nothing else you wanted to do with your life?"

"No. Well . . ." Dan's shrug was awkward. "I wanted to work with wood. Shop class was my favorite in high school, and I took woodworking classes after school at an art center. I've even got a small studio in one of the sheds behind the house."

"No shit." Ash was grinning as he poured the vegetable oil into the pan. "What kind of things do you build?"

"Smaller household items, mostly. Jewelry boxes, small coin bowls, and . . . Actually, here." Dan reached into the last bag he'd brought and came out with a small brown box. He handed it to Ash. "This is for you. As a thank you. For tonight. For your hospitality."

Could he sound anymore awkward?

"For your hospitality," Ash repeated with a smirk. "You make it sound like you're a guest at my hotel."

"Shut up, asshole. Just open it."

Ash did, pulling out a sun catcher shaped like a crescent moon with a round crystal hanging from the top. His eyes widened as he brushed a thumb over the logo of his AHL team that Dan had painstakingly burned into the moon's widest part. The entire sun catcher was about the size of Dan's palm, and the widest part of the moon was only about an inch wide, meaning the logo was itty-bitty. If someone didn't know what it was, it probably looked like a bunch of squiggly lines with an S in the middle. Dan was proud of it nonetheless.

"You made this?" Ash asked softly.

Dan's shoulders hiked up to his ears, the awe on Ash's face too much, too potent. "Yeah."

"You even put the year I started playing for Syracuse. How'd you know it?"

"You must've told me at lunch at some point."

Dan had looked it up online.

Same thing.

"This is amazing. These are the kinds of things you make? You should sell them online."

Dan waved a hand. "I doubt there's much money to be made in that kind of thing."

"Is that why you went into the family business instead?" Ash left the kitchen to hang the sun catcher on a hook in the window in the living room. "Looks good here, yeah?"

"Yeah," Dan echoed hoarsely. "It looks good."

They finished preparing dinner, making enough to feed six people. Or two people, if one of those was Ashton Yager. By the time they finished eating, there was just enough left for one person—Ash's dad, who, according to Ash, was due home any minute.

"That was the perfect amount of spicy," Ash announced as he transferred the leftovers onto a plate for his dad, then brought the pan to the sink. "My mouth is on fire. It's amazing."

"It'd probably feel better with my tongue in it."

Standing at the sink, Ash froze, hands in the water, Dan's words playing on repeat in his head.

It'd probably feel better with my tongue in it.

It'd probably feel better with my tongue in it.

It'd probably feel better with my tongue in it.

Yes! Ash wanted to scream. *Yes, it would!* He'd spent weeks pretending that Dan was just a friend, that he didn't feel anything for him beyond friendship. Catching Dan's eyes lingering on him more than once didn't mean anything. Ash was a big guy; people looked twice all the time.

But the way Dan looked at him . . . There was heat there that Ash hadn't wanted to acknowledge, and not because he didn't feel the same way. Dan was . . . Frankly, Dan was beautiful. Ash had been surrounded by athletes his entire life—he'd certainly admired another guy's physique before. Had even been attracted to guys before, in a yeah-I-could-do-you kind of way.

This was more than that. He was attracted to Dan on

a deeper level. Dan was shy even though he pretended he wasn't. Slightly awkward, though he covered it well. Generous and kind. A bit of a nerd, though you wouldn't know it by looking at him. And the hint of vulnerability made Ash want to protect him.

No, the reason he hadn't wanted to acknowledge what was between them was two-fold: First, they lived four hours apart. Second, Ash played professional sports. One did not come out in professional sports unless one wanted to be bullied and ostracized.

Nobody said he had to come out, though.

And since Dan had thrown down the gauntlet . . .

Ash turned from the sink to do exactly what Dan had suggested—stick his tongue in his mouth—only to find Dan on the other side of the kitchen, the island between them.

"I'm sorry." Dan's eyes took up half his face, and he held his hands up, ready to defend himself against . . . against Ash? "I'm sorry, I didn't mean to say that."

If he hadn't meant to say it, then . . . "What did you mean to say?"

"I . . ." Panicking. Dan was panicking, his breathing fast and choppy. But why?

Ash took a step toward him. "Dan—"

Dan took a step back, eyes getting bigger, if that was even possible.

Ash held his own hands up, sudden clarity stopping him in place. "I'm not going to beat you up for being gay."

"Bisexual, apparently," Dan whispered. "If that makes a difference."

"Yeah, well." Ash lowered one hand, keeping the other raised. "Same here." No *apparently* about it, though. He'd known he was bisexual for a long time but never felt the need to act on it. Or come out. Why did his sexuality have to be a defining characteristic of who he was?

There was certainly a need now. Lots of it. Most of it centered in his pants.

"You . . ." Dan's gaze swept Ash from the top of his brown-haired head to his size thirteen feet. It was an assessing sweep, no hint of heat, but it still made Ash's blood sing. "Guys who look like you aren't . . ."

Hands on his hips, Ash cocked his head. "Pretty sure that's a stereotype. That guys who look like me can't be gay, or bi, or whatever."

"You're right." Dan rubbed his forehead. "You're totally right. That was dumb. I'm sorry. I'm sorry also for what I said. Before."

"Sorry, huh? Does that mean you don't want to kiss me?"

"I . . ." Dan's gaze landed on Ash's mouth.

Ash raised an eyebrow.

Dan blushed.

It was a good look on him.

Ash took a step toward him, but Dan stiffened. What was going on in that head of his? Was he embarrassed by what he'd said? Surprised that Ash felt the same way? Freaking out that he'd laid it all out there in the first place?

All of the above. Definitely.

Ash might freak out later himself. Knowing he was bisexual was one thing. Acting on his attraction to men—to Dan—after spending his adolescent years in locker rooms where the words *gay* and *fag* and *homo* were used as insults by clueless teens? It was like getting used to a new coach after playing for the same one for years. Like climbing the Himalayas after practicing solely in Yosemite.

It'd take practice. Lots of practice. Lots of practice

kissing Dan.

He was so on board with that.

Dan was no longer looking like the top of his head was about to fly off. Ash chanced another step closer, and Dan watched him, not moving, not even blinking.

Was he breathing? Ash certainly wasn't.

It was Dan who closed the distance between them, tentatively, hands curling around Ash's upper arms. Ash snaked his arms around Dan's waist, bringing them chest-to-chest and lifting Dan up onto his tippy toes, making Dan's breathing hitch and his hands clamp onto Ash.

Holding a man was different than holding a woman. Dan was harder, sturdier, curved in different places. But it was nice not to have to watch his own strength for once. Dan looked like he could take a pounding.

Fuck. When had he gone from kissing Dan to pounding him?

Now that his brain had gone there, it was impossible to rein it in, and he kept picturing Dan on his back underneath him, head thrown back against the pillow, mouth open in an O of ecstasy, sweat dampened curls clinging to his forehead.

Jesus. The air was sucked out of the room, and yes, that was his dick thickening in his pants, right up against Dan's thigh. There was no way Dan could miss it.

And he certainly didn't. Gasping, his gaze snapped to Ash's, eyes dark and wide. His hands came up to Ash's face. "You do want to kiss me," he breathed.

"Yes. Yes, I really, really do."

Dan reared up, nuzzling Ash's face with his nose, breathing him in. Ash returned the gesture, arms banding iron-like around Dan as he inhaled. Dan smelled mostly of soap and a little bit of aftershave, scents Ash had never been turned on by before. But on Dan, it made him want to pull him even closer.

Ash pressed a tiny kiss to Dan's cheekbone, the skin warm and soft. "I've never kissed a guy before."

"Me neither." Dan pulled back, just a bit, and smiled quietly at Ash. "Hi."

Something soft and warm tumbled in Ash's chest. "Hi."

He leaned in and—

A key in the lock, then the door being thrown open, and a loud voice proclaiming, "It smells great in here! I hope you left me some of whatever that is."

Huffing a frustrated breath, Ash's hands clenched on Dan's hips. "Are you kidding me? Way to suck the fun out of the evening, Dad."

"What was that?" his dad called from the front, where he was no doubt removing his work boots.

"Nothing," Ash called back.

Dan's shoulders shook with suppressed laughter, and he fell forward into Ash, laying his forehead on Ash's shoulder.

"I'm glad one of us is finding it funny," Ash grumbled, pressing a quick kiss to the top of Dan's head. "Parents have the worst timing."

Footsteps came closer, and with a final squeeze, Ash stepped back from Dan. Nothing like a parent to kill an erection. Dan appeared to be in trouble, though. He scrubbed his hands over his flushed face and remained behind the island, hiding his boner from view. The grin he shot Ash was self-deprecating and open and a little bit naughty, and promised all sorts of things Ash would've given his left nut for had his dad not walked into the kitchen.

"Hey, kid."

Ash took a steadying breath and leaned back against the counter. "Hey, Dad. This is my friend, Dan."

"The one from your office building you've been lunching with? Nice to meet you, Dan."

"You too, sir," Dan said as they shook.

"Sir?" Ash's dad's eyebrows flew up and he smiled at Ash. "I like this one. I'm no sir, though," he told Dan. "It's just Eddie."

"Okay, just Eddie. You're even bigger than Ash."

At six-foot-four, Ash was tall, and he was wide. Eddie was both taller and wider, his hair a thick, shocking silver, laugh lines bookending his eyes and mouth.

A booming laugh from Ash's dad. "His mom's tall too, so between the two of us, he was going to be a giant. He was always the tallest kid in his class. You should check out the pictures in the photo album on the coffee table."

"Dad . . ."

"What? Dan wants to see."

Dan turned to Ash. "Yeah, I want to see."

Ash pointed at his dad. "You're not allowed to meet my friends anymore."

Eddie Yager didn't appear too concerned about it.

In the living room, Ash took the photo album off the coffee table and handed it to Dan. Plopping onto the couch, Dan opened it to the first page. Ash sat on the armchair, the clink of silverware on a plate resounding around them.

Couldn't his dad go away? Couldn't he see that Ash was trying to woo someone?

Dan chuckled and scooched forward, holding the album out between them. "What's this?"

"My first hockey game." Ash moved forward too, the album resting open half on his lap, half on Dan's.

"You look deranged."

"Yeah," Ash said with a laugh. "I couldn't wait to play. I was awful. I mean—" He waved at the picture of his relatively pint-sized self in a hockey uniform and skates. "—I was four, so it's to be expected."

"How does someone from Florida end up playing hockey? Why weren't you at the beach?"

Ash glanced over his shoulder at his dad and lowered his voice. "My parents both have demanding jobs. They worked nights and weekends sometimes, so I'd find myself at the rec center down the street with my babysitter more often than not. One of the instructors there must've seen me admiring the skaters, because he found me a pair of used skates in the lost and found, put me on the ice, and from there . . . there wasn't any going back."

Their gazes met over the album, something heavy and soft, terrifying and thrilling settling between them. Dan perched on the very edge, his hand resting on the arm of Ash's love seat.

A throat cleared loudly. "I'm going to take my dinner into my room," his dad announced at full volume. "And watch some TV. Very loudly."

Neither of them acknowledged his departure.

Silence descended between them. Ash could've sworn he heard his own heart beating in tune with Dan's. The night felt surreal, as if Ash was looking at it through a gauzy curtain. He stood to place the album on the coffee table, and when he turned back, Dan was standing right behind him.

"Should we have dessert now?" he asked.

Ash reached for his hand and drew him those last few inches closer. "Does dessert involve kissing?"

"Yes." Dan rose onto his toes, arms threading around Ash's waist. "Definitely yes."

He kissed the corner of Ash's mouth. Ash hummed in frustration. Chuckling under his breath, Dan placed another tiny kiss on Ash's jaw.

"No more of that," Ash growled, chasing Dan's lips with his own, hands clamping onto Dan's hips.

Finally, their smiling mouths met, clinging with no sign of hesitancy. Dan tasted faintly of the beer they'd had with dinner, and his mouth was alternately hard and soft on Ash's. One of Ash's hands found Dan's lower back, fingers spreading wide onto the top of his ass; the other carded through those amazing curls Ash had been dying to touch for weeks.

Perhaps they'd never kissed men before, but they got with the program fast enough.

Kissing Dan wasn't unlike kissing a woman. Except where Ash might've hesitated before biting a woman's lower lip, thought twice before cupping an ass and squeezing, banked the desire to just *let go* and fucking take . . .

He didn't do that with Dan.

And Dan groaned and bit back, and his nails dug into Ash's shoulders through his T-shirt, and he gave and took with as much enthusiasm and desire as Ash.

They separated, but only for a second to catch their breaths. Dan cupped Ash's face with a hand, thumb brushing along Ash's lip. Ash sucked Dan's thumb into his mouth, swirling his tongue around it, enjoying the rough edge of a nail against his tongue so much it tantalized his senses. Dan's eyes went so hot, his cheeks flushing with hunger, and Ash growled in the back of his throat.

Then they were kissing again, harder, messier, teeth clicking, tongues sweeping in to take control. Clenching hands and hungry moans. Dan's leg wound around Ash's hip, bringing them even closer, nudging their erections together.

Breathing hard, Ash tore his mouth away. "Fuck." He dropped a kiss to the corner of Dan's mouth, on the underside of his jaw, down to his collarbone.

Dan's head fell back with a gasp and he clung to Ash's shoulders.

Ash's hands had somehow found their way up the back of Dan's T-shirt, and he ran them along heated skin, brushing the tips of his fingers along Dan's spine, making him tremble.

"Fuck," Dan breathed, echoing Ash's sentiment. His own hands clenched on Ash's shoulders. "Fuck, Ash, I don't . . ."

"Don't what?" Ash mumbled into Dan's neck. He bit the soft skin between Dan's neck and shoulder, making Dan shudder so violently that he buckled. Ash caught him, then stumbled onto the love seat behind him, taking Dan with him. Straddling Ash's thighs, Dan rested their foreheads together as they got their breaths back, both hands cupping Ash's face.

"Don't what?" Ash asked again.

Dan's low laugh was self-deprecating. "I don't know what to say to you right now."

Ash ran his hands soothingly up and down Dan's sides. "Hopefully not *That was awful, let's never do it again.*"

"No. If anything it's let's do that again. And again. As often as possible."

So they kissed again. And again. As often as possible.

TWELVE

SEPTEMBER 2009—PRESENT DAY

THEY DIDN'T AWAKE TANGLED IN EACH OTHER, BUT it was close.

Ash squinted his eyes open to gentle yellow sunlight. He was warm and cozy, and his feet weren't hanging over the end of the bed. He snuggled further into the pillow.

A pillow he shared with Dan. Nose to nose, on their stomachs, Ash breathed deeply and inhaled Dan's sleep-musk scent.

They weren't tangled together . . . but they were half on top of each other.

Ash found he didn't care.

Dan's face was relaxed in sleep, cheeks flushed from heat, mouth slightly parted. The corner of his lips were crusty on one side where he'd drooled. He slept the way he had six years ago, with an arm folded up under his pillow. He'd wake up with a kink in his elbow if he didn't move it soon.

Ash ran the back of his fingers over Dan's jaw, the warm skin tingling his fingers.

Leave. He should leave. He shouldn't have stayed in the first place.

But this was Dan. His Dan. A little more subdued, a little less quick to smile, a lot harder on himself. Still his Dan, though. Same crazy hair. Same flash that sparked in his eyes when he was angry. Same habit of rubbing his forehead when he was nervous or unsure. Same underlying vulnerability.

Same ability to get under Ash's skin.

He should leave. But he didn't want to.

So he stayed. No matter how bad of an idea it was.

He ran his fingers over Dan's jaw again. Because Dan was still sleeping. Because he could. Because cocooned under the covers together felt like old times, felt like past Sunday mornings they'd spent together, breathing each other in and wishing the day would never end.

Dan snuffled, sinking further into his pillow. Ash yanked his arm back, which was what woke Dan fully. His eyes cracked open, and he blinked blearily at Ash. Sighing, he closed his eyes again, only for them to spring open a second later.

"You're still here," he said, voice rough with sleep. He touched Ash's bare shoulder, as if assuring himself he was real.

Ash sucked in a breath at the barely there touch. "Yeah."

"How come?"

He should've hedged.

I was comfy and didn't want to move.

Your bed's bigger than mine.

The alarm on my phone didn't go off.

But if he expected honesty from Dan, it was only fair to reciprocate.

"I didn't want to leave."

Dan's hand jerked on Ash's shoulder. "And now?"

"That's a loaded question," Ash said, rolling onto his back and scrubbing his hands over his face. "I should go."

"You don't—"

"I do have to. Otherwise I'm going to jump you, and I don't think either of us is ready for that."

He got out of bed, a choked sound coming from behind him as he gathered the sweat pants, T-shirt, and hoodie he'd discarded last night.

And fled.

The numbers in the spreadsheet didn't make sense. And not because Dan was too distracted with thoughts of Ash returning to jump him. But because the numbers didn't add up.

After Ash had run out of his room like he was being chased, Dan had showered, dressed, and gotten to work. He should've slept longer given the time they'd gone to bed, but he'd been wide awake after Ash's words and couldn't think about anything except Ash jumping him.

He'd even left his door open a crack in case Ash came back.

Seated in one of the lounge chairs next to the window in his room, laptop on his thighs, he checked his spreadsheet for a third time, frowning when the numbers still didn't make sense.

He wasn't distracted.

His math wasn't wrong.

Which meant . . .

Well, he wasn't sure what it meant.

Just like Ash's parting shot. He didn't know what that meant either.

I do have to. Otherwise I'm going to jump you, and I don't think either of us is ready for that.

Dan was ready. More than ready. He'd been born ready. He ached with how ready he was.

But Ash was very obviously not ready. And more than that . . .

Possibly not interested.

No, he was definitely interested. That had been a

full-on erection in his running shorts when he'd left, tenting the front and making Dan's mouth water just remembering it. Remembering how it'd felt in his hands once upon a time, smooth and silky and hard. The sounds Ash had made as Dan licked the underside, nibbled the tip, and then sucked him into his mouth.

So, yeah. Ash was interested. His body, anyway. The rest of him . . . his mind, his heart . . .

That was what Dan needed to work on. Because he didn't just want Ash's body—he wanted the whole package. He'd had it once. He'd had every part of Ash once, and he wanted that back.

But what if he'd fucked things up too badly last time? What if there was no coming back from that? Second chances were all well and good unless the person you wanted a second chance with didn't want you back. Had written you off as a mistake.

He'd just ask Ash what he wanted. He could do that, right?

Or . . . Even better, Dan would lay it all out there. Everything he felt, everything that was in his heart, he'd hand it to Ash with a bow for Ash to accept or reject.

It was the least he could do.

His gaze snagged on a swath of denim-blue fabric on the chair across from him. It had the Syracuse AHL team's logo on the front—faded and almost entirely gone. Dan sighed. Ash had caught him wearing his old sweatshirt a couple nights ago. Would he never stop embarrassing himself in front of that man?

"What'd the laptop do to piss you off?"

Forced out of his thoughts, he found Ash leaning against the doorjamb, wearing a pair of jeans and a T-shirt and looking so edible that Dan had to swallow past a dry throat. "Huh?"

Ash waved at his own forehead. "You're frowning at your computer."

"Oh. It's not the computer so much as the spreadsheet on it."

"Spreadsheet? Why are you working on a Sunday?"

"I always work on Sundays."

"Why?"

"Why not? You work Sundays."

Ash crossed his arms. "That's different."

"Why?"

"Because that's the nature of my job."

Dan glared back at him. "And this is the nature of *my* job."

"Still?"

"Still," Dan confirmed. "And much more frequently."

"Why?"

"Because I was only a junior analyst back then."

"And now?"

"Now I'm the manager of financial planning and analysis."

"I don't know what that means, but it sounds boring." Ash straightened and gave a jerk of his chin. "Let's go have breakfast."

"I need to send an email to the auditors about—"

"Do the auditors work on Sundays?"

Dan huffed. "No."

Ash merely raised an eyebrow.

Saving his work, Dan closed the laptop and stood. "Breakfast it is."

THIRTEEN

PACING THE LENGTH OF HIS BEDROOM AT THE
B&B, Ash refreshed the web browser on his phone
for the umpteenth time. The article on *Sport
Check* would be up any minute.

After tossing and turning all night, he'd finally given
up with a muttered curse. He refreshed the browser again.

"Still nothing," he told the spider in the corner.

He paced some more, narrowly avoiding conking himself on the sloped roof. Stared cross-eyed at a landscape
painting on the wall. Inspected a loose thread in a pillow
cover. Buffed his nails against his boxer briefs. Downed
half a bottle of water. The other half. Flossed.

He was about to come apart.

Again, he refreshed the page.

Oh god. Oh shit. Oh damn. There it was. Right on the
Sport Check homepage, at 7:00 a.m. on the dot, as promised. Stomach rolling, he clicked on the link.

NHL Player Comes Out as Bisexual

*Ashton Yager, NHL defenseman for Tampa Bay, has
come out as bisexual, hoping that it will inspire others to be
true to who they are.*

*"Being gay or lesbian or bisexual or transgender or
whatever else," Yager said in a telephone interview, "it's seen
as a stigma in professional sports. But why? At the end of the
day, your team is relying on you to bring your skills to the
table and to play the best you possibly can."*

Yager, who played for Tampa's affiliate AHL team in

Syracuse prior to his move to Tampa in 2004, isn't shy about admitting his nerves.

"Of course I'm nervous about coming out," Yager told Sport Check *with a laugh. "And there's a part of me that doesn't understand why I have to. Why can't I just live my own life? But I understand that the world isn't like that yet."*

Yager, 27, told Sport Check *that an LGBTQ friend of his has been bullied at school, and that this friend's story inspired Yager to step up and, hopefully, "kick stereotypes in the ass."*

"What I really want is for LGBTQ kids out there to realize that they can make their dreams come true, no matter what. Maybe, by coming out, I've made it easier for the next person."

As a final word of advice, Yager had this to say to LGBTQ youth: "You're not alone."

"Wow." Sinking onto the edge of the bed, he read it a second time. Then a third. "Okay, that wasn't so bad."

His phone buzzed. And again. A Twitter notification. Seven Twitter notifications. A phone call. Staples from the Toronto team.

Ash let it go to voicemail. Then promptly listened to the voicemail.

"Dude, what the hell? You could've told me. I've got your back, man. Call me if you need anything."

"What the . . .?" Ash muttered to the room at large.

And hung up to a dozen more notifications.

He threw the phone onto the bed. Covered it with a pillow. Backed away from it slowly.

Christ on a hockey stick. What the hell had he done?

Dan was packing the last of his toiletries away when a loud bang on his door made him fumble his tube of toothpaste.

"Dan!" came a muffled voice.

"Ash?"

Flinging open the door, he found a giant, rumpled hockey player wearing tiny underwear.

Ooh la la.

Ash's eyes were wild and he was struggling to breathe. Dan's lusty thoughts came to a halt. "What's wrong?"

"I . . ." Ash took in the toothpaste in Dan's hand and the open suitcase behind him on the luggage rack. "You're leaving?"

"It's Monday. I've got to head back to Burlington for work."

"Oh." A pause. Then, "Can I have this room?"

"Really? That's where you went?"

"I did a thing." Ash thrust his cell phone into Dan's hands, forced his way past Dan, and hightailed it toward the bathroom. "I gotta go throw up now." The door slammed closed behind him.

What the ever-loving hell?

Ash's phone was lighting up with one notification after another. Emails, texts, Twitter, Facebook, missed phone calls. Had he messed up somehow?

Tapping a random Twitter notification brought up a message in all caps from one of Ash's followers: *CONGRATULATIONS!!*

"Didn't mess up, then," Dan mumbled to himself.

Had Ash won an award?

Scrolling through Twitter, he found messages of a similar theme.

You're a pillar of hope!

Dude, you've just made history!

Wow, that took a lot of guts! Congratulations.

Love is love.

Such an inspiration.

On and on, but . . . why?

Finally, one follower had a link to something with the words *Have you seen this? It's a great day for the LGBTQ community! Congrats to Ashton Yager for coming out.*

"The fuck . . .?"

Sure enough, the link led to an article on *Sport Check* and—

"Holy jumping cheeseballs, Batman."

Right there, for all the world to see, was his sexuality exposed. Oh god, had he been outed?

No. There was an interview with Ash. Which meant Ash had known this was coming. That must've been what had him distracted all weekend. And here Dan had thought it was the hurricane. They'd spent most of the weekend to-gether—why hadn't Ash said anything?

Dan shook his head to dispel the thought. This wasn't about him. Not even a little. Swallowing the hurt, he cocked an ear toward the bathroom and listened for sounds of . . .

Not throwing up. In fact, all was silent.

He rapped on the door. "Ash?"

"Go away." Ash's voice was grouchy and annoyed with an underlying tinge of fear. "I'm busy questioning every de-cision I've ever made."

Pressing his lips together to keep in a laugh, Dan slid down to sit on the floor, back against the wall next to the bathroom door. "Why? You should see all the support you're getting." He went back to Twitter. "You've got hun-dreds of new followers, and a lot of the people sending you supportive messages have that little checkmark next to their name." That meant it was an official account or something, right? "Athletes, former athletes, athletes from other hockey teams. Hell, other sports. Celebrities, TV personalities."

One message caught his eye. *No fags in hockey.*

"Oh, *hell* no," he muttered. Tapping on the guy's name redirected him to the fucker's profile. Thirty-eight followers. "Yeah, we won't worry about that guy." Besides, Ash's other followers were already blasting him.

The phone rang in his hand. *Private number.*

"Don't answer that," Ash said. The bathroom door opened and he stepped out, skin too pale. "I'm not supposed to answer anything from the outside world until tomorrow."

Momentarily distracted by Ash's nearly naked state, Dan cleared his throat. "Why's that?"

"That's the plan we put together."

"Who's *we*?"

The phone had stopped ringing and now it pinged with a voicemail.

"Well?" Ash waved a hand. "Check it."

"You just said—"

"I need to know." He strode away with a wince, face tight, and wrapped his arms around his torso. "Just play it."

"Okay."

Dan tapped the button and put the phone on speaker.

"Mr. Yager, this is Daniel Curtis."

Dan boggled at the phone. Shit, Daniel Curtis, the league commissioner. This could be really, *really* good or really, *really* bad.

On the far side of the bed, Ash froze and appeared to stop breathing.

"Congratulations, son. You're the first out bisexual NHL player."

Ash whimpered.

"Things might be tough for a while. There'll be a lot of good, and some bad, but know that the organization is behind you one hundred percent. If there's anything I can do to help, just ask."

Ash fell face-first, crosswise, onto the bed, long legs hanging off one side. He muttered something Dan didn't catch and buried his head in the bedcovers.

Muting the phone, Dan stood and made his way over to the bed, collapsing on his back next to Ash. "What are you thinking?"

"I'm thinking," Ash said, flipping onto his back, "that I just tanked my chances at that new contract."

"Really? But the chairman said—"

"I know what he said, but whether the NHL backs me or not isn't the point. Think about it—I'm sure even a non-homophobic exec would rather have a player no one hates for his sexual orientation than one with all this baggage."

Dan didn't consider a person's sexual orientation *baggage*, but he could understand why an exec might. "What did Curtis mean when he said there's going to be some bad?"

Ash turned his head toward him. "There's generations of fans who grew up in an era where being gay in sports is wrong. That's not gonna go away overnight."

"Look at it this way, though. This'll blow over in a few weeks, by which point there'll still be months left in the regular season. Still lots of time for them to decide to offer you a new contract."

"True." He didn't sound convinced.

"Ask you a question?" Dan said.

"Mm-hmm."

Brown eyes like bricks of chocolate regarded him lazily, making Dan lose his train of thought.

"What's up?" Ash prompted.

Dan ran his tongue along his teeth, forcing moisture into his dry mouth. "I read online once that homophobia is pretty rampant in professional sports. Do you see a lot of evidence of that?"

Ash's lips kicked up on one side. "You sound like a reporter."

"Sorry, I didn't—"

"I'm just teasing you." He knocked his shoulder against Dan's, and Dan's stomach went giddy. "Truth is, I haven't. Not at the professional level, anyway, but I question whether that's because I just didn't notice. At the same time, though, the entire team knows about Alex. The coaches and management too. Maybe they've been on their best behavior, I don't know." He rubbed his hands over his face. "I feel like I'm talking in circles. Should I be worried that my phone stopped making noise?"

"I silenced it." Dan handed it over.

"Oh. That's a good idea. Thanks."

Dan rolled onto his side and propped his head up. "I admire you, you know."

Ash's snort of laughter was anything but amused.

"I'm serious." Dan punched Ash in the bicep and bruised his own knuckles in the process. God, the guy was *jacked*. "I get claustrophobic if there are too many eyes on me when I go out for a jog. And you . . . You've just put yourself in front of the entire world, given youth someone to look up to. That's amazing, Ash."

Mouth slacking, cheeks flushing, Ash's hand inched closer to Dan. Dan took it in his own and twined their fingers together.

"Thanks," Ash whispered.

His lips were red and slick. Skin tight and warm. Torso

cut and defined. Legs strong and thick. Underwear clung to hairy thighs and stretched taut across his pelvis.

Did someone turn the heat up in the room?

Dan swallowed hard against the desire to rub himself all over Ash like a fevered cat. Resisting didn't get any easier when Ash licked his lips and dropped his gaze to Dan's mouth.

Jerking away, Ash leaped off the bed. "I, uh . . ." Back to Dan, he coughed once. "I should get out of your hair. Let you finish packing, get on the road."

Dan stood too and discreetly readjusted himself in his dress pants. Not that the discretion mattered; Ash wouldn't look at him.

"Um . . ." At the door, Ash turned halfway, upper body toward Dan, feet pointing toward the exit. "Thanks. For . . ." He waved ineffectually. "Just. Thanks."

"I didn't do anything."

Ash huffed a laugh. "Feels like you talked me off a ledge. You have this way of remaining calm under pressure that makes it seem like everything's going to be okay."

Dan averted his gaze. Calm under pressure? Him? If only Ash knew why Dan had left him six years ago, he'd be singing an entirely different tune.

Ash reached for the door handle and Dan panicked, not wanting to let Ash go so soon. He said, "Ash? Do you think it's possible for us to ever be friends again?" He held his breath, the words to argue his case just waiting, poised, on the tip of his tongue.

Ash's cautious smile outshone the rising sun. "We already are." He gave Dan one of those leering up-and-down looks, taking in Dan's black dress pants, dark-purple shirt, and lavender tie. "You look good, by the way." Then he was gone with a wink.

FOURTEEN

Ash's departure gate at the Burlington International Airport was sleepy and sparsely populated. He and Alex had breezed through security forty minutes ago and still had another twenty to go before boarding. Nobody was flying anywhere on a Wednesday morning except business executives, and even fewer people were heading to Tampa. But Ash and Alex were due back today—their canceled preseason game had been rescheduled to Saturday evening at home given that Amalie Arena hadn't been damaged—so here they were.

Straightening from his half slouch, he squinted at the display board through his sunglasses. Nineteen minutes until boarding.

He wanted to go home; he was afraid of the condition he'd find his home in.

He wanted to stay; Dan was here.

He missed hockey. He missed home. He missed Dan.

We already are.

Not a lie. But he should've clarified. Because the words had made Dan's eyes light up, and it was clear that he wanted more from Ash than friendship.

Was Ash willing to give it to him? He wasn't so sure anymore that the answer was no. Hell, he'd gone to Dan on instinct Monday morning when his phone was blowing up, knowing Dan's steadiness would smooth him out. That had to mean something, right?

A few months ago, Ash had asked Mitch what sex with

a guy was like, mostly because he wanted to see how Mitch would react. If Mitch got fired up over the question, then he clearly wasn't the guy for Alex, who was the most laidback person Ash knew. But Mitch had barely hesitated before rebutting with a question of his own: "What's it like to have sex with a girl?"

Truth was, Ash's first time with a guy was years ago with Dan, before he'd even met Alex or Mitch. He didn't know why it was on his mind right now—possibly because of how Dan's intention to kiss him had been written all over his face on Monday morning. Ash had almost let him too. Dan was wearing him down, and Ash had no idea how it had happened.

It wasn't fair that Dan could come back into his life and make him feel again. To be honest, though, Ash didn't think Dan had done it on purpose. Ash was the one who'd sought him out—taking him out for milkshakes, making LEGOs with him, waking him up in the middle of the night because Ash was bored, sleeping in the same bed. Dan had been . . . not distant, but respectful of Ash's space. As a result, Ash had sought *him* out.

Dan was a fucking genius. Or a mastermind. Or a manipulative asshole. Or curiously considerate.

Ash thumped the back of his head against the window once, twice.

"Here."

He opened his eyes to find Alex holding out a takeout cup of coffee. "Thanks, man."

"It's very gray out there," Alex said, peering past Ash.

Ash grunted. Everything seemed gray to him. He even felt gray.

On the bank of television screens hanging from the ceiling to his left, the latest baseball highlights were replaced with talking heads and the headline *Ashton Yager: first out bisexual player in NHL history.* Ash tugged the bill of his ball cap lower, shading his face.

Alex sat to his right, leaving an empty chair between them, and laid his own head back against the window with a sigh.

"You worried about what you'll find?" Ash asked.

"I talked to my landlord yesterday," Alex said by way of response.

"What'd he say?"

"That it could've been worse."

"Not exactly reassuring."

Ash's landlord had given him a brief rundown of the damage to his own apartment, and, well . . . Actually, *it could've been worse* wasn't far off the mark. And, it turned out, he did have insurance. Or his landlord had insurance that covered him, or they both did, or . . . something. Ash had understood the specifics in his paperwork enough to know that he was covered, one way or another.

"Want to talk about it?" Alex asked.

Ash opened his eyes and looked down at himself. Jeans, running shoes, navy-blue hoodie, too hot coffee held in the hand braced on his thigh. All perfectly normal and mundane. Nothing that would prompt Alex's question.

"Talk about what?"

Alex removed the lid to his cup and set it aside to let his coffee cool. "Whatever's been bugging you lately." He nodded at the televisions. "Is it that?"

"No, that's . . . Most people have been surprisingly supportive." There were, predictably, unsympathetic assholes out there as well as the requisite jerks touting that bisexuality wasn't a thing, but Ash's fans were quick to castrate them. It was awesome to watch. But only on Twitter. There was only so much damage someone could do with a hundred and forty characters. Ash hadn't been on Facebook in days. Who knew what he'd see when a person had the freedom to write full paragraphs?

Thanks, but no thanks.

"I think I'm even more worried about Saturday's game," he told Alex, "than I was about the article. Facing the fans for the first time?"

There were going to be some haters in the crowd, he had no doubt.

Alex sipped his coffee. "Yeah. But we've got your back."

"I know. Tony called me yesterday."

"The VP of ticket sales?"

Ash grunted an affirmative. "He's only had one fan wanting to return his season tickets, and two dozen more who *want* season tickets. And Rachel's gotten calls from media and sponsors who want to know how they can be more involved with the club. And with me." His agent was fielding calls too, from two different major clothing companies that wanted Ash for their new line of commercials.

His life had become a circus, and all he could do was hold on for the ride of a lifetime.

"I've been thinking about it the past few days," Alex said, his own ball cap shading his face. "Coming out. I feel like I'm letting you down by staying closeted to the public."

"What? Dude, no. I appreciate it. Really, I do. But don't you dare do anything you're not ready for. I know you've got my back."

Leaning forward, Alex braced his elbows on his knees, coffee cup cradled in both hands. "If it was just me, I'd consider it more seriously. But it's Mitch too."

"I get it." Ash squeezed Alex's shoulder.

Alex squinted at him. "You sure there isn't anything else you want to talk about?"

"Other than the public exhibit my life has become and possible hurricane damage?"

"You tell me."

Ash glanced at the display board again. Sixteen minutes until boarding. "I'm gonna get some snacks for the flight," he said, standing.

"Uh-huh."

Taking his coffee with him, he found a convenience store not far from his departure gate and perused the snack options. The snack options that could rob people of their livelihoods. Jesus. Five ninety-five for a tiny bag of crackers? Four fifty for a two-pack of Oreos? Airports were thieves. Who'd be that desperate for snacks?

Hungry travelers, that was who. Ash grabbed a few packs of crackers and cookies, a couple bottles of water (four dollars each!), then wandered aimlessly through the souvenir aisle. He poked at jugs of maple syrup that cost more than his snack loot combined. Upended plastic snow globes with cows or covered bridges inside. Crouched to peer at keychains in the shape of the state. Tried on a couple of zip-up hoodies with *Vermont* stitched across the front, both of which were too snug in the shoulders. There were pens, mugs, maple candy, T-shirts, coasters, teddy bears, hats, posters. All Vermont-branded and many in various shades of green.

He glanced at his watch. Eleven minutes until boarding.

Not that boarding would deter Alex from asking his questions—they were sitting next to each other on the flight—but the distance gave Ash time to figure out how to tell Alex about Dan without telling Alex about Dan.

Ash didn't have any intention of telling anyone about Dan. He liked having Dan all to himself. As if Dan belonged to him, a secret gift Ash didn't want to share with anyone else. Not that Dan belonged to him now, but he had, once. Just like Ash had belonged to Dan.

They'd belonged to each other.

Maybe it was a stupid thought. People weren't possessions, and that wasn't at all how he meant it. Dan wasn't a *thing* Ash had owned. They'd just fit so well together, had complimented each other like nothing Ash had ever experienced before, and *belong* was the best word he could find to describe their relationship.

Leaving the souvenirs behind, he paid for his snacks with seven minutes to go until boarding, and strolled back to his gate leisurely, sipping his coffee and trying to ignore how every man he saw reminded him of Dan.

Wait.

"Dan?"

Because that *was* Dan striding toward him, the corners of his mouth tipped upward uncertainly, wheeling a small, hard shell carry-on behind him. Dark, fitted jeans hugged his legs, and the collar of a white shirt peeked out of the neck of a light blue sweater. The whole outfit, topped with a royal blue blazer, was very men's fashion magazine.

Damn, he looked good.

"Are you heading back to New York today?" he asked when Dan stopped in front of him, smelling like some kind of masculine aftershave and coffee.

Dan threw his shoulders back. "I'm coming to Tampa with you."

"You're—Why?"

"If you think I'm going to let you face the potential damage to your home alone, you're crazy."

Suddenly, the veil smothering Ash's morning lifted, and the gray dogging his mood was replaced with bright fluorescents and pale pastels.

It really *could* have been worse.

There wasn't any storm surge damage, for one—there'd been flooding in plenty of areas, but not Ash's neighborhood. He'd lost some siding, but that was covered by his landlord's insurance, apparently. Chunks of drain pipe stuck out at odd angles, and other sections appeared to be missing entirely. The windows were all still intact thanks to the storm shutters and the extra plywood he'd hammered on top of them. His door hadn't been blown in.

His yard, however, was another story entirely. It looked liked a child had played with a backhoe. Luckily, the stone outdoor cooking area was still in one piece, although the heavy piece of what was possibly rebar or a lamp post would be difficult to remove from where it rested half on the cooking area and half on the grass. All but one massive, sturdy tree had either been uprooted or snapped in half. And he was pretty sure that was siding off of someone else's house wedged against the fence.

It really, *really* could have been worse.

On the other hand, his hometown was a disaster.

He'd white-knuckled the drive home from the enclosed parking garage he'd parked his SUV in before leaving, taking backroads and side roads that added almost an hour to an otherwise short trip home, avoiding flooded zones, areas with downed power lines, and others where trees blocked the way. Some homes had fared worse than others, just like some neighborhoods had fared better. Ash honestly didn't want to know what it looked like closer to the ocean.

Driving home had been disheartening, and Dan's muttered "Jesus Christ" from the passenger seat as they passed a demolished and flooded trailer park summed up Ash's feelings perfectly.

Extreme weather fucking sucked.

Why were they even playing in this city so soon after the storm? Roads were impassable, power was still out in some areas, and thousands had probably lost their homes. Nobody was thinking about hockey right now. Yeah, yeah, the game must go on and all that shit, but they should've played elsewhere until the city had time to recover.

Dan sidled up next to him, hands in his pockets, and they gazed out the sliding back door together. "Where do you want to start?" he asked.

"Good question." Ash contemplated the backyard again; the mess was so daunting that he turned his back on it and surveyed his apartment instead. With half his stuff in storage on the sixth floor and his large furniture clustered in the middle of the living room and covered in tarps, his place felt oddly barren and disorganized.

Something off must've been written on his face, because Dan took one look at him and announced, "We'll start with lunch."

So they started with lunch.

Down the street from his building was an Irish pub—or maybe English or Scottish. With a name like The Tavern on the Bay it was hard to tell. Not that it mattered; Ash knew the important stuff, like that they had the best fish and chips in the city and spicy chicken quesadillas with extra spice that made his mouth water and his heart burn just thinking about them. A dozen customers sat at the tables on the covered patio, most in business attire.

One lone asshole in a pair of cut-off shorts and a sleeveless T-shirt sat in the far corner of the patio, as far away as he could get from everyone else, reading a book and smoking a cigarette. His slouched posture told everyone louder than words to leave him alone. He blew smoke over his shoulder, in the direction of the street.

"That shit'll kill you," Ash said as he walked by, tapping the *No smoking within 10 feet of this building* sign bolted to the brick above Kinsey's head.

Kinsey gave him the finger without looking up.

"That's just Kinsey," Ash explained at Dan's eyebrow raise. He held the door open and waved Dan inside.

"Yeah, I recognize him. Didn't realize he was so . . . standoffish."

"Kinsey's an asshole." They might play for the same team, but they weren't friends. Kinsey didn't appear to have friends. In fact, they were so not-friends that Ash constantly forgot that they lived in the same neighborhood. "He lives a couple of blocks that way." Ash waved vaguely east and chose a four-seater table away from the window, away from Kinsey's pierced face and tattooed arms and general scowliness.

"Maybe he's just misunderstood."

Ash squinted disbelievingly at Dan and handed him a menu from between the salt and pepper shakers. "Or maybe he's just an asshole."

"You could try getting to know him."

"Give me some credit. I've tried. We've all tried. But if the conversation isn't about hockey, Kinsey doesn't say much. And when he does, it's with grunts and glares."

Dan still wasn't convinced about Kinsey's assholishness, it seemed. He leaned sideways, trying to see out the window.

Ash sighed and tried again. "He got his secret Santa a gift card to the grocery store last year."

"You say that like it's a bad gift."

"Dude. It's a *gift card*. To the *grocery store*."

"Okay?" Dan's brow pinched. "Everybody needs to eat, though. How is that a bad gift?"

Ash didn't have anything to say to that except a mumbled, "He didn't put any thought into it."

"How do you know? Maybe food is important to him."

A rebuttal sat on the tip of Ash's tongue, but he remembered the plate on Kinsey's table—not a crumb left on it. And he remembered every event they'd attended together, the buffet-style ones specifically—Kinsey piling his plate high with as much food as it could hold, inhaling it all like it'd rot if he didn't get to it fast enough.

Huh. Dan might be on to something. But—

"He's still an asshole."

Dan was laughing at him. "Plays good hockey, though."

After lunch, they tackled Ash's living room, moving the couches and coffee table back into position, the bed and dressers into the bedroom, the desk and office chair into the spare bedroom.

"I swear if I break my back on this," Ash huffed as they carried a four-drawer dresser into the bedroom, muscles laboring, "I'm gonna kill you."

"Me?" Dan huffed back at him. He'd changed out of his fashion magazine clothes and into shorts and a T-shirt, and his biceps strained again the black fabric. "It's your stuff." He grunted and sweat dampened his curls.

He probably had no idea how damn good he looked.

Distracted, Ash rammed his elbow into the bedroom doorjamb. "Ow, fuck."

Speaking of fuck, with Dan's hair clinging to his forehead and his mouth open as he breathed roughly and the sweat dripping down his temple and—

"Ow, *fuck*." That was his heel hitting the doorjamb now.

"Are you even paying attention?"

They were both flushed with heat despite the air conditioning and irritable despite the full bellies.

"Fuck you," Ash grumbled.

"Fuck *you*," Dan retorted. "Watch the bedpost! Seriously, it's like you forgot where everything is in your own home."

"Stop for a sec. I need to reposition my hand."

The glare on Dan's face would kill a lesser man. "Are you fucking kidding me?"

"There. Done." God, his fingers *ached*. He had practice in a couple of hours too. How was he supposed to hold his stick?

His stick. He chuckled to himself. Likely he wouldn't be able to hold *that* stick either. Oh well. He could go a day without a jerk off in the shower, right?

He glanced again at Dan.

Then again, maybe not.

"How did you get this out there by yourself in the first place?" Dan asked.

"Adrenaline?" Finally they made it to the other side of the room. "Bend with your knees."

"No shit, genius."

The dresser finally back in its original spot against

the wall perpendicular to the bed, they straightened with groans and creaking knees, stretching their fingers out.

"God." Dan flopped onto the bed, arms akimbo, legs hanging over the end, and blinked at the ceiling. "Everything hurts."

Ash collapsed next to him. "Thanks for the help." *Thanks for being here.* Facing the semi destruction of his hometown was somehow less unsettling with Dan here. He still couldn't believe that Dan had come. Out of his own free will. To be here for Ash, he'd said.

"We'll tackle your backyard tomorrow."

"Don't you have to work?" Dan had told him on the flight over that he still had to check in with his boss every once in a while.

Dan gave a low grunt. "I'll get some work done in the morning," he said, his words slurring, "and come back in the afternoon to help. 'S why I'm here anyway."

"Is it?"

"Mm."

Why was Dan *really* here? As friendly support, like he'd said? Some other reason? Was he expecting something from Ash? At the airport this morning, he'd told Alex that he was heading to Tampa to try out Westlake's office, the one in Burlington having not worked out for him. Alex had eyed them both shrewdly and muttered an unconvinced, "Uh-huh."

They were clearly not fooling Alex. It was anybody's guess why he hadn't called them on it yet. Or what had given them away.

Ash exhaled and inched his hand closer to Dan's where it lay on the bed. Dan's shoulder was warm against his, and Ash swore he could almost feel Dan's leg hairs from where their legs dangled closely—but not touching—off the end of the bed. His hair was a golden crown spread out around him, and with his eyes closed he—

He looked like he belonged in Ash's bed.

Ash nudged him with an elbow. "Don't fall asleep on me."

"I want a milkshake," Dan declared, apropos of nothing.

"I don't have any ice cream."

Dan's sigh was hugely fake. "Such a disappointment."

For some reason, that set them both off, sniggers turning into full belly laughs. A release of tension Ash hadn't known he was carrying.

"Seriously, though," Dan said after they'd caught their breath. "I could nap. I think the fish and chips made me lethargic."

"Deep fried foods'll do that."

Dan crab walked up the bed, then fell onto it once again, this time with his head on a pillow. "I think I am gonna take a nap."

Ash tilted his head back and regarded him upside down. "I wanna nap too."

Dan patted the empty spot next to him as if it was his bed, not Ash's.

"Can't," Ash said with a sigh. "Got practice in a couple of hours, and given how much time it took us to get here from the airport, I should probably leave now to give myself enough time to get there. I can drop you off at your hotel on the way. Dan?"

Dan was already asleep. His chest rose and fell gently. He lay on his side, one arm tucked under his pillow, the other outstretched, palm out. Beckoning Ash to join him.

And Ash wanted to. He really, *really* wanted to. And if he didn't have to leave, he might've caved. Might've sprawled right there next to Dan, face-to-face. Breathing the same air. Sharing a pillow.

His heart went soft and liquid. Shifting onto his side, he reached a hand up to hook a pinky around Dan's while Dan slept. He wished there was a way that Dan could stay here forever.

But wishing for Dan was like wishing for a new contract with his club. Pointless.

Ash spent the entire practice being scrutinized by Alex. Actually, he spent the time *before* that being scrutinized by Alex, *and* the time after. It was annoying.

"You're annoying," he told Alex.

"I'm just standing here," Alex said from where he stood in front of his cubby next to Ash's, towel around his waist, chest and hair still wet from his shower.

"Standing there probing me with your mind."

Alex made a face.

"Yeah, I heard how that sounded too," Ash said with a wince. "If you have something to say to me, just say it."

"Nah." Alex stepped into boxer briefs with a grin. "Don't want to spoil your pleasure at eventually telling me."

"Telling you what?"

"You know what."

So annoying. "I don't know what you're talking about."

"Because you're either delusional or in denial. I'm going with denial."

"I'm not *in denial*—"

"Everybody listen up for a second!" That was Coach Ness's deep voice thundering through the locker room, the door swinging shut behind him. "I've got an announcement from Bridget Snyder, and I need you all to pay attention."

Bridget was their community and outreach coordinator. She was efficient, smart, recently graduated, and completely tongue-tied in front of any of the guys on the team. It was sweet in an adorable sister kind of way.

"We just heard from Teri at Try Out," Coach Ness said. "Sadly, the center was badly hit by the hurricane and won't be able to reopen for the kids until it's rebuilt, and that . . ." He blew out a hard breath. "That could take some time. They need to dip into the reserve emergency fund, but they need approval from the board to do that first, and as you can imagine, the board is, for the most part, still out of town."

Damn. If the center had been destroyed, where were the kids supposed to go?

Ash stepped forward. "How can we help, Coach?"

Coach Ness said, "They need donations, and they need volunteers. Whatever you can do yourselves, whichever of your sponsors, fans, social media followers, and friends you can lean on . . . Do it. The more people who know about this, the better. Thanks guys." He rapped once on the door before pulling it open. "See you tomorrow."

"Want to head over?" Ash asked Alex.

"Definitely."

He followed Alex out of the locker room, through the maze of Amalie Arena's hallways, and out to the parking garage. Once at his car, he leaned back against the driver's side door and rubbed his eyes with a thumb and forefinger. Alex, possibly sensing Ash's need to talk, joined him.

"What's up?" Alex asked.

And Ash blurted, "Dan and I used to be together," without thinking too much about it. Because he was tired of keeping it to himself. Because he wanted someone to talk to, someone removed from the situation who might see it more clearly. Because he could trust Alex not to judge him or lie to him.

"You don't say." Alex's voice was bland.

Ash turned his head to stare at him. "How'd you figure it out?"

"You look at each other as if you're looking at something you know you'll never have, but you want it desperately anyway, even though it could hurt you."

Was Alex implying that Dan was afraid Ash would hurt him? After what Dan had done, *he* was worried about getting hurt? That was rich.

"I wouldn't have known you had a past," Alex continued, "if you hadn't once mentioned a curly haired guy who looked like Mitch that you dated in New York. Thought it was just attraction at first until I put it together."

"Mitch is right—you really do notice everything."

Alex smiled softly and crossed his ankles.

"Does Mitch know?" Ash asked.

"Doubt it."

"You haven't told him?"

Alex side-eyed him. "It's not mine to tell."

Ash sighed and stared at himself in the reflection of the car window next to him, listening with one ear for sounds of their teammates entering the parking garage.

Fuck, he was tired and wired all at the same time.

"It was six years ago," he said. "And it didn't end well."

There was a pause, then, "Six years?"

"Why do you say that like it means something?"

"Because it does," Alex said slowly, choosing his words. "Something happened between Mitch and Dan six years ago and . . . It stands to reason that whatever happened between you and Dan is somehow related."

"You know what that something is."

"I do. I'm not telling you."

"I didn't ask you to."

No, Ash wouldn't ask him to. As much as he'd pushed against Dan at first, pushed against the explanations, the excuses, the apologies Dan so obviously needed to get off his chest, now Ash wanted to know. Needed to know. But he only wanted to hear it from Dan.

Dan's words from a few weeks ago came back to him: *I lost the two people who meant the most to me.*

Those two people being Mitch and Ash, if what Alex said was true.

Everything I did was for nothing, Dan had also said. *That* Ash almost asked Alex about. Processing the words now, though, when he hadn't bothered to weeks ago, made him realize just how much Dan had to live with, especially paired with the other thing Dan had said: *I couldn't see a way out of the corner I'd been put in.*

Ash tried to organize his thoughts and put everything in order based on those bits and pieces.

Dan had been manipulated into doing something.

Whatever it was had led to him breaking up with Ash *and* Mitch because he hadn't seen any other way out.

In the end, it hadn't made a difference, and he'd clearly been living with the regret ever since.

Question: What had Dan been manipulated into doing? And who'd done the manipulating?

Theory: Greta Westlake. It made the most sense given Dan had gone to see her before they were supposed to meet at the airport.

Follow-up question: When Dan had realized he'd been duped, why hadn't he reached out to Ash right away?

"Mitch and Dan seem to be okay now, though," he said.

"Yeah. Dan came forward a few months ago. When

Mitch passed out? Remember? Some things came to light then and . . ."

A few months ago . . .

"And you can't say more without revealing Dan's secrets?" Ash said.

"Sorry, I just—"

"No, I get it. You don't have to explain. Did it take Mitch a long time to forgive him?"

Alex chuckled quietly. "About four minutes."

Ash's eyes snapped over to Alex. "Are you serious? After six years, why so fast?"

"Because Dan's his brother. And Mitch missed him."

Dan had been Ash's boyfriend. Ash's everything. And Ash had missed him.

He'd spent the past few weeks not forgiving Dan, while Mitch had been able to in minutes? Obviously Mitch was the bigger person.

"Not necessarily," Alex rebutted when Ash said so. "They're family. That's a different kind of relationship than anything else."

"Maybe."

"Why hasn't Dan already explained what happened?"

Ash shuffled on his feet. "I . . . maybe haven't let him?" He'd been too angry to listen at first, and then he'd told himself that it didn't matter—it'd been six years. Except it *did* matter; he'd just been afraid of the truth. What if Dan had left him because he didn't love him anymore?

But if Ash was right about Dan having been manipulated or tricked . . . That changed things.

Alex cocked his head. "How do you expect to move forward with him if you don't have all of the information? Assuming you want to move forward with him, of course."

He did. He really, really did. His head, though, couldn't

stop remembering that text: *I'm sorry, I can't.* Could he go down that path with Dan again?

"Think you'll ever forgive him?" Alex asked.

Closing his eyes on a sigh, Ash said, "I think part of me already has."

Try Out Center for Youth wasn't quite as bad off as Coach Ness made it out to be. They'd had some flooding on top of suffering from missing siding and roof tiles and a few blown out windows, Ash found out when he and Alex and a handful of other guys on the team arrived half an hour later. Teri took them on a tour that started with the art room turned shower. Bubbles protruded from the ceiling where water had pooled, the paint and plaster cracked and slimy as water dripped down into strategically placed buckets.

"This sucks," one of the guys muttered.

Scratch that. It *was* as bad as Coach Ness had made it sound. It might even be worse.

The only part of the facility to have survived was the ice rink, and even that had a chunk of roof torn off in one section above the east bleachers. The workout room was in the same condition as the art room, the locker rooms smelled of mildew, the walls were cracked and stained across the facility, and inside the huge gymnasium, light fixtures hung precariously by their wires in the corner. Midway through the gym, four of those yellow A-frame caution signs formed a weak barrier.

"Don't go behind them," Teri said as she concluded their tour, waving in the direction of the signs and what lay behind them: a storage room housing mats, basketballs, baseball bats, and other sports equipment as well as various tools like hammers and nails and measuring tape. "Obviously those could come down at any moment. Someone's coming in to look at it tomorrow."

"Was anybody hurt during the storm?" Ash asked.

"No. Thankfully there weren't any staff or kids here at the time." Teri led them back through the gym to the waterlogged front lobby and out the front door. The rest of the street hadn't fared much better, debris and broken buildings lining the sidewalk. Ash swallowed hard and wished he were back in bed napping with Dan.

He'd never seen anything like it. Never seen a more solemn group of hockey players. The devastation was unreal and it was home and it affected people they knew and cared about.

The front of the building had lost a lot of its siding, and the painted *Try Out Center for Youth* above the door now read *Tr. .Out C. .ter for. .ou h.*

"As you can see," Teri said, posture flagging, "it needs a lot of work, so I'd appreciate any help you can give me, even if it's volunteering to remove some of the debris."

Yeah. Definitely yes. This was . . . This was horrible.

Ash withdrew his phone from his back pocket and snapped a few pictures of the *Tr. .Out C. .ter for. .ou h* sign. He knew someone who could help with that.

Dan awoke to a quiet apartment, his skin goosebumped from the air conditioning. Fuck, he was cold. Why couldn't Floridians find a comfortable indoor temperature to battle the heat outside?

Oh, there was a note from Ash propped on the night table.

DON'T TACKLE THE BACKYARD WITHOUT ME!

He sniggered at the all caps. Message received.

If you want to be useful, the note continued, *maybe get my boxes out of storage?*

It was signed simply *A*. As if it was too hard to add *sh*. So lazy.

There was a separate piece of paper with a key taped to it and instructions on where to find the storage room and what section of it contained Ash's belongings.

Not that Ash's belongings were hard to find. The sixth floor storage room used the sophisticated organizational system of masking tape on the floor forming dozens of neat twelve by twelve squares. Apartment numbers were written on the top left corner of each square. He found Ash's assigned square not far from the door. Patio furniture was stacked on top of itself—chairs on top of the table and a cute love seat wedged underneath that—with a hideously creepy gnome between the chair legs. Boxes and small potted plants were stacked around it.

After propping the storage room door open with a box, Dan settled in for some snooping.

The first box contained a DVD player and a gaming console. Boring. He brought that down to Ash's apartment and hustled back up. The second had some lawn ornaments, decorative rocks, and outdoor garden lights and the like. With the state of Ash's yard, he wouldn't be needing these anytime soon. Dan left them where he'd found them and moved on to the next box.

Jackpot! A box of framed photos. Many of them were of Ash with his team, both current and former. Dan managed to put the photos in somewhat of an order based on Ash's hair color: brown, brown with gray at the temples, brown with gray streaks, gray with brown highlights, and finally fully gray. Dan liked that Ash wasn't vain enough to dye his hair. There was an assortment of pictures of Ash with his mom, with his dad, and a handful of the three of them together from when he was a kid. One photo in particular caught Dan's attention and held it: Ash and his parents, recently going by the state of Ash's hair, on a beach somewhere with blue ocean and seashells and warm sand.

Ash's parents hadn't been able to make their marriage work but they were still friends, whereas Dan's parents didn't want to be in the same state together.

Putting the pictures back in the box with a sigh, he brought it downstairs and tackled the rest. He found books, old hockey equipment, trophies, a few pucks, various knickknacks no doubt collected from Ash's travels, sun catchers, several pairs of dress shoes—

Wait.

Sun catchers.

Ash still had his sun catchers.

His breath caught. Stilled. Released in a rush. Carefully, he removed them from the box and set them down in front of him. Six in total. Half moons, suns, and stars. Most plain with crystals hanging from the top, but the two that were his favorite had a small design burned into the wood.

The first was the logo of Ash's AHL team in Syracuse. It still looked like a blob of squiggly lines. The second simply had *A+D*. Cheesy, but honest.

He didn't know what to think about these sun catchers. On the one hand, he was amazed and touched and honored that Ash had kept them. It was like reaching adulthood and realizing that Santa Claus really was real. The fact that Ash had kept them had to mean something, didn't it? On the other hand, it was possible Ash had forgotten all about them, buried at the bottom of this box that contained other random odds and ends—bookends and a pencil holder and a pile of stickers for some reason.

But he still had them. Maybe it meant nothing. Maybe it meant something. Dan chose to believe the latter.

Dan repacked the box of sun catchers and brought it downstairs, but froze outside Ash's apartment door, which wasn't latched properly.

"Why would you come back now?" Ash was saying. Silence, then, "But, Mom, half the roads are impassable, power's still out in some places, and—"

On the phone, then. Dan hovered, biting his lip, the corner of the box digging into his belly. When the conversation continued, Ash trying to convince his mom to stay put wherever the heck she was, Dan gave up, bored, and was elbowing the door open when he heard Ash mutter, exasperated, "Mom, I'm not calling Laura. She knows where to find me if she needs help."

Laura was the ex-wife. Dan backed out again, quietly, leaving the door ajar. But guilt hit him instantly; he couldn't *eavesdrop* on Ash. He'd promised himself nothing but honesty with Ash from now on, and eavesdropping wasn't just dishonest—it was sneaky.

Making as much noise as he could to announce his presence, Dan shouldered his way inside with an apologetic smile. Ash smiled back and gestured at his phone with an eye roll. *Moms*, he mouthed. And Dan . . . had no idea what he meant. What about moms? Dan had never met Mariana Tessler in person, only via phone when he and Ash had been together, but even through the phone, Dan could tell that she was Greta Westlake's polar opposite. She badgered Ash about his love life, asked about his friends, questioned him on his food choices, if he'd done his laundry, what touristy things he'd seen in the Big Apple, if he'd found a new chiropractor. It was meant with love and Ash accepted it like it was normal. For him, it was.

Greta Westlake never badgered. She coldly demanded and then expected everyone to exceed her expectations. She'd once fired one of Westlake's delivery companies because one of the truck drivers continually forgot to capture a signature upon delivery.

Ash wandered away for a bit of privacy, but Dan still heard his annoyed, "I don't know what makes you think I want Laura back in my life."

Well, it was nice to hear that Dan wouldn't be competing with an ex-wife. But by that same token, if Ash didn't want his ex-wife in his life again, in what universe would he want an ex-boyfriend?

Annoyed with his own thoughts, he went back up to the sixth floor to lock the storage room door. Downstairs again, he left the key on Ash's counter.

"Thanks, man," Ash said, coming out of the bedroom. He pocketed his phone and headed for the sliding glass doors, but he didn't go outside. Just stood staring out, hands on his hips, exactly like he had earlier.

Sad. A bit lost.

"How was practice?"

Ash turned from the door. "Good. Actually, I wanted to talk to you about it."

"About . . . practice? Did something happen?"

"Not at the rink. After, I mean. This," Ash said, pulling his phone out and scrolling through something, "is the Try Out Center for Youth downtown." He turned the phone to Dan, and—

"Jesus."

"Yeah," Ash went on as Dan thumbed through the photos. "It's pretty bad."

"The kind of damage that this city sustained . . . I've never seen anything like it except on the news."

"Me too."

Dan passed the phone back. "How can I help?"

Ash's smile was slow in forming, but when it did, it was a thing of such beauty that Dan forgot to breathe.

"That's what I wanted to talk to you about. See this?" Ash showed him the phone again. On it was a picture of the front of the center, a thick metal door with a white patch above it, and on that, chipped and faded red paint that must've spelled a word or a phrase before the storm. "It used to say the name of the center, but it was pretty tacky even before the storm. Could you build something nicer? Something friendly and inviting, but also sturdy? You know, like those pub signs? The ones that stick out from a metal rod from the front of the building and have a swinging sign on them?" He swung his hand side to side.

Dan rubbed his jaw, ideas and concepts already forming. "I could do that, yeah. I'm guessing it's not a huge rush since they need to renovate first? Do they have a logo?"

"Um . . ."

"Never mind. I'll check online."

"Um." Ash fidgeted. "About payment . . ."

Dan shot him a dirty look. "Please. As if I'd charge a non-profit for something like this. I don't have anywhere to work here, though, or any tools or materials. Maybe there's a trade school nearby I could work out of," he said, thinking out loud. "I'll need to go to the center and take measurements and talk to the owner or director or whoever about what they want—"

"I can take you next week."

"Yeah? Great."

"Thank you." Ash squeezed Dan's arm, and the

sensation traveled through Dan's blood and locked in his stupid, hopeful heart. "Really."

"You're welcome." Dan's voice was hoarse and his palms were sweating. They stared at each other for a moment, the air between them dense with everything Dan wanted to say. What would Ash do if Dan leaned forward to kiss him? The intention must've been written on his face, because Ash stepped back and smiled faintly. "I'm beat. Can I take you to your hotel?"

Disappointment gnawed at Dan, an empty chasm of regret, but he pushed past it. If Ash needed time, Dan would give it to him.

FIFTEEN

JULY 2003—SIX YEARS AGO

"**S**O. YOU AND DAN, HUH?"

Ash froze, backpack in hand. On the bed was a brand new box of condoms and an unopened bottle of lube.

He quickly dropped the backpack, covering the evidence of tonight's activities to come—ha ha!—and whirled to face his dad. "Huh? What?"

His dad leaned against the doorway and made a *nice try, but you can't hide from me* face. "You and Dan. You've been hot and heavy for weeks."

"Ugh, don't say hot and heavy like that. Ew."

"Your mom and I were hot and heavy once."

"Oh my god, why?"

"I'm just trying to say that maybe you shouldn't rush into things."

"I'm not . . . We're not . . ." Well, they *were*, but still. Not rushing, that was, but doing things. They'd started small and they'd discussed the succession of their sexual activities ad nauseam. Frankly, for two guys in their early twenties, they talked *a lot* and about *everything*.

"How come you didn't tell us you're gay?" his dad said, changing the topic. Clearly he could see that talking about *sex* with his *dad* was freaking Ash out, and obviously the subject of his sexual orientation was *so* much better.

God. Parents.

Ash shrugged and crossed his arms. "Never mattered. It's always been women up until now."

"I get that. But what about once you started seeing Dan?"

"Because it still didn't matter. Not that Dan doesn't matter, that's not what I'm saying," he explained to his dad's shocked face. "I'm saying my sexual orientation doesn't matter. Why do I have to come out? I am who I am and everybody else can just deal with it. I'm not hiding him. Oh shit." Horror struck as he realized what he'd just said.

I'm not hiding him.

His arms fell to his sides. Fuck. Now, there was something they hadn't talked about. How had Ash not thought of it until now? Because he'd been living in Happyville with Dan, that was how. Riding on roller coasters and free falling into something beautiful and real and unexpected.

He sunk onto the bed heavily. The lube rolled off and landed on the floor. Ash snatched it up, shoving it in his backpack while his dad studiously looked elsewhere.

"What is it that you've just realized that made you panic?"

Flopping backward, Ash stared at the ceiling. "I can't have a boyfriend in professional sports. I mean, I can, but . . ." But they'd have to hide.

"You're only just realizing that now?"

"I've been living in Happyville," he mumbled.

"What?"

"Nothing."

"It doesn't have to be one or the other," his dad said. One or the other: hockey or Dan.

"No." Ash sat up. "No, it doesn't. But having both means asking Dan to hide. And that's not fair to him."

"That's his choice, don't you think? Talk to him. But

first, go have sex." His dad picked the box of condoms off the floor—which apparently had also fallen off the bed, Jesus—and tossed it at Ash.

"Oh my god, how are you a parent? That's so inappropriate."

"Do we need to talk about safety and STIs and—"

Ash held up the box of condoms with a glare.

"Right." His dad nodded once. "Glad we had the gay sex talk."

"Oh my god." Ash fell back on the bed again with a groan.

Anal sex 101 wasn't as easy as it sounded. According to websites Dan had found, you couldn't just glove up, add some lube, and push your way in. There was preparation so it didn't hurt, and even then it would probably hurt even with tons of lube, but not for long (or so they said). There might be poo and there might be blood, and most importantly—*real life sex does not look like porn.*

Okay then.

With all of that, part of him didn't want to have anal sex ever. According to his research, not all gay men enjoyed it. But then Ash showed up at his apartment, tall and muscled and smiling like Dan was the best thing since ice skating, and Dan's hormones went haywire. Ash's too, which honestly the best part.

They'd started small after that first kiss on Ash's couch last month, graduating from kissing on the couch to kissing in bed. Then kissing while half-naked, and then entirely naked. And then kissing other body parts. And then humping and grinding and rubbing, with clothes on but more often with clothes off.

And blowjobs. Those were . . . Dan's dick jerked just thinking about it. Heat overtook him and his entire body flushed.

"We don't have to do this," Ash said from beside him, misinterpreting Dan's shaky inhale.

Sitting naked next to each other on a towel on Dan's bed with Dan's clunky laptop in front of them was not how Dan had envisioned their first time. But Ash was as ignorant as Dan when it came to anal sex. They'd managed to find a how-to video on one of the porn websites that had some comments à la the *this was so useful* variety from other anal sex first-timers. So they were going with it.

"No, I want to," Dan said, pausing the video. On screen, one tall, buff guy—a supposed expert in anal sex between men—was rimming a second tall, buff guy. "Not sure about the rimming, though."

"Yeah. Maybe we come back to that later?" Ash jumped forward in the video. Buff Guy 1 and Buff Guy 2 were already fucking. "Whoops. Too far."

He cued up the video to where they needed it, post-rimming (which was not a necessity—apparently not everyone liked it—but could be fun, according to Buff Guy 1) and pre-prepping, and urged Dan to lie back.

"You sure you want to bottom first?" Ash asked, settling between Dan's spread legs and moving the laptop up near Dan's head, angled so they could both see it.

"Yup." Dan twined his legs around Ash's waist and pulled. Ash landed on top of him. "Kiss me first."

Ash grinned at him and did as told, his smiling mouth meeting Dan's.

The last few weeks had been the best of Dan's life. Ash stayed over more often than not these days. Dan was no longer going in to work early and leaving late. He had someone to see and things to do and he was going to spend every free second with Ash that he could. Ash had about six weeks left before he had to return to Syracuse, and while it was true that it was only four hours away and they'd still see each other, it was also true that it'd be much less frequently.

Dan was going to milk every last second.

Ash's kisses led from Dan's mouth to his jaw and down to his neck. But Dan wanted his lips again; he palmed the back of Ash's head and guided him up, where they met in a lazy kiss that was mostly lips and sighs.

"Ready for this?" Ash asked before planting a tiny kiss on Dan's cheekbone.

Dan melted. "Uh-huh."

Ash unpaused the video.

"If you have gloves," Buff Guy 1 said as he slipped a thin nitrile glove over his right hand, "use them."

Ash and Dan exchanged a glance. They did not have gloves.

"They're not mandatory," Buff Guy 1 continued, "but they're helpful for preventing your nails from accidentally hurting your partner. They're also easy to slip off once you've lubed yourself and your partner, and if you run into some poo—" He shrugged. "—no biggie."

If you run into some poo, Ash mouthed, eyes huge.

Dan cracked up.

"Everything just got so much more real," Ash muttered, and he sounded . . . not horrified, but like the concept of running into poo while going into someone's butthole hadn't occurred to him.

Clearly, he hadn't done his research.

"Jerk." Ash heaved himself onto his knees and swatted Dan's thigh. "Stop laughing."

Dan couldn't. "I'm sorry," he wheezed, tears of laughter beading in the corner of his eyes. "This is just so much funnier, and so much more un-sexy, than I thought it was going to be. We really don't have to do this."

"I'm not letting normal bodily functions stop me from going in there." The expression on Ash's face was so fierce, Dan couldn't stop the snigger. Ash pointed at him with a fake scowl. "I'm watching you."

"I should hope so."

God. *God*. Dan hadn't laughed so much during sex in his life. Before Ash had arrived, he'd been all nerves and jerky actions. But he was so comfortable with Ash, and Ash made him feel safe and desired. It constantly shocked him how little time they'd known each other—only a couple of months. If pressed, Dan would've been tempted to say years. There was something about Ash, something about their fast friendship and gentle slide into a relationship that spoke of a knowing. Dan had read something online once about friend chemistry. How there were people you met that you formed an instant friendship with, and it felt like you'd known them forever. Like sexual chemistry, you were attracted to that person, but purely on a friendship level.

That was Ash. Dan was attracted to him as a friend. They had excellent friend chemistry.

Also excellent sexual chemistry, if Dan did say so himself.

"Why don't we watch the video," he said, "get all the tips and tricks, and then do the thing?"

"Yeah, okay." Ash lay down on top of Dan, propping an elbow next to Dan's head to hold his own head up, and restarted the video.

They watched Buff Guy 1 prep Buff Guy 2 with one finger, two, three, using so much lube it dripped from Buff

Guy 2's wide-open hole and onto the towel underneath him. Buff Guy 1 talked throughout the whole thing, about angles and prostates and safety. He continued to talk as he lay down on the towel and Buff Guy 2 straddled his thighs, explaining that it was sometimes easier for first-timers and newbies to sit on a penis as an introduction between it and a butthole. It was all so clinical despite Buff Guy 2's groans and sighs and curling toes, and Dan's erection had flagged by the time the video finally ended.

"Okay, then." Ash pushed the laptop lid closed and moved off Dan only as far as needed to drop the computer onto the floor next to the bed. "Let's do the thing."

Dan snorted a laugh.

Ash kissed his nose. "Don't even start that again. I can't do the thing when you're giggling in my ear."

"Giggling? I do not *giggle*. I—I—I—Oh, *fuck*, Ash."

Because Ash hadn't waited for Dan to finish explaining that he didn't giggle. He'd already started the thing.

He licked and sucked Dan's dick until Dan was so hard he could slice butter. Then he followed Buff Guy 1's directions, slicking his fingers and using one, then two, then three to stretch Dan open. Dan felt so full with three fingers he had no idea how he was going to take Ash's dick, but fuck if he wasn't willing to try.

"Am I doing this right?" Ash asked with a scowl at Dan's ass.

"Gah!"

"I'm gonna take that as a yes."

By the time Ash was shakily putting on a condom and slathering himself with lube, Dan was such a hot mess of pleasure and lube and desperation that he couldn't move except to clench the pillow under his head.

"Fuck, Ash."

"'M just following directions," Ash said gruffly. He fell onto his side next to Dan, wiped his hand on the towel, and pulled Dan with him as he flipped onto his back. "Get up here."

Dan went up here.

And tensed so badly the head of Ash's cock couldn't get past his ring.

"Hey." Ash ran his hands up and down Dan's thighs. "Easy."

Dan hung his head, trying to get a grip. "Sorry."

"We don't have to do this. We can stop here." Ash heaved himself up, and now they sat face-to-face, Ash's concerned gaze on his.

"No," Dan said, forcing himself to relax. Buff Guy 1 said it was important to relax. His fingers loosened from their death grip on Ash's shoulders. "No, sorry. I just panicked for a second. Are you sure I'm open enough?"

"No?" Ash's brow furrowed, and now his hands clenched on Dan's thighs. "I've never done this before either, and I don't want to hurt you—"

"It's okay—"

"You're right, though, I should keep going. Here, switch spots with me."

"Ash, stop. Stop." Dan cupped Ash's face and forced him to meet his eyes. "I trust you."

That was all it took for Ash to soften, bones going liquid. Dan pushed him back onto the bed and followed him down. Because he wanted a kiss, and he wanted to feel Ash against him, and he wanted to reassure Ash that he was fine. The moment of panic had receded to the back of his mind; he wasn't sure if it was because Ash's panic had calmed him, or if them both panicking had canceled it out, or if he'd simply realized that he was being an idiot.

This was *Ash*. Of course they were going to take care of each other.

Ash's erection poked Dan in the stomach, and he reached between them to hold it, stroke it, and generally make Ash go crazy.

Ash wrenched his mouth away from Dan's. "Jesus, fuck. Fuck." Growled through clenched teeth with his head thrown back, it made Dan grin in satisfaction. Sweat gleamed on Ash's skin, making him glow.

"God, you're gorgeous."

"Let me in you." Ash flung an arm around Dan's neck and dragged him closer, muttering against his lips, "Let me in you."

"Yes. Yes."

Scrambling upward, Dan was so turned on he couldn't have tensed if he'd been paid to. He lifted himself onto trembling knees, lined up Ash's cock, breathed out slowly, met Ash's gaze . . . and sunk down, taking Ash's length into him.

It wasn't smooth and it took some patience and it hurt. By the time Dan was fully seated on Ash's dick, he had to pause for a minute to adjust and breathe and marvel at how damn stuffed he felt. Ash was panting beneath him, hands gripping Dan's thighs so hard it'd leave marks. For some reason, that made Dan's mouth water.

He leaned forward, bracing a hand on Ash's sweaty chest and one on the bed. "Okay. I'm ready. Do the thing."

Ash grinned and did the thing.

And it did *not* hurt.

They started slow, tentative, getting a feel for one an-other. When Dan's head fell forward because he couldn't hold it up anymore, Ash picked up the pace and Dan met him thrust for thrust, and shit, fuck, damn it was good, so good, a blow job and endless kisses and his birthday and Christmas all rolled into one. It was so good that he couldn't hold himself up anymore, and he fell onto Ash, burying his face in Ash's neck. Ash squeezed Dan's ass cheeks, grunting beneath Dan, breathing hard in his ear.

"Gonna come soon," Ash gritted. "Gonna come fast."

Dan wanted to come too, but he needed something, needed—

"Fuck!" He groaned, almost flying off the handle when Ash read his mind and palmed his leaking cock, squeezing. "Oh, fuuuuuuck, Ash." His blood ignited and he came, shooting on Ash, on himself, toes curling as his body went rigid, and he clutched the towel under Ash in a fist. God, he was done. He was so done, except Ash hadn't come yet. Ash was straining, panting, eyes tightly shut. Dan bit his chin—and evidently, that was all it took for him to come with a yell, head thrown back.

They lay there for a long minute, puffing and damp and sticky and sore in odd places. Dan eventually made himself move, if only to stop squishing Ash, giving the man room to catch his breath.

"Easy," Ash wheezed.

"'M good." Ash slipped out of him, making him wince a little, but the discomfort lasted only until he could fling himself onto his belly next to Ash, close enough to share air space and a pillow. "Holy fuck. Holy, holy fuck. My bones are liquid."

"Mm."

"We did the thing."

Ash chuckled. He turned his head toward Dan, eyes soft and tender. "Was the thing okay?"

"So good. You?"

"So good."

It was nice, lying side by side, not exactly cuddling, but coming down from the high together. The air was stuffy and humid and it smelled like sex, Dan's body was JELL-O, and Ash kissed his forehead.

It was perfect.

"I gotta pee," Ash announced. He removed the condom carefully, knotted it as best he could, and placed it on a corner of the towel.

"Me too. You go first."

Neither of them moved. Finally, Ash heaved a breath, rolled over onto Dan, making him laugh and mumble, "Get off me, asshole," rolled off him onto the other side, and swung himself out of bed and into the bathroom with a salute, come crusted onto his stomach. He was back a second later to snatch the condom off the bed.

Rolling his eyes—really, he couldn't have gotten off the bed on his side and walked around it to the bathroom?—Dan got himself up too, used the towel to wipe come off his stomach and lube off his ass and thighs—seriously, that shit got everywhere—and chucked it into the laundry bin in the closet. He should send an email to Buff Guy 1 thanking him for the towel tip. Still naked, he hustled into the kitchen to warm up the oven and pop in a frozen pizza. That done, he collapsed onto the bed again just as Ash was coming out of the bathroom.

Ash raked his eyes up and down Dan's body. If Dan wasn't so lethargic and hungry and satisfied, he might've been able to get it up again. He was so lazy that he couldn't be bothered to move to pee. He held out an arm, beckoning Ash to join him.

Lying side by side on the same pillow, Ash booped Dan on the nose. "Hi."

"Hi."

It was a muggy night outside, and Dan's piece of crap window air conditioning unit didn't always work properly; in spite of that, his body had cooled enough that he was no longer sweating profusely and was now comfortably warm.

"So." Ash's lips twisted and he glanced away. "I need to talk to you about something."

"Okay."

Silence.

"Should I be worried?" Dan prodded.

"No. No, no. I'm just . . ." Ash ran a hand through his hair. "I'm not sure where to start."

"Okay."

More silence. It was so unlike Ash not to know what to say that Dan felt a kernel of worry anyway.

"The pizza'll be done by the time you figure it out."

Ash sniffed the air. "There's pizza?"

"In the oven."

"Thank God. I'm starving. Oily Dude didn't have *that* tip, did he?"

"Oily Dude? Oh, you mean Buff Guy?"

Ash threw his head back and laughed.

"He was oily, though," Dan murmured. "Why is that a thing in porn?"

"I'm sure you'll look it up online later."

"Hmm."

"So, listen." Ash was more serious than Dan had ever seen him. "Full disclosure first up: I want you in my life."

Time stopped. "Ash—"

"Wait, just . . . Hear me out before you say anything. I can't come out." His eyes were regretful but determined. He didn't like what he was saying, but it needed to be said. "Not with the way the professional sports climate is. If I come out, my career is over. No team will want me." He shook his head, his jaw clenched so tight it threw his cheekbones into sharp relief. "And that means that if we're together, we can't tell anyone except closest friends and family. I'm sure you've noticed that I never hold your hand or kiss you when we're out in public together."

"I've noticed. It doesn't bother me."

Ash's eyes narrowed. "It doesn't?"

"I've never been into public displays of affection. My feelings are my business and my partner's, not anyone else's."

"Being with someone who can't be out, though . . . that's different. I couldn't take you to benefits and fundraisers, and—"

Dan cupped his cheek. "I don't care."

"You say that now, but—"

"Ash. I don't care."

"You don't understand." Ash was getting agitated, but Dan very much understood: live with the secrecy or lose Ash. "This isn't short term. Unless I get injured or my contract doesn't get renewed and I don't get picked up by another team, I'm going to be playing for a long time."

"Ash. I know. You're not saying anything I haven't heard from my brother. I get it."

Mouth working, Ash rubbed his eyes with a thumb and forefinger. "O . . . kay? That means when I go back to Syracuse in a few weeks, we'll keep seeing each other when we can?"

Dan kissed him gently, slowly. "I'm not losing you. I'm not. If that means we keep this a secret for five years, ten years, twenty years, then so be it."

Ash wiggled closer until their foreheads were touching. "I can't ask you to do that."

"You didn't ask. I'm telling you—that's how it's going

to be." Dan didn't say the words. Didn't know if he could yet even though he often felt them so deeply that it made him want to laugh and cry at the same time with the over-whelmingness of it all. But he could give Ash something else. "I'm yours. Always."

SIXTEEN

DAN KNOCKED ON ASH'S DOOR AFTER LUNCH THE next day. After his early morning jog, he'd spent the remainder of the morning alternately putting together a report for his boss and on a conference call with the analyst from the Chicago satellite office. He'd had the television on in the background and had stopped everything—even moving—when a live interview with Ash had played on the sports network.

"What made you decide that now was the right time for you to come out as gay?" the interviewer, a gentleman in his fifties with a full head of dark hair—totally dyed—had asked.

"Bisexual," Ash corrected mildly.

"Of course, sorry. Are you seeing someone that you wanted to show off to the world?"

"No, it's nothing like that," Ash had explained, appearing comfortable and relaxed in front of the camera in jeans and a polo shirt. "Truth is that if I'd had an out NHL player to look up to as a kid, I might've been more comfortable with my sexuality growing up. I never thought my sexuality was wrong; but neither did I act on my attraction to men except for once a few years ago. If I can show the youth of today that you can be true to who you are and still make your dreams come true, I'll have done something right."

"Speaking of the youth of today"—the interviewer

looked into the camera—"we're standing in an athletic and recreational facility that caters to underprivileged and at-risk youth in downtown Tampa. Ashton, can you tell us a bit about Try Out Center for Youth?"

Oh, he was brilliant, his Ash. Conducting the interview at Try Out meant it a) kept the focus off himself, and b) highlighted Try Out's desperate need for donations.

Ash had taken the interviewer around the facility, pointing out the different areas that required repair and how donations were needed for the renovations.

"Without this center," Ash had said, "a lot of kids don't have anywhere to go after school."

Dan was so damn proud of him it was overwhelming at the same time that it made him furiously happy, and he'd grinned during the entire interview, hugging the pillow to his chest.

He was jittery when he knocked on Ash's door, unable to stand still. His feet kept moving forward as if Ash had opened the door already. If he didn't stop, he'd end up on top of the damn thing and—

The door swung open and—"Whoa!" Ash jerked back . . . because Dan *had* pretty much been on top of the damn thing. "Eager beaver," Ash said around a grin.

And Dan almost did it. Almost leaped at Ash, who stood there holding the door open in shorts and a tight T-shirt, his feet bare on the hardwood floor. Something about those feet made Dan's vision go swimmy, and he was still staring at them when he followed Ash inside and into the living room.

"Do I have toe fungus or something?" Ash asked, staring perplexedly at his feet.

"Huh? What? Who has toe fungus?"

Head tilted, Ash regarded Dan for a moment like he'd

never seen him before—or . . . maybe like he was contemplating kissing Dan too? The lines around his eyes got more pronounced when he smiled. "Hi," he said.

"Hi," Dan whispered back, heart beating madly. What was that expression on Ash's face? Ash hadn't looked at him like that in six years. What had changed?

And how could Dan ensure it wouldn't go away?

"Saw your interview this morning."

"Yeah?" Ash grabbed the key to the storage room from the counter and gestured upward. "What'd you think?"

"I think holding it at Try Out was a stroke of genius," Dan said, frowning at Ash heading for the door. "Wait. Aren't we going to clean up your backyard today?"

"Nah. That hunk of metal—" Ash nodded in its direction. "—is too heavy. Alex and Carlie are coming over tomorrow to help us move it."

"Speaking of Alex." Dan trailed Ash out of the apartment and down the hallway to the stairs. "How damaged is his place?"

"Pretty damaged. He had some flooding, so the baseboards and the flooring on the first floor are going to need to be replaced, and his backyard's way worse than mine. A lot of debris. He's staying at a hotel for now."

Dan pushed on the handle of the stairway door; Ash pushed the button for the elevator.

They stared at each other for a second.

"I don't take elevators," Dan eventually said.

"Ever?"

"Ever."

"Since when?"

"Since the day we met." Dan's tone held a heavy dose of *duh*.

"But . . . Don't you work on the eighteenth floor of that building?"

"So?"

"So?" Ash mimicked. He followed Dan up the stairs. "What if you wanted to go up the CN Tower or something?"

"Why the hell would I ever want to be up that high?"

"You really haven't been on an elevator in six years?"

"Nope."

Exiting the stairwell onto the sixth floor, Dan led the way to the storage room and held his hand out behind him for the key.

"Is that why you jog?" Ash asked, slapping the key into Dan's hand.

"I've been jogging since high school." Unlocking the door, Dan pushed it open and flicked on the light. "All that cardio came in handy, though. Where do you want to start?"

"Well." Ash surveyed his belongings, hands on his hips. "Might as well leave the patio stuff here since the yard's still a mess. Guess we'll just bring the rest of the boxes down."

They grabbed a couple of boxes each, relocked the storage room, and went back downstairs. Dan stared at Ash's back the entire time—his wide shoulders that could handle anything, his strong back that flexed as he readjusted his hold on the boxes, his waist that led to hips that led to a firm butt.

There was an itch under Dan's skin. A temptation to touch, to stroke. To run his hand down Ash's arm, over the warm skin, and twine their fingers together. To lean against Ash's shoulder. To unburden himself of everything that still weighed on him—how he'd treated Mitch the past few years, his discontent with his job, his need to build and create, the anger at his mother that was always there, simmering under his breastbone. Ash wouldn't be able to fix anything; Dan didn't want him to. But it would be nice to talk to someone about everything that sometimes made it hard to motivate himself to get out of bed in the morning.

Ash's arms had always made Dan feel safe.

But Ash had thrown a wall up between them from the get-go. Dan didn't know how to knock it down except to keep proving to Ash that he wasn't going anywhere. It was what made him follow Ash to Tampa in the first place—he needed to show Ash that he was here to stay.

After bringing down the remaining boxes, Ash announced that he wanted to clean his place before unpacking. Probably it was something they should've done before bringing the boxes down. Too late now, though. So they dusted everything from the top of the coffee table to the top of the fridge, vacuumed every corner and under every piece of furniture, moving the boxes to one side of the apartment to vacuum where they'd been, and then moving them again to get into that corner.

Obviously they hadn't planned well.

They dusted between and on top of books, vacuumed closets, rearranged furniture, destroyed dust bunnies Ash hadn't known he had, and purged the kitchen junk drawer.

"I think there's something growing in this dust bunny." Dan stood on a stepladder and reached into a corner of the ceiling next to the TV with a long Swiffer duster thing.

"It's not a spider, is it?" Ash said, swiftly relocating to the other side of the room.

"I think it's a whole colony of spiders."

Ash made gagging noises.

By the time they were done, they were sweaty and dusty and hungry, the place was sparkling, there was a bag of trash by the front door, the spider colony had been transported outside and across the street as per Ash's directions, and they hadn't even started to unpack the boxes.

Dan collapsed onto the armchair in the living room. Ash dropped face-first onto the couch.

"I'm starving," Dan said, wiping his filthy hands on his shorts.

"I—"

"I swear, if you tell me you have cauliflower pizza, I'm gonna come over there and beat you."

Ash chuckled into the couch cushion. "I was gonna say that I can make pasta."

"What do you have to go on it?"

A pause, then, "Cheese?"

Dan sunk deeper into the chair.

"We could go to The Tavern," Ash suggested.

"'Kay."

Ash yawned. Dan lifted his feet onto the coffee table.

"Do they deliver?" he asked.

"Sadly not."

"Tell me about your favorite meal."

Ash heaved himself onto his elbows to stare at Dan.

"What?" Dan shrugged lazily. "I figure if you tell me about good food, it might motivate me to get up and find my own."

"Medium rare steak," Ash said with a smirk.

"Mm."

"White wine peppercorn sauce."

Dan's mouth watered.

"Mashed potatoes with chunks of garlic."

"Gargh."

Laughing, Ash rose to his feet and grabbed Dan's hand. "Come on," he said, pulling Dan off the chair. "Let's get some dinner."

The Tavern on the Bay was packed with singles, couples, groups of friends, and families alike. A table to their right, against the window, opened up. An older couple and what was presumably their granddaughter were rising, and Dan and Ash inched their way closer, ready to snag it before someone else could.

Once they were seated, the remainder of the previous guests' debris moved to the end of the table for the server to remove—a couple of rolled up napkins and water glasses—Dan plucked a menu from between the salt and pepper shakers and turned it to face Ash.

"This," he said, pointing at the restaurant's logo. "You want to talk about unoriginal names for establishments?" He tapped the logo.

"The Tavern on the Bay," Ash mused. He reached for his own menu. "It's about as unoriginal as Greyson's Woodworking."

Dan gave him the finger.

"I did think of a new name, you know."

Dan flipped his menu open. There better be steak in it. "For what?"

"Your woodworking studio. I did tell you I'd find a new name for it," Ash said when Dan blinked at him blankly.

"Oh. Right! What is it?"

"I'm not telling you."

"You—" Dan's jaw dropped. "What? Why not? It's my studio."

"But it's my name."

"Why would you tell me you had one and then not tell me what it is? Asshole." He threw one of the dirty napkins at Ash.

Ash caught it and threw it back. "I'll tell you on one condition."

Dan put the napkin into one of the used glasses. "What's that?" What was Ash up to?

"You start making things again."

"I already have."

Eyes narrowed, Ash played with a corner of his menu. "When?"

"A few weeks ago," Dan said, quietly, because it felt like something crucial had shifted between them. Leaning forward with their forearms on the table, inches of space between them, neither of them acknowledged when a busboy cleared the debris off their table. "When I got back from Toronto. I've been stuck in a rut the past few years, just trucking along, doing what's expected of me. Working with wood again was like bumping into an old friend." He scoffed. "Sounds cheesy, I know."

"It doesn't," Ash said. "That's how I feel every time I step onto the ice for a game."

"Speaking of the game . . . any news on the contract?"

"I spoke with my agent yesterday." Ash stared at his hands. "He says they're revisiting my contract."

"What does that mean?"

"Your guess is as good as mine." He threw Dan a partial smile. "On the bright side, I just signed a contract to shoot a series of commercials for Sport U Apparel."

Dan's eyebrows winged up. "Shut up."

Ash sat back with a grin. "I kid you not."

Not only was Sport U Apparel the biggest line of athletic wear in the country, rumor had it that they were about to branch out to sports equipment too. They had an excellent reputation for community engagement and sourcing ethical materials, and for the last several years a portion of their sales went to LGBTQ charities.

"I am so, so sorry." Their server appeared, blonde hair

escaping a high ponytail, sweat glistening at her temples. "It's a zoo in here tonight and a table of eight just arrived . . . Can I get you something to . . . Oh my god! You're . . ." She burst into quiet tears. "Oh my god, *thank you.*" She shook Ash's hand so hard his whole body shook. "My sister . . . She's been so moody and withdrawn the past few months and we couldn't figure out what was wrong. And then earlier this week she told us she's gay after reading your article, and, and, and *thank you.*" She put her small pad down and wiped her face with a laugh. "Oh god, I'm so sorry. I'm such a mess. What can I get you guys? Anything. Anything at all. It's on me."

"Oh no, that's—"

"No, truly." She sniffled hard. "You have no idea what the past few months have been like."

Ash stared at her, mouth agape.

"Anything you want. What can I get you?"

Dan picked up his menu. "I haven't even looked yet."

"You want this." Ash flipped back a page and pointed at something.

"Surf 'n' turf? Yes. Yes, I want that."

"Make it extra spicy," Ash told the server.

Dan grinned at him.

After taking their orders, the server went away with another *thank you* and a promise to be back shortly with their drinks.

They chatted while they ate. About some of Ash's most memorable games—some of which were memorable to Dan too, having followed Ash's career and all—and some of the best cities he'd visited. About movies and travel and family. About the pros and cons of living in Syracuse versus Tampa.

"Less threat of hurricanes in Syracuse," Ash said,

toasting Dan with the last of his beer.

"True." Dan gazed out the window. It had gotten dark while they ate. Some streetlights were lit; others weren't. Bright fairy lights strung along The Tavern's covered porch illuminated the area. This street corner would be pretty if half the shops and restaurants weren't boarded up. Storm damage was everywhere.

The server returned to clear their plates. "It was such an honor to meet you, Mr. Yager."

"It's Ash, and really, the honor was mine. Thank you for telling me about your sister."

"Just . . . Just . . ." She backed away with their plates, getting teary again. "Just have the best life."

"She's sweet," Dan said once she'd gone.

"Yeah." Ash smiled to himself, and it was both bewildered and beatific. Taking something out of his wallet, he placed it underneath the saltshaker. "Gotta use the restroom," he said, standing. "Be right back."

He'd left a one-hundred-dollar tip.

Running a hand over his face, Dan glanced over to the hallway Ash had disappeared down, and then kept staring, waiting for Ash to reappear again like some smitten teenager who couldn't control his hormones.

He was so very cool.

Tearing his eyes away, he scanned the restaurant, his gaze snagging on a woman sitting with a group of friends. In her early twenties, she had brown hair to her shoulders and purple glasses were perched on her nose. She sunk into her chair with a grimace when Dan caught her ogling him, her lips twitching up in embarrassment. Dan smiled back at her despite the across-the-room flirting doing nothing for him. All he could think about was Ash. Ash's arms streaked with dust; Ash's muscles straining as they moved furniture around; Ash's laughter when Dan nearly swallowed a dust bunny; Ash's mad scramble to the other side of the apartment when Dan came down the stepladder with the spider colony; Ash's expression when he talked about hockey; the emotion in Ash's eyes when Dan had shown up earlier.

It was Ash. It had always been Ash.

Dan's smile grew when the man himself reappeared next to him.

"Who are you smiling at?" Ash stood next to the booth, hands on his hips. His scowl would scare small children away.

"Um, you?"

Assuming they were leaving, Dan stood . . . and ran into a wall of muscle when Ash didn't budge. Ash was warm and big and strong, and Dan forgot all his words. He swallowed hard and told himself the shiver was from the air conditioning.

Ash looked over his shoulder, scowled some more, and growled, "We're leaving."

They left. The walk back to Ash's apartment was silent but for Ash's stiff shoulders proclaiming his unhappiness with Dan, dinner, or the world at large. Who knew.

"Are you okay?"

"Just . . ." Ash gestured wildly, arms flying. "I'm trying to sort some stuff out. In my head."

"O . . . kay." Whatever that meant.

Reaching Ash's apartment, Ash slammed the door behind them and whirled on Dan, hands on his hips. "Do you want to date women?"

"Like, right this second?" *I only want to date you.* "Not particularly."

"What about the woman from The Tavern?"

"Who?"

"You know." Ash's gestured. "The one you were smiling at."

"Why are you being weird?"

"*I'm* being weird." Ash huffed and paced away. "You were the one eye-flirting while I took a two-minute bio break."

"I have no idea what you're talking about."

"No idea what I'm . . ." He trailed off, jaw ticking, his eyes fire and fury. Pacing back to Dan, he clamped a hand behind Dan's head, pulled him forward, and kissed him.

Ash kissed him.

Ash *kissed* him.

Ash kissed *him*.

Dan stood shocked and immobile.

"Gonna kiss me back?" Ash murmured against Dan's lips, walking him backward until his back hit the wall next to the door. "Or just stand there like a corpse?"

Pushing against Ash, Dan reversed their positions and kissed him back.

God. Yes. More. More. But why? Oh, who cared. He shut his brain off and went with it, consequences be damned.

Ash's mouth was hot and wet and firm, and his hands were everywhere at once. Every part of him Ash touched and stroked felt like it was being touched and stroked for the first time. Parts of him he'd thought dead flared to life.

Ash bent his knees and sank down on the wall, bringing their heights in line. Dan could feel Ash's heart beating furiously between them, just as fast as his.

He was light-headed and his tongue was in Ash's mouth and the world was a million times brighter than it'd been mere minutes ago.

Ash kissed as if he was starving. Dan met every kiss with hunger of his own and held on for dear life.

Finally, *finally* he could run his hands through Ash's hair. The gray was coarser than the brown had been; Dan couldn't get enough of it. Ash inserted a leg between Dan's thighs, igniting his senses. Dan ripped his mouth away to gasp in air, making Ash smile against his throat. Hands at Dan's hips encouraged him to move, and the pressure of Ash's thigh on his erection made him see stars.

"God."

He dragged Ash's mouth back to his.

Gentler this time. Quieter. More sensuous than frantic. Kiss after kiss after kiss.

Dan pulled back to look at Ash, breathing ragged, and ran a thumb along Ash's jaw and over his lips. Ash sucked his thumb into his mouth, tongue swirling around the tip.

"You kissed me," Dan choked around a gasp.

"Mm-hmm."

"Why?"

Ash let Dan's thumb pop out of his mouth. "Felt like it."

It . . . wasn't exactly what Dan wanted to hear. It wasn't *I missed you so much I had to kiss you before I died*. It wasn't *You're everything to me and I couldn't wait another second*.

Ash had felt like kissing him. Which, actually, wasn't as bad as he thought. Ash had felt like it, so he'd gone for it. Dan could work with that. It was as good a start as any.

"Feel like kissing me again?" Dan asked, and he moved in, anticipating Ash's response.

"Uh-huh." Ash kissed him once, fast and hard, and stood in one smooth motion, hands going to Dan's ass. "Feel like doing more than that."

They were shirtless by the time they reached the bedroom.

Pantsless by the time Dan shoved Ash onto the bed.

Completely nude four seconds later.

Ash lay down and Dan straddled him, bringing their mouths together again. Ash had surprisingly fine chest hair between his pecs and a trail that led to his crotch.

"How is it," Dan said, trailing his lips down Ash's throat to the vulnerable area between his neck and shoulder, "that your chest hair is still brown?"

Ash hissed when Dan bit his nipple, hands clamping onto Dan's butt. "I don't really think about the logistics of it."

They shouldn't do this. Nothing had been resolved between them. But Ash flipped them over, spreading Dan's legs apart and settling between them, licking a fiery path from Dan's navel to his crotch, winding his tongue around the tip of Dan's cock, and—

"Fuck, Ash. Please."

Dan fisted the bedcover and held on for the ride.

It took all of his strength to keep his hips from gyrating, from fucking himself into Ash's mouth when Ash swallowed him, sucking and sucking, and it had been so long, so long between them, that Dan was close to coming but he didn't want to, not yet.

"Ash." He tugged on Ash's hair. "Ash, please. *Please*."

"So impatient," Ash said, crawling back up Dan's body, hands running up Dan's sides, making Dan giggle helplessly. "Still ticklish."

Dan scowled at Ash's smirk. "Don't even think about it. Tell me you have stuff."

"I have stuff."

Ash reached into the nightstand and Dan groaned at the full-body contact. Ash was hard and built and hard and so warm and hard and his skin was damp with sweat. Did he mention hard? Dan was six years starved for Ash's touch, Ash's attention. The small niggle at the back of his mind that warned him that this was going to blow up in his face wouldn't go away, but as Ash found the lube and a condom and started to prep him, Dan found himself uncaring of anything that might happen past this moment.

He was a sobbing mess, hips unable to remain still, flushed and overheated, by the time Ash finished prepping him and was putting on a condom.

"Now, Ash, now, now."

Ash's hands trembled as he widened Dan's thighs and lined himself up, pushing in slowly, so slowly. Fully seated, Dan held his arms out and Ash fell on top of him, bracing himself on his arms.

Gazes met. There was desire in Ash's eyes and pleasure and . . . fear? Before Dan could decipher it, Ash ducked his head, bit Dan's collarbone, and said, "Can I?"

"God, yes."

And then he moved.

He'd forgotten. Dan had completely forgotten what being with Ash was like. Or, if not forgotten, then he'd muted the knowledge. Being with Ash was equal parts amazing and terrifying.

Amazing—it felt like his entire body was going to come apart, his belly clenching, his heart pummeling his ribs, his hands urging Ash faster and faster, his skin hypersensitive, his nerves tingling . . . he was consumed with Ash.

Terrifying—the past collided with the present, and for one moment, one overwhelming moment, he couldn't tell where he was, when he was. It didn't matter, though. None of it mattered. Ash was finally opening up to him—if only with his body—and Dan gave him everything in return.

"I love you. I love you."

Ash didn't appear to have heard. He kept pumping, swearing against Dan's neck, straining. Dan carded his fingers through his hair. "Come inside me," he whispered in Ash's ear.

"Fuck, Dan, gotta . . ."

"Yes, do it."

Dan grabbed his own cock as Ash went rigid above him and groaned, limbs shaking. Watching Ash fly off the handle was better than any external stimulation, and Dan came right behind Ash.

SEVENTEEN

FUCK.

Fuck.

What had he done?

Before he opened his eyes the next morning, Ash knew exactly what he'd find: Dan sprawled on his side next to him, face soft in sleep, one arm tucked under the pillow, the other outstretched toward Ash.

So much for pleasant, yet distant. Pleasant, yet distant had smacked him in the face with *do me baby one more time.*

Goddamn it. Ash scrubbed his face and swore under his breath.

Dan let out a little noise Ash refused to find adorable.

As quietly and quickly as he could, he dressed and left the bedroom, closing the door quietly behind him. He left a note on the counter—*Gone to practice*—grabbed his bag of gear, and was out the door less than three minutes after he'd awoken.

He consoled himself with the fact that he wasn't hiding—he really did have practice.

Last night had been . . . Fuck. He shouldn't have let it happen. Shouldn't have let it get that far. But he'd seen that girl—woman—flirting with Dan at The Tavern, and he hadn't been able to think. Dan wasn't his; Ash didn't have a say about who he did or didn't date. But jealousy had roared, green and ugly, and he'd gone all caveman *nobody can have you except me.* It hadn't helped that Dan had been so infuriatingly calm last night while Ash railed at him about the eye-flirting.

Twice more they'd had sex after that first time—a mutual blow job and then a lazy grind after Ash had gotten up to pee in the middle of the night. His dick was raw and sore, but the rest of him felt fucking amazing. He hadn't had sex like that in a long time. His stomach tangled with adrenaline just thinking about it. He was a fucking superhero!

His head, though . . .

His head was still trying to get on board with the situation.

What did this mean for them?

And how was he supposed to figure it out when Dan was right there, in his space? Ash needed some alone time to sort shit out, but he couldn't exactly send Dan away when the reason the man was here was to help him clean his place, could he?

Fuck. Maybe Dan would head back to his hotel this morning and he'd still be gone by the time Ash returned, giving Ash time to think. To breathe. To untangle his head and his heart and figure out what the hell he wanted.

What *did* he want? If he was honest with himself, what he really wanted was to turn back time six years, find out what Dan had been manipulated into doing, and then help him dig his way out of it.

Barring a sudden, miraculous appearance of a DeLorean capable of time travel, he wanted . . .

What?

He arrived at his team's practice rink and was no closer to figuring it out. Practice ended, and he was no closer to figuring it out. He drove home with Alex and Carlie, carpooling in Alex's car behind him, and he was no closer to figuring it out.

Dan's rental car was still parked outside of Ash's building on the street. Ash's hands grasped the steering wheel so tightly his knuckles turned white with the strain. His chest felt like a bowling ball sat on it. Really, it was nice of Dan to stick around, but Ash's head was about to blow off.

By now, Dan had probably showered in Ash's shower; he'd smell like Ash. His shorts and T-shirt from yesterday were sweat-stained and filthy; he was most likely wearing Ash's clothes.

Alex and Carlie followed him inside, where they found Dan in the kitchen cooking enough food to feed an army. Or three hungry hockey players. As Ash had predicted, Dan was indeed in a pair of Ash's sweatpants and one of his T-shirts, both of which were much too big on him. His curls looked recently washed and clean and soft, and for some reason Ash couldn't name, he resented Dan a little bit for making himself at home in Ash's place. This was Ash's space, his apartment. His house, his sanctuary, where he could unwind and take a load off away from the public eye. Dan's level of comfort here, before Ash could make sense of his feelings, was making him twitchy.

"Hey!" Dan grinned at them from the stove where he was frying sausages. "I remembered you said Alex and Carlie were coming over today to help with the yard," he said to Ash, "so I made lots."

Lots included scrambled eggs, bacon, blueberry pancakes, and fruit, spread out on the island like a feast. Next to it all was a small stack of plates, four sets of cutlery, a handful of napkins, four empty glasses, and a jug of orange juice. Coffee was brewing on the kitchen counter. Everything looked and smelled amazing. Ash bit the inside of his cheek. He felt caged in, pressured from all sides.

"It's Evan, right?" Dan extended a hand to Carlie. "I'm Dan."

"I remember."

Alex was trying to catch Ash's eye.

Avoiding his gaze, Ash said, "Where'd you get all this food?"

"The grocery store," Dan said, going back to the sausages.

"You went grocery shopping this morning?" By the tone of his voice, one might've thought he'd asked *You murdered someone this morning?*

Alex and Carlie appeared to want to blend in with the wall.

"Yes?" A question was written on Dan's face, his good mood replaced with confusion and caution. "All you had was condiments and eggs."

Alex shot him a smile. "This looks great, Dan, thank you."

"Sure. I, uh . . . I mean, I figured you'd be hungry after practice, so . . ." Now everyone was trying to catch Ash's eyes. "Anyway, dig in, I guess? While it's warm? Everything's ready."

Damn it. Ash was being an ass and taking it out on Dan.

Space. He needed space.

He lifted the bag he'd dropped on the floor, and as much as he tried, he couldn't dredge up a reassuring smile for Dan. "You guys go ahead and start. I'm just gonna put this in the bedroom."

The bedroom. It smelled like sex. It *reeked* of sex. A small stain on the bedcover drew his attention, lube or come or both. Piled on the floor next to the dresser were their dirty clothes from yesterday, as if waiting for one of them to do the laundry. As if they lived together. The bed was haphazardly made, the covers rumpled. A condom wrapper was on the floor, half hidden by the nightstand. In the bathroom, a wet towel that wasn't his hung over the shower door.

Every muscle in his body locked, and he only realized his fists were clenched when the strap of his bag dug into his palm.

It was too much. All of this was too much, and it was messing with his head, and what would happen when Dan went back to New York? Huh? Did Ash really think this would work out between them? It hadn't the first time. What had changed in Dan's life to make the possibility of them a reality for a second time? Nothing Ash had learned proved to him that things wouldn't end just as badly this time as they had last time.

He was staring down a black, depthless hole with the knowledge that he had to go in, yet also knowing that he'd never find his way back out.

"Hey."

Tension and an overwhelming sense of dread froze him in place at Dan's voice. A cold ball formed in his stomach and radiated outward to his extremities.

"Are you okay?" Dan tugged the bag from Ash's grip and set it aside. Then he took one of Ash's hands, unballed the fist, and straightened Ash's fingers out, one by one, massaging them as he did. "Did you have a bad practice?"

He'd had a great practice, actually, receiving nods of approval and pats on the back from the coaches. They had two back-to-back games starting tomorrow, a third game midweek, and then two back-to-back games in Orlando at the end of next week. Five more preseason games to prove that he deserved to play this year, that he was good enough to keep for next year.

He was ready to play for his life.

But he couldn't do that when Dan was jumbling up his head and confusing him.

"What are you doing here?" he asked, and even to himself his voice sounded harsh and mean.

Dan's brow furrowed. "I wanted to make sure you're okay."

"No, I mean . . . What are you doing *here*? In Tampa?"

"I told you, I . . ." Dan was no longer massaging Ash's fingers, though he still held his hand in both of his own. "I wanted to be here for you. After the storm."

"Why? I didn't ask you to come here. I don't need you."

"You . . ." His face paled and his hands went lax. Ash's arm fell to his side. "I was . . . trying to help. I wanted to . . . Oh." His entire body sagged with that *oh*. "But you're right. I . . ." The way he said it—*You're right*—it was like he'd just realized that he'd forced his presence on someone when it was unwanted in the first place. And even though that was exactly what Ash had meant with his words, he didn't actually *mean* them. As Dan stepped back, bumping into the bed and bracing himself with a hand on it, which he immediately jerked back as if the cover had scorched him, Ash burned with shame hotter than the sun and—

"Dan—"

"No, you're right, I . . ." Still appearing dazed, Dan searched Ash's face for something. Ash had no idea what his expression said right now; whatever it was, it wasn't what Dan was looking for. His entire body wilted. "I'm sorry," he whispered roughly. "I didn't mean—I just wanted—" He took in the room as if seeing it for the first time, wondering where he was and how he'd gotten here.

Ash knew he should do something, say something.

Apologize, at the very least. But his words were a sand-bank—dry and coarse.

"I'm sorry," Dan repeated. With one last glassy look at Ash, he left the room. As if in a fog, he headed down the hallway, his posture the picture of bewilderment and anguish.

When he'd turned the corner and Ash could no longer see him, Ash slumped against the wall of his bedroom and took what felt like the first breath since he'd woken up this morning. It was tainted with regret and remorse and . . . loss. He hadn't felt this way since *I'm sorry, I can't.*

"Damn it."

He moved fast, but it was too late. Dan's shoes were already gone from where they'd rested next to the front door, and the sound of a car starting outside reached his ears.

Alex and Carlie—damn, Ash had forgotten they were here—gaped at the front door.

Ash punched the side of the fridge. "Damn it."

Had he not known Alex as well as he did, known that the man had a heart of gold, the scowl on his face would've sent Ash running. "What the hell did you do?"

Defeated, he told them everything.

The hotel room door swung closed behind Dan with a quiet click, the latch catching sounding too loud in his quiet room. He'd blindly followed the GPS's directions back, not paying attention to where he was going or what he was seeing.

Sinking onto the edge of the bed, he stared at him-self in the mirror on top of the dresser. This morning he'd looked at himself in the mirror in Ash's bathroom after his shower, surprised to find himself smiling at nothing. Happy. Anticipatory. He'd even played teenager and drawn a heart in the foggy mirror. Now, he was haggard, his eyes hollow, his skin too pale.

Last night had been amazing, if wholly unexpected. Ash had been alternately sweet and desperate, careful and rough. But there'd also been a lack of . . . warmth. Like Ash wanted it, but was holding a part of himself back. The whole thing had felt off from the moment Ash kissed him. Dan had ignored it at the time, too willing to go along with whatever Ash was ready to give him. He'd fooled himself into believing that the awkward tension between them was due to their years apart, to timidity as they relearned each other.

Truth was that Ash was horny and Dan had been a convenient, warm, willing body.

What had he thought would happen? A sigh escaped him. His chest felt concave, empty. What had he expected? That he'd cement himself in Ash's life, become a constant, and Ash would miraculously forgive him and they'd be together again? Everything all hunky dory and better than ever?

Yes. Naively, that was exactly what he'd expected.

Stupid, really, to think that they could go back.

God, he was such an idiot. To think that he could prove to Ash that he wasn't the same person anymore, that he was here to stay. Ash was understandably protective of himself; he wasn't letting Dan in.

Maybe he needed more time.

Or maybe all the time in the world wouldn't change anything.

The problem was that Ash had moved on. He'd left Dan in the past, exactly where Dan belonged if he was being honest with himself.

And Dan . . . Well, Dan was stuck in the past. Overwhelmed with guilt. Dwelling to the point of obsession over what he'd done and how to fix it.

But there was no fixing, only going forward.

Could they move forward? Together?

He almost did it then. He pulled his suitcase out of the closet while his laptop booted up, prepared to pack up, book a flight, and head home to admit defeat.

Go big and fail epically. Story of his life.

What would bailing prove, though? It wouldn't prove to Ash that Dan was sticking around this time; it would only show, beyond a doubt, that Ash was right and Dan wasn't to be depended on.

So he was staying. For a little while, at least. He'd said he'd help Ash and he would. He'd stay as long as that took. After that . . .

He changed out of Ash's clothes and into his own, then brought Ash's down to the hotel laundromat. No doubt Ash wouldn't want his clothes back smelling like Dan. While he waited, he sat on his bed in his room with the TV on, but he couldn't see anything past the expression on Ash's face when he'd told Dan he didn't need him—angry and frustrated, ready to vibrate out of his skin.

And because the universe didn't think he was hurting enough, his mom called.

"Jesus."

He considered not answering, but as the phone continued to ring in his hand, a pounding started in his ears, loud as a drum. Here was the cause of all of his troubles. Her call couldn't have been more timely.

"Mom."

"Dan." The sound of a door closing echoed through the

line. "I've just returned home from brunch at the Millers where I bumped into Mark. He said you're working in Tampa now?"

"Uh-huh."

"Were you going to tell me?"

"Why? You don't keep track of other employees who transfer offices."

"Well, no. Of course not. But you're my son. I worry about you and your brother."

"You *worry*?" Dan's hard laugh stung his throat. "Really? Is that why you visited Mitch after he fainted earlier this year?"

Silence answered him. They both knew she'd done no such thing.

She sounded oddly subdued when she said, "I didn't think he'd want to see me."

"He wouldn't have. But since when do other peoples' feelings stop you? Mine certainly didn't six years ago."

"Dan—"

"Do you remember?" he whispered past the knot in his throat that stung his eyes, made his nose burn. "I told you my plans, my dreams. And you shit on them like they were as much of a nuisance as the phone bill."

"I . . . Yes, well . . ." She cleared her throat delicately, a little *ahem* that reminded him of all those times she'd made the same sound at the dinner table to get his and Mitch's attention while they debated something or play-fought or Mitch jabbered on about this or that hockey something. "I know you don't believe this, but I really was doing what I thought was best."

"Whatever." All of the fight went out of him—if he'd had any to begin with—and his body went limp, sinking into the pillows. Exhausted to the point of oversensitivity, he just wanted to curl into a ball and nap until things got better.

"When are you coming home?"

Woodenly, done with everything, he said, "I don't know. I gotta go. Bye." He hung up on her protests and turned off his phone.

He was out of ideas.

Worse, he was out of hope.

He was lying on the bed with an arm flung over his eyes when the room phone rang. His clothes were dry. Taking a deep breath that did nothing to loosen the grip on his chest, he pocketed his wallet and keys, went down to the laundromat to fold Ash's clothes, then got back into his rental car.

Twenty minutes later, he knocked on Ash's door, unsure of his welcome. He swallowed hard and fidgeted while he waited, holding Ash's clothing out in front of him, a bad peace offering.

The door swung open so fast Dan's hair bounced.

"Hey, man," said Evan—Carlie. Whatever he liked to be called.

"Oh. Uh, hi. Is Ash here?"

"Yeah, he's out back." Evan jerked a thumb in the backyard's direction. "Come in and I'll grab him."

"I'll wait here." He was never forcing his presence on Ash again.

Evan frowned at him but merely shrugged. "Okay. Yo, Yager!" he yelled as he headed for the patio doors, thrown open to the summer sunshine. "You've got a visitor."

"Who is it?" Ash asked.

Just the sound of his voice made Dan choke on a breath.

"Dan?"

He couldn't have mustered a smile if he'd tried. "Hi." God, Ash looked good, all sweaty and dirt-stained from working in the yard. It seemed the anger had passed, or the frustration, or whatever. Instead, there was confusion in his gaze, a little bit of uncertainty as his lips tilted up in a small, tentative smile. It reminded Dan of the expression on Ash's face when Ash had first spotted Dan at the bookstore in Toronto during Alex's book launch last month. Back before Dan's hope had been killed.

He handed Ash his bundle. "I brought your stuff back. They're clean. I washed them at the hotel."

"Oh. Thanks." Ash's penetrating gaze narrowed on Dan. He stepped forward, onto the front stoop, and the world shrunk in size to just the two of them.

Dan took a step back.

"Are you—"

Okay, Ash no doubt meant to ask, but Dan cut him off at the quick. Because no, he was not okay, and he didn't want to have to lie.

"I came to help. If . . . If you'll have me, that is. I said I would, so . . ." His shoulders jerked. "Put me to work. If you want."

"Okay, thanks. That's . . ."

Ash moved forward again; Dan countered with another step back.

Ash licked his lips. "Listen, about last night—"

Ugh. If ever there'd been a more inauspicious start to a conversation . . . "We don't have to talk about—"

"I just wanted to say—"

"Really, there's no need—"

"—that I didn't mean to make you feel bad—"

"It's fine, I get it." Dan spoke loudly, making himself heard. "Messaged received, loud and clear."

Scowling, Ash blew out a hard breath through his nose. "Are you going to let me talk?" he growled.

Dan took another step back and bumped into the porch post. "Like you've let me talk?"

Ash's mouth opened, ready for a pithy rebuttal knowing him.

Dan held up a hand. "Do you want my help or not?"

Yes.

Of course Ash wanted Dan's help.

More than that, he wanted five minutes to explain where his head had been this morning.

It was only fair, though, that Dan didn't want to listen. A taste of Ash's own medicine, so to speak.

Fuck, they sucked at communicating.

"Let me get this straight," Alex had said this morning after Ash had finished telling them everything. *Everything.* From their first meeting in the elevator to last night. "You slept together—"

"Three times," Carlie had piped in, the jerk.

"Three times. He told you he loved you and you kicked him out?"

"I didn't—" Okay, that was a lie. *I don't need you* was a very loud, very definitive *get the fuck out.*

Hours later, he was still kicking his own ass for it.

"You've got a second chance here," Carlie had said, "and you're blowing it."

"If you want that second chance." Alex had squinted at him. "Which, judging by our conversation the other day, you do."

Yes. Yes, he fucking well did. Just that everything had happened so fast and he couldn't get his head around it.

He'd spent the entire time during Dan's absence

convinced that Dan was going to hop on a plane any second, leaving Ash's stupid ass behind. Yet had he called Dan and explained? Asked him to stay?

Nope. Apparently he was a chickenshit in a hockey player's body.

Smart, his head chirped. *You were smart. If Dan left, that'd just prove what you've known all along.*

But Dan hadn't left. No, he'd shown up all sad and determined, and then had proceeded to unpack all of Ash's boxes, sorting all of his stuff into piles so that Ash could clearly see what needed to be put away. Neat piles too, all stacked against the wall in the living room, out of the way so that nobody tripped on anything as they went in and out from the backyard to the kitchen for a snack or a water refill.

And he'd left half an hour ago for the grocery store, declaring that Ash and Alex and Carlie needed dinner that was more sustaining than frozen pizza.

Ash didn't know what to make of it.

Dan hadn't left. *He hadn't left.*

Ash was so confused that he couldn't even make sense of Dan's need to make them dinner when he hadn't stuck around to eat his own breakfast earlier. Ash stared at his neat piles of stuff, seeing Dan's handsome face and his light brown eyes the color of good whiskey and his blond curls tumbling all over the place.

I love you. Did Dan realize what he'd said? Did he remember? Had it been uttered in the heat of the moment and he didn't mean it at all?

"Told you he wouldn't leave." Alex plopped onto the couch.

"Yeah, well. You know more about the situation than I do."

"And whose fault is that?"

Ash gave him a black look.

Alex merely raised an eyebrow, the know-it-all.

A knock on the living room window came from outside and had them both turning toward it.

"Why am I the only one still working?" Carlie called through the glass. He wore a bandana to keep his hair out of his eyes and a pair of well-used gardening gloves.

Alex rose and headed for the patio doors. "Don't let Dan leave without talking to him first," he said over his shoulder. "The key to any good relationship is communication."

Said the guy whose only—and longest—relationship was a whopping nine months.

"We're not in a relationship."

Alex's don't-be-stupid face was truly spectacular. "If you believe that, you're a bigger idiot than I thought."

Left alone, Ash sighed. Alex was right: he and Dan needed to talk. It was time.

A car door slammed, and he headed to the picture window that overlooked his street.

"For fuck's sake."

Despite divorced parents, being left at the "altar," and a cheating wife, Ash had never considered himself one of those jaded I'm-never-gonna-love-again types. Yes, he was protective of himself. And it was true that he hadn't let himself get attached to anyone since Dan and Laura. There was someone out there for him, though, he knew that. When he found that person, he was going to open himself up entirely and lay it all on the line. He wasn't hiding from love, just from being hurt.

Watching Dan and Laura hike up his walkway together, Ash's stomach went hard and he found himself unashamed of the image that crossed his mind. One where he went out the back, crossed the yard, snuck out the side fence, and headed to The Tavern to get shitfaced.

This was one of those moments that would be better dealt with if alcohol were involved.

Dan and Laura's walk up to the door was that unpleasant, hesitant *hey, we parked in front of the same house, are you going here too, let's walk up together and make awkward small talk until someone answers the door, ha ha, strained smiles everywhere.* Ash might've laughed if the situation wasn't so ridiculous.

He reached the door before Dan and Laura did and opened it wide, then blocked most of it with his body, allowing a small gap for Dan, with his paper bag of groceries, to slip through and inside. Small enough for Dan to brush up against Ash as he passed—in fact Ash purposely moved closer—but Dan somehow managed to keep them from touching, which made Ash feel . . .

Sort of panicky.

Damn it. They needed to talk and it had to be today.

"Laura," he greeted.

He heard Dan freeze behind him. Ash couldn't remember if he'd ever mentioned Laura to Dan; either way, Dan clearly knew the name.

"Wow," Laura said as Dan unfroze and wandered off into the kitchen.

"Wow what?"

"I totally misread the situation." She laughed without humor.

"What situation?"

"I thought, when you helped me board my place up last week . . . But you've never smiled at me like that."

Ash pulled his gaze away from Dan unloading his

groceries. "Sorry, what?" Who was smiling at who?

Laura's snort was as small as her stature. "Is that—" She jerked her chin. "—the person you were texting when I saw you last time? Your new boyfriend?"

"He's not my—" Alex's words came back to him. "I mean, he's . . . It's complicated."

"Does it have to be?"

Ash opened his mouth to respond, but a chuckle took him by surprise instead. "No. No, I don't suppose it does."

Laura's eyes lingered on him for a second, and then she was backing away. "See you later, Ash."

"Wait. What'd you come by for?"

"I was going to ask if you wanted to—Never mind. Doesn't matter. Hey!" This last she yelled in the direction of the window above the sink in the kitchen. From his vantage point at the door, Ash saw Dan lift his head from where he was washing carrots. "Good luck with this one!" Laura gestured at Ash, turned, and was gone.

Dan looked at him, a question mark on his face.

Ash shrugged.

Dan surveyed him for a moment, and said, "I'm making stew."

"Stew?"

"Yeah. Meat and potatoes. I figure it'll go over well with this crew."

"You're not wrong. Can I help?"

"No." And he started peeling carrots.

"Okay, then. I'll . . . put my stuff away?"

"You do that."

Amusement tickled Ash's belly despite the circumstances. "You're very irritating."

"Are you actually insulting the guy making you dinner?" Setting the carrots aside, Dan reached for a purple and white vegetable at his elbow. "You don't like rutabaga, if I remember correctly?" he asked as he started peeling.

"That's just mean."

Dan's lips twitched.

Leaving him to it, Ash headed back into the living room, fervently hoping the rutabaga wouldn't end up in the stew, yet knowing full well that if Dan was peeling it, then the recipe called for it, and if the recipe called for it, Dan would include it. Dan didn't deviate from a recipe.

He didn't deviate from a lot of things.

Which was why the way he'd left Ash at the airport made no sense.

There was no figuring anything out right now, though, so he left Dan to his stew and concentrated on putting his stuff away.

As an hour passed, and Alex and Carlie came and went, asking Ash for his opinion on this or that, and as Ash slowly cleared the living room, he was always aware of Dan's presence mere feet away in the other room. Dan was the last piece of cheesecake at the restaurant—Ash wanted a taste even though he knew it was bad for him.

In that hour, Ash achieved very little. He spent too much time sorting his books into two piles—read and un-read—useless minutes hooking up his DVD player, and a few sentimental moments placing his trophies in chrono-logical order. Then he started categorizing everything into piles depending on which room they belonged to. The re-sult was that he ended up with a living room that looked like a bomb had gone off.

So much for Dan's neat piles.

Speaking of Dan, Ash had heard him banging through cabinets a little while ago, and then silence, and now it smelled like . . . fresh baked bread?

Ash leaned over the couch to see what he was up to. "Are you making bread?"

"Biscuits," Dan said, elbow deep in water as he washed dishes in the sink.

"Why?"

"Because you need biscuits to go with stew."

Feeling light as air, Ash said, "Do you?"

"Well, yeah."

"Who told you that?"

"None of your biscuits."

"Oh my god." Ash fell onto the couch, charmed by him, yet embarrassed for him at the same time. "That was so bad."

"You're laughing, though."

"Only so that you don't feel bad about how bad that pun was."

Dan's laugh made Ash's belly slip and he grinned up at the ceiling. Hauling himself up, he got back to work.

Finding the hockey puck from his first goal in the NHL, he weighted it in his palm. When you stopped to think about it, pucks were tiny things—only three inches across, one inch thick, and weighing about as much as a couple of apples. And yet they meant so much to so many people. Whether he was passing the puck to a teammate, setting up a shot, or flipping one over the glass for a fan, it was odd to think that this little piece of rubber had driven him for most of his life.

As hard as he'd worked to get where he was, it sucked that it could all get taken away if his club decided it didn't want him.

"What's wrong?" Dan said from behind him, appearing on silent feet.

"I was just thinking . . ." Shaking his head, Ash placed

the puck on the shelf next to the television. "Never mind."

Dan's eyes fell shut on a wince, fingers closing gently around the item he held. His eyes opened after a few seconds, and he stared glassily at the wall as if seeing something else entirely. Swallowing hard, he cupped whatever it was in both hands, then looked Ash straight in the eye with a gaze that was hopeless and bleak. It made Ash's heart thrum with nervous fear, not unlike what he'd felt upon returning home after the hurricane.

Dan's voice was whisper-soft when he spoke. "We're never going to get past what happened between us, are we?"

Ash's breath stopped.

"You hold yourself back. You think I don't see it, this wall between us, but I do. And I don't know how to knock it down." Self-deprecation twisted Dan's lips. "I've been trying, but . . . I know I fucked things up a long time ago, but I've been trying to make things right. I just . . . I don't know what else to do to prove to you that I'm not going anywhere this time. That I'm not who I was. I don't know how to get you to trust me again. I don't even know if I should keep trying. Do you want me to go? Is that it? You know how I feel about you, Ash. And there's a part of me that's just waiting for you to tell me to leave, to get lost . . . and another part that's dying for you to love me back. But I don't know what else to do. I wish you'd tell me where I stand with you so I can stop guessing."

"Dan, I . . ." It hurt, seeing Dan like this. Rubbed Ash raw and knotted his insides. Felt like there was sandpaper at the back of his throat. "I want to trust you. I do. My heart says I can, but my head . . ." His head was smart. His head remembered trusting this man once before and ending up heartbroken. His head knew that going down that path again would only lead to hurt.

Dan was already nodding, like he'd expected that answer. He took a deep breath. "I think . . . I'm gonna go."

"You're . . . What? No. But . . . dinner."

"Oh." Dan glanced toward the kitchen, as if he'd forgotten he'd cooked them an entire meal. "It's mostly ready. Just need to let it simmer a bit and take the biscuits out of the oven in a few—"

"No, I mean . . . You should stay. For dinner. You made it. You didn't even get breakfast this morning, either."

"Oh. I'm, uh, not really hungry." He firmed his jaw and lifted his head. "Thank you for letting me back into your life. I wish . . ." He trailed off. Clearing his throat, he went on. "I wish things could be different between us, but I understand why they can't be. I really missed you." His words were low and unsteady. "And I'm glad I got to be in your life again, even if—" He hiccupped and wiped away a stray tear, slicing Ash through the chest. "Even if only for a little while." He set his item down on the table, gently, so tenderly . . .

And then he was gone.

The sandpaper turned into claws and Ash couldn't swallow past it, couldn't breathe past his burning nose. His skin itched and pulled, and it felt like he'd tumbled into a dark, ugly, bottomless pit of heartache.

On the table lay one of the sun catchers Dan had made him a lifetime ago, a crescent moon made of some type of pale wood. A round crystal hung from the top point of the moon on a clear string. *A+D* had been burned into the widest part of the moon. Next to the sun catcher was the small pile of Ash's clothes Dan had brought back. On the very bottom was a familiar denim-blue sweater with the faded logo of his old AHL team in Syracuse.

Dan had returned his sweater in a silent, final good-bye to what they'd once been.

I'm not that person anymore! Dan had wanted to yell at Ash. *I promise! Please see me!*

Actions spoke louder than words, however. But hadn't Dan proved that he wasn't running away this time? What else did he have to do?

As he pulled into the hotel parking lot for the second time that day, eyes blurry with tears, throat aching with the effort of holding them back, he admitted to himself that there wasn't anything else *to* do. Maybe Dan's actions six years ago would always be between them, an immovable wall of pain and loss that Dan tried to climb but that Ash couldn't see around.

Which meant that what they'd been doing lately, getting to know each other again, the sex, sharing a bed, trading texts . . . It wasn't meant to lead anywhere. Dan had thrown his whole heart into it, his whole self, laid it all out on the line, hoping that, like him, Ash was done living in the past. But when Ash had picked up the puck, something clearly on his mind, Dan had known as soon as Ash refused to share that Ash was never going to share anything important with him ever again.

Was this what Ash had felt like back then, when Dan had left him? Like someone had stolen all of his dreams? Without Ash, Dan was facing a future that was gray and dull and fuzzy along the edges.

His jaw ached from clenching his teeth to hold off the tears. His hands hurt from gripping the steering wheel too tightly. A headache pulsed at his temples, part lack of food and part tension.

It was nothing compared to the black, empty hole in his heart that reminded him too much of the past.

Heading inside, Dan firmly—finally—shut the door on that part of his life.

EIGHTEEN

AUGUST 2003—SIX YEARS AGO

TAKING A LAST LOOK AROUND HIS APARTMENT, Dan admitted to himself that he'd miss it. Before Ash, he hadn't had any emotional attachment to it. It was sparsely furnished and belonged to Westlake Waterless Printing, one of the company's handful of apartments in the city that housed visiting employees and stakeholders from out of town.

He and Ash had made a lot of memories here these past few months. Cooking and watching movies on the laptop and relaxing. Kissing and sleeping and having sex.

So yeah, he'd miss it, but not enough to stay.

The decision to drop out of school and follow Ash to Syracuse had been a surprisingly easy one to make. They'd flown to Syracuse every weekend for the past month and had found a two-bedroom apartment near the university that they'd co-signed the lease on just last week. They were moving in in two weeks. On top of that, Dan had found a woodworker twenty minutes outside of the city who was willing to take him on as an apprentice.

Everything had come together so easily and now it was time to go. Their flight was in a few hours.

He was looking forward to exploring a new city and building things full-time and making a life with Ash. He'd miss Mitch, though. Ever since Dan had moved out of their home in the Hamptons two years ago to attend college in

Manhattan, they hadn't seen each other as often as they used to. Holidays and the occasional weekend. So basically, nothing would change there. Mitch was going to be happy for him, Dan had no doubt. So was their dad.

Their mom, however . . .

"All set?"

Ash stood in the doorway separating the kitchen and the bedroom, his wide shoulders taking up almost the entire space. He'd slowly moved his stuff back to Syracuse over the past few weekends; all he had left now was a backpack with a few toiletries, T-shirts, and underwear.

"Yeah." Dan nodded. "All set."

"And you're still sure about this? It's not going to be easy for you, having to hide our relationship—"

"It's not going to be easy for you, either."

"No, I know, but—"

"Ash."

Ash stopped talking.

Dan held out a hand. "I'm sure."

"Okay." Ash took his hand and reeled him into a hug. "Okay."

Nosing his way to Ash's neck with a sigh, Dan twined his arms around Ash's waist. "You give the best hugs."

"I'll put that on my resume."

"No. Only I get them."

Ash pulled away with a quiet laugh, but it wasn't long before his expression pulled down again. "Sure you don't want me to come with you to talk to your mom?"

"Yeah." Dan patted Ash's chest, then turned to lift his suitcase. He'd packed the essentials; everything else he'd already shipped to Syracuse. "I'll be fine."

"I know, but I can be your backup in case things get heated. I'm a defenseman, you know. That's my job."

"Thank you. Really," Dan said through a chuckle. He placed a small kiss on Ash's jaw. "But it's probably best if I do this alone. You head on to the airport; I'll be right behind you."

They separated in the lobby, getting into different taxis in the early afternoon drizzle. Ash threw Dan a wink and a grin before getting into his own. It wasn't until Dan was ensconced in his that his heart started to pound and his upper lip beaded with sweat. *I'm dropping out of school and quitting my job to move to Syracuse to be with my boyfriend* wasn't going to go over well.

He should leave out the boyfriend part—his mother wouldn't understand it—and make it about himself and his desire for a career of his own choosing.

Yes, that was definitely the way to go. Keep it professional, leave out the personal.

The drizzle turned into a downpour, thundering onto the top of the cab, raining down the windows like tears. Dan rehearsed his speech on the drive, hands clenched into fists. It made him a coward that he'd waited until the very last second to talk to his mom, but this way he could say his piece and then leave, escaping the fallout.

And the fallout would be ugly. Greta Westlake didn't like being said no to.

He left his suitcase at the security desk in the lobby of Westlake's office building, shaking water out of his hair, and took the stairs up eighteen floors. If he was sweating before, it was nothing compared to the lakes his armpits had become by the time he reached Westlake's floor, his face gleaming with perspiration. He was out of breath; possible it had more to do with the upcoming conversation than with the climb.

Slipping into his mother's outer office two minutes

before his scheduled meeting time, he fell into a chair to wait and made inane small talk with Elise. Elaine? Elena? Erica? His mother went through executive assistants so fast Dan could never keep them straight.

Right on time, his mother ushered someone out of her office and gestured Dan inside with a quick word to Elise/Elaine/Elena/Erica. Inside his mother's inner sanctum, it was cool and spacious and bright. The corner office's two walls were made up entirely of windows that looked out onto other office buildings' windows. It should've made him claustrophobic; instead, it gave him a false sense of security, like being enclosed in bubble wrap.

He took a seat in one of the two chairs facing the sturdy wooden desk, knowing full well that the little round two-seater table in front of the window was only for show. A large dresser behind the desk was actually a fancy filing cabinet, dry cleaning encased in plastic hung on a hook next to the door, a mini fridge hummed obnoxiously to his left. As well as a computer, the top of the desk held papers, folders, a notebook open to a to-do list, a cup of pens, an empty coffee mug, what was possibly a mint wrapper, and one of those palm-sized daily calendars with a saying for each day. Dan turned it toward him while his mother was still in the outer office with Elise/Elaine/Elena/Erica.

It was a word of the day calendar. Today's word was *unacknowledged—not recognized, accepted, or admitted.*

Dan gulped.

"Dan." His mother came in and shut the door. "I know you know this, so I'm not sure why I should have to tell you, but that's not the way we dress at the office."

No, a polo shirt, dark, pressed jeans, and loafers weren't appropriate except on casual Fridays, which today was not. "I took a vacation day. I only came in because I need to talk to you about something."

"Oh?" She steepled her fingers.

Standing, he took a folded sheaf of paper out of his back pocket and handed it to her.

"What's this?"

"My resignation," he said. Her eyes flew to his. "I know I should give it to Mark technically, since I'm interning under his supervision, but . . . You're my mom and it's your company, so . . ." He sat with a helpless shrug.

"I see." She unfolded the letter and spent so much time reading it over that he was sure he'd lost her attention.

He cleared his throat. "I'm moving to Syracuse."

"Syracuse?"

The way she said it, one would think he'd said Siberia.

"Yeah. There's a woodworker there who's agreed to take me on as an apprentice."

She scoffed and tossed the letter aside. "Woodworking. Dan, how many times do I have to tell you that it's not a real career?"

Should he mention the dozen pieces of one-of-a-kind wooden furniture at home she'd had specially commissioned?

"I know you think that," he said, slowly, almost placating. "And maybe I won't ever be a household name, but I have to try."

"You'll fail."

It was his turn to scoff. "So what if I do? At least I'll have tried."

"No."

"No?" With some amazement, he found himself quietly amused. He smiled gently. "Mom, it's not up for debate. I've already got the apprenticeship set up, and I signed the lease on an apartment last week."

"Something wrong with your apartment here?"

"Um . . . It's four hours from my apprenticeship?"

"And you couldn't find someone here to apprentice with?"

"No, actually, I couldn't." Hadn't tried, but that wasn't the point. "Mom, look, I didn't make this decision lightly. But the truth is that I don't want to study business and accounting. It's fine. I'm good at it. But I don't love it like I love woodworking. *That's* what I want to do. I don't . . ." He stalled out, then took a deep breath and said, "I don't want to work for the family business. I hope you can understand."

"I understand."

Shoulders loosening, he huffed out a relieved breath. That was easier than he'd expected. "Good."

"I understand that you don't appreciate how hard I've worked to expand and elevate this company to where it is today. How hard I've worked to ensure we stay relevant to current needs. I understand that *you don't understand* why it's important for this company to remain a family-run business."

Mouth agape, Dan reared back in surprise, shoulders hitting the back of the chair. "What? I . . . I understand that you want this to remain a family business. I do. But isn't that an archaic way of looking at things? Do you know how infrequently family businesses actually remain in the family these days?"

His mother narrowed her eyes. "We will not be one of those companies."

"So you'd rather pass it along to me or Mitch even though we may not be the best bet for the company? We might not be the best ones to run it. Could even run it into the ground. Wouldn't you rather pass it on to someone who has the knowledge and experience and entrepreneurial drive to see it succeed?"

"Once you graduate and have a dozen years working here under your belt," his mother said, sitting back in her chair, calm and unruffled, "you'll have everything you need to keep this company successful."

"I appreciate your vote of confidence in my abilities." Dan stood and wiped his palms on his thighs. "But my decision's been made. My flight leaves for Syracuse in a couple of hours."

"No."

It was an effort not to roll his eyes. Where previously he'd been amused, now he was exasperated with her refusal to listen. "Mom—"

"Did you know that I had to pay my own way through college when I was your age?"

The sudden change in subject threw him. "Okay?" Where was she going with this?

"My parents could afford it, but they wanted me to learn hard work and perseverance. You're very lucky that I'm paying your tuition."

"I know that." Was she implying that he owed her somehow?

A perfect eyebrow raised. "Do you? I don't think you understand how difficult it is to work one, sometimes two jobs to pay for tuition, books, and living expenses, all while maintaining your grades."

Ah. He got it now. She was threatening to take away his tuition if he didn't do what she wanted. He almost laughed in her face—he was dropping out, so none of it mattered, anyway.

"If you don't complete your degree and come work for me, I'll take Mitch's college tuition away." Her voice was indifferent and cold. She could've been telling him to eat his greens or pick his dirty socks off the floor.

Every urge to laugh fled. "What? You wouldn't do that."

"You think not?"

"You want us both to have a good education. There's no way you'd do that."

"Daniel Greyson." The use of his full name stilled him. "If I don't see you back in this office tomorrow morning, ready to work, and if you don't start classes again in September as expected, Mitch won't see a penny of college tuition from me."

She didn't look away from him the entire time, didn't blink, didn't fidget. Her expression, her entire body language, was remote and frigid. It didn't invite debate or discussion.

Realization hit Dan with the force of a truck—she was serious. There was not an ounce of indecision or wavering, no indication that she'd take the words back.

She was dead fucking serious.

"Wow." He slow-clapped, the skin around his eyes feeling tight. "Congratulations. You clearly know my weak spot." To his own ears, his voice was strained.

She had him in a corner and the slight widening of her eyes told Dan that she knew it too.

How fucking dare she? Did she have no shame? No principles? Of course he'd stay now. There was no way he'd make Mitch the unsuspecting victim of his decisions. So fine, he'd show up for work tomorrow and go back to school, unless . . .

"Dad." His dad. His dad could fix things. "Dad'll help with Mitch's tuition."

"You think he'll be able to afford four years' worth if he suddenly finds himself unemployed right before Mitch is due to start college?"

Jesus. Now she was threatening his dad too? Who was this person he'd called mom his whole life?

Dan would pay Mitch's tuition himself! Oh, fuck him, who was he kidding? There was no way he could afford it. He might live in the Hamptons, he might come from money, but he didn't *have* any damn money himself except for some savings from part-time jobs when he was in high school and the little he made as an intern. His parents were of the *you have to earn it* school of thought. He quickly did some mental math . . . When Mitch graduated high school in three years, Dan would be a year out of college and theoretically making a decent wage. But with the cost of living in this city, he couldn't count on having the funds Mitch would need.

And Mitch certainly couldn't pay his own way. School was fucking expensive, and if Dan didn't have any money, Mitch had less. When he wasn't in school, Mitch was either studying, completing homework, or playing hockey. He didn't have time for a part-time job, and even if he took a full-time summer job for the next two summers, at minimum wage he *still* wouldn't have enough to afford college.

There were student loans, but they were based off parental income.

He lowered himself back onto his chair slowly, as if every bone hurt, throat scratchy, entire body clenched. "Looks like you've got yourself a deal." To his own ears, his voice was flat. Dead. "But you've lost everything else."

His mother tapped a pen on the desktop. "Meaning?"

"I had a lot of respect and admiration for you, for what you've managed to accomplish with this company. You've just lost all of that. I will never trust you or confide in you again. You're a virtual stranger to me." Truth. There was so much truth coming out of him and he couldn't make it stop. A single tear fell onto his cheek. He dashed it away. "I'm *ashamed* to call you my mother. I wish Dad knew about this so he could see you for who you really are." He stood, keeping his movements slow and controlled. "You've shown your true colors. I hope you can live with the consequences."

Seconds later, he was closing the office door behind him with a barely heard *snick*, then the outer office door, and then he was in the stairwell, feet thumping on the metal stairs. His heart hurt—he couldn't breathe. His eyes stung—he couldn't see. The walls of the stairwell pressed in on him from all sides, and he was seconds away from coming apart at the seams.

How could she be so heartless and cruel? What was so wrong with him wanting his own career? With giving the company to someone who would take care of it?

His vision blurred further as he thought of Ash at the airport waiting for him, of the new apartment they'd leased together, of the life they were going to build. But okay. It was okay. Ash would go back to Syracuse and Dan would stay here and they'd do the long-distance thing until . . . until whenever they didn't have to and *then* they'd build a home together. In the meantime, they'd see each other every weekend they could and every holiday. Syracuse wasn't *that* far from New York City.

God. Thank God he hadn't told her about Ash. If she was willing to use his own brother against him—her own son—she wouldn't hesitate to use a complete stranger.

The thought froze him near the ground floor and he sucked in a breath, hand braced on the wall. Shit, what if she did find out about Ash? She would at some point, right? Dan couldn't keep him hidden forever. Then what? Would she threaten Ash's career if Dan fell out of line?

Yes. Unequivocally yes.

Did she have the power to carry out a threat against Ash?

Uncertain, but probable.

He couldn't let that happen. Ash was just starting out in his professional hockey career and Dan couldn't jeopardize that. Wouldn't.

The walls were inches away on all sides. It was like being stuck in that playground tube again when he was a kid, shaking and crying and struggling to draw breath, desperate for help. For someone to save him.

But no one could save him from this.

He was trembling when he exited the stairwell, vision hazy. Crossing the lobby, he went out the front doors and gulped down a breath that stung the back of his throat. It was muggy, and the rain wet his shoulders, his hair, as he picked a direction and started walking, unseeing. The only thing he saw was Ash's wink and grin before he'd gotten into his taxi less than an hour ago.

Dan took his phone out of his pocket and did the only thing he could to protect Ash.

I'm sorry, I can't.

Can't come with you.

Can't put your career on the line.

Can't be with you.

At the airport, Ash was in line at a Starbucks on the other side of security when his phone vibrated in his pocket.

Dude, what time do you and your friend need a pick up from the airport?

He sent a reply back to his teammate and glanced up

to find himself next in line. Tucking his phone away, he ordered, then moved aside to wait for his coffee. His phone buzzed again, but he let it go. Probably his teammate with an *okay, see you soon* reply. Ash was tempted to get a coffee for Dan too, but Dan was probably only now leaving Westlake's offices.

Taking his coffee to his gate, he found an empty row of chairs against the window overlooking the runways and settled in to wait the—he checked the departure board— hour and four minutes until boarding.

Ugh. He was going to go out of his skull with boredom. Flying was the worst, for exactly this reason. All the *waiting.*

He people-watched for a bit. A few people clad in business suits spoke into cell phones. Parents attempted to corral wayward children. A mom tried to sooth a fussy baby. A man about Ash's age juggled a carry-on, a coffee, a paper bag likely holding some kind of pastry, a magazine, and his boarding pass.

Boring. He removed a magazine from his messenger bag and started to read.

Forget it. He couldn't concentrate anyway.

His summer had been a hundred times better than expected. A thousand times. No, a million times.

First, there was the job at Goal. When he wasn't at their facility coaching kids in everything from hockey to soccer to bowling, he was in the head office helping stuff envelopes for fundraising letters or brainstorming ways to raise donations for new sports equipment.

Second, there was his dad. Ash hadn't spent so much time with him in one go since his parents divorced. It had been an adjustment at first, getting used to telling someone where he was going and with who and when he'd be back. But once they'd settled into a routine and things had smoothed out, it had occurred to Ash that his dad was pretty cool. Possibly he worked too much, though, which just meant that Ash would have to visit more often to get him to take some time off.

Finally, there was Dan, who'd burrowed under Ash's skin, dug his fingers in, and cemented himself as part of Ash's life forever. It had been fast too, impossibly fast. But they'd just . . . clicked. They fit, like a perfectly broken-in pair of ice skates. Dan made him stop and think before powering through. Made him consider all of the angles. It was why Ash felt like a tool asking Dan if he was sure about this move, as if Dan hadn't considered it from every angle, weighed the pros and cons, and made the best decision for himself. But Ash had to be sure that Dan was sure. Because, frankly, hiding their relationship was going to suck big time.

Could he come out? Of course he could. Could he come out without it impacting his career?

Not a chance.

Maybe a few years from now, being gay—or bisexual in his case—wouldn't be such a huge deal in professional sports. But a few years was a lot to ask of a guy.

God, he hoped he didn't fuck this up.

Although it was hard to think of fucking up when he was just so stinking happy. He'd do a little victory dance if he had any rhythm. He moved his feet to an unheard beat instead, and smiled at nothing.

He started to worry when Dan still hadn't shown up thirty minutes before boarding. Possibly he was stuck in traffic. If there was anything Ash had learned in the past three and a half months, it was that traffic in New York City was the worst and drivers honked at everyone. *Everyone.*

Twenty minutes and still no Dan.

Ten minutes and still no Dan.

It wasn't until boarding started that Ash thought to check his phone.

Fuck, he had a text from Dan from over an hour ago.

I'm sorry, I can't.

The hell did that mean? Worried that Dan would miss the flight, Ash tried calling him.

Straight to voicemail.

Okay, don't panic. He sent a text: *What does that mean? Are you going to miss the flight? Just let me know when you rebook it for and I'll come get you at the airport. Unless you want me to wait and come with you? I can do that. I don't actually have to be back until Saturday for a team meeting.*

No response.

He was pacing now. Half the travelers had boarded.

Dan? Is everything okay?

What couldn't Dan do? What was he sorry about? Ash sent a flurry of texts.

Dan? What's going on?

What happened?

Please talk to me!!

Are you hurt?

By the time everyone had boarded and Ash was the only one left, boarding pass in one hand, phone in the other, he admitted to himself the thing he hadn't wanted to acknowledge since *I'm sorry, I can't.*

Dan wasn't coming.

But . . . It didn't make sense. Dan wanted to do this.

Didn't he?

Yes! He'd even shipped the bulk of his stuff to Ash's tiny apartment in Syracuse. He'd written a two weeks' notice and was planning on working remotely to finish out his last two weeks. He'd co-signed the lease on their new place. He'd found himself an apprenticeship with a woodworker he was looking forward to studying with.

What had happened after he'd gotten into his taxi? Had he . . . Had he changed his mind?

Sick to his stomach, Ash fell into a chair. The airport hustle and bustle continued around him; for Ash, his world had stopped. His heart sank. His skin felt stretched too tight, ill-fitting. Stomach aching as if someone had whacked him with a hockey stick, he hung his head and tried to think.

All he could see was Dan's smile, wide and white and happy. All he could feel was the last kiss Dan had given him, a tiny thing on his jaw. All he could hear was Dan telling him that no one else could get his hugs, that they were for him alone.

He wanted to turn back time to this morning, when they'd woken in each other's arms in Dan's bed. Ash loved Dan's apartment. It was the size of a shoebox, but in it, they could relax, and make dinner, and be themselves.

"Attention passengers, this is the last call for flight number 2021 to Syracuse at gate forty-seven. If there are any passengers still needing to board, please make your way to gate forty-seven immediately."

That was him. The boarding pass shook in one hand, his still-silent phone in the other. He was already at the gate, but he couldn't make himself move. He didn't want to go back to Syracuse without Dan, without the future they'd planned together for themselves.

Why wouldn't Dan just tell him what was going on?

If he didn't want to move, why didn't he just say so?

If he was breaking up with Ash . . .

Ash pressed his lips together to keep the pained sound at the back of his throat at bay.

"Attention passengers, paging traveler Ashton Yager. If there's an Ashton Yager in the airport, please head to the nearest gate and announce yourself to a flight attendant."

He stood. The flight attendant behind the podium at his gate caught his eye as she hung up. "Sir? Are you Ashton Yager?"

He checked his boarding pass for a name. He couldn't remember anything. Everything was unraveling around him. "Yes."

"Great." Her smile was too big for his soul. "Let's get you boarded."

"I . . ."

"Sir? Mr. Yager? Can I see your boarding pass and ID?"

Leaving his heart behind, he handed them over.

NINETEEN

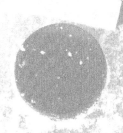

IT WAS FREEZING IN HIS HOTEL ROOM. DAN COULDN'T be bothered to get up from his curled position on the bed to turn off the air conditioning. He was cozy in his onesie anyway, and he'd pulled the sleeves down to cover his hands. The only part of him that was hot was his face, where he'd scrubbed the tears away.

He stared at the wall and tried to keep his mind blank; it proved impossible, especially with nothing to distract him.

He'd done everything right, hadn't he? Ash was simply too smart to allow himself to be hurt again.

And that was fine. That was ... well, smart. Except that it left Dan in a shitty position.

Tucking his nose into the pillow, he contemplated what to do now. Head back to New York? There wasn't anything there for him, but he did miss his apartment, particularly now when he felt the need to comfort himself with the familiar. Back to Vermont? He'd enjoy a visit with Mitch, and Mitch's brattiness was a surefire way to keep him distracted.

There was nothing for him in Tampa either, although he did like the city. No doubt he'd like it even more once the storm damage was cleaned up. The humidity made his hair frizzy but he could live with that. He was tempted to get on the computer and run a search for woodworkers in the area, but he was pretty sure that asking for an apprenticeship while the city was still in shambles was an asshole move. Not that any of them would want him anyway, not after a six-year hiatus.

He lay on the bed, staring at the wall. His little balcony overlooked a cute indoor village with a village square complete with a water fountain, shops, restaurants, and cafés, and he'd left his balcony doors open a crack. The muted sounds of conversation six floors below him made him feel less alone.

Sighing, he rubbed his chest. Fuck, he was wiped. Just done. Crying took a lot out of a person.

The last time he'd cried was a few months ago when he'd learned that Mitch had fainted and why. Before that? Not since the day everything had gone to shit.

His phone rang. He rolled over to reach for it on the nightstand, hope blooming despite everything, like a phoenix coming back to life.

Mitch was displayed on the screen along with a picture of the two of them from Alex's book launch last month.

Dan swallowed hard and answered with a hoarse, "Hey."

A pause, then, "Are you okay? You don't sound okay. Are you sick? Alex said I should call you 'cause something was wrong, but he didn't say you were sick."

That was actually really nice of Alex, but then Alex had never been angry with Dan. Alex seemed to understand better than anyone the crappy position Dan had been forced into.

"I'm not sick. Unless heartsick counts."

"Heartsick? Wait, were you seeing someone? Did she dump you? Who was she?" Mitch sounded so upset on Dan's behalf that Dan couldn't help but smile.

"Not a she."

"But you just said—"

"It's a he."

Silence reigned again for a moment. Dan actually pulled the phone away from his ear to make sure they were still connected.

"I did not see that coming," Mitch finally said. "So you're . . ."

"Bisexual."

"Okay. There was a guy, then. And he dumped you? What the hell? Who is he?"

"It's a little more complicated than that."

"Explain."

Mitch must've had him on speaker because a voice in the background—Cody—clearly said, "Dude, Alex told you not to push."

"I'm not *pushing*," Mitch grumbled. "I'm encouraging."

Despite himself, Dan laughed softly, but he sobered fast. "You remember when I came to see you in March?" he said. "After you fainted? And I told you what went down between me and Mom six years ago? I may have left some details out."

"You said Mom blackmailed you into staying in college by threatening to take my tuition away."

"Yeah."

"Okay." Mitch's tone was wary now, as if he was expecting a blow. "What'd you leave out?"

"Nothing that pertained to you and me. But . . . there was someone else. I was seeing someone that summer."

"You were? So what happened?"

Mitch listened attentively, occasionally muttering under his breath as Dan explained everything, leaving out Ash's name. There was no reason for Mitch to know, not when Alex and Ash were teammates and friends. It'd just complicate things.

"Man, I'm sorry." The sound of couch springs reached Dan's ears. "I had no idea. But why did you break up with him?"

Dan scrubbed his face. "I didn't want Mom to use him against me too."

"And this is the guy that dumped you today?"

"No. He didn't—I mean, we weren't—It's complicated. Ash didn't—" Whoops. Shit, fuck, damn!

"Ash? Is that your guy?" Mitch paused for a second, and Dan winced, knowing Mitch was too smart not to put it together. "Wait, *Ash*? As in *Ashton Yager*?"

"Um . . ."

"Holy shit! You were the guy in New York?"

Dan stilled. "He told you about me?"

"No, but he told Alex and me once that he had a guy in New York years ago when he was working there, and that it could've been something but that it didn't work out. Holy, *holy* shit. No wonder he was looking at you like he wanted to eat you up then spit you back out."

"That's disgusting. And slightly disheartening."

"I meant that in a good way."

"Uh-huh."

Mitch went quiet again and then, with vehemence, "I am going to kick his fucking ass."

"Mitch—"

"He doesn't get to hurt you like this and get away—"

"I hurt him first," Dan interrupted, blinking up at the ceiling. "And much worse. And . . . And it was my choice. At the end of the day, I chose to hurt him." A realization he'd come to while lying in a cold hotel room indulging in grief and rejection and self-pity. His mother had issued the ultimatum, sure, but everything that had come after was a result of his decisions, his choices. Maybe they'd been wrong—

No. In hindsight, there were other options he could've chosen, other decisions he could've made. But what good was hindsight unless you had a time machine? He'd made the best possible choice he could at the time, which, in the end, made it the right one.

If he could convince himself of that, he might be able to move on.

"I hurt him badly," he told Mitch passed the lump in his throat that refused to go away. "It's not really a surprise that he doesn't want to try again, even though I hoped for something different."

"Dan . . ."

Thickly, he said, "I'm fine," and wiped his face with his sleeve. "Or I will be, I guess. Eventually."

"You still love him."

"Yeah." His jaw hurt from holding back tears. "He always saw me, you know? Not the sophisticate who grew up in Mom's world, but the guy underneath who just wanted to get his hands dirty. He made me not take myself so seriously. Made me want to try new things and make mistakes."

"I'm sorry, Dan."

"Yeah, me too."

"I want to help."

Dan mustered a smile. "Thanks, but there isn't anything for you to do. Talking helped, though. Thanks."

Mitch huffed, displeased with that answer. "So . . . On a different yet somewhat related topic . . . How come you never told me you're bi?"

"Didn't realize it until I met Ash," Dan said, rolling onto his side, facing the balcony.

"Huh. Okay. But what about recently?"

"I don't know. I guess there was never a right time for me to bring it up. And since there's never been a guy except Ash, I never really saw the point. Besides . . . I liked having Ash to myself."

"I really am gonna kick his ass," Mitch growled.

Dan snorted.

"Why is that funny?"

"He's, like, four times your size."

"He does have biceps that go on forever, doesn't he?"

Dan sighed. "Yeah."

"Ew. I don't wanna hear my brother make lovesick sighs, gross. I'm hanging up now."

"Okay," Dan said with a laugh. "Hey, thanks for calling. It helped a lot."

"Call me if you want to talk more, okay?"

"I will. Bye, Mitch."

They hung up and Dan sat up. Mitch's honesty and uncensored reactions had made him feel a bit better, although there was a headache pulsing at his temples. Had he eaten today? Little bites of fruit this morning when he'd made Ash and the guys breakfast, but nothing since then.

He got up to fetch the room service menu off the desk and was debating between a burger and fries and something a little healthier, like a chicken salad wrap, when someone knocked on his door. It was probably one of the hotel staff coming by again to give him a heads up about some noise as they did repairs a couple floors up. He opened the door without checking the peephole—

And found Ash on the other side.

Dan's breath left him in a whoosh, leaving him concave and frail as surprise and hope made him light-headed. White knuckling the doorknob, he managed a breathless "Hi."

"Hi," Ash replied, equally as breathless it seemed. Dirt crusted his shorts and T-shirt, his hair was a tousled mess, and he was wearing two different flip-flops—one gray and blue, one black.

Dan had been at the hotel for less than an hour and it was a fifteen-minute drive from Ash's . . . which meant Ash hadn't waited very long before coming to find him.

God, that stupid, *foolish* hope. It made his pulse race and his hands tremble.

Ash squared his shoulders, and said, "Okay. Tell me."

Ash stepped into Dan's hotel room and surveyed his surroundings. It was a clean but generic little room: two double beds with a nightstand between them, a dresser with a TV atop it, a desk with a hotel-branded notepad and pen, a bathroom with a tub, and a small balcony. Abstract art hung on the walls, two of the lamps were lit, and Dan's suitcase was tucked against the wall next to the unused bed, no doubt empty with his clothes sorted in the dresser drawers.

Dan was fairly vibrating. He clutched a laminated menu to his chest; the other hand convulsively clenched and unclenched at his side. The reappearance of the onesie made Ash soften toward him—as if he needed a reason to soften toward Dan.

He'd spent the drive here preparing a speech; truth was that there was nothing else for them to say to each other until Ash learned a truth he was finally ready to hear.

"Why now?" Dan asked. He sat on the edge of the furthermost bed.

Ash sat on the edge of the other bed, facing him. "Because I realized that if we're going to move forward together, I need to know the truth."

Dan nodded. "That's fair."

Ash braced himself.

Dan picked at a thread in the bedcover.

Ash waited.

Dan scratched his knee.

Ash waited some more.

Dan placed the menu on the nightstand.

"Why do I get the feeling that you don't want to talk about it?" Ash asked.

"It's not that I don't." Dan lifted tired eyes to Ash. "It's just that I don't think it'll change anything at this point."

Well, that was dire.

"And I'm tired, Ash. I just got off the phone with Mitch and I told him everything, and . . . I'm drained."

He did look exhausted. Purple bags under his eyes, lines bracketing his mouth, a downward curve to his lips. He looked like he'd fought with life and lost.

"You talked to Mitch about us?"

Dan shifted. "I had to talk to someone, and you weren't listening."

Fair enough. Not that Ash would've had a leg to stand on anyway—he'd told Alex and Carlie everything. "I'm listening now."

Closing his eyes, Dan blew out a breath. "Okay. Here goes."

The story he told was ridiculous, something Ash would expect to see on one of his mom's soap operas, not in real life. Blackmail and threats and manipulation. Ash got up to pace as Dan talked, useless anger burning a red path to his sternum.

From the little Dan had said about it over the past few weeks, Ash had suspected some kind of coercion, but this

. . . This was heartless. No wonder Dan hadn't wanted to introduce Ash to his mother back then.

Ash paced between the beds, from the nightstand to the dresser and back, like a goldfish in a tiny aquarium, until Dan got to the part where Mitch fainted. Ash remembered that. He'd been with Alex when Alex had gotten the call from Cody. Mitch had passed out from exhaustion after a game, ending up in the hospital. Ash had watched Alex quietly panic—quietly, because for a large guy, Alex didn't do anything loud—until he'd pulled himself together, booked a seat on the next flight out, and fled to the airport.

"What does Mitch's passing out have to do with what your mom did?"

"She went back on our deal." Dan's palms were flat on the bed next to his thighs, bringing his shoulders up to his ears. "Turns out she did deny Mitch his college tuition when Mitch told her he wanted to play hockey and study kinesiology instead of something that would benefit the business. He has a partial hockey scholarship, but he passed out because on top of classes and labs and homework and practice and games, he was working two jobs to make ends meet. He could barely afford food some weeks, and . . . I didn't know about any of this until last March."

"Jesus." Falling onto the bed, Ash stared at Dan. He'd known Mitch had passed out from exhaustion, but not *why*. Alex had never shared the details. "That's . . . Are you . . .? Why aren't you angry?"

"I've been angry for six years, Ash. Now I'm just tired."

Ash took a breath and forced his muscles to loosen. He was so angry on Dan's behalf, and he itched to get onto the ice and take his anger out with a puck and a net. "Not to be insensitive, but what does all of this have to do with you and me?"

Dan gave him a sad smile. "I was trying to protect you."

"From what?"

"If she was willing to use her own son against me, I have no doubt she would've used you too when she found out about us. There's no way I could've kept you a secret from my family forever. She would've hurt your career, threatened to out you before you were ready. I wasn't about to let that happen."

Ash's entire body went cold at the thought of what coming out six years ago would've done to his career. Would he be where he was today?

And then a rush of heat swept through him as he processed Dan's words, and he stood to pace again. He couldn't sit still; there was too much energy thrumming under his skin. "You didn't think that you should talk to me about this before making a decision for the both of us?"

"No."

Shock froze him and he gaped. "No? Dan, I could've helped. Hell, *I* could've paid Mitch's tuition!"

"You think I don't know that?" Dan stood too, face flushed, angry lines marring his forehead. "You think other options haven't occurred to me in the past six years? Options that would've saved us both a lot of heartache? I made the best decision that I could at the time, and as much as I wish I could change things, I can't. All I can do is ask you to understand why I made the choice that I did and ask you to forgive me. Beyond that, there is nothing else I can do except admit that I made a mistake. I really was just . . . I was . . ." Eyes wide, he sat heavily. "I was doing what I thought was best," he said on a whisper. He'd gone unhealthily pale.

"Hey." Ash nudged his foot. "What's wrong?"

Dan laughed without humor, a harsh sound that grated

Ash's ears. "Do you know how often my mom's said that? 'I did what I thought was best for you and your brother.' Without asking, without considering our feelings or opinions. And I . . . I did the same thing."

"Dan." Ash squatted in front of him. "You are not your mother."

"But I am, don't you see? We both charge ahead without consulting other people, so sure that we know what's best for everyone."

"Hey." Taking Dan by the shoulders, Ash shook him. "The difference is that you can admit that you were wrong. Your heart was in the right place."

Dan touched Ash's face. "All I wanted was for you to be safe."

"And all I ever wanted was you."

Dan's face collapsed.

"It's always been you, Dan," Ash said, choking up as Dan's tears absolutely gutted him. "My career was never as important as you and me."

"I'm sorry." Dan leaned forward, cupped Ash's face, and pressed their foreheads together. "I'm sorry."

Ash squeezed his wrists. "I know. I know." Dan smelled like generic hotel soap, and his breath was slightly stale, and his hair tickled Ash's forehead. He was warm and he was here and—

You made me feel like I could fly.

Dan's words from their stay at the B&B hit him like a boulder, nearly knocking him senseless. The choice Dan had made six years ago wasn't one he'd made lightly. And it wasn't only Ash's heart that he'd broken.

He'd broken his own too.

Desperate for room to think, Ash jerked away and started pacing again, this time up to the door to give himself more space. When he turned back, Dan was standing next to the bed, hands outstretched toward Ash, stricken eyes practically taking up his whole face.

"I'm not . . ." Ash glanced at the door behind him. "I'm not leaving. Needed to think is all."

Dan gulped. "Okay."

To give him some peace of mind, Ash returned to the bedroom proper and leaned back against the desk. "So I figure it's all about choices."

"I . . . Yes, that's true."

"Six years ago, you made a choice that broke my heart. Broke yours too."

Dan glanced away.

"And now we have another choice—a choice on how to move forward."

"You know what I want, Ash. You know how I feel." Dan's arms flapped like he didn't know what to do with them. "Ball's in your court."

Meaning it was all on Ash. The choice, it seemed, was his.

He could choose to thank Dan for explaining, thank him for his willingness to help get his home back in shape, and then go his separate way. Dan was half right—knowing the truth didn't really change anything.

Except it made Ash see Dan more clearly. Ash wasn't the only one who'd suffered. To be placed in such a tight spot that the only choice among bad choices was to break both their hearts couldn't have been easy. It was a lot of guilt and regret to carry around for six years. Dan had asked him to understand, and Ash did—to a point. He understood that Dan had felt the need to protect. He understood that Dan had thought the worst of his mother—probably for good reason. He understood that Dan had taken the only course of action he could see.

He didn't understand why Dan hadn't talked to him when it had happened. They'd been stronger than that, hadn't they?

Was Dan's fear of his mother's possible actions stronger than his faith in their relationship?

No. That wasn't right. Ash reordered things in his mind and came to a different conclusion. Inasmuch as he could tell, Dan's fear of his mother's possible actions was stronger than Dan's belief in himself, in his ability to keep the people he loved safe.

By that token, Dan's choice had nothing to do with their relationship and everything to do with his faith in *himself*.

Ash could walk away. Wipe his hands clean of Dan and move on with his life.

Ball's in your court, Dan had said.

It was all about choices.

And Ash chose Dan.

"I want to trust you again," Ash said. "I really do."

Dan's sigh was so miserable Ash could taste it. "Okay." He took a step back, clearly expecting the worst.

"If we do this," Ash continued, and Dan's head snapped up, "I need to trust that you'll talk to me when things get tough. I want to help you, but I can't do that if I don't know what's going on."

"I will, I promise."

"Don't just say that because I'm saying what you want to hear."

"I'm not, I . . . Do you know that I've spent the past six years pretending I was fine? I couldn't tell Mitch what was going on, I barely spoke to my mother, I put on a brave face for my colleagues at work and at school before that. I promised myself that I wouldn't bottle everything up anymore, but . . ." He shrugged. "You should know that it's a work in progress. It's not easy for me to open up sometimes."

"Okay." Ash could accept *work in progress*. He smiled at Dan, butterflies tickling his ribs. "So . . . Want to be my boyfriend?"

"I . . ." Dan's eyes searched his, looking for sincerity. "It's been a long time since I've been someone's boyfriend."

Ash cocked his head with a playful smile. "Is that a no?"

"Of course it's not a no. Asshole."

Amused by him, Ash chuckled.

"But I don't . . . I don't know how to do this." Dan sounded lost, his tone a blend of wonder and fear.

"I don't either." It had been a long time since Ash had been someone's boyfriend too. "Let's take it one day at a time. See where it takes us." He held out a hand. "What do you say?"

The way Dan took his hand, so tentatively . . . It was as though he expected Ash to take the words back. But once their hands were clasped, Dan hung on tightly, not letting go, even when Ash pulled him in flush against his body. His slouch against the desk put them at the same height, and up close like this, Ash could see the tears swimming in Dan's eyes. So afraid and so nervous, more so than Ash even, which was sad and amazing at the same time.

Ash leaned forward, tucking one arm around Dan's waist as Dan sucked in a shaky breath. The sound shredded Ash, made him want to keep Dan safe.

Their lips met so hesitantly one would think they hadn't had sex three times last night. That they hadn't had their first kiss six years ago after Dan's Thai chicken curry.

It was entirely possible to have two first kisses with the same person.

This kiss was soft and gentle and sweet, everything

last night's angry mash of mouths should've been. Dan moaned, and the hand not holding Ash's went to the back of Ash's neck. His body was hard underneath Ash's hands. Ash's dick twitched, but it was more of an oh-hey-nice-to-see-you-again rather than a lusty let's-do-it-baby. It was a reawakening, a relearning, a desire for touch and intimacy rather than a need for orgasm.

Their kisses grew more heated and wet, but still languid. Ash's breathing sped up, and he fit Dan more firmly against him, his hand trailing down to cup Dan's—

The loud thump of music had him jerking back. "What the—" He looked toward the balcony.

"There's a, uh, nightly light show, at eight," Dan said, breathing just as hard as Ash. "Want to watch?"

They watched.

They sat on the little balcony, arms crossed on the railing, chins propped on their arms. Down below, the fountain, spotlighted in blue and green and red, stopped and sputtered, rose and shrunk in tune to the music that changed from pop to hip hop to country to an oldies song. A verse from Lady Gaga's "Just Dance" transitioned to the chorus from "See You Later, Alligator" to a snippet from a Blake Shelton song.

This travesty went on for fifteen minutes.

Ash scooted his chair closer to Dan's and bumped their elbows. "Ever been to Disney World?"

"No. Key West once when we were kids."

"I'll take you sometime. Those guys know how to do a light show. This?" He waved at the fountain. "This is your grouchy Uncle Frank at Christmas, smoking a pipe and complaining about the dry turkey—all bark and no bite."

Dan's laughter lit him up from the inside. Ash smiled back, helpless to do anything else.

They might crash and burn again, but Ash would never forgive himself if he didn't try. He owed it to himself, and to Dan, to give them a second chance.

He ran his fingers along Dan's elbow discreetly, conscious of other balcony spectators, and stifled a grin when Dan shivered. "Did you eat today?"

Dan shook his head.

"Come on."

Inside, Dan left the doors open but closed the curtains. Ash picked up the menu off the nightstand. "What do you feel like?"

Dan walked into his arms and nosed his collarbone. "A chicken salad wrap."

Ash snorted. "Nobody ever feels like a chicken salad wrap." He kissed Dan's temple. "What do you actually want?" He could feel Dan's smile against his skin.

"A burger and fries."

"Now we're talking."

The clock on the nightstand ticked over to 5:00 a.m. Ash sat with his back against the headboard, Dan resting against his chest. "Will you tell me the real reason you quit woodworking?"

Dan tilted his head back against Ash's shoulder to look at him upside down. "I didn't have anyone to share it with anymore."

Ash touched their foreheads, wishing he could make all the promises, knowing they weren't there yet. "I looked for you."

"When?"

"After you sent me that text. I almost got on the plane,

but . . ." Ash swallowed hard against the memories. "I didn't want to go without you. So I rented a car and I went to your apartment and your office building and every grocery store we'd ever shopped at together. Even drove into the Hamptons looking for a gothic monstrosity. But I couldn't find you."

It made Dan cry, but Ash didn't take the words back. Dan needed to know.

"And when I finally arrived in Syracuse and I went to my apartment . . . all your stuff was there, the stuff that you'd shipped ahead of time. Seeing it there and knowing . . . knowing that . . ." His arms tightened around Dan's chest.

Dan turned and burrowed into Ash, his tears wetting Ash's throat. "I'm sorry. I'm so sorry."

"No." Ash pushed him away by the shoulders so he could see his face. "You don't need to keep apologizing. That's not why I'm telling you. I just need you to know how it felt, living in a place surrounded by your things but without you there. Having to get out of the lease we signed. I was in a fog for a long time after that. Couldn't figure out what I'd done to make you go."

"Ash . . ." Dan cupped his face.

"It didn't make sense. After the summer we had, for you to just disappear? I couldn't make sense of it. For a long time I thought I did something to drive you away, but then I remembered you were going to talk to your mom that day and I figured she managed to change your mind somehow. Turns out she did, just not how I ever would've expected."

Dan sat up and leaned against the headboard facing Ash, their legs tangled.

"I need you to know all this," Ash said, "because your leaving gutted me." He soothed Dan's forehead when he winced. "And it might take some time for me to open up to you again."

Face tense, Dan nodded. "Okay. I'm so—" He cut himself off.

"I know." Ash nuzzled his face. "I know you are. And I forgive you, I do. I'm not so blind that I can't see why you made the choices you did." He squeezed Dan's thigh. "I'm sorry too, you know."

"What do you have to be sorry for?"

"For not listening when you first wanted to talk."

"It's okay."

"No. It's not. I should've listened. And I'm sorry for yesterday morning too. I was a jackass."

Dan played with Ash's collar. "Why?"

"Because things happened so fast. We hadn't talked—my fault, I know—and all I could see was us repeating past mistakes. I needed to wrap my mind around the fact that we're different people now. I just needed space to think, and I went about it the wrong way."

"I don't think I'm that different than I was," Dan said.

"You're . . ." Ash searched for the right word. "You're more melancholy than you used to be. It's almost as if you expect things to turn out badly, so you prepare yourself for the worst. You smile less." So much less that it was sunshine when Dan did smile. Ash had a feeling that Dan had had a very lonely six years.

"There hasn't been much to smile about," Dan said, confirming Ash's thoughts.

"You have a nurturing instinct as long as my arm, though." Ash ran a hand through Dan's curls. "I don't know how I didn't see that back then."

Dan pouted. "No, I don't."

"Are you kidding? You came all the way out here to help me even though you weren't sure of your welcome. You keep cooking me food you haven't even eaten. You broke your heart to protect me, to protect Mitch. And even though it's been months since you found out the truth, you still, for some inexplicable reason, haven't told your mother to fuck out of your life."

Dan smiled weakly and wiped his nose on his sleeve.

"Why is that?" Ash asked.

Blowing out a breath that puffed his cheeks, Dan's mouth opened and closed a couple of times. "I guess because she was the only one who knew the truth, which made it feel like she was the only person who knew me. I had to hide from everybody else and . . ." He played with the pocket of Ash's shorts. "That's probably what made me start bottling everything up inside."

"That's not healthy."

Dan just shrugged. "And you."

"What about me?"

"You're not the same as you were six years ago, either." He placed a palm on Ash's chest, over his heart. "You're so much more protective of yourself now."

"Yeah. That's what happens when my boyfriend breaks up with me via text and my wife cheats on me."

"She—" Dan jerked back, eyes shooting sparks, fingers digging into Ash's biceps. He was so pissed that had Ash been a lesser being he would've been burned. As it was, he grinned like a lunatic. Dan was fucking *hot* with his face all flushed and his lips pulled tight.

"*That's* why you divorced?" Dan said. "I couldn't find anything online."

Ash smirked at him. "Did you follow my career?"

A pause, then, "No?"

Ash cracked up, and fuck, it felt good to laugh with Dan again. They really weren't the same people, and maybe they'd changed so much that this would never work between them . . . Or maybe this was exactly the second chance they needed. What kind of miracle was it that had made Alex and Mitch meet, thus forcing Dan and Ash back into each other's lives?

"Stop laughing." Dan punched his arm. "Jerk."

Tickled pink, Ash rolled them until he was on his back with Dan tucked into his side. "I love that you followed me. It's—Oh, shit." He winced as a thought occurred to him. "Oh fuck, Dan, you must've been so sad when you found out I was getting married."

Dan remained silent, one finger scratching at Ash's T-shirt.

"I'm sorry. I shouldn't've teased you."

Very softly, Dan asked, "Did you love her?"

Ash sighed. "I loved the idea of her. When I got sent to the NHL, and it turned out I'd be staying there, she came with me. And at the time, it meant everything. But the truth is we were horrible for each other. Fought *all* the time. Not, like, cute married couple bickering. We were like those two dirtbags from the Muppets. Just . . . mean."

Propping himself up on his elbows, hair tumbling into his eyes, Dan kissed Ash's shoulder and said, "Is it bad that I'm not sorry you broke up? I'm sorry it happened the way it did. I can't believe she cheated on you." That last was mumbled to himself, and he shook his head as though he couldn't believe it. "But I'm not sorry you're single now."

Something was very wrong with Ash for him to feel so desperately pleased by that statement. "Come up here and kiss me."

Dan did.

The next time Dan awoke the clock read six thirty and Ash was slipping into his flip-flops. They were accurately named, because at the sight of Ash getting ready to go, Dan's belly flip-flopped. He sat up with a gasp.

"Hey." Ash's smile was lazy and warm, no hint of exhaustion after being up talking most of the night. Hopefully exhaustion didn't catch up with him during tonight's game against Carolina. "I was just about to wake you. I've gotta go home and get my gear and then head to practice. Wanna check out of here and come stay with me?"

Dan blinked at him.

"Hello." Ash waved a hand in front of his face. "Anybody in there?"

Slapping Ash's hand away, Dan rose and pressed a fast kiss to his lips. "Give me two minutes to pack."

"'Kay. You might want to change too. I mean, the onesie's adorable, but you look ridiculous."

Dan flipped him off over his shoulder as he withdrew clothes from the dresser and threw them into his suitcase.

"Why would you bring a onesie to Florida, anyway?"

"Because Floridians have an incessant need to keep indoor temperatures at minus a zillion."

Ash squinted at the thermostat. "This says sixty-seven."

"Sixty-seven!" Dan's arms flailed. "That is not an appropriate room temperature." He changed quickly, conscious of Ash's eyes on him. His chest puffed out. It made him feel like a million bucks that Ash still found him attractive, but it really was freezing, so it wasn't long before he was dressed again in jeans and a T-shirt. Making a noise of disappointment, Ash headed into the bathroom and came out less than a minute later with Dan's toiletries. Dan threw everything into his suitcase and made one last pass to ensure he didn't forget anything. "Okay," he said. "I'm ready."

Ash's amused gaze settled on Dan, then on the suitcase, Dan again, back to the suitcase.

"Okay," Dan said, holding up a finger. "One sec." Re-opening his suitcase, he organized his toiletries in his toiletry bag, tucked his dirty clothes into the suitcase's inside pouch, and roughly folded his clothes so they wouldn't wrinkle too much. "Now I'm ready."

"Uh-huh. Come on." Ash took Dan's suitcase in one hand and Dan's hand in the other. "Let's go home."

TWENTY

ASH STOOD IN THE LOCKER ROOM WITH THE REST of his team, suited up in full uniform, helmet and gloves on, skates tied, and tapped his hockey stick against the floor.

"I'm gonna beat you with my pads if you don't stop that," Carlie snapped.

"Sorry, sorry." They were due on the ice any minute for the pre-game warm up, and Ash's nerves were frayed. He was about to face the fans for the first time since coming out. It was cool in the locker room, yet he was sweating through his jersey.

Typically, the arena was only about one-third full when they stepped onto the ice for the pre-game warm up; according to Coach Ness, today it was already packed to capacity, recent hurricane be damned.

Their preseason games *never* sold out.

Everyone was here.

There was nothing left to do but face the music.

"Dude." Taylor punched him lightly in the arm. "We got your back."

"Yeah, man," Greer piped in. "Nobody messes with this team."

"That should be our new motto," someone else said.

Alex winked at him. "You got this."

He had this. Totally.

"Hey, guys!" Masterson ripped into a clear plastic bag of rainbow-colored somethings. "They arrived right on time."

Whoops and hollers followed, and Masterson handed out what turned out to be rainbow armbands. Dumbfounded and just in complete awe of his friends, Ash stood stupid, face uncomfortably warm, chest full of gratitude, while his buddies tied the armbands around their upper arms. Even Kinsey put one on, and Kinsey was an asshole.

Masterson thrust one at Ash, but he could only stand there astounded, staring at it. "You guys, I . . . I don't . . . This is . . ."

"Aw, we made him cry."

True, his eyes were prickling, but Greer didn't have to so gleefully point it out, the asshole.

"Here." Alex came to his rescue, removing the armband from where it rested on Ash's glove, and tied it around Ash's upper arm, ensuring the Velcro was securely fastened. "Now you're ready for your big game."

Ash let out a wet sigh. "I hate you guys so much right now."

The guys cackled madly and hugged him from all sides.

One over-emotional Ashton Yager, coming right up.

"This is really cool, guys, but we're not allowed to wear them." League rules prohibited any kind of adornments or changes to the uniform unless previously approved.

"We're good," Masterson said, pulling on his gloves. "We got league approval."

Releasing a helpless laugh, Ash shook his head and grinned all the way out to the ice.

Stepping onto the ice in front of a sold-out crowd was cathartic. The smell of the ice, the chill in the air, the fit of his skates on his feet, his teammates at his back. Playing hockey in front of so many people always felt like he was giving away a piece of his soul to every person here.

Tonight that was magnified times a thousand.

Coach's advice had been to ignore the fans. Rachel's too. Alex's. Basically everyone. But he wouldn't do that on any other day. The fans were the heart of them. Cheering, bringing signs, donning jerseys. Ash had thrown more than one puck over the glass for a fan, stopped to sign autographs countless times after a game, and he wasn't about to be coached into doing differently. He had to believe the best of the fans, otherwise what was the point?

He wasn't disappointed. The roar of the spectators was louder than he ever remembered hearing it, and from what he could tell, there were a dozen rainbow themed signs across the stadium.

Yager's #1 fan.

Hockey pride.

I love you, Yager!

Marry Me, Ashton Yager.

Yager, can I hold your stick?

That one cracked him up.

"That's mildly inappropriate," Carlie said as Ash came around the net.

"I think it's hilarious."

"You would."

What didn't amuse him was the booing coming from a small section in the three hundreds on the northwest side of the arena. Like hell was Ash going to let that continue. There were kids in attendance.

He couldn't quite tell—the three hundreds were way the fuck up there—but it looked like there were only a handful of booers holding up a *Hockey is a man's sport* sign.

Ash stopped next to the net and stared them down.

One by one, his teammates came and stood behind him, giving him gentle helmet taps and soft raps on his shin guards with their hockey sticks.

And then the opposing team did the same.

Ash's jaw dropped, and for the second time tonight, he stood dazed and overwhelmed, limbs tingling, tension easing out of his neck. Around the upper arms of every white, red, and black Carolina uniform was a rainbow armband.

God, oh man, oh shit. Ash needed to go home so he could have a good cry.

With two teams staring them down, the booers quieted. A hush fell over the rest of the arena, the quietest Ash had ever seen it during a sold out game. Some of the Tampa and Carolina players eyed the rest of the crowd, all *Anyone else want to mess with us?*

It was surreal.

And then a shouted "I love you, Yager!" got the crowd cheering again and everything was, once again, copacetic.

Ash choked on a laugh. Wow. Just . . . wow.

A sign pressed against the other side of the glass near the blue line, held by a teenager who couldn't be more than fourteen, caught his attention. *Ashton, I'm bisexual too! Can I have a date? Or a puck?*

Ash tossed him a puck. Hard no on the date.

Speaking of dates, Dan was in the crowd somewhere, not that Ash would ever be able to spot him. Since Dan had waited until nearly the last minute to purchase a ticket, he'd paid what he'd said was a "stupid" price for it, which Ash took to mean that it'd cost a small fortune. Ash could've given him his comp tickets since his mom was still out of town and wouldn't need them, a fact that Dan hadn't been all that impressed with when Ash told him, seeing as he'd already paid for them.

"Next time," Dan had said. Ash loved that there was going to be a next time.

The game itself passed in a blur of plays, blocked shots,

elbows to the solar plexus, and streaks of white-red-black and blue-white. It moved in slow motion; it went by too fast. He broke up a big play; he let a shot through. Tampa received a penalty; Carolina too. Neither scored on the power play.

Toward the end of the third period on the Carolina side of the ice, Masterson passed him the puck, and he sent it to Alex, who came up behind him, took off toward the net and its single defenseman, did a truly beautiful spin-o-rama around him, and shot the puck into the net on the backhand.

It was only the preseason, but still—the assist felt awesome.

Later, after they'd won 3-2 and Ash had showered and changed into his suit, he announced that he was treating the guys to a late dinner and drinks at The Tavern.

"Someone go tell the Carolina guys that they're coming too," he shouted into the ensuing chaos.

"I'm on it!" Greer disappeared.

Before he could go find Dan, first Ash had to talk to a bunch of reporters who wanted to know what it was like to play his first game as an out gay player.

Bisexual, Ash corrected more than once, like nobody wanted to acknowledge that bisexuality was a real thing, which was annoying and probably something that he'd have to deal with for the rest of his life, which was also annoying.

Oh, and playing his first game as an out player felt like it did every game maximized by a thousand thanks to the amazing support of the fans.

Finally freed of the press's clutches, he headed toward the back exit that led to the secluded employee parking area. A handful of WAGs waited for his teammates by the door; Ash only had eyes for the lone male in the group.

WAGs really needed a new name. SASOs maybe? Spouses and significant others.

HTSTKBTTDAHP? Humans too stupid to know better than to date a hockey player. Professional athletes didn't exactly lead quiet lives.

That last one was maybe too long.

He was chortling to himself when he reached Dan.

Dan's smile grew, creasing his cheeks. "You look happy."

"I am happy." Ash pecked Dan's lips with a chaste kiss, ignoring the dropped jaws of the WAGs. Dan rose onto his toes, twining his arms around Ash's shoulders. Maybe Ash hadn't been able to see him in the crowd tonight, but just knowing he was here had been enough.

Dan nuzzled Ash's cheek. "Hi."

"Hi." Ash smiled stupidly and squeezed his waist. "How was your first NHL game?"

"My first . . ." Dan trailed off, dropping onto his heels. "Um, this wasn't my first game."

"No? I guess I just assumed." Threading their fingers together, Ash led Dan into the parking lot. The night air was hot, and although not overly humid, still too humid for his suit. "What was your first one then?"

Lips pursed, Dan cleared his throat. "Tampa versus New York a few years ago."

"Wait." A few years ago? Ash stopped, right there in the middle of the lot. "You went to one of my games?"

Dan suddenly found a nearby beige sedan very interesting. He swung their arms between them. "Um, all of them?"

"Full stop. You've been to all of my games in New York City?"

Pressing his lips together, Dan shrugged, his eyes lit from within.

They'd been in the same building together? More than once? Instead of dwelling on the past, Ash shook his head and laughed, heading for his car. "I'm treating the teams to dinner and drinks at The Tavern. You in?"

"Teams, plural?" Hopping into the car, Dan slid on his seatbelt and shot Ash the side-eye. "That's going to be quite the hefty bill."

"Worth it."

"Yeah. That was the most . . . interesting game I've ever been to."

Ash started the car, but then sat with his hands loosely resting around the bottom curve of the steering wheel. He blew out a breath. Dan massaged his neck, fingers sinking into his hair. Felt so fucking good, Ash let out a grunt.

"You okay?" Dan asked, his voice quiet in the dim interior.

"I'm . . . kind of confused. I think I expected today to go a lot differently."

"It's nice when people can surprise you for the better."

Ash turned his head on the headrest to look at Dan. "Did I ever tell you why I came out?"

"No." Dan's thumb traced a path behind Ash's ear, making Ash's neck erupt in goosebumps. "But I saw your interview from a couple of days ago. You said you wanted to show kids that they can be who they are and still achieve their dreams."

"Yeah, that was part of it." Ash laid a hand on Dan's denim-clad thigh. Dan shifted closer, and in the quiet confines of the car, it felt like they were the only two people in the world. "There's this kid at Try Out. Grant. He gets bullied at school for being gay, and . . . I guess I wanted him to know that he isn't alone."

"That's really brave."

"Or really stupid, considering I might've tanked my whole career in the process."

"If you have, will it have been worth it?"

Ash frowned, squinting at Dan, and thought about the donations Teri said were pouring in to Try Out, and his new contract with Sport U Apparel, and the supportive emails from the teenagers he coached at Try Out, and all of the positive commentary that overshadowed the bad. "I think so, yeah."

"Well then," Dan said, a corner of his mouth kicking up.

"Well then."

"The Tavern?"

"Fuck yes. Let's go get drunk."

TWENTY-ONE

FOUR DAYS LATER, ASH FELT LIKE HE WAS STILL drunk. Or maybe he was overly tired to the point where it mimicked being drunk.

True to his word, he and Dan—as well as most of the guys on his team and the Carolina team—had gotten hammered at The Tavern on Saturday night. Put a bunch of twenty-something men at a bar after a game, when the adrenaline was pumping, and the outcome was fairly predictable.

They'd been paying for it ever since.

First, there'd been the early morning Sunday flight to Raleigh for game two against Carolina, not to mention the game itself, where Carolina had put them through their damn paces.

Second, there was his team's coaches, none of whom had been particularly impressed that their players had shown up hungover for the flight. They'd put them through a grueling late morning practice on Sunday, an extra-long practice on Monday once they'd returned to Tampa, and had them running drills first thing Tuesday morning until the rookies were puking.

After last night's game against Florida, his team finally had a day off today before they flew to Orlando tomorrow for the final two games of the preseason, but Ash was so exhausted he could barely keep his eyes open on the way to . . . wherever Dan was taking them.

Pulling his travel coffee mug out of the cup holder, he

took a hefty sip and looked out the window.

The further out of the city they drove, the more the storm damage changed from downed power lines, busted out windows, sagging fences, and missing siding and roof-top shingles to uprooted trees and swampy fields. The damage to the city was costly, but not as bad as it could've been had the hurricane landed as a Category 5 as predicted. And, due to the mandatory evacuation, there'd been minimal loss of life.

It was a reminder of how fragile life was and that it should be taken by the balls at every opportunity.

Dan pulled into the driveway of a boxy one-story home near the wilderness preserve and came to a stop. Stepping out, they met in front of the SUV.

"Now do I get to know what we're doing here?" Ash asked.

Dan looked like a fallen angel: blond curls, black polo shirt, and pressed dark jeans. *Dress casual* Dan had said this morning, yet he hadn't taken his own advice. Although, for Dan, this *was* casual. Ash was tempted to tumble him into the mud pit that was the front lawn, just to dirty him up a little.

Dan took his hand and they walked up the paved walkway to the front door. "I want to show you what I've been up to while you've been working the past few days." He pulled a keyring with a single key on it from his pocket and opened the front door.

The house was not a multi-room home like Ash had thought. Instead, most of the walls had been torn down to form a square workshop. There were multiple counter spaces; a zillion tools that hung on wall pegs, burst out of drawers, or sitting in doorless cabinets; hand saws and electric saws; an entire shelf of rulers; and some kind of tube thing that was either used to suck out brains or dust, one or the other. Wood shavings clung to every piece of furniture, and an air conditioning unit chugged near the back. To the left of the entrance, a door led to what Dan said was a small kitchen and a bathroom.

Dan gave him a tour of the space, then stood in the center, hands on his hips, grinning. "So? What do you think?"

"I think I'm . . ." Ash ran a finger over a counter. It came away full of dust. "Confused."

Dan rubbed his forehead and blurted, "This is my new workshop."

"Your new . . . What?"

"I found Mrs. Sebastien on Kijiji. She's the owner. This is her place." He picked up a short, thin tool Ash couldn't identify and tossed it from hand to hand. "She wants to semi-retire, and she was looking for someone to share the costs of this workshop with—mortgage and air conditioning and lighting and all that. We met on Sunday when you were in Raleigh? And we hit it off, so . . ." He shrugged. "She's going to have the papers drawn up to make me a co-owner."

"Co-owner?" Ash scrubbed his hands over his face. "But don't you have a workshop in the Hamptons?" His foggy brain couldn't make sense of anything.

"Yeah," Dan said. "I do. The entire thing is about the size of that counter over there. Mrs. Sebastien said I could use any of the tools, but I have a whole bunch of my own I want to have shipped here and—"

"Dan." Ash sucked in a breath scented of dust. "Are you moving here?"

Dan set the tool aside, gently, slowly, like he was buying time, and shoved his hands into his back pockets. Meeting Ash's gaze head on, he said, "Yes."

Ash's lungs caved in, and as much as his head wanted to throw him back to the last time they were supposed to live together, he kept himself firmly rooted in the present. He cupped Dan's face. "Are you sure about this? Your entire life is in New York."

"No. My life hasn't been in New York for a very long time."

"What about Mitch?"

Dan's brow creased. "What about him?"

"You transferred to the Burlington office to be closer to him. I guess part of me thought you'd head back there at some point."

"Yeah, I did, but . . . I realized I don't have to be geographically near him to be close to him. Mitch and I are on different paths, always have been. And that's okay. My life is wherever you are. If you'll have me." Dan winced. "And I know I probably said something similar six years ago, but—"

Ash kissed him.

And then he kissed him again.

Dan chuckled into his mouth and pulled away. "I'm going to take that as a yes."

Ash kissed him again, fast and wet, because he could. "No more living in the past, okay? For either of us."

"You and me against the world?"

"Damn straight."

A woman—Mrs. Sebastien, Ash presumed—emerged from the other room a few minutes later while Dan was telling him about his plans for his website. She was tall, with skin tanned the color of walnuts, a long face, and long hair that was either red or brown—Ash couldn't tell which. She leaned into Dan for a hug and patted him on the back before extending a hand to Ash. "You must be Ashton. Dan's told me a lot about you."

"All lies."

Her laugh was surprisingly deep. "I somehow doubt it unless you aren't a talented hockey player who happens to be the love of Dan's life." Before Ash could parse through that, she turned to Dan. "Dan, while you're here, can I show you the design for an armoire I've been commissioned to build? There are some intricate designs I think you might be better suited for."

Dan leaned into Ash with a smile. "Do you mind?"

"Course not." Ash kissed his temple. "Go crazy."

He leaned back against a counter. Dan was shoulder to shoulder with Mrs. Sebastien at the counter opposite, talking as he sketched something on a sheet of graph paper. The sun shone in from the window in front of him, highlighting the dust motes that bobbed and danced, and when Dan laughed, appearing ethereal and delicate, Ash's knees turned to water.

"Ash? Ash!" It sounded like it wasn't the first time Dan had called his name.

"Huh? Yeah?"

Dan and Mrs. Sebastien were now on the other side of the workshop admiring long planks of wood in different colors. Dan was flushed, and he had a dark smudge on his collarbone, wood shavings on his jeans, and dust patches on his T-shirt. Wearing that grin and holding those sheets of wood, he looked like a cross between an exuberant child and a sexy calendar model.

No. Given the way Ash's mouth dried up and his dick started to plump, Dan was definitely more sexy model.

288 | AMY AISLIN

"Ash? Seriously, are you okay?"

"Sure," Ash croaked. "Why?"

"You've been staring at me for ten minutes."

"Maybe don't look so sexy and I wouldn't stare."

Dan went pink.

Mrs. Sebastien giggled.

Oh god! Mrs. Sebastien! She was *right there* and all Ash could see was Dan. Dan, Dan, Dan. As if they hadn't spent Ash's every available free second together the past couple of days. For fuck's sake, Dan was *living* with him—temporarily. Maybe—and Ash couldn't stop staring.

"Um, sorry about him," Dan said to Mrs. Sebastien with a shrug. "Hockey players. I don't think they have a filter."

"Except in front of reporters," Mrs. Sebastien corrected.

"Sometimes not even then. You should hear some of the things my brother's said."

And they were off again, chatting like teenagers gossiping in a school cafeteria.

Ash went outside for some fresh air before he gave in and stalked over to Dan to kiss him silly. That giddy smile on Dan's face was making his heart do a fucking tap dance in his chest.

Heading to the car, he leaned against the hood. While he waited for Dan to finish geeking out over an armoire, he pulled his phone out and called his agent, only to get his voicemail.

"Scott, it's Ash. Just calling to see if you've heard anything about a new contract. Give me a call back when you can. Bye."

Sports blogs and TV channels were starting to speculate on why he hadn't been offered a new contract yet and if it was related to his recent coming out. Having a boyfriend would no doubt complicate things further. Now he wasn't just the guy who'd come out as bisexual; he was the guy who'd come out and lookie here! A boyfriend! Interest in Ash was starting to die down—slowly, but he could see it in how his phone no longer blew up as much—but as soon as he and Dan went public, the media circus would begin all over again. It'd put every lens on Dan, who was uncomfortable being the center of attention. Uncomfortable to the point of claustrophobia.

That being said, he shot off a quick email to Rachel giving her a heads up about him and Dan in case their relationship came to light before they were ready to come out.

The door to the workshop swung open.

"See you soon, Ash!" Mrs. Sebastien waved at him from the doorstep. "Dan, I'll see you tomorrow." She went inside and shut the door.

Dan walked up to Ash, grabbed his face, and kissed him smack on the mouth. "That armoire is going to look amazing once we're done with it. I am *pumped*! Where to next?"

Next: Try Out Center for Youth.

Almost as soon as they arrived, Ash got voluntold by Masterson to order, pay for, and pick up lunch for everyone. On top of the Try Out staff, there were three contractors, nine of Ash's teammates, and two teenagers who'd come in to help remove peeling wallpaper on their high school lunch hour.

Too bad neither of those high schoolers was Grant. Ash wanted to talk to him, make sure everything at school was okay. Judging by the email Grant had sent him, though, Ash was pretty sure he was no longer being bullied for his sexuality. *Coming out in front of a reporter was really dumb,* Grant's email had said. *But the jerks at school have left me alone since then, so . . . thanks?*

290 | AMY AISLIN

Leaving Dan with Alex for Alex to give him a tour and introduce him around, Ash did as instructed and took the many lunch orders. For a guy who didn't enjoy meeting new people, Dan was chatty and engaged. Maybe because Try Out existed for a good cause, or because Dan was in a good mood, or because these were Ash's teammates and he wanted to make a good impression. Knowing Dan, it was a combination of all three.

Between Ash's demanding schedule and the few hours Dan spent working daily on his laptop or checking in with his boss on the phone, and finally, *finally* organizing the crap in Ash's living room and fixing up his yard, they'd watched movies, made dinner—not cauliflower pizza, god no, never again—taken jogs together, and spent a lot of time talking.

Oh, and one of the things they *hadn't* done between the practices and the work and the cleaning up? Had sex. Or done anything of a sexual nature. If it was possible to die from blue balls, Ash was nearly there.

They'd indulged in lots of touching and kissing and more than one hot and heavy makeout session that left them both breathless. But as soon as clothes started coming off, Dan pulled back and made I'm-hungry or I-gotta-pee or I'm-tired noises. Ash had a plan to sit him down later and ask him WTF, because he was going crazy. If Dan needed more time before they slept together again, that was totally fine, but Ash needed to know so that he didn't inadvertently pressure Dan or misstep in any way.

An arm came around his shoulders, and he looked over to find Alex grinning at him.

"What?"

Alex ruffled Ash's hair. "The sappy smile's a good look for you."

"Fuck you, I'm not sappy anything. I'm an emotionally stable guy."

Alex kept grinning.

"Fine," Ash said on a sigh. "I have no idea what I'm doing."

"Most people don't when it comes to relationships."

"You seem to be doing fine."

"Please." Alex snorted. "I've been taking it one day at a time since Mitch and I met. Things are even harder now that we're living in different states again."

"Still." Ash elbowed Alex in the ribs. "You seem to be doing pretty good with the long-distance thing."

Alex took his arm back and ran a hand through his hair. "I worry about him. Part of the reason he passed out last spring was because he was keeping himself extra busy because he missed me, and he wasn't getting enough sleep. I don't want him going back to that place."

It had never really occurred to Ash how hard Alex and Mitch had it. Right now they were in different states because Mitch attended college in Vermont, but what about later? When he graduated? If he ended up playing in the NHL like he wanted—like he most certainly would. The man was too skilled a player not to—he could end up virtually anywhere, meaning that for however long Mitch and Alex played for the league . . . Jesus. They could be navigating a long-distance relationship for *years*.

When he pointed that out to Alex, Alex just shrugged and smiled softly. "What's the alternative? Breaking up?" He shook his head. "I'm sure I could live the rest of my life without him. But I don't want to."

Ash didn't want a long-distance relationship. He'd do it for Dan, no question. But he had a feeling it was something Dan didn't want either.

Alex elbowed him. "You're grinning again."

"And you're annoying again." Ash elbowed him back. "I'm gonna go pick up lunch." He did a quick scan of the lobby, but Dan wasn't where he'd been a few minutes ago talking to Teri. "Can you find Dan and tell him I'll be back in twenty minutes?"

"No problem."

It was more like thirty minutes by the time he got back from the restaurant. Apparently, it took a while to put together two-dozen BBQ chicken lunches and associated sides. It also took a while to haul the entire load inside from his SUV. Four trips to be exact. It was a humid day and he was hauling hot chickens. By the time he finished distributing everyone's orders in the air conditionless building, he was sweaty and cranky and ready to chow down on his own meal and gulp his ice tea in one sip . . . but he couldn't find the guy he wanted to have lunch with.

"Yo, Greer. Where's Dan?"

"Huh? Who?" Sitting against the wall in the lobby with two of their teammates, Greer was already digging into his BBQ chicken with a side of fries and a house salad.

"Dan. About yay high, curly blond hair."

"Oh, he went to find a measuring tape."

"Where? Did he walk to the hardware store down the street?"

"Nah, man, the equipment room in the gym."

Ash left his and Dan's meals with Greer with a pointed *Don't touch my food* and went in search of his boyfriend.

The caution signs in the gym had been removed and the light fixtures that had previously been dangling from the ceiling were now fixed. Everything appeared to be back in working order in this room, except that it smelled a bit mildewy. With the lights off, shadows cast an eerie pallor across the walls, reeking of decay and places best left undisturbed.

No Dan. In fact, the gym was eerily silent. The light was on in the equipment room in the corner. Ash headed toward it, his sandals flapping against his heels the only sound in the room.

"Dan?"

Dan poked his head out of the equipment room. "Hey!" He disappeared again. "Just a sec," he called from inside. "I'm looking for a measuring tape so I can measure the sign outside."

"Wanna leave it for later?" Ash called back across the cavernous space. "Food's here. Get it while it's—" *hot*, he meant to say, but a loud screech from outside interrupted him. Panicked shouts reached his ears, the sound of tires squealing on pavement, metal grinding against metal.

"The hell?"

A groan made him freeze. Sounded a bit like a rollercoaster reaching the crest of that first big hill. And then a sound not unlike the rollercoaster plunging down that same hill.

The earth shook, throwing him off balance and onto the floor. Dust rained down from the ceiling above him, followed by tiles and wood and whatever else held up a roof. Ash covered his head, the crash echoing in his ears, rubble hitting his back and arms. When everything settled, there were shouts from the lobby, dust swirled in the air, Ash was covered in detritus . . .

"Yo, Yager! You okay?"

And the back end of an eighteen-wheeler lay on its side through the equipment room, smoking and belching crates of whatever it'd been transporting.

"Oh my god." Pulse skyrocketing, Ash shot forward,

half crawling, half running, his heartbeat thrashing in his ears. Oh god, oh shit. He scrambled over and under piles of debris, shoving things out of his way, uncaring of the nicks and cuts he was surely giving himself. When he reached what he thought was the front of the equipment room—it was hard to tell with everything in ruins—it was to find a sheet of metal and wood blocking the entrance.

"Dan?"

Nothing.

"Dan!"

Dan sneezed, shooting dust into the air from where it had settled over every available inch of space, including his person. What the hell had happened? He'd been reaching for the box of tools on an upper shelf when something had hit him in the back, shoving him forward, and then it had felt like every shelf in the room had toppled on top of him, including various pieces of equipment.

It was dark. His ears rang. He couldn't move. At first he thought some part of his body must be pinned, but when he looked up, he found that he was trapped in a small bubble of empty space just large enough to sit in without hitting anything in any direction.

Oh god.

His throat closed off. The walls were pressing in.

An elephant sat on his chest. He couldn't move.

His vision went cloudy, and every muscle locked.

He was back in that stupid playground in California. No way out. No room to move. No one to hear him. Alone and terrified.

A keening sound reached his ears, and he imagined the

rest of the room falling on top of him. Took him a minute to realize that it was *him* sounding like a lost animal.

He unburied his face from where it was pressed into his knees, loosened his arms from where they were wrapped around his legs. His limbs were trembling as he took in his surroundings.

Behind him, a shelf upon which—miraculously—still sat a dozen basketballs. To his left, a shelf that had collapsed; baseball gloves and helmets were scattered around him. To his right and front, wooden beams, metal piping, destroyed shelving, tree branches, shattered light fixtures. He had about two and a half feet to move around in.

Taking a deep breath, he took stock of himself. No missing body parts. A few cuts on his arms. Somehow he'd lost a shoe. He was covered in bits of wood and water and grime. The dust was dense, making it hard to breathe. His back hurt where something had crashed into him. There was nowhere to go and the semi-darkness was cloying.

But he was alive.

Sound started to reach his ears as he shoved the panic and claustrophobia aside. Dripping water. Settling debris. His harsh breathing.

The loudest of all? Ash's voice.

" . . .and you're going to be fine. Dan? Okay? You're going to be fine. I know there's probably not a lot of room in there, but I'm right here. We're all right here. And the fire department's here too. Okay?"

Holy shit, was that *Ash*? Sounding wheezy and shaky and like *he* was the one with claustrophobia?

Wait, fire department? They were here already? Fuck, how long had Dan been on the brink of a panic attack?

"Ash . . .," he choked out.

" . . .said to stay out of the way, okay? If there's a corner you can hide in . . ."

"Ash."

" . . .make yourself as small as possible. Okay? Dan?"

"Ash!"

"Dan?" And then with relief so profound Dan could've swam in it, "Oh, thank god. Are you okay?"

"I'm stuck."

"I know. The fire department's here. They're going to get you out safely, okay?"

"I can . . ." Dan pressed against whatever was blocking his way. It was grainy; some type of wood perhaps. It shifted a little bit, but something fell with a *smash* where he couldn't see.

Frantic shouting ensued.

"No, no, no," Ash said, sounding hysterical. "Dan, no. Whatever you're doing, stop. One wrong move and the entire corner of this building is going to fall on top of you."

Dan froze, his lungs hardening. The very air he breathed was thick and soupy.

"Dan? Did you hear me?"

"Yeah," Dan whispered.

"Dan!"

"Yes," he said, louder.

Oh god, he didn't want the building to fall on top of him. He stayed as still as possible, tense with worry that one exhale too hard might . . . might . . .

Fuck, he was gonna die in here. In some dark room full of used equipment that smelled like someone's ass. All he'd wanted was the damn measuring tape. Ash had only asked one thing of him, one stupid, easy thing since he'd been here . . . and Dan was going to die before he had a chance to build the damn sign.

"Dan? You still with me? Dan! You've gotta get him out

of there; he's claustrophobic."

Another voice answered Ash.

Okay, okay. They couldn't both freak out. One of them needed to stay relatively calm, and no matter how much his mind wanted to cower, Dan had to keep it together for the both of them.

"Ash?"

"Dan! You okay?"

"Yeah. I'm moving into the corner against the shelves on my left. Your right." He did so, very slowly, careful not to touch anything or bonk his head.

"Okay. Okay, good." Ash's voice was gravel. "Stay there. I've gotta get out of the way so the firefighters can work—"

Dan moaned.

"—but I'm still here, all right? I'm not going anywhere. I'm gonna keep talking to you."

And he did. About nothing in particular—how he re-gretted buying his SUV in silver because "every fucking car on the road is fucking silver," and how impossible it was for someone with his ass and thighs and calves to find jeans that fit properly, and how his tailor was a gift from the heavens, and how the girl at the order counter at the restau-rant had asked him to sign a napkin, and how, according to Mitch, scientists knew more about space than they did about Earth's oceans and "how does that even make sense? Why wouldn't you explore your own world first," and how he'd read something about the government putting together a secret space army to fight the aliens that would eventually come visit for "nefarious purposes." Mundane things, as though he knew Dan just needed to hear his voice to stay in the present.

"Are you kidding?" Dan murmured loud enough for Ash to hear. "We're the assholes with words like *queue*—it uses five letters when one would do. Aliens are gonna fly right fucking past us."

Laughter outside of his bubble made his lips twitch, and he reached out, palm flat, as if Ash was right there waiting for him.

There were other voices too, shouting instructions and observations. The firefighters, no doubt. Underneath the voices were loud clatters and softer tinklings as materials were carefully moved and discarded.

Finally, what felt like hours later, a small opening near his feet cleared, letting in light and fresh air. Dan took a deep breath and sobbed it back out.

"Sir? Dan?" a foreign voice said. "Is this a big enough crawl space or do you need us to make it bigger?"

Fuck bigger. Dan wasn't spending another second in this dank shithole.

He crawled out slowly, conscious of his every extremity. *Don't touch anything. It'll fall on you.* He didn't want to die by heaps of metal.

Emerging from his cocoon into a sunlit-yet-messy world was like walking outside after seeing a movie at the theater. He blinked against the brightness and let the firefighter guide him out and then away from the equipment room.

"Ash?"

"Right here." And then there he was, sinking to his knees in front of Dan, tugging Dan into his enormous arms. "You're okay, you're okay." He ran his hands over every inch of Dan, assuring himself that he was unhurt.

Dan's heart cracked and broke and put itself back together. "I'm fine," he tried to reassure, but Ash kept muttering, "You're okay, you're okay, you're okay," over and over. His eyes widened at the blood on Dan's arm. "You're bleeding. He's bleeding! I need an ambulance!"

"I'm fine," Dan told the hovering firefighter. "Just cuts and bruises."

"We'll get you checked out anyway, sir."

"You're *not* fine, are you kidding?" Ash's hands hovered over Dan's arm. "Your arm is bleeding, and your hand, and there's a scratch on your forehead, and, and, and you're missing a shoe. Where's his shoe!"

"Ash. Hey." Dan cupped Ash's face and forcibly turned his head toward him. Ash's pupils were so huge they took up half his clammy face. His entire body shook. "I'm fine. Look at me." Ash's eyes snapped to his. "I'm fine. See?" Dan took Ash's trembling hands and brought them up to his face.

Gently, oh so gently, Ash ran his fingertips over Dan's jaw, his cheeks, his eyebrow, the scrape on his forehead he hadn't known about, couldn't feel. His choppy panting ghosted over Dan's lips.

Dan latched onto Ash's T-shirt, right above his heart, which was beating madly, and tried not to cry. "See? I'm fine."

"You're fine," Ash said, as if he really believed it this time. He sagged against Dan, touching their foreheads together. "You're fine." He kissed Dan's lips, the corner of his mouth, his cheek, frantic little kisses until he buried his head in Dan's neck, arms banding steel-like around Dan's back.

Dan let him take what he needed and held on.

There were too many thoughts in Ash's head, keeping him awake in the middle of the night. He was getting on a flight in a few hours for two back-to-back games in Orlando, but he couldn't make himself sleep.

He lay on his side in bed, facing Dan. On his stomach with one arm tucked under his pillow, Dan looked like a sleeping cherub. Ash couldn't stop staring at him, memorizing the way he breathed in sleep, the curve of his nose, the pout of his lips, the angle of his cheekbones.

Ash could've lost him today.

Closing his eyes, he sucked in a lungful of air and forced himself to make like Wendy, John, and Michael and think happy thoughts to settle his heart rate. Dan was fine. Other than a scratch on his forehead, a cut on his arm, and some bruising on his lower back, he was fine. Hell, Ash had injuries of his own—his hands were all beat to shit with nicks and cuts from shoving debris out of his way. They stung, but it was nothing compared to the sheer terror that had overtaken him when he'd reached the equipment room and found a twelve-foot long section of roof hovering precariously right above it, heavy enough to crush a person to death. And when Dan had done whatever he'd done on his side that had made it slide down?

Sitting up with a gasp, Ash folded himself in half, sticking his head between his knees. Shit, he was going to throw up. Swallowing hard past the bile, he clutched the bedcovers in one hand and his hair with the other.

Not in a million years would he ever tell Dan how close he'd been to death. The man was already terrified of small spaces.

But Ash would never get that image out of his head.

Alex's words floated around in his skull. *I'm sure I could live the rest of my life without him. But I don't want to.* Ash knew he could live without Dan—the last six years proved that. But he really, *really* didn't want to.

Arms came around him and a bare chest pressed against his back. "I'm fine," Dan whispered in his ear.

"I know." Grasping Dan's arms, Ash leaned against him. "I don't know why I'm still so scared hours later."

"Imagining all of the possible scenarios? Things that could've gone wrong?"

Ash swallowed, the sound clicking loudly in the silent bedroom. "Yeah." Turning his head, he pressed a kiss to the underside of Dan's jaw. "Why aren't you more afraid?"

"I was." Dan kissed Ash's temple. "But it was okay because you were there."

All of the tension in Ash's body released. He lay back down, face-to-face with Dan, sharing a pillow. Dan ran a thumb over the corner of Ash's eye. "Hi."

"Hi," Ash whispered back, just *gone* over this man.

"I love you."

Ash went breathless. "Dan—"

"It's okay, you don't have to say it back." Dan ran a hand over Ash's chest, soothing him. "I know I said it before and you didn't say it back, and that's okay. I just wanted you to know. I love you. Always have. It's always been you."

Ash kissed him, slow and sweet. A tangling of tongues, a savoring of moans, a brief clash of teeth. "I love you, Dan."

Dan's smile was quick and easy, but then he bit his lip. "You don't have to say that because I almost died today."

"I wouldn't say it unless I meant it."

Grinning, Dan nuzzled Ash's chest. "I wanna tell you something," he told Ash's pecs. "But I'm afraid it'll make you sad."

Ash played with his curls. "Tell me anyway."

"A few months after I . . . after you . . ." Pulling back, Dan stared at Ash's collarbone, his eyes pools of black in the darkened room. "Once I started realizing I'd been an idiot and acted rashly, I was going to call you. But then I saw a picture of you somewhere . . . online or in a sports magazine, I can't remember . . . and you were with Laura. I didn't think anything of it, but then there were more pictures of you and Laura turning up, and you looked . . . happy. And so I didn't call you, but I wanted you to know that I was going to."

Dan was right, it did make Ash sad. Regretful too. But also happy that Dan hadn't forgotten about him.

"I just wanted you to be happy, Ash. Were you?"

"I was, for a little while. But then . . ." *Laura cheated on me.* "There was the divorce. And frankly, that was a pretty shitty time."

"Did she ever tell you why she cheated?"

"She felt . . . neglected, I guess? Said I loved hockey more than her, which—" Ash jerked a shoulder. "—is true. Part of me doesn't blame her. Who'd want to come second to a job?"

Crazy thing was, even six years ago, Dan had never come second.

"But after the divorce was behind me," Ash continued, "I was happy, sure. I'm playing for my hometown team, and I like my teammates. They're family. Except Kinsey."

Dan chuckled. "I was talking to Kinsey while you left to get lunch, and he's not the asshole you make him out to be."

"That's 'cause you saw him without all the hardware. He's less intimidating that way."

"Hardware?"

"The piercings, remember?" Ash waved at his own face. "Eyebrow, lip, nose. He only wears them when there aren't cameras around."

"Like at The Tavern the other day."

"Mm."

"He reminds me of Mitch," Dan mused. "Lots of attitude to hide what's really going on inside. Except Kinsey's attitude comes with more anger."

"Can we stop talking about Kinsey while we're naked in bed?" Ash grumbled.

"You're the one who brought him up, but sure." Dan pushed Ash's shoulder with a lewd smile. Ash took the hint and lay back, surprised and delighted when Dan climbed on top of him. "Wanna do something else instead?"

Yes! I'm so on board I can't see straight.

His dick was on board too. But . . .

"Whoa, hold the fort there, hot stuff." He tapped Dan's thigh where it was slung around his hip. "Wanna tell me what changed?"

Curls fell over Dan's forehead when he cocked his head. "Huh?"

"The past few days, you've been pulling away when things get . . . intimate between us."

"Oh. Right. It's just, I . . ." He trailed off and looked everywhere but at Ash.

Needing to be closer, Ash sat up and wrapped his arms around Dan, bringing them face-to-face. Dan slid down Ash's stomach, nudging Ash's dick.

Ash nearly swallowed his tongue. "Gargh."

"Sorry," Dan said, chuckling. "Did it to yourself, though."

Ash groaned, nerves tingling. "Pretending you're not sitting on my dick . . ." He pecked Dan's lips. "Talk to me."

"It's stupid." Dan kissed Ash's shoulder where the skin there met his neck, making Ash's eyes cross when his tongue came out to play. "Just that the last time we had sex, I got kicked out."

Oh, fuck. Damn, Ash was an idiot. Of *course* his actions

had left their mark. They'd had sex, during which Dan told him he loved him, and not twelve hours later, Ash was telling him to get the fuck out. Would they never stop hurting each other?

Truth was, probably not. Even two people in a relationship hurt each other sometimes. They simply needed to learn to work through things together.

Like right now.

"I'm sorry." He hugged Dan closer. "Shit, I'm sorry."

"No, don't. You already apologized, that's not why I told you. My head's just been dealing with it, I guess. It's stupid."

"Not stupid."

It was about as stupid as Ash holding himself back and not getting too close to anyone the last few years. They'd been instinctively protecting themselves.

"We can have sex now, though?" he asked for clarification, falling back against the pillows, bringing Dan with him.

"Uh-huh."

Cupping Ash's jaw, Dan tilted Ash's head to the right angle and kissed him silly.

The sound of their stubbled jaws scritching made Ash crazy, and he hooked one leg around Dan's hip. Letting Dan set the pace, Ash ran one hand down Dan's back, avoiding his bruised lower left side, and squeezed his asscheek. Fuck, Dan felt so fucking good in Ash's arms—better even than he had when they'd done this days ago. Because now they were on the same page.

Dan pulled his mouth away with a groan and slid his lips from Ash's jaw to his neck to his chest. "God. What you do to me."

"Feeling's mutual. Get back up here." Ash carded his fingers through Dan's hair. "I want your mouth."

Obliging with a hot sound, Dan swept back in and took Ash's lips again. Ash's stomach tumbled on itself, and his nerve endings went haywire with desire.

They kissed for a long time, sometimes slow and sensual, other times fast and messy. Hands found sensitive spots, skin flushed and heated, eyes met for a beat before the kissing began anew. Kissing Dan was like meeting a kindred spirit.

"Always loved kissing you," Dan murmured before gently biting down on Ash's lower lip.

"Fuck."

Throwing his head back, Ash gasped as Dan made his way down his body and caressed every inch of him he could find. Ash's skin was burning, and he hissed in a breath when Dan sucked him into his mouth and played with his ballsack.

It was both torture and pleasure.

"Dan . . . Fuck."

"Mm."

The moan around Ash's erection made him see stars. "I need . . ." He reached into the nightstand and blindly fished for a condom and lube. His hand jerked and hit the top of the table when Dan licked into his slit. "Dan. Fuck, please."

Dan must've heard his desperation, because he climbed up Ash's body. Grabbing what they needed from the nightstand, he handed Ash the lube and left the condom on the pillow.

"Roll over," Ash demanded.

How beautiful Dan was, all loose-limbed with passion and slick with sweat. Hearing his breath catch as Ash prepped him with one finger, then two, then three, made Ash's blood boil. With one hand, Ash held Dan's thigh open, and the sight of Dan with his lips parted, fists clutching the pillow behind him, legs shaking, lungs heaving . . . Ash bit Dan's hip and tried not to come on the bedcovers.

Once he deemed Dan ready, Ash kneeled between Dan's legs and rolled on the condom.

Dan kicked him gently in the thigh. "On your back."

Obeying, Ash laid back and watched with glorious wonder as Dan straddled him for the second time that night.

"Like this," Dan said, voice hoarse, sweat matting his hair. "Like the first time."

Oh god, yes.

Then Ash was inside him, and all of a sudden it was six years ago and they were doing "the thing" for the first time in Dan's tiny apartment in Herald Square. Fuck but Ash missed that apartment, and as much as he hadn't wanted to, he'd thought about it a lot the last several years. Their safe space, their haven, their home. Where they'd learned and laughed and loved.

And here they were now, after so much time apart, and if anything, Ash loved Dan more than ever. But there was a fear under his breastbone that was new; a fear that Dan would disappear from his life again with nothing but an *I'm sorry, I can't.*

What was fear, though, if he wasn't willing to face it? Once, he would've thought he was smart for protecting his heart. Now it seemed braver to let go of the past and hold on tight.

So he did.

Sitting up, he clamped his arms around Dan and swallowed Dan's moan with a kiss. Dan placed a hand against Ash's neck and used a thumb to nudge Ash's mouth open wider.

Fuck, that was hot as sin.

They were both panting when they pulled back, and at the same time, they said, "I love you," making them chuckle gruffly.

Dan buried his face in Ash's neck. "Ash," he sobbed.

"I got you." Lying back again for more leverage, Ash planted his heels against the bed . . .

And pumped.

"Oh!" Dan's eyes squeezed shut, and he gasped and moaned and swore as he met Ash thrust for thrust, falling forward onto his hands. One fell onto the bed; the other was braced on Ash's chest, fingers curled, nails digging into Ash's skin.

"Fuck, yeah, keep doing that." That little bite of pain meant the marks would last long enough for Ash to see them in the mirror tomorrow morning. Tiny nail-shaped crescents. Evidence of this night.

Ash took Dan's hard-as-a-steel-pipe cock in his hand and jerked him off, earning him a choked off shout as Dan came, his whole body going rigid. Ash followed right behind him, toes curling.

Dan slumped forward onto Ash's chest, shaking as he came down from the high. They were both drenched in sweat and sticky with lube and come, but Dan cuddled close and Ash wasn't letting go for anything.

Except to throw out the condom, which he did a few minutes later. Crawling back into bed, he cleaned Dan up, running a warm washcloth over his belly, his soft cock, and between his thighs while Dan ran the backs of his fingers over Ash's cheekbone.

Once he was done, Ash threw the cloth in the direction of the bathroom, where it landed on the tile with a wet *splat.* He curled up next to Dan and laid his head on Dan's pillow. He kissed Dan's temple once, twice, then again. Dan smiled at him softly.

Now Ash could sleep.

"Hey," Dan said a few minutes later when Ash was starting to drift off. "Were you serious about that government space army thing? Because I feel like that could be a perfect opportunity to propose Sparklepants Space Station to the president."

Ash laughed so hard his stomach hurt.

TWENTY-TWO

DAN AWOKE THE NEXT MORNING FEELING LOOSE and languid and like he could take on the world and win. Also, he was freezing, as he often was while indoors in this state. Pulling the covers up, he brought it over his head, tucking himself into a blanket burrito.

Better.

Except Ash was missing.

He could hear the blender and smell bread toasting. Likely Ash was making himself breakfast before getting ready for his flight that left in . . . Dan extended an arm for his cell phone on the night table. Three hours.

Which meant they had about an hour before Ash needed to head to the airport. They could do a lot in an hour.

His phone rang in his hand before he had a chance to implement any of his many fantasies, most of them featuring shower sex, and he swiped to answer before noticing whose name was on the call display.

"Damn it."

"Dan?"

He sighed. "Hi, Mom." He'd been avoiding her calls since hanging up on her last week and any second now he was going to hear about it.

"Dan, do you know what day it is?"

His sleepy brain stalled. That wasn't at all what he'd expected and he had to think about the answer for a second. "Um, Thursday?"

"Thursday, the first of October to be exact. Meaning you've been away from the office for two and a half weeks. I expected you back by now."

"What?" Maybe he was still half asleep, but he didn't remember ever telling her when he'd be back.

"I expect my employees to show up at the office."

"I'm working out of the Tampa office for now," he said, knuckling one eye.

"I happen to know for a fact that the Tampa office is temporarily closed until the water damage can be repaired. Employees have been working from home."

"Right. Like I have. Well, from—" Ash's. "—the hotel, but still."

"I expect you back in the New York office on Monday."

Expect, expect, expect. As if everything revolved around her. She was ruining his good mood. "Yeah, that's not gonna happen."

"Dan." She didn't sigh; she never showed that much emotion. But she did make a sound in the back of her throat. "If you don't come back to work, I'm going to out your brother."

He scrubbed a hand over his face. "Huh?" Were they having two different conversations, or what?

"If you're not in the office first thing Monday morning, I'll let your brother's sexuality slip." Her voice was so matter of fact, it was taking him a moment to catch up. "Not sure how many NHL teams will want a gay player. Monday, Dan."

She hung up.

So much for taking on the world.

Suddenly awake, he sat up, the cover pooling at his waist. His skin pebbled from the cold but with the fire boiling in his veins, he couldn't feel it. There was just a swell

THE NATURE OF THE GAME | 311

of fury as he stiffly swung out of bed and started throwing clothes at random into a small suitcase.

Twice! This was the second time she'd used Mitch against him, and fuck her if she thought she could get away with it again. Underwear joined a pair of jeans and a couple of T-shirts. Socks. A light jacket. His laptop went into a messenger bag.

Why was it so important for him to be physically present in the office that she'd threaten Mitch to get him to cooperate? As if he couldn't work from anywhere. Jesus, he was so fucking done.

"What are you mumbling about?"

"Huh?" He turned, finding Ash in the doorway in only a pair of loose sweats, hair sticking straight up, a tall glass filled with a pink-colored smoothie in each hand.

"I could hear you talking to yourself from the kitchen," Ash said, placing the glasses on the dresser. "What's going on?" His dark gaze landed on the suitcase on the bed. He stilled. Tone cautious, he asked, "Are you going somewhere?"

Even Ash's half-nakedness couldn't quell Dan's anger. His stomach burned with resentment. "I have to go home for a couple days."

"A couple days?"

"Yup." He marched into the bathroom and started the shower. "I'll be back Saturday night, latest."

"What's so important that you didn't even fold your clothes before putting them in your suitcase?"

Jumping into the shower, Dan said, "There's no time for niceties."

"I don't know if I'd consider that—"

"God, I can't *believe* her!" He shampooed his hair, then rinsed it out quickly, surely leaving most of the shampoo behind. "As if once wasn't enough, she has to go and black-mail me a second time."

"Ah. Your mom, then," Ash said from the other side of the shower stall.

Dan briskly ran the bar of soap over himself, rinsed, and turned off the water. The faster he got ready, the sooner he could head to the airport, and the sooner he could con-front his mom.

"Where does she get off? Huh?" Stepping out of the shower, he wrapped a towel around his waist.

Ash leaned his ass against the bathroom counter, arms crossed. "What'd she do this time?"

"I can't even with her right now." Marching past him, Dan went back into the bedroom and pulled clothes out of the drawer Ash had given him.

"Okay, stop." Ash's hands landed on his shoulders. He turned Dan to face him. "Take a breath." Dan did. "Now tell me what happened."

Looking into Ash's concerned gaze, Dan took a second lungful of oxygen. Admittedly, it did help settle him. "My mom threatened to out Mitch if I'm not back in the office on Monday."

"Okay," Ash said slowly, brow creasing. "And you're go-ing back to . . ."

"To give her a damn piece of my mind."

Ash's mouth kicked up. "Okay, baby, come here. Keep breathing."

Sinking into Ash, Dan let out a long breath into his shoulder. "I'm so tired of fighting her, Ash."

"I know." Ash kissed his temple. "Can you wait? I'm back Saturday morning. We can fly out together that after-noon. That way I can come with you."

"Thank you." Dan pulled away to kiss Ash's unshaved

jaw. "But I don't think I can wait that long. I want to be done with it." He winced. "Look, I know this reeks of six years ago—"

Ash cupped his face. "No." His gaze was intense and steady. "We're done living there, remember?"

Something that felt like permanence settled over Dan's bones. "Okay."

"Okay. Now tell me why you can't be done with it from here."

"I need to face her. Look her in the eye and tell her she's lost."

"That's . . . kind of evil."

Dan scoffed. "Nah. Just necessary. Besides." He ran a thumb over Ash's lower lip. "While I'm there, I can start packing my apartment, hire movers . . ."

Ash's eyes lit up. "Now you're talking. I just wish you didn't have to go."

"It's only for a couple of days. And you won't even be here anyway." Dan patted Ash's chest above his heart. "Don't worry, though. My heart's staying here with you."

As if suddenly weightless, Ash fell onto him, arms banding around his waist. He kissed Dan's neck. "I love you, you know that?" A second kiss to Dan's neck, then he pulled back to meet Dan's gaze. "Okay. Go to New York. Break up with your mom."

Dan's snorted laugh felt freeing.

"But first, since this involves Mitch . . . maybe give him a call first?"

Eight hours after his mother's phone call, Dan stepped into the lobby of Westlake Waterless Printing in Manhattan. In that time his ire had cooled, so it was with a calmer head that he aimed for the stairwell behind the bank of elevators.

Mitch's response to Dan's news had been a pithy "Fuck her" followed by "Doesn't she watch the news?"

Men and women in business attire sat in the lobby typing on laptops, crossed the marbled floor with heads bent and thumbs arcing across tiny telephone keyboards, waited aimlessly for the elevator. The hustle and bustle of New York City. It was jarring after a few weeks away. Dan had once prided himself on being one of them—flitting from appointment to meeting, always being *on*, dealing with every little detail as if they were all emergencies that needed immediate handling.

Tampa had a slower rhythm to it, was more social, and had little lizards sunning themselves on Ash's front porch. Despite the traffic being as miserable as it was in New York, Dan was looking forward to making a permanent move there. Well, as permanent as could be when his boyfriend could be traded anywhere.

Stopping in front of the door to the stairwell, he turned and observed the elevators, their bland silver doors opening with a quiet whoosh to belch out passengers and closing on new victims moments later.

Fuck it.

He sweat on the entire trip up, swallowing against a dry throat. Tucked into a back corner, he kept one eye on the little display that told him what floor he was on, and ignored the rest of the passengers. Fifth floor, sixth, seventh. Pause to vomit passengers. The walls were too close, but if he kept sight of his own reflection in the mirrored back wall, it made the tiny space feel a smidge larger.

Why couldn't everyone get off and leave him the six-by-six space? The car wouldn't seem so small then, and he might be able to breathe.

Then again, if you plunge to your death, you won't be alone.

There was that.

Finally expelled onto the eighteenth floor, Dan sucked in a large breath of fresh air and wiped his forehead. If he could ride in that death trap, he could do anything.

Making straight for his mother's office, he announced himself to his mother's executive assistant, then sat to wait. Tapping his heel impatiently, his mind went to Ash. They'd driven to the airport together, and Ash had dropped him off at his terminal with a kiss and a wink before jetting off to the private terminal celebrities, sports teams, and rich people flew out of.

"Hey." Dan had leaned into the SUV before shutting the door. "I'll see you in a couple of days."

Ash had leaned across the center console to kiss him. "I know."

Those two words were even better than *I love you.*

"Mr. Greyson," the EA said now, jolting him out of his thoughts. "You can go on in."

Inside his mother's office, nothing had changed in years. Same sturdy wooden desk and matching round table. Same dresser, same mini fridge. Different dry cleaning hanging on a hook next to the door, but dry cleaning just the same. The clunky desktop computer was now a sleek laptop, but still. Everything was the same down to the word of the day calendar.

Today's word was *hearken—to listen with respectful attention.*

Huh.

"I didn't think you'd be back until Monday," his mother said from behind her desk, coiffed to perfection as always.

Were the lines around her eyes and mouth more pronounced, or had it just been so long since Dan had seen her? Either way, she appeared tired and stressed.

"I'm not back." He didn't sit. "Just here for a short visit before I head back to Tampa."

Subtle lines creased her brow. "Excuse me?"

Dan handed her the file folder he'd brought in with him.

"What's this?" His mother flipped it open.

Inside was a single sheet of paper.

"My resignation," he said. The same one he'd handed her six years ago with the date updated. Seemed fitting.

She set the folder down with a jerk. "Daniel—"

"Don't." He held up a hand. "I heard you this morning. I did. But the truth is that you don't have a leg to stand on."

"You think not?" She leaned back in her chair, crossing her legs. "Do you know of any teams who'd want a gay player?"

Actually, yes. "Okay, first of all—what is wrong with you that you'd use your own son like this? Second—I spoke with Mitch this morning and he refuses to be used like this again. And third—do you not watch the news?" He pulled his phone out of his pocket, opened the internet browser, and brought up Ash's article with its tell-all headline. *NHL Player Comes Out As Bisexual.* "Here."

She took the phone from him. "What is this?" Dan waited as she put on a pair of reading glasses and gave her time to read the article, tempted to smirk but determined to hold it together.

His mother leaned forward, elbows on the desk, phone held in both hands. It took her so long to read the article, Dan suspected she did so two or three times. Finally, she set the phone down and ran a hand over the front of her blouse before rising. "I see."

He waited for more. Some sign of acquiescence or regret or . . . just something. Instead, she handed Dan his phone back, closed the file folder with his resignation letter, and said, "What do you intend to do with yourself now that you're jobless?"

That, apparently, was as much acceptance as she was going to show.

"You don't need to worry about it," he responded. "I don't intend to share my plans with you because no matter what they are, you won't approve. So." He shrugged. Now the next part. He cleared his throat and looked his mother in the eye. "I wanted you to know that I forgive you."

Her lips parted.

"For what you did back then," he continued. "And this morning. You said you did it for the good of the company and because you wanted what's best for us. Maybe that's true, maybe it's not, I don't know. But I'm going to choose to believe you."

It had taken him some time to realize that if he could forgive himself for his actions six years ago, he could forgive his mother too. Whether or not she'd acted with good intentions would no doubt remain a mystery forever. But it was like he'd said—he was going to choose to believe her. He didn't want to move forward with his new life with Ash carrying this anger around, and choosing to believe his mother was the only way to let it go.

"Anyway." He knocked once on the desktop. "That's all I came to say. See you around, Mom."

Part of him was tempted to end with *You did this to yourself* or *I did tell you you'd have to deal with the consequences of your actions.* But he didn't want to burn those bridges. People could change. Inside him was a small hope that Greta Westlake could too.

"Did it ever occur to you," he said, hand on the door-knob, inches from escape, "that had you not pushed so hard, I might've ended up working here of my own volition? And I might've actually enjoyed it?" He could even picture himself at the helm of the company. Maybe that was another reason why he hadn't quit sooner—because, under better circumstances, he could've been happy here.

"And did it ever occur to you," his mother said, voice softer than he'd ever heard it, "that everything I've ever done, I've done for you and your brother?"

"Sure. But you know what they say—actions speak louder than words."

He left.

TWENTY-THREE

THE TAMPA INTERNATIONAL AIRPORT WAS crowded late on a Saturday morning. Dressed down in jeans and a T-shirt, baseball hat on, Ash had so far remained unnoticed as he leaned against the wall in baggage claim, playing a game on his phone while he waited for Dan.

It didn't escape his notice that he was once again waiting in an airport for Dan after Dan had taken on his mother face-to-face. They'd come full circle.

Things would end better this time. He'd thought a small part of him would expect to be left behind again, but there was nothing except the knowledge that they were solid. He'd meant it when he'd said the past should stay there.

He hated that Dan had gone to New York without him. Not to break up with his mom as Ash had joked, but to distance himself from her in the only way he knew how. According to Dan, it had been cathartic, which could only be a good thing. It felt like Dan had finally let go of a part of himself he'd been holding onto for years.

His phone rang in his hand, interrupting his game, showing his agent's name on the caller ID. Another interview, no doubt, and he groaned. He shouldn't complain. The feedback and commentary on his coming out had so far been overwhelmingly positive. Maybe it'd inspire others, maybe it wouldn't.

It allowed him the freedom to be in a relationship with Dan without hiding, which was a selfish perk, but humans were selfish creatures. So there.

He swiped to answer his phone. "Hi, Scott."

"Ash, you won't believe what I have in front of me."

"An interview request from Ellen DeGeneres?"

A pause. "No? Is that a thing you want? Because I can try to get in contact with—"

"I'm kidding, I'm kidding. Thank you, but no. What've you got?"

"Your new contract offer."

Ash sucked in a breath.

Scott blathered on about the length of the contract and the signing bonus and the average annual value. Ash chuckled quietly and listened with half an ear. His club was offering him more than he was currently making, which wasn't necessary, but it was nice. Raises typically meant someone was doing well in their job. Just that most people's raises weren't usually in the millions.

Oh, and they'd like him to be part of an NHL-led focus group on new LGBTQ policies and engagement programs.

"Yes," Ash interrupted.

"You . . . don't want to read it, first?"

He probably should.

"Why don't I fly to Tampa early next week?" There was the sound of a keyboard being vigorously tapped. "I don't know what your schedule looks like off-hand, but if I rear-range a couple of things, I can be there Tuesday through Thursday."

"Sounds good, Scott."

They hung up shortly after, and Ash didn't have much time to marvel at life and how it could surprise you with the unexpected when Dan appeared near one of the baggage carousels. Wearing form-fitting jeans and a teal polo shirt, he was lifting a large black suitcase off the carousel. He'd left with a carry-on and returned with a suitcase full of clothes. He'd hired movers, he'd said, to box up the rest and drive it to Tampa.

Dan seemed brighter somehow. His steps were lighter, his shoulders were loose, and as their eyes met across the room, his face lit up in such a huge smile that Ash forgot all about the new contract. There were more important things, and for the first time in what felt like forever, Ash's world was complete.

Wheeling his two suitcases behind him, Dan headed for him. Ash dodged other travelers and met him halfway and grinned at the expression on Dan's face. Happiness and relief and amazement. He seemed to be restraining himself from throwing himself into Ash's arms.

Ash could relate. However, they hadn't discussed coming out as a couple, so he restrained himself and settled for squeezing Dan's forearm.

"Hi, baby," Ash murmured.

Dan's smile grew. "Hi."

"Ready to head home?"

"Yeah." Dan held out a hand—an offer, a statement. "I'm ready."

Hand in hand, they walked out into the Florida sunshine.

EPILOGUE

JUNE 2012—THREE YEARS LATER

THERE WERE PEOPLE IN DAN'S STORE. ACTUAL customers. And they were *buying things*! Young ladies and older ladies and husbands looking for gifts.

Dan stood off to the side, in front of a display of thin wooden bookmarks. Behind him, Mitch was taking a customer's payment at the register. She was buying two sun catchers and had commissioned a third smaller one for her new granddaughter.

He had *commissions*!

He had *customers*!

Here he'd thought he'd get two drop-ins on opening day, max.

"Are you kidding?" Ash had said this morning while Dan panicked. "You advertised everywhere. I advertised everywhere. Hell, so did Mitch and Alex and most of the guys on their teams *and* mine." Alex had been traded to Toronto last year and Mitch had gone on to play for Boston after graduating last spring. Ash was right—including his own team, that was *a lot* of NHL players pimping his grand opening on social media.

The worst part had been the press this morning. Dan still wasn't convinced that his grand opening was especially newsworthy, but people wanted to see what the hockey player's boyfriend was up to. It was a human-interest story.

Probably many people had shown up today because they wanted to meet said hockey player, which was fine. Dan didn't care where his customers came from as long as they came.

Anticipating that development, he'd crafted some hockey-themed pieces that had gone over remarkably well with today's crowd. Keychains and sun catchers in the shape of hockey sticks, the Stanley Cup, and various NHL team logos; coaster sets; Stanley Cup replicas; coat racks shaped like hockey sticks; sun catchers shaped like hockey pucks. That one had been interesting—turned out it was rather difficult to make a round piece of wood look like anything but a round piece of wood.

They'd come out publicly right before Christmas three years ago when Dan had attended a charity gala with Ash. As much as he hated the spotlight, it hadn't been as bad as he'd feared it would be. Part of that was because Dan was a nobody compared to Ash. Former manager of financial planning and analysis at a print house based out of New York and currently unemployed? He couldn't possibly be less interesting. At the time, he'd been on exactly zero social media platforms, and the only public information about him had been his under-construction website that listed a short biography and a contact form.

One thing that Dan hadn't expected was the focus on Mitch. Someone somewhere had dug up Dan's family tree and when sportscasters found out Mitch played college hockey, a lot of attention shifted in his direction, the talk all about Mitch's skills and his potential in the NHL.

Mitch, of course, had eaten it up.

And that was fine. Let Mitch have all of the attention. It freed Dan up to live his life—for the most part—free of scrutiny.

At the front of the store, Ash stood framed by the window, chatting with a couple of women Mitch's age who were clearly here to see the hockey players. They wore Tampa's jersey and held an autograph book each that had already been signed by Mitch and Alex. Ash signed the book, then, like he had all morning, he picked one of the hockey-themed items—a wooden mortar and pestle this time—and, with a wink in Dan's direction, showed off the detail on the Tampa logo that had been burned into one side.

Dan grinned at him and surveyed his store.

It was magic.

From the ceiling hung a dozen crescent moon-shaped wooden sun catchers adorned with pieces of crystal that caught the light and diffused every color of the rainbow onto walls purposefully painted white. Artfully arranged on tables he'd built himself were sun catchers in other shapes and sizes—suns, stars, hearts, oblongs. One piece was shaped like the state of Florida with a row of crystals hanging from the bottom. If it was a popular item, he'd think about making similar ones shaped like the rest of the states. Countries even. He had larger pieces too, like one three-foot plank of sanded cherrywood inset with a dozen globes of colored glass, as well as jewelry boxes, palm-sized coin bowls, and treasure chests.

It'd taken him a long time to get here considering he'd first had this dream in high school. But every struggle and setback had been worth it. He was so fucking proud of his place, of what he'd made happen with Ash's help. Even better was the fact that it was—loosely—associated with Try Out Center for Youth. The after-school part-timers were all kids from Try Out, and anyone who wanted to learn some skills in woodworking were welcome at his workshop for lessons.

Ash was spending more time at the center in the off-season too, sort of unofficially working for Teri. He wanted to learn the ropes so that he could be more involved with Try Out, and other programs like it, once he retired from hockey. Whenever that would be.

A lull in customers late in the afternoon left Dan alone in the shop with Ash, Mitch, and Alex. Blowing out a breath, he leaned against the customer service counter. There were gaps in his displays; where once there'd been merchandize, now it was empty.

"If all of these people come back tomorrow to return things they don't need, I'm taking the difference out of your pay checks," he said.

"Nah," Ash said with a smile, throwing his arm around Dan's shoulders. "They'll just put it up on eBay."

"Yeah," Mitch said, and in a high-pitched voice, "Oh my god, Ashton Yager touched it!"

Ash cracked up.

"In all honesty, though," Alex said, standing in the center of the store, hands on his hips. "This is really cool."

"Yeah, I think so too," Dan said. "But I'm biased."

Ash kissed his temple. "As you should be."

"Dad just texted," Mitch said, nose buried in his phone. "Says he'll be back once we've closed to take us all out to dinner to celebrate."

He'd been here this morning—along with Ash's entire team and their families—but he'd hurt his back last week and had left after an hour to head to his hotel to rest.

"Sounds good," Dan said.

"And Cody says he'll—" Mitch broke off, and Dan found him scowling at the door, brow furrowed, eyes nothing but slits. "What's *she* doing here?"

She being Greta Westlake.

Huh.

"Mom," Dan greeted once she'd stepped through the door, setting the little bell jingling. "I didn't think you'd make it."

He met her in the middle of the room, Mitch at his side, shoulder to shoulder. Their defensemen stood several feet away at their backs, ready to protect.

Their mom's hair was twisted up off her neck and pinned to the back of her head. A breezy red top was tucked into a pair of skinny white pants, and a pair of crystal-studded sandals completed the outfit. She seemed . . . tiny. Dan had always imagined her as an immovable mountain, formidable and titanic.

Right now she just looked . . . small.

"I was visiting Westlake's Tampa office yesterday," she said, hiking her bowling ball-sized tote bag higher onto her shoulder, "and I decided to stay an extra day so I could attend your grand opening."

He'd sent her an invitation, half expecting her not to show up. But he had to admit, she'd made an effort the past few years. Baby steps.

She hadn't attended Mitch's graduation last spring, but she'd given him a check as a graduation gift, the amount totaling to four years of college tuition.

"Too little too late," Mitch had said. Dan still didn't know what he'd done with the money.

She'd attended Mitch and Alex's wedding last summer, sitting in the back. She disappeared after the ceremony.

She'd gifted Dan a subscription to a woodworking magazine and another to *Entrepreneur*.

Every couple of months, he received a new book on small businesses—his mother's way of subtly pointing out that his business degree was actually good for something.

She'd donated a large sum to Try Out after the hurricane on behalf of Westlake Waterless Printing.

And she'd shown up today—under the pretense of being in the neighborhood, but still.

Mitch wasn't impressed.

Dan elbowed him in the ribs. If she was trying, so could they.

"Why do you even want her in your life after everything?" Mitch had asked once, months ago, when Dan had invited her for a weekend visit so she could see his and Ash's new Craftsman-style house in Hyde Park. He was still waiting for a response.

"Because it's Mom," Dan had said inanely, not knowing how to explain. "I've spent a long time being mad at her, Mitch, and . . . I'm tired of it. It's exhausting being angry for so long."

"Thanks for coming," Dan said now.

"Yes, well." She looked everywhere except at him and Mitch, mouth a tight slash, blinking rapidly. "It's very lovely, Dan. Congratulations. You're in a great location, and—" She picked up a business card off the table to her right. "—you came up with a beautiful name."

Sun Catcher Studios. Ash's name, which he'd finally coughed up after Dan signed the lease on the building.

"Thank you," he said. Mitch kept scowling. "Let me give you a tour."

She waved a hand. "Oh, I only have a few minutes; I'll take a quick look around myself. You—" She was interrupted by the bell on the door. "You greet your customers. I'll be just fine." She patted him on the arm and wandered away.

Ten minutes later, Dan glanced up after he finished ringing up his customer; the door was closing gently on his mother's retreating back.

Shaking his head, he chuckled softly. Typical.

"Hey." Ash came up next to him and pulled him into his arms. "You okay?"

"She came."

"Told you she would. And how about that excuse?"

Dan snorted a laugh. "Yeah, she just happened to schedule a visit to the Tampa office for the Friday before my grand opening?"

Outside the picture window at the front of the store, a young couple came to a stop. The woman pointed at something in one of Dan's displays and gestured to her partner, mouth forming a shape Dan interpreted as *ooh ooh ooh I want it*!

"How do you feel?"

And here was Ash, the part of Dan's life he liked the best.

Dan kissed him. "I feel really fucking awesome."

Go big and fail epically?

Not this time.

ABOUT THE AUTHOR

Amy started writing on a rainy day in fourth grade when her class was forced to stay inside for recess. Tales of adventures with her classmates quickly morphed into tales of adventures with the characters in her head. Based in the suburbs of Toronto, Amy is a marketer/fundraiser at a large environmental non-profit in Toronto by day, and a writer by night. Book enthusiast, animal lover and (very) amateur photographer, her interests are many and varied, including travelling, astronomy, ecology, and baking. She binge watches too much anime, and loves musical theater, Julie Andrews, the Backstreet Boys, and her hometown of Oakville, Ontario.

Stop by and say hi:

Website: www.amyaislin.com

Newsletter: bit.ly/AmyAislinSignUp

Instagram: www.instagram.com/amyaislin

Facebook: www.facebook.com/amy.aislin

Facebook group: www.facebook.com/groups/amyaislin

Facebook page: www.facebook.com/AmyAislinAuthor

Bookbub: www.bookbub.com/profile/amy-aislin

Twitter: twitter.com/amy_aislin

Pinterest: www.pinterest.ca/amyaislinauthor/

Goodreads: www.goodreads.com/author/show/16693566.
Amy_Aislin

QueeRomance Ink: www.queeromanceink.com/mbm-book-author/amy-aislin/

TITLES BY
AMY AISLIN

Printed in Great Britain
by Amazon

45455906R00192